Web Design Tools and Techniques

2nd edition

Peter Kentie

Peachpit Press

Web Design Tools and Techniques, 2nd Edition
Peter Kentie

Peachpit Press
1249 Eighth Street
Berkeley, CA 94710
510/524-2178
510/524-2221 (fax)

Find us on the World Wide Web at: www.peachpit.com
To report errors, please send a note to errata@peachpit.com
Peachpit Press is a division of Pearson Education

Editors: Whitney Walker, Becky Morgan
Production Coordinator: Kate Reber
Cover design: Be One
Cover illustration: Sander Kessels (concept), Peter Kentie (execution)
Interior design: Peter Kentie
Production: Peter Kentie

Colophon
This book was created with QuarkXPress 3.31 Passport on an Apple Macintosh 8100/110. The fonts used were FF Scala from FontFont, FF Meta from Fontfont and Myriad from Adobe. Final output was on a CREO CTP Prinergy Work Flow at Commercial Documentation Services in Medford, Oregon and was printed on 70# Sonoma Matte paper.

ISBN 0–201-71712-3

9 8 7 6 5 4 3 2 1

Printed and bound in the United States of America

For my dearest Marjan,
Thank you for your dedication and endless patience.

ABOUT THE AUTHOR:

Peter Kentie is Director of Content & Marketing at Ilse Media in The Netherlands. Peter is a graphic designer and marketeer who has created and developed Web sites for organizations and professional companies since the beginning of 1995. He has worked on Internet projects for companies such as Philips, DAF Trucks, VNU, Merck, and others. In addition, he writes for *Publish* magazine, and has authored a successful book on desktop publishing for Pearson Education. Peter and his wife Marjan live and work in Eindhoven, the Netherlands.

FOREWORD

Probably every foreword of a substantial reference work is written as the last step. That applies to this foreword, too. The technical standards of the Internet are developing at such a merciless pace that a book on Web design can, in theory, never be finished. Can it even be written? Recently, there was a posting on a newsgroup expressing sympathy for someone who was advertising himself as a Web designer. "How can you design for a medium over which you have no control as a designer?" was his complaint. There is, of course, a grain of truth to this bold statement. Theoretically, because the Web is based on a structured formatting language, a designer's options are limited. But time doesn't stand still, and the Internet is increasingly becoming a rich graphics and multimedia-oriented communication medium.

Aesthetic considerations of Web pages are also playing a role in the development of design standards. Because the medium is developing into a fusion of radio, television, and telephone, image quality is also becoming important. The Web is more than just text and a few pictures, however; its multimedia and interactive capacities are increasingly determining the success of a Web site. Consequently, the techniques available are also becoming increasingly complex. Can graphic designers, who already work with formatting and drawing software, also create multimedia productions? In practice, this would seem to be quite a serious obstacle, notwithstanding the effective use of a programming language such as Java or even Lingo. Should a successful Web designer have to learn to write code? Probably not. What they do have to learn, however, is the opportunities Java, Flash, and XML can offer Web designers.

That is why, in this book, I teach you more than just the most recent HTML tags. I also discuss relevant layout and Web design techniques. Whether it concerns image processing, Java and JavaScript programming, Macromedia Flash animations, or even the production of a QuickTime VR movie, you will find the basis of every significant Web design technique in this book. Design and production tools and techniques for mobile phones and TV browsers have also been given attention. The Internet is eventually coming to every screen near you!

Web design techniques are developing at a lightning pace and the learning curve for aspiring designers is becoming increasingly steep. And just when you think you have mastered the trade, the rules of the game change again. In that respect, the Internet is truly a "living organism." To provide you with additional support, a companion Web site has been created for this book. Also all relevant HTML code and images are accessible online. The address is: **www.kentie.com**. For questions and comments concerning this book, you can always send me an e-mail at: **peter@kentie.com**. I wish you enjoyable reading and hope I have inspired you to create your own online publication!

Peter Kentie

	Table of Contents	With the assistance of:	Page
▶ **Functional**	10 Web Design Rules		**1**
Web Design	Marketing and Web Design	Advice: Paul Keltjens	**7**
	HTML for Designers	Advice: Rob Kouwenberg, Edwin Martin	**23**
	Building a Web Site	Illustration 'Hacker Tracker': Albert Kiefer	**35**
	Basic HTML Concepts		**47**
	Basic Table Design		**75**
	Frames and the Meta Tag	Illustrations: Frits Bonjernoor	**85**
	Typography and the Web	Illustration 'Scrabble': Wouter Betting	**99**
	From Copy to HTML		**113**
	Usability Design	Illustration 'Knot': Sander Kessels	**127**
	WYSIWYG Web Design		**133**
▶ **Creative**	Adjusting Colors for the Web	Advice: Victor Engel, Douglas Jacobson	**147**
Web Design	GIF and JPEG Images		**153**
	Tiled Background Patterns		**165**
	Background Lines and Patterns	Illustrations: Jay Boersma	**171**
	Large Background Pattern		**177**
	Clickable Image Maps		**181**
	Interactive Navigation on the Web	Illustrations: WDS, Bitmap Brothers	**187**
	Aligning Text and Images		**195**
	Seamless Tables		**201**
	Foreground and Background Integration		**207**
	Integration of Text and Image		**215**
	Shadow and Pattern in HTML		**225**
	Corel Painter: Image Hose and Patterns		**233**
	Creative Picture Frames	Illustration 'Quad': Cor Steenstra	**241**
	Graphic Web Pages	Illustration 'face': Marijke den Ouden	**247**
	Corel Bryce Splash Page	Illustration 'Counter': Eric Bruinewoud	**253**
▶ **Advanced**	Optimal GIF Animations		**259**
Web Design	Shockwave Flash Animations	Advice: Marc de Kruijf	**269**
	Shockwave Movies	Director programming: Marc Hagers	**291**
	Banner Advertising		**297**
	Adobe Acrobat and PDF		**305**
	Working with Sound	Advice and Web Design: Maarten Schutjes	**313**
	QuickTime VR and Video	QTVR production: Mark Ossen	**319**
	The Web in 3D	Advice and Web Design: Thomas Marzano	**327**
	Web Design and XML	Text and programming: Eric van der Linden	**335**
	WAP Design and WML		**351**
	Programming with JavaScript	Illustration 'Candle': Eric Bruinewoud	**357**
	Dynamic HTML and TV Browsers	Programming: Jeroen Ritmeijer, Martin Mes	**363**
	Java Programming	Spacemen JavaApplet: Richard Heesbeen	**379**
		Illustration 'Java': Eric Bruinewoud	
	All About ActiveX Controls	Text and programming: Jeroen Ritmeijer	**387**
	Filemaker Database Publishing		**395**
	Database Linking with ASP	Text and programming: Jeroen Ritmeijer	**401**
▶ **Index**			**411**

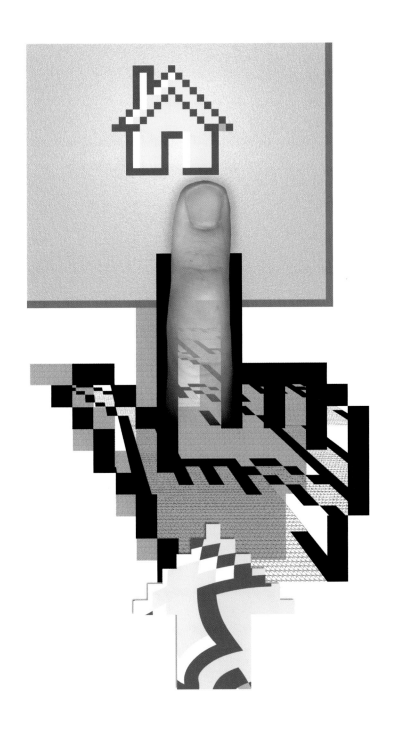

Functional Web Design

The Web offers ▶ every kind of page imaginable —from a KISS (keep it simple, stupid) design, almost entirely in HTML, to a predominantly visual design.

With the field of Web design changing at breakneck speed, it's good to know that some rules always apply. This chapter offers ten rules garnered from practical experience that will help you keep the development and construction of your Web site on track.

10 Web Design Rules

Rules and laws apply to all professional areas. Whether you hammer nails into wood or drill for oil in the ocean, every field has rules that are generally accepted and respected by its workers. In professional Web design, some might assume that these rules are still under development.

In practice, the professional Web designer cannot ignore generally applied user interface design laws or screen communication laws. Concepts such as font display size and navigation structure are the same for all digital media. However, the Web has its own rules.

And although they continually change as technology advances and designers become increasingly inventive with their digital creations, Web site builders must respect certain basic principles.

▶ Rules and Regulations

A well-constructed Web page contains a number of features that let the user efficiently assimilate information—both what is conveyed via the digital highway and the content on the page itself. Of course, the rules presented here are not enforceable; given the constant innovation on the Web, nothing is sacred anymore.

All the same, there are a number of design principles the Web designer must take into account. The objective of your site should determine whether or not you follow them.

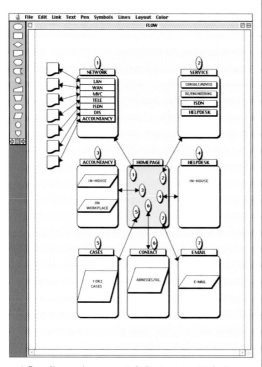

▲ A flow diagram is one way to help structure a Web site.

Rule 1: First Create a Structure

■ Before you reach for the mouse, pick up a pencil. A simple storyboard or a diagram specifying the different parts of a site is enough to provide structure for the information. Later in this book we will delve into this subject more deeply *(see the chapter "Interactive Navigation on the Web")*.

Rule 2: Put Valuable Content on Every Page

■ A second element of Web site planning is collecting content. Know in advance what the site will communicate. What information will be displayed and is it digitally available? And most important, do not create unnecessary pages that merely provide links to other Web pages—that just frustrates visitors. They're looking for information, so make sure every page displays meaningful information that's tailored to their needs.

Competition on the Web is intense, and Web site visitors' patience lasts as long as a click, so you must give your public their money's worth. Someone coined the expression "catching eyeballs." How effectively you grab the reader's attention and how much time you can entice him to spend on a page or at a site largely determine the income the site owner earns.

Your biggest enemy is the Back button! The switching barrier is very low on the Web. Millions of alternatives are just one click away.

Rule 3: Test the Site Before and During Design

■ A commercial organization does itself a great service by conducting a user test during the design development phase. If possible, give your potential visitors a preview of the site's form and contents and ask for their opinion. Of course, make sure the profile of these users closely resembles that of the site's target group.

You can also perform the test "virtually" by putting a design in the form of a GIF file online and presenting the the Web page address *(the URL)* to visitor candidates along with a questionnaire. Whichever way you offer the test, you can integrate the results into the next iteration of your Web design.

Unless you're creating a personal Web page, this is an investment that will pay for itself over time.

▲ Herman Miller's site is a model of efficiency.

Rule 4: The First Impression is Key

■ The home page is the most important page on your site. Depending on the impression this page makes, a visitor will decide to continue surfing or leave. So make sure the site's function or objective is clear. "At this site you will find information about. . . " must be communicated not only in words, but also visually. The trick is to strike the right balance between an introductory message and navigation elements to subsequent pages. The quality and clarity of the navigation is just as important as the visual impression the site makes. Important links must be displayed clearly and products for sale have to be attractively presented.

Rule 5: Use Common Sense Technology

■ It's tempting to include the newest Web technologies on your site in order to fulfill the promise of a multimedia medium.

However, site visitors are not amused when they're confronted with the broken icon that represents a missing plug-in—not to mention a crash caused by an experimental applet. The lack of uniform Web standards and the multitude of browser and system versions require caution when implementing state-of-the-art technology.

Rule 6: Offer Alternatives

■ If you do decide to use specific plug-ins or ponderous graphics, it is important to give visitors the option of experiencing your site the way they like. An introduction presented in Macromedia Flash is only great if you perform a browser check in advance to ensure that the corresponding plug-in has been installed. If not, a replacement image must be displayed automatically.

A site that uses "heavy" images *(those that take a long time to draw on the screen)* must have a "light" alternative as well. In a site with a great deal of service-content, such as an online investor site, this is an absolute must because it saves time.

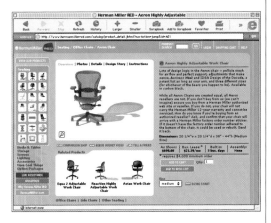

▲ Herman Miller's store is crispy clear and easy to navigate.

▲ E*Trade's investors have a choice between versions.

Rule 7: Design with Intelligence and Restraint

■ Even though the newest computers are equipped with 56Kbps modems, and Internet via cable is here to stay, this does not mean you can let your Web site grow infinitely. Your visitors want to see information on the screen quickly, preferably within 10 seconds. Although this standard could never be enforced, a designer cannot ignore the user's need to see something onscreen immediately after connecting.

Thus the site designer must set up the page to quickly display some textual information that the visitor can absorb, and then the images will flow in at a speed that depends on the user's Internet connection. One way to guarantee this works is to assign both width and height for all your images. The browser needs this data to display the text on the HTML page. After the text is read in, the corresponding images are displayed one by one.

Sites that retrieve content *(images or scripts)* from external servers, such as advertising banners from external sources, run the risk of delays caused by the external connection. Try to isolate the banner in the layout, so that the entire page does not have to wait for it.

▲ Web browsers display HTML text first. With a lot of information visible right away, the reader can get on with it.

▲ The rest of the page appears after the images have been added.

▲ An ad banner slows up the rest of a download.

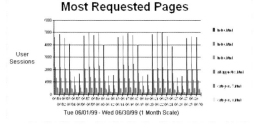

■ Your site's statistics are extremely valuable data that you can include in the design and maintenance process. Categories and functions that have a high priority for the visitor are reflected in the statistics, and you can modify the site design accordingly.

Rule 8: Clear and Consistent Navigation

■ However beautiful first impressions may be, the home page is only the beginning of a site visit, since the pertinent information is usually displayed on subsequent pages. That means you must let the visitor get to the content easily. It also means that subsequent pages must have the same navigation structure as the home page. This kind of consistency ensures that users will find their way without obstacles, enticing them to stay at the site longer and giving them a reason to return.

When a visitor leaves the home page and starts clicking through the site, he needs to know where he is in the site's hierarchy and how he can get back to the home page.

The relationship to other subpages or topical pages must also be clear. Tabs have become popular navigation elements because they make it possible to use screen space economically, and they serve simultaneously as location indicators. The height of a navbar using tabs is usually small. But in this tight space a range of navigation options can be presented.

▲ Tabs are becoming more and more popular on the Web.

■ **All links on the left hand side!**

This seems to be the convention for most public sites. A recent study of the top 50 American media and entertainment sites revealed a striking result: Almost three-quarters of all sites have a column on the left side containing all the navigation elements. This placement works well, but the number of links in the margin needs to be restricted; otherwise, visitors will click on only the top few choices.

Alternative navigation methods, such as a search engine, can best be placed at a prominent, fixed spot on the page. A Quick Search function is ideal for the Web surfer who wants fast results—he can enter his search word immediately without first clicking on the search page, and the search result is the same.

Rule 9: Web Design Is Dynamic and Proactive

■ A Web site is like a living organism; pages are constantly being added to and deleted from it. The design also needs to be critically reviewed on a continuing basis: Can the page be made "lighter" for faster screen draws? Should we modify our site to keep up with any online trends? Visitor behavior changes and so do the circumstances under which the pages are viewed. Monitor sizes grow and modem speeds increase, but alas, so does online traffic. When it comes to Web design, standing still means moving backward. This can be illustrated by the "before" *(above)* and "after" *(below)* views of Amazon.com's home page. Thus, the ultimate tip is: Control-E, or View Source...

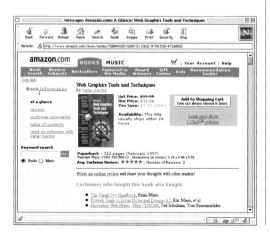

Rule 10: And Above All, . . .

■ Avoid busy, cluttered backgrounds that make the text in the foreground hard to read.

■ Adjust the background color to suit the background pattern. This prevents a shock effect when opening the page.

■ Avoid Web pages that merely offer screen-filling plug-ins without providing an alternative HTML version for the user who does not have that plug-in.

■ Always make background music an option; unwanted sounds are annoying.

■ Ensure readable text sizes, and do not use too many different fonts and font sizes on the same page.

■ Avoid unneccessary GIF images when the same information can be offered in text only HTML.

■ Be conservative with all-uppercase text — it's difficult to read and is associated with shouting.

■ Do not turn your site into "brochureware"; try to avoid reusing existing information. The Web is an interactive medium and requires a different approach.

■ Be wary of actions your visitors won't expect. They won't appreciate an applet that loads suddenly or an unannounced pop-up window.

■ GIF animations are cool and frequently the only dynamic element on the page. However, too many of them are not at all cool, and speed suffers as well.

■ Regularly check your site. Pages that can no longer be found and Java or JavaScript error messages aggravate the user.

■ Adjust your window size to the user's screen size. Do not make pages too wide and avoid extremely long pages. Scrolling is nobody's favorite pastime.

■ Create pages where the most important information and the necessary informational and navigational hyperlinks are clearly recognizable and easy to find.

■ Finally, be sure to renovate your site and make updates!

Microsoft ▸ Internet Explorer uses a special icon in your Favorites list.

It's not just design that determines the success of a Web presentation.
Just as important are the techniques applied in the creation process, the scope of user interaction, and practical service matters such as the quality and consistency of e-mail follow-up.
In short, the marketing of your Web site, as well as the attention devoted to the information and how it is presented, ultimately determine the site's success.

Marketing and Web Design

It is the designer's fate to have to deal with a number of Web environment–specific factors not relevant in other media during the design and production process. The designer must be thoroughly familiar with the medium's technical possibilities and— just as important—its limitations, so that he can find the best bridge between concept and execution. And he must do all this in a way that serves the target group for which the site is being constructed in the first place.

A number of external factors that determine how comfortable visitors feel with a Web site are also crucial to the site's success. For example, what is the value of a brilliant Web site if no one can find it? And how successful is a 3-D animation if only a few people can view it, because certain plug-ins are missing? For the Web designer and marketer alike, the trick is finding the right balance between the Web's technical requirements and its creative possibilities.

This challenge can be compared to that which arose with the advent of desktop publishing. When the DTP concept started to appear in the graphic industry, I felt as if my designs were being hampered by technical limitations, in particular the lack of fonts and computing power. Of course, this was the wrong attitude. My father taught me to concentrate on the original concept and worry about its technical realization later. It's the same situation in Web design now. The limitations of HTML and the abundance of codes and technical details often lead to boring productions with similar designs.

It does not have to be this way. If you decide to deepen your knowledge of basic Internet technology a bit, and master common rules and laws with the help of this book, any design can be translated into a professional-quality HTML document. And let's be honest, we have it a lot easier today than in the old DTP days. HTML is much simpler than the cryptic PostScript programming language that was the basis of the DTP revolution. Incidentally, both revolutions in the communication industry, DTP and the Internet, are based on one programming language and one uniform standard. However, the Web goes one step further by being completely system-independent.

▶ **Push and pull**

Whether you're publishing on paper or onscreen, one thing is certain: content and form determine the impact, and thus the success, of your message. And the Internet presents more possibilities for communication because we are in direct contact with the reader. A well-designed Web site doesn't just present information, it also establishes a connection with the visitor. Direct interaction is one of the Web's most powerful instruments! This is true especially because it

Here is the Philips Semiconductors site before (top) and after its redesign. ▶

is the reader who approaches the party sending the message. Out of all the millions of Web pages, someone takes the trouble to type in your Web address *(URL)* to read your message. This is a completely different form of communication than a TV commercial or a newspaper ad, for instance. People usually receive these messages passively, because their eye is simply confronted with the offer.

How do visitors get your address in the first place? Printing it on your business card and in advertisements produces visitors, of course. A search engine can also specify your URL. And you can generate more visits via a Web site dedicated to giving referrals based on a search by keyword or name. Naturally, there are other ways to lure Web surfers to visit your home page. But first of all, the visitor has to make the effort to stop by.

▶ Take me Home-page

The Web site must reward the visitor for her efforts. A messy site with inconsistent typography and use of color will make a negative impression. A business Web site normally presents information that's included in a neat brochure. If you choose the Internet to communicate your commercial message, you need to consider certain priorities.

The level of interaction and the way the visitor is guided through the site are extremely important. Unclear references and buttons needlessly complicate this process. Some companies have a Web site with a representative who is available 24 hours a day. But this representative cannot direct the customer to click on certain buttons or hyperlinks so that she can get the requested information. Thus the interaction and logic that are fundamental to the Web site must be built into the design and its execution.

One of the Web designer's key jobs is not only to create an attractive and informative Web site, but also to make it easy to navigate. This spares him from discovering later from server statistics that a special Web page, nested some what deep in the site, has hardly ever been visited.

▲ The Philips Semiconductors home page contains a unique navigation feature that lets the visitor link directly to a Web page many layers deeper in the site. The site's target group consists mainly of engineers looking for specific product information. Thanks to this dynamic HTML solution, the target group is served quickly.

▶ Target Group and Scope

As with all marketing activities, advertising focuses on target groups. First, one conducts a study to learn to whom the commercial message must be geared, and then one makes a presentation based on the profile for this target group. If you want to do more than merely inform, a good Web site must also satisfy these criteria. Perhaps you also want to convince the digital visitor to purchase something by filling an electronic form.

As I've mentioned, this option is unique to the Internet medium: just imagine a TV commercial with an order form! The Web gives you direct interaction with your potential customer, who can then go on to make a purchase without the intervention of other parties *(read: retailers)*—every marketer's dream. The Web has made one-to-one marketing possible, and this form of customer relationship marketing has enormous potential.

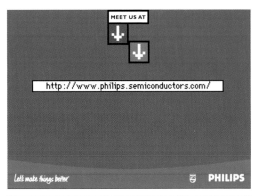

▲ The Philips flyer describes the most important site elements.

▶ Am I on Your Bookmarks List?

The Bookmarks or Favorites list is an enormously powerful instrument. This feature lets users store a number of Web addresses in a separate menu in their browser. When they select a name from the Bookmarks menu, the correct URL location is automatically placed in the 'Go to' window, and contact is automatically established with the selected site.

The trick is getting users to include you in their list. The willingness to purchase is not the problem. First you must ensure that people check out your site and that they are willing to come back a second time. A good Web site is appealing enough to entice the reader to come back again. The Web designer must strive to convince customers in the target group to include the Web site in their bookmarks list.

Do not underestimate the power of this function; bookmarks are, in fact, a user's hotlist—they reflect a Web surfer's personal hobbies, interests, and preferences. If you took a look at a friend or colleague's bookmarks, you would learn a lot about that person. The bookmark list could be viewed as the contemporary mirror of the soul.

▶ Measuring the Medium's Reach

The more technical the communication medium, the easier the measurement. All sorts of measurement instruments have been envisioned and developed over the years for calculating and charting a medium's effective reach. Since the invention of television, people have been looking for systems that provide insight into the medium's effectiveness and its reach.

Thanks to companies such as Nielsen Media Research, we can now determine with some precision how many viewers have watched a particular program by working with representative random samples. By extrapolating the figures to total population figures, we can get a realistic image of the medium's reach. These figures are extremely

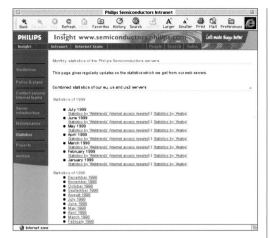

▲ Current data about visits to Philips' SemiconductorsWeb site are available to the people in the company on the Philips Semiconductors intranet, both in visual form in Webtrends, as well as in text-only form.   ▼

important for advertisers, since they want to have their commercials aired during programs that attract a lot of viewers.

The techniques used for television cannot be applied to the Web. Nor are they necessary, because the medium measures itself: The HTTP protocol automatically records each visit to a Web page. Visiting a Web site, in fact, means using a standardized technical protocol that requests the server to transmit an HTML file and all its corresponding images, animations, Java scripts, and applets. These components are sent one by one via modem or a fixed connection. The Web browser *(the reading program on the Web)* does nothing more than display the HTML document and its images.

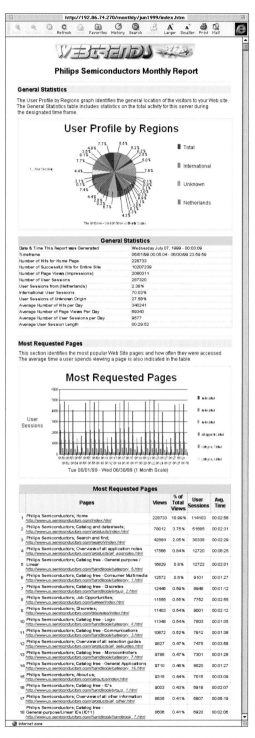

▲ The statistics show the number of visitors, where they came from, and what pages they looked at.

▶ Numbers Don't Lie

With every visit to a Web page, it is the server's logbook that shows exactly when and how frequently each HTML document was transmitted. If the home page is named "index.html," which is the normal convention, you can interpret these numbers as a correct reflection of the number of visits.

Note: These are not the "hits" that are so frequently mentioned in Internet publications. That figure actually provides much less insight into the number of visits, because each Web page *image* sent counts as a hit. As you can imagine, one visit to a complex page with a large number of images produces quite a number of hits, and that number doesn't mean there were many visitors! The designation "page views" or "impressions" is a better indicator because it records only actual visits.

▶ Anonymous Visitors

One of the features of the Internet is that a site's visitors remain anonymous. The server cannot tell who has viewed a particular home page. What the server does register is the location from which the visit was made. In other words, the "host" is marked for every visit. That means if a visitor logs onto the server at Philips, the software registers that a visit was launched from the domain "com.philips." The number of files sent is also registered, as is the visitor's browser and what files were viewed.

This means you also get a clear overview of which software was used to surf the Web. Given that the different browsers support different standards, you can get a picture of surfer behavior. If you analyze and plot this information, it provides interesting material for the Web site owner. In the examples shown in this chapter, the owner is a manufacturer of high-quality semiconductor products. The site uses scripts that dynamically generate pages from different databases. The big advantage of this design is that the

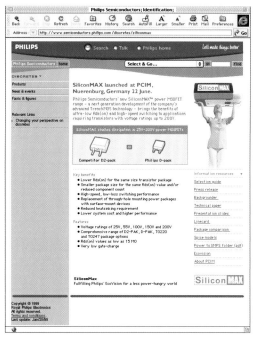

▲ Special feature pages are used to promote new products, services and events.

site offers specific visitors their own page tailored to their preferences. A distributor, for example, could have special pages showing its modified prices.

▶ Unique Contacts Are No Good

A single hit is a flash in the pan. This music-industry motto means that an artist who has had only one successful hit record is not a star. The same is true for the Web—what good does it do if a surfer visits a Web site only once? If the visitor has seen it all in one go or is put off by factors such as boredom, illustrations that take too long to load, or a very poor interface, it will be difficult to entice this person to come back a second time.

Let me say it again: The visitor has taken the trouble to log in and he must be rewarded for his efforts. A consumer-sensitive approach is a must for the long-term success of any commercial site.

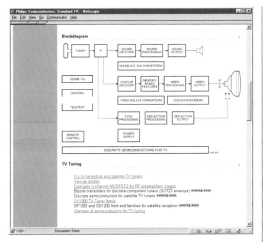

▲ The engineers can use the diagrams interactively; the individual boxes link to specific product information pages.

▶ **Super Zapping**

The phenomenon "zapping" is familiar from television. If a program is boring or there are too many interruptions for commercials, the viewer has the urge to move on to another channel. This is a simple operation that requires only the push of a button. The same phenomenon applies to the Internet: If a Web page is not interesting enough, the visitor can jump to another Web site with one mouse-click. But on the Web, people can visit millions of pages, multitudes more than the number of channel options on TV. You can visit a Dutch Web site one minute and a second later log on to an American record company. This is truly super zapping! Thus it is not easy for a site to stand out, certainly if you want to build a site that must appeal to a large online public. The competition is infinite.

▶ **Vertical Markets**

The Web sites that fare best in this enormous competitive field are those geared to niche markets or those that primarily have niche applications. *Niche* is a marketing term for a specific, limited market segment. A typical example is the semiconductor

application illustrated in this chapter. The members of the Philips Semiconductors target group, primarily engineers in the electronics industry, spend a great deal of time on the Web *(two hours per day, according to studies)* and use this medium to request information. The target group evaluates a site based on its structure and its accessibility of information. That has been the primary principle behind the design and technical setup of the Philips Web site. In total, the site consists of 18,000 pages that are dynamically created from a database. That also means the form of the Web page and its contents are actually separate; at the moment the site is published, the two information streams come together.

▲ This page consists of separate "scripted" text modules, compiled from several databases.

▲ The request form for eNews, Philips Semiconductors' weekly e-mail newsletter, has been kept short and concise.

These peripheral conditions influence the Web designer's flexibility to a large degree, but simultaneously provide unique possibilities. For example, the 18,000 pages can all be modified at once by modifying the basic template. Database-driven Web design has become a condition for maintenance-intensive Web sites.

▶ E-mail Is King

The number of hits or the frequency of visits to a home page are not the only good measurements of a Web site's success. The quality of the e-mail *(electronic mail)* that visitors send to the Web site manager is just as efficient a measuring stick for the Web marketer. A positive response, both quantitative as well as qualitative, clearly indicates that the site's message is reaching the target group. In spite of the size and worldwide scope of the Internet, it can address the individual user. Of course, this also offers possibilities for segmentation, for it is impossible to create a Web site that reaches everyone. This is reserved for the big search engines such as Google, Lycos, AltaVista, Excite, and HotBot.

▶ Follow-up Is Crucial

Getting an electronic reaction is one thing; responding to it is another. So-called Netiquette, an unwritten standard, dictates that e-mail must be responded to within

▲ In each Philips Semiconductors eNews mailing, the content originates from the same database as the site.

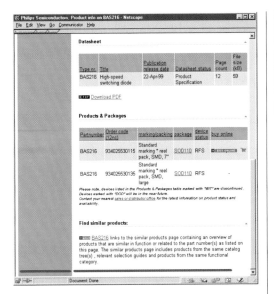

▲ Customers can select and buy products direct from the Philips Semiconductors product information page.

(via a bookmark or search engine) more often than through the home page.

Thus if you are considering a site with a design based on frames, keep in mind that only users with Microsoft Internet Explorer version 5.0 or higher can bookmark specific subpages. Every other browser returns to the home page where the basic frame set was defined. This is an important point you must keep in mind when designing the site, and it is why very few large scale public Web sites use frames.

24 hours. This means that if you wish to exploit a Web site commercially, your organization must provide the proper structure to ensure appropriate and timely follow-up to e-mail messages.

The Web site requires equal involvement from the Webmaster, the technical manager, and the Web marketer. This marketer, frequently a product or communications manager, is responsible for both the site's contents and the prompt follow-up on electronic leads and contacts. More often the answers come from within the organization.

▶ Every Web Page Is Relevant

Many companies focus all their attention on the home page and let the rest of the Web site languish. An appealing facade attracts visitors, but a successful Web site requires more than a home page with pretty images and fine words. You must figure out how to attract visitors to return to your site. Consistent navigation is thus an absolute must. In a technical environment, visitors may reenter the site through a subpage

▶ Prepared for E-commerce

When a Web site visitor takes the trouble to type in a URL or click on a hyperlink that takes him to a site, we can assume that the visitor is interested in the supplier's message.

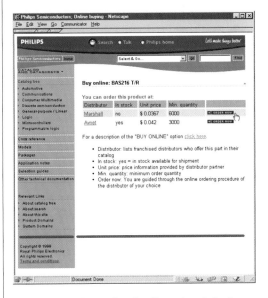

▲ Products can be purchased online; selected distributors handle the actual sales.

It also means the visitor has specific expectations, which you must anticipate.

Appealingly presented information and up-to-date news are a requirement for any site. These do not necessarily have to be press releases; editorial contributions are also appealing to the user.

Thanks to the Net's direct distribution possibilities, online shopping has become generally accepted, and not only in the consumer market. The Web has found its second calling in the business-to-business (B2B) world, as well. The Internet is shifting from a communication medium to a direct-marketing instrument.

Through data-exchange standards such as Edi and EdiFact, e-commerce has been adopted quickly in the B2B world and is now a fast-growing source of income. The Web site occupies an important role in this process, that of profit generator.

▶ Eliciting Responses

Thus a Web site's appeal is not determined by form alone, but also by content and visitor interaction. Depending on the nature of the site, playing games is another way to attract visitors. With the help of Shockwave and Java applets, you can create many opportunities for interactivity.

Good responses can be obtained only if you give visitors room to express their opinions, whether or not it's in the form of multiple-choice questions. A well-designed form contributes significantly to the quality and quantity of your responses, but you must also consider how to follow up on them effectively.

▶ Promotional Elements

A Web site element geared toward generating responses is the most effective instrument for a Web marketer. By integrating a unique action into the site, you can add value to your Web site. A personal newsletter tailored to visitors' preferences is a perfect example.

Philips Semiconductors' weekly eNews newsletter gives customers information tailored to their needs. The company sending the e-mail builds a relationship with existing and potential customers and adds valuable customer information to its database.

▶ One-to-One Marketing

Respondents must be arranged in a database so that their data are not lost. It is advisable to set up a direct marketing database, so that respondents can be categorized by their specific needs and interests. That way, each customer can receive information and offers attuned to his specific needs—the idea behind one-to-one marketing.

All the tracking techniques the Web makes possible let you tailor information to a user behind the scenes. Simply by analyzing surf or click patterns, you can offer the user content that is customized to her surfing patterns. This smacks a bit of Big Brother, and consumer's privacy rights must be honored, but it is the future of marketing. Compare it to a visit to the corner baker in the old days—he also knew exactly which bread his customers wanted and how much they consumed.

So e-commerce is actually old wine in new bottles. The issue is whether a company can deal with the new rules. If a company is set up for bulk deliveries, how will it process onetime sales to an individual customer? The idea is to avoid constantly opening cartons containing 1000 pieces and then repacking the items. If a Web site needs to let customers order products and/or services, you must ensure in advance that the organization is set up to deal with those orders. A direct link to the warehouse administration and booking system can create a workflow that will pay back the investment in Web site development.

An e-commerce Web site that is set up ad hoc creates many administrative headaches,

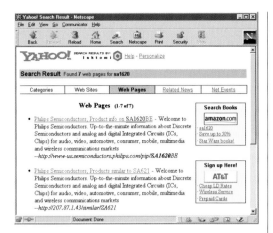

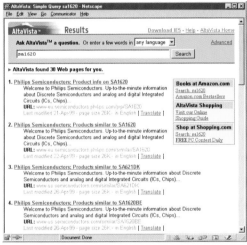

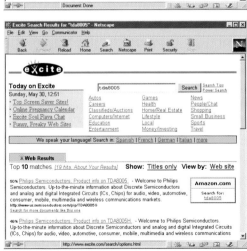

▲ With three of the most popular search engines, the Philips Semiconductors site scores high in a search by industry-standard component number.

since a Webmaster is not really qualified to deal with bookkeeping and logistics issues. In that case, the Web site can do more harm than good.

▶ The Power of Search Engines

Search engines, or search robots, are the real muscle of the Web. In the unstructured virtual world of the Internet, search engines are the only tools the user has for finding the information he is looking for. Search engines have expanded beyond their primary function and have now become portals.

For a supplier of commercial information this means that a high ranking in search results of the most prominent search engines is worth a great deal. In fact, it is worth more than an online advertisement, since fewer people click on banner ads than use search engines for their information needs.

Studies show that more than 70 percent of Web surfers primarily use search engines to navigate the Web. Bookmarks are used in more than 75 percent of cases, while less than 20 percent of the users click on online advertisements. The percentage of users who click on an advertisement *(the "click-through ratio," in Web lingo)* is barely one percent.

Advertisements in other media offer better prognoses. Acquiring a high position in a search engine depends on many factors, and not all laws apply equally to AltaVista, Yahoo, and Excite. A search engine specialist knows how to influence positions and is thus an indispensable member of your Web team.

▶ No Contact?

Online communication on the Net can be disrupted for technical reasons. Keep this in mind and record these disruptions. There is also occasionally a problem in the site itself. Make sure you have an error message page that apologizes to users for your inability to serve them at the moment. And include an alternative search method on the page so the user always has another option.

▶ Online Project Site

A Web site's design and navigational features must be consistent throughout all its sections, especially in complex sites that require a great deal of maintenance *(a basic principle discussed earlier in this chapter)*. When several parties work on a site—editors, technical developers, content builders, and the like—you should create a site guideline, as well.

This document, which is more extensive than a house style guide *(see below)*, can be used to specify all the relevant data about the site, and it may contain confidential company information that is not intended for everyone. The most appropriate medium for distributing the information is in this case an *intranet*, since the document must remain secure behind the company firewall.

An online site guideline is more than just the source of information about templates used and statistics scored. Ideally, all information regarding the site can be found on the project site: the project descriptions, who the content "owners" are, and so on.

In larger organizations such as Philips Semiconductors, several functional groups are involved in the site—the media relations department, for example, which manages press releases, and the finance and accounting group, which is responsible for the

Investor Relations section of the site. All of these groups contribute to the site guidelines.

▲ A product information page consists of separate scripted text modules brought together on the page.

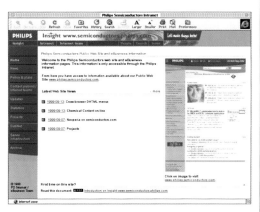

▲ The corporate intranet is used as a central information point for the public Web site and e-business strategy. ▶

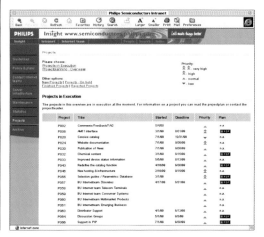

▲ The home page is described on the company's intranet.

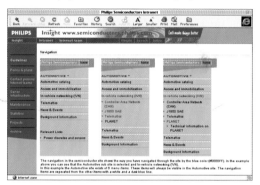

▲ The navigation structure is displayed in the left margin.

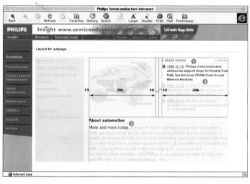

▲ The site's dynamic HTML navigation is explained.

▲ Each icon has a corresponding function.

▶ Online Style Guide

The forms for the various Web pages that appear on the Philips Web site have been recorded in minute detail in the style guide shown on this page. The reasons for this are clear: to guarantee consistent design and simplify the creation of new content. Using this stringent standardized approach, the company recoups its investment over the long term. The style guide also ensures that geographically diverse parties can work on the site simultaneously. The end result is that a subsite created in the U.S. is attuned to the pages created in the Netherlands. In these examples, not only are the grids specified down to the last pixel, but the use of the navigation elements, the icons, and so on are also specified. All of this information has been published on the company intranet project site in a clear, comprehensible manner.

◀ The layout is described down to the last pixel.

▶ Intranet and Extranet Design

For some Web sites, the number of hits and e-mail responses are not the core elements. Its connection with the outside world is not the first priority; rather, the internal communication is the focal point. These Web sites have become known as intranets. The primary advantage of intranet technology for a company lies in the fact that different computer platforms and operating systems can communicate with one another. The Internet protocol TCP/IP is universally supported in the computer world. As a result, you automatically have a common standard for the company network.

The basic principle on which the Internet runs—system-independent communication—is a godsend for the internal company network: a virtual internal company network. Using a browser that is available on all platforms makes the user interface identical for all workstations. This yields obvious advantages in terms of training and maintenance.

▶ Paperless Office?

Companies that use an intranet will quickly adopt a different course of communication from that used in its pre-intranet days. If Web servers are set up within the company as well, the information streams can be managed even better. For example, the marketing department can put its reports and prognoses on its own network, making them easily accessible to all the interested parties within the company. This work method requires a complete turnaround from the paper world. Communication via e-mail is a step in the right direction, but messages must be sent to recipients. With an internal Web server, it's the other way around: If you want information about a specific project, you only have to look on the intranet—all the information is continuously and uniformly available.

▲ An intranet must be secure, but a gateway to the outside may be needed for remotely located staff.

▲ The start page of Philips' intranet magazine, Insight, offers all Web-connected employees a variety of relevant subjects.

Setting up an intranet poses different design requirements than a public Web site. Looks are less important than the site structure and the interface. A good search engine is also indispensable, since experience has shown that an intranet grows at an amazing rate. Typical paper information sources—for example, the internal telephone directory, training manuals, and job openings—are eventually placed on the server. Over time this represents a considerable savings in the amount of paper circulating through the company. The location of the employee who wants to gather information becomes less relevant. Employees have access to the network, and thus to the information they are looking for, from any location.

▶ Intranet-Specific Conditions

Since it uses the existing infrastructure, setting up the intranet Web server is a standard task for an IT department. However, the creation and management of the Web pages is another matter. Not only must a structure be created for the pages, but also the relationship between them must be managed. The Web designer is involved in creating a basic HTML grid in which fixed page elements are arranged and structured within the company's style guidelines. The designer can apply the rules for paper communication to the intranet.

The fact that everyone on the intranet uses a Web browser is a good starting point. This provides intrinsic guidelines for the computer programmers and designers. On the Web, everyone uses the same simple yet extremely effective conventions. For example, a hyperlink is displayed in blue and accented by underlining the text. This convention is not only generally accepted, it is also easy to teach when introducing a new user to the intranet.

▶ Templates

The content of Web pages is much more important than how the HTML document looks on the intranet. The designer should strive to create simple, easy-to-print pages for those employees who still need paper copies. The use of simple, pictogram-like GIF images can make the navigation easier.

If your own staff has to create the Web pages, the master-page design must not be complex. Using a WYSIWYG - HTML editor such as Microsoft FrontPage 2000 or Netscape Navigator Gold is one way to make the layout work as accessible as possible. The HTML house style manual can specify the consistent use of the same GIF images in the same size.

By designing fixed template (grid) pages and distributing them among users, you ensure consistent quality in your Web pages. For example, you can specify in the template that a document title must always be indicated by the tags <H2></H2>, or that a subheading must be indicated using the boldface tag <B></B>. By adhering to these layout rules, a homogenous image is created even though different people are creating the pages.

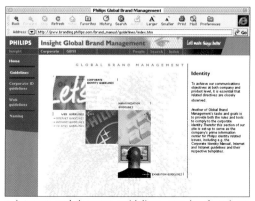

▲ Internet and intranet guidelines can be found on Philips' intranet.

▲ Complete templates are downloadable.

▶ Database Links

Every company has an internal database *(or perhaps several)* in which an enormous amount of information about products or services is stored, information that clearly should go on the intranet. Linking internal company databases requires a great deal more expertise. But there are standard solutions for this task—for example, products from Oracle, Microsoft, and Sybase. Most of these packages support the familiar open database connectivity *(OBDC)* database file format.

▶ Extranet

Shielded from the outside world, an intranet site doesn't need to contain any publicity. However, many corporate Web sites have both a closed section and an open section. It is entirely possible to seal off certain Web pages from the outside world. When you put both accessible and protected pages under one domain name, the site is called an extranet.

Extranets are ideal for setting up a separate area for protected external communication, with distributors and customers, for example. Of course, this requires absolute security on your site.

A firewall—a computer that keeps uninvited guests out—is a requisite, just as is strict compliance with the security requirements. The difference between the Internet, intranets, and extranets is, in fact, the difference in access privileges that visitors enjoy.

The Internet ▶
has its own
language and
writing
conventions.

Acronyms such as HTML, HTTP, URL, and FTP may seem like code language. But every profession has its own jargon, and each of these acronyms stands for a technical Internet term. This chapter discusses the basic concepts of these terms, illustrated with practical examples.

 ## HTML for Designers

Hypertext Markup Language, commonly known as HTML, is nothing more than a set of layout codes added to ASCII text that specify the way the text is displayed. Moreover, HTML commands add references that link a document to other Web documents or e-mail addresses. HTML is derived from the coded markup language SGML, which stands for Standard General Markup Language.

The words *language* and *code* may give the impression that HTML is a programming language, a description that immediately creates resistance and may frighten off many a Web designer. Actually, HTML is simply a markup language in which logical codes, always placed between angle brackets (< >), determine the appearance of the Web page and all the text it contains.

Users of the page-layout program QuarkXPress who have worked with layout programming software will be quite familiar with these codes.

In short, do not be put off by the seeming complexity of Web vocabulary. Designing and laying out Web pages using HTML is definitely not a high-tech task that requires learning all sorts of codes by heart.

The HTML editors currently available make the work much more pleasant without sacrificing quality. For those who refuse to type in a single line of code, there are even WYSIWYG *(what you see is what you get)* HTML editors available. This book offers examples of what you can do with Web site creation programs such as Adobe GoLive and its competitors, Macromedia Dreamweaver and Microsoft FrontPage, which fulfill the WYSIWYG promise on the Web.

▶ Learn the Basics to Get Better Results

Why, you may ask, don't I restrict myself to this WYSIWYG category of layout programs? Well, there are two important reasons for learning HTML theory. First, having a sound basic knowledge of the HTML commands is an advantage during the layout process. If you understand the structure and underlying principles of a technology, you can gauge and perform your actions better. Compare it to driving a car: If you know what the clutch does, you can learn how to use the clutch pedal faster and more efficiently. The same applies to creating a document using HTML codes. The second reason HTML knowledge is indispensable lies in the WYSIWYG editors themselves. These software programs do not support the complete arsenal of HTML commands, so the designer must gain extensive knowledge of HTML and its conventions if he wants to create a well-structured, creative Web site.

▶ HTML's Ancestor, SGML

The foundation of HTML was formed on the basic principles of the general markup language SGML. This language takes into account that on the Internet, all computers and operating systems must display informa-tion uniformly. Whether you have a computer that runs on Microsoft Windows operating system, an Apple Macintosh, or a Unix-based system, the Internet knows no boundaries in terms of system diversity—one of the reasons for the explosive growth of the Web.

The two pillars of the Web are HTML and TCP/IP, the Internet's communication protocol that handles data transfer in the form of "packets." Since system independence was a must from early on, the creators of HTML scrounged around for a standard at the International Standards Organization, or ISO, Institute—and SGML was its contribution. ISO is known for its certification activities—for example, the ISO 9000 and 9001 norms—but the institute has also contributed a large number of standards to the world, and one of them is SGML. This general markup language is used by numerous American government agencies to structure documents.

SGML is also found in page-layout programs such as Adobe FrameMaker. SGML's logical construction served as the starting point for the developers of the HTML code set, since it was an ideal basis for system-independent markup. The installed fonts and basic settings of a Web message recipient's system have little or nothing to do with the Web itself, but a markup language that makes logical formatting a priority is a must. Mind you, the reader is the one who determines the display font and the font size in her browser. If you could specify that a Web page must be read using Helvetica, what about the poor users who have other fonts installed instead? This limitation is the price we pay for the total system independence of the Internet and, specifically, Web protocol. The universality of the Web allows everyone to choose their own settings and fonts so they can more easily read the information. Until document-sharing programs such as Adobe Acrobat are used on all computer platforms, we will have to go on living with this restriction.

◄ What a difference a browser makes: Here's the same Web page viewed with Netscape Communicator (left) and the Lynx text browser, shown below.

Welcome to Philips Electron Optics

PHILIPS | Philips Electron Optics

You have entered
Innerspace
Domain of Philips Electron Microscopy

Welcome to Philips Electron Optics' home page. From here you can reach out for news, views and information about the exciting world of electron microscopy.

This page is Netscape 2.0 enhanced. Latest update February 29, 199...

NEW This update features:

- Just a few words from our MD Bill Whitward
- CompuStage animation sequence
- Dialogue with Philips Electron Optics

 Look into Philips Electron Optics
...and learn the secrets of over 50 years suc...
microscopy.

 News You Can Use
Read all about the very latest techniques, d...
one of the world's market leaders in scannin...

 SEM & TEM Product Programme.
We have one of the most complete program...
electron microscopes in the industry. And if...
needs, we'll tailor a microscope so that it do...

 Customer Support Services
Our microscopes are designed with service...
services of unsurpassed quality are the hid...
manufacture and sell.

 Education & Training
New to electron microscopy? Studying mate...
staff need training in EM operation, mainter...
Electron Optics has all the answers.

 3D Electron Micrography
Philips Electron Optics introduce a new dim...
This page features a unique WWW Art Gall...
many in 3D. But don't take all of them too s...
made purely for the sake of "art" or fun. Why...
PEOs Art Gallery?

 Around the World in 80 Clicks
Click here for an international listing of Phil...
Optics addresses.

If you are using NCSA Mosaic for X 2.6, see this page without tables.

Address any questions or comments to Philips Electron O...
Copyright © 1996 Philips Electronics. All...

---

igate.wise.nl 4

Welcome to Philips Electron Optics

Philips Home Page Philips Electron Optics Home Page

You Have Entered Innerspace

Welcome to Philips Electron Optics' Home Page. From here you can enjoy complete access to news, views and more information about the exciting world of electron microscopy.

This page is HTML 2.0 enhanced.

THIS UPDATE OF FEBRUARY 29, 1996 FEATURES:

"Cool" micrographs in our microscopic Art Gallery Download our "Let's make things better" screensaver SCOPE magazine No. 4 EO bulletin No. 134 Philips Electron Optics at SEMICON Europe '96 Philips' State-of-the-Art Products at Pittcon '96

INFORMATION

Site history Site guide Dialogue with Philips Electron Optics

Look into Philips Electron Optics
...and learn the secrets of over 50 years success in innovative electron microscopy.

News You Can Use
Read all about the very latest techniques, developments and applications from one of the world's market leaders in scanning and transmission microscopy.

SEM & TEM Product Programme.
We have one of the most complete programmes of scanning and transmission electron microscopes in the industry. And if we still don't meet your specific needs, we'll tailor a microscope so that it does!

Customer Support Services
Our microscopes are designed with service in mind, because customer services of unsurpassed quality are the hidden assets in every product we manufacture and sell.

Education & Training
New to electron microscopy? Studying materials or life sciences? Does your staff need training in EM operation, maintenance, new techniques? Philips Electron Optics has all the answers.

3D Electron Micrography
Philips Electron Optics introduce a new dimension in TEM & SEM micrographs. This page features a unique WWW Art Gallery of electron microscope images, many in 3D. But don't take all of them too seriously, some of the images are made purely for the sake of 'art' or fun. Why not exhibit **your own image(s)** in PEOs Art Gallery?

Around the World in 80 Clicks
Click here for an international listing of Philips Electron Optics addresses. Wherever you are, you're never far, from Philips Sales & Service.

If you are using NCSA Mosaic for X 2.6, see **this page without tables.**

Address any questions or comments to **Philips Electron Optics, marcom@eo.ie.philips.nl.**
Copyright © 1996 Philips Electronics. All rights reserved.

-- press space for next page --
Arrow keys: Up and Down to move. Right to follow a link; Left to go back.
H)elp O)ptions P)rint G)o M)ain screen Q)uit /=search [delete]=history list

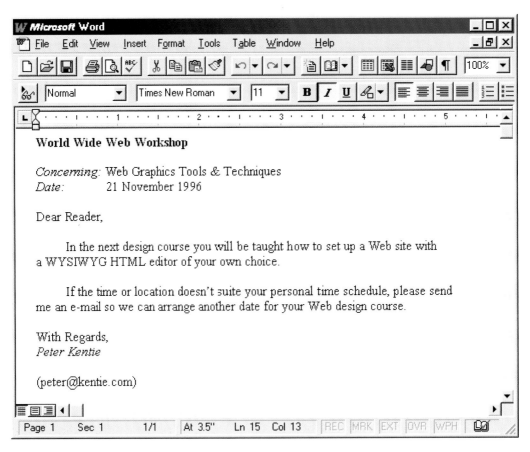

▲ If you read formatted text from a word processor in a Web browser, the layout vanishes—spaces and hard returns have no effect on the display.

The browser displays the text in the standard font size specified in the Preferences window. HTML codes are desperately needed to structure this page's information and make it readable. ▼

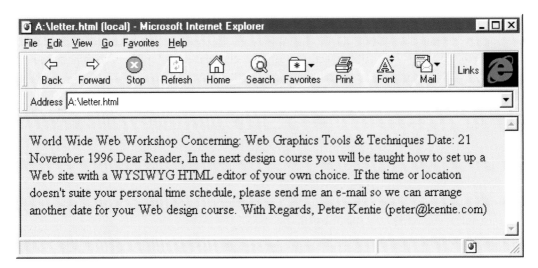

► **Code Language**

HTML files are pure text or ASCII documents to which markup labels or "tags" have been added. Tags can be divided into two categories:

■ "Styles," for the visual layout
■ "Anchors," for references to other HTML documents, audio or film clips, e-mail addresses, and the like.

Anchors are unique to the HTML language and form the basis for the hypertext options on the Web: By merely clicking on a bit of text or an image rather than typing in complicated codes and addresses, the user instructs the computer to retrieve another HTML document. Of course, this technique is not restricted to the Web; CD-ROM and CD-I media also use hyperlinks.

The methodology was discussed as early as 1945 by Vannevar Bush and later worked out by Alan Kay and his associates in the Xerox PARC laboratory. Obviously, tags are not displayed on Web pages viewed on a browser, since visible markup codes would disrupt the legibility of the text. To make a distinction between the textual ASCII text and the coded ASCII text, all markup codes are placed between two angle brackets—the less-than (<) and greater-than (>) characters.

This technique has been used for years by typesetting systems and was even built into word processors such as WordStar, one of the first word processors from the early '80s. QuarkXPress also uses its own markup tags, with which copy can be precoded in a word processor.

► **Solo and in Pairs**

HTML tags are generally used in pairs— one tag to turn the instruction "on" and a second tag to turn it off. The latter can be recognized by the slash (/) character placed immediately after the first angle bracket. If you want to display a bit of text in bold,

in HTML it must be coded as follows:

```
<B>text</B>
```

The first tag, <B>, indicates that the text that follows must be displayed in bold. The second tag, </B>, cancels this style so that the text following it is displayed as normal *(unformatted)* text. Without the closing tag, all the remaining ASCII text on the page would be displayed in bold.

Clearly, it's a must to create a Web page with precision—tracking down an incorrect or missing markup label can be quite a chore. It's just as it was with photographic typesetting in the past: If the typesetter forgot to cancel the typesetting instruction "font corps 24" with a second instruction, an endless roll of paper *(or, even costlier, a roll of film)* came out of the developing machine and would have to be thrown out immediately. Fortunately, if incorrect codes are entered while creating an HTML page, the designer can still check the page by opening the Web browser.

Complex HTML pages that contain lists and tables may require a lot of searching. The huge number of tags that go into forming a table means that you quickly lose any overview of the table, and one incorrect revision can create serious problems. It always helps to insert comments tags (<!-->), which are invisible on the actual Web page, at crucial places within your coding to explain formatting details.

▲ Basic HTML code is fairly simple to read.

▶ HTML Dialects

Not all tags are used in pair combinations. Some tags occur alone; examples include the end-of-paragraph tag, <P>; the end-of-line tag, <BR>; and the horizontal-line tag <HR>, none of which need to be cancelled by a second, closing tag.

So, you see, the HTML standard has some flexibility. In fact, the HTML standard is modified and added to regularly. All Web browsers support the standard HTML 3.0 commands; however, at the end of 1994 Netscape began introducing "extensions," which of course were supported only by the company's own Netscape Navigator browser. The extensions were partly an expansion on the existing HTML standard and included, for example, tags for right-justifying images. Moreover, other new tags replaced the earlier HTML 2.0 tags. Netscape's move was controversial because it apparently opposed the basic principle of the HTML standard: to allow the exchange of documents worldwide without any system dependency.

The HTML language itself is "backward compatible" because of the enormous diversity of hardware and software the data must be able to interpret. Even a Lynx browser, which can show only text, not images, must be able to display the information *(you can imagine how strange a Lynx page looks with all sorts of cryptic and peculiar commands)*.

▶ HTML>XHTML>XML

Practically all browsers are compatible with HTML version 3.2. The specifications for its official successor, version 4.0, are complete and supported by Microsoft Internet Explorer version 4 and later, and by Netscape's Navigator version 6 and later.

In the meantime, the World Wide Web Consortium *(W3C)* is working hard on a new standard called XHTML—hoped to be the mother of all HTML versions. In principle this is a fantastic goal, but why introduce yet another abbreviation that causes confusion? *(XHTML, not to be confused with XML, stands for "eXtended HTML.")*

Besides, unauthorized extensions are being added to the HTML specifications. Since people use these extensions, and because of the success of Netscape Navigator, they have become unofficial additions to the HTML standard.

Microsoft's browser, Internet Explorer, enjoys such broad acceptance by the market that it is the absolute market leader. Its close integration with Microsoft Office components and the dominant position of the Windows operating system have ensured the market position of this browser. The most popular browser on the market, it is used by nearly 80 percent of all Internet users.

Microsoft has also taken advantage of its position by adding its own extensions to the HTML language, aiming to increase the popularity of Internet Explorer. The functionality these new tags introduces cannot be dismissed as merely a clever marketing ploy. Typical Microsoft Web innovations such as background sounds, colored table cells, and built-in video images are now supported by the competing browsers Netscape and Opera.

Practical Web TIP

▶ If you want to keep track of browser developments, check out BrowserWatch, a Web site that lets you find such information conveniently displayed, including a list of available plug-ins. The Web site is maintained by Dave J. Garaffa and published by internet.com.

The URL is:

http://www.browserwatch.com

▶ Competition or Collaboration

The browser war between Microsoft and Netscape creates an additional worry for Web page creators, who now have to take the browser market into account even more. You would have to maintain an administrative staff just to keep track of what extensions which browser supports.

It would be better if Netscape and Microsoft collaborated—or, better still, adopted each other's most successful extensions. Undoubtedly, time will tell how the browser market will develop. Given the interests involved, the browser companies will undoubtedly chart their own paths.

(The W3C acts as the referee and publishes the latest suggestions for and extensions to the HTML standard on its Web site at www.w3c.org.)

▶ HTML Containers

Back to basics: Each Web page has a fixed fundamental design that consists of three sections, or containers. The entire page always starts with the <HTML> tag and ends with the </HTML> tag. There can be a second subdivision, the <HEAD>, in the header section, where the title of the document is placed. Depending on the browser, this text is displayed at the top of the page or in a separate title bar. The text also serves as a Bookmarks entry. The head tag is ended by the HTML command </HEAD>.

The rest of the page is specified using the <BODY> tag. This contains all the text and images in the page display. The </BODY> tag ends the third container. In 1996 Netscape introduced a fourth container, Frames. We will discuss this markup variant in a separate chapter.

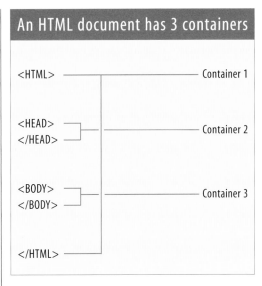

▲ A schematic of the three basic HTML containers, their relationships, and their sequence.

The goal of the Web Standards Project is to advocate system-independent tags and conventions. ▶

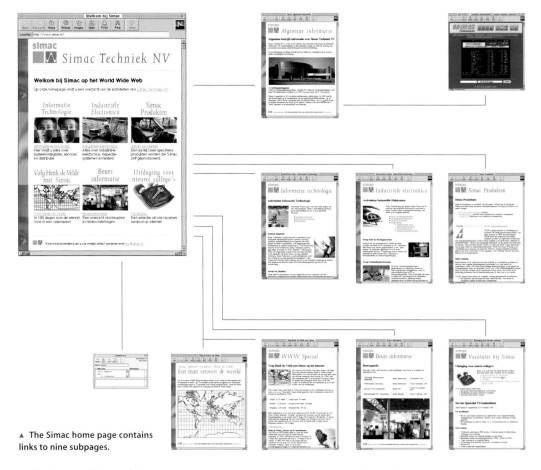

▲ The Simac home page contains links to nine subpages.

▶ **The Power of Hyperlinks**

The overwhelming success of the Web isn't easy to explain. A number of factors have played decisive roles in the spread of this medium, such as its system independence and its worldwide scope. But something else has contributed enormously to the speedy acceptance of the Web: anchors, or hyperlinks.

Since HTML is a hypertext system, documents can refer to one another by means of links, thus allowing interaction unrivaled by any other medium. It is possible to create links not only to text documents, but also to video images, audio clips, illustrations, photos, e-mail addresses, and even animations *(thanks to Sun's Java and Macromedia's Shockwave)*.

The user doesn't have to type in or remember any complicated commands. One click on a colored word or text fragment is all that's needed to establish a connection with another HTML document on the same computer or on the other side of the world. If the Net surfer didn't occasionally glance at the HTTP address, he wouldn't even realize that he was exploring the world from his keyboard and monitor.

If you could read this book's page in hypertext, you would only have to place the mouse pointer on one of the hyperlinks, and with one mouse-click you could read the chapter containing this text. But since you're reading mere paper pages, you don't have that option. With the paper medium, a reference such as "see the chapter about Shockwave" serves the

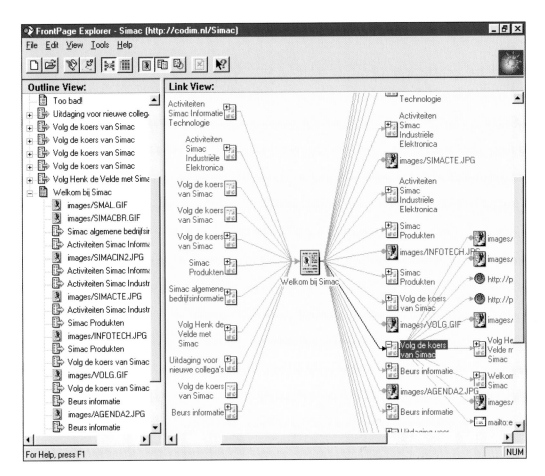

same function. However, this requires more effort on the reader's part, since he must page through the book to find the reference. Interaction with other media is virtually impossible—you cannot play an animation or an audio clip with the paper version. HTML's ability to create links to all available forms of media, combined with the limitless possibilities the Web offers, is unparalleled in traditional communication.

The codes you must include in an HTML document to create hyperlinks are relatively simple. The overview in the example shows nine references to subpages made from Simac's home page index.html. The references range from general information pages to an overview of job openings within the company. To make the Web site more

▲ Microsoft's FrontPage can display the Simac site schematically including the hyperlink text and images that lead to the various URLs.

attractive, a hyperlink to an action element is included. Simac is sponsoring a sailor's round-the-world voyage, which visitors can follow via the Web site. Each day the Web page shows a new position on a map of the world, and a bit of text is included describing the sailor's latest experiences. The Web site offers added value with up-to-date news, and at the same time visitors can get familiar with the services and products being promoted on the site. Of course the home page includes a reference to Simac's e-mail address, which is also displayed in a "footer" on all the subpages, along with a button that lets visitors return to the home page. This is a great navigation element, especially on long pages like the overview of job openings.

In addition to interactivity, a good site must offer high-quality content. In spite of the gigantic number of Web pages out there, only a few sites have content that's as carefully crafted as the graphic design.

A firm that invests a great deal in its house style wants to see this cost and effort reflected in the Web site design. A site that has the character of a paper brochure won't get a great response. After examining it once, the visitor won't come back a second time; the site will suffer the same fate as a brochure, ending up in the trash can. The Web must have added value—otherwise, why have a site? The fact that you can establish an ongoing interactive relationship with the reader makes the Web unique. And this relationship is not limited by time or distance; you can communicate with your target group anytime, anywhere.

▶ **URL and HTTP**

Each Web page has a unique address by which all computers connected to the Internet have access to the page. The ability of different computers to find one another is one of the pillars of the Internet.

Web surfing is simple because one click on a word or image is all the instruction the computer needs to access another computer and retrieve the requested Web page. This technique is based on a protocol called uniform resource locator, or URL, which refers to a specific address on the hard disk of a particular computer. Technically, this protocol also specifies how the information exchange between the different network sources must be handled.

The best-known protocol on the Web is the Hypertext Transfer Protocol, or HTTP. This always refers to a hypertext document *(that is, an HTML file)*, and it's the prefix for many URLs. There are now legions of other protocols online, such as the Mail To protocol, which establishes a connection to send e-mail.

This function is extremely important for generating and measuring Web site responses. The Mail To option ensures that an e-mail window is invoked in the browser. The recipient's e-mail address and the name and e-mail address of the sender are entered automatically; the user simply types his message and sends it. This prevents a great deal of bother, since Internet protocols require great precision.

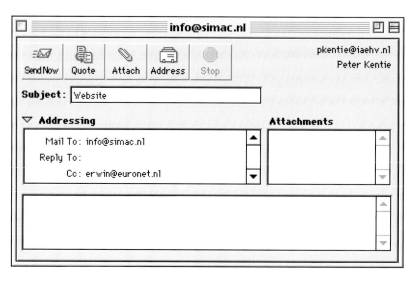

◀ With an e-mail address, viewers can send mail from their browser.

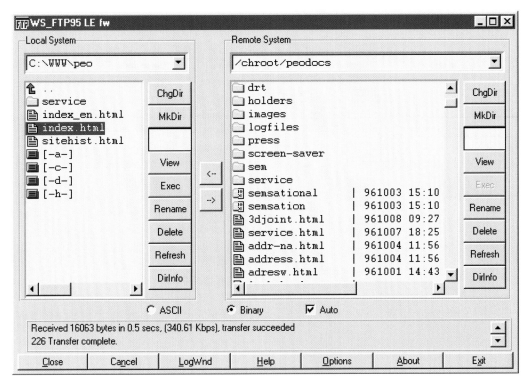

▲ WS-FTP is an extremely effective Windows FTP client.

An attempt is made to contact the external Unix server by ▶
means of an FTP client.

▶ FTP

Another cornerstone of the Web is the long-standing File Transfer Protocol, or FTP. If you want to publish your HTML pages and their related images on the Web, the data must be placed on a Web server. The most common way to transfer the data is by using a stand-alone FTP program or an HTML editor containing a FTP component.

FTP offers two modes of transferring files: binary and text. Binary mode transfers raw data as is, while text mode includes a translation step from one platform to another. For Web content, it's usually safer to transfer data via binary mode; then you can be certain that your data will remain unchanged when it reaches the server. This is especially important for PDF files and multimedia files such as Shockwave and audio files.

▼ After the name and password are accepted, the user is "in."

Name	Size	Date	Zone	Machine
📁 .elm	–	30-08-1994	1	iaehv.iaehv.nl
📄 .forward	1k	16-05-1995	1	iaehv.iaehv.nl
📄 .forward.oud	1k	16-11-1994	1	iaehv.iaehv.nl
📄 .history	3k	24-01-1996	1	iaehv.iaehv.nl
📄 .html	–	01-02-1996	1	iaehv.iaehv.nl
📄 .login	1k	03-10-1994	1	iaehv.iaehv.nl
📄 .newsrc	1k	27-10-1994	1	iaehv.iaehv.nl
📄 .newsrc.bak	4k	05-10-1994	1	iaehv.iaehv.nl
📄 .nn	–	05-10-1994	1	iaehv.iaehv.nl
📄 .pdksh_hist	1k	16-05-1995	1	iaehv.iaehv.nl
📄 .tcshrc	1k	30-08-1994	1	iaehv.iaehv.nl
📁 homepage	–	01-02-1996	1	iaehv.iaehv.nl
📄 index.h	32k	06-06-1995	1	iaehv.iaehv.nl
📁 Mail	–	30-08-1994	1	iaehv.iaehv.nl
📁 News	–	30-08-1994	1	iaehv.iaehv.nl

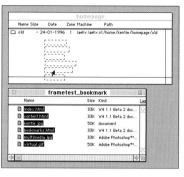

◀ The new content of the home page is moved to the server using drag and drop.

This progress bar is visible during transmission. ▼

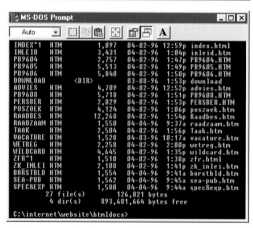

▲ When converting between platforms, the index.html file appears on the disk under the name INDEX~1.HTM. Different line feeds also cause problems. ▼

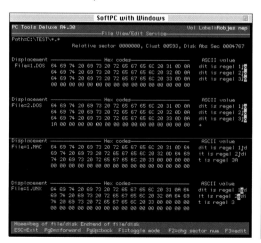

▶ Filename and Writing Conventions

With Web site content developed on both Windows PCs and Apple Macintoshes, communication problems arise because of the two operating systems' different file-naming conventions. Windows 95 has an additional problem: Not all programs comply with the Win 95 file structure. That means a Windows 95 file named index.html could be saved as INDEX~1.HTM if it was downloaded by a browser running on DOS or Windows 3.1 *(though few people use those systems today)*.

Problems can also arise when the browser downloads the files for a Web page, because Windows uses long filenames. Though most operating systems can handle long file names, it's safe to use the "8.3" filenaming convention, which involves using a name of 8 characters, followed by a period plus a 3-character extension such as .doc. Avoid using spaces in filenames; they may create difficulties when trying to access the file in a Web browser.

To ensure that your files can be safely served on and downloaded by browsers running on: UNIX; Windows 95/98, NT, and 2000; and Macintosh OS *(taken together, these cover 99 percent of the Web browsers now in use)*. Obey these rules for naming files:

- Keep your filenames to 31 characters or fewer, including extension
- Don't use these characters: \ / * : < > ? | "
- Use lower case characters only
- Don't start a filename with a period
- Don't use spaces; use _ (underscore) to separate words

3D-model: David Merck, Specular

When someone creates a Web page or site, it's for a reason. They may want to share personal information or preferences with the Internet community or develop an interactive business application. Whatever the motive, the same rule applies: Think before you act.

Building a Web Site

No matter why you're creating a Web document, you need to get to know your target visitors so you can create the style, layout, and content with them in mind. You also need to decide whether the Internet is the right medium for your goals. The Web is experiencing continuous growth, but you should know what those areas of growth are. Naturally, it's not a good idea to build a Web site for people who rarely use the Web—in that case, you may want to consider a medium that would provide better coverage for your target group.

▶ Printing Pixels

It's been said that the World Wide Web is, in fact, an electronic press; bits and pixels are replacing paper and ink as publishing tools. Now several years into the Internet boom, we know there's truth to this statement. Many of the rules that apply to paper publications also apply to the Web, and we need to take some of them into account when designing a Web site. But there are differences too.

As with a paper brochure, it's a must to identify a source or company name on a Web site. But since Web surfers can arrive at a site from any of a number of different places and they won't necessary arrive at your home page, you should be sure to include the company name on each page of the site and give visitors an easy way to reach the various areas of the company. Paper communication is initiated by the company, conceivably to a specific target audience. A Web visit is initiated by the visitor, and the company doesn't know how he got there or what he's looking for, so it is important to provide easy access to various areas of the company's Web site.

▶ Content and Information

When it comes to content, it's not really important whether your online visitor arrives at your Web site via a hyperlink, by using a search engine, or by finding the URL in another medium. The crucial issue is this: What do you present to the visitor?

We can assume that your potential visitors are looking for specific information. And the Web is an excellent medium for this transfer of knowledge. However, this doesn't mean you can simply paste the company brochure into the site.

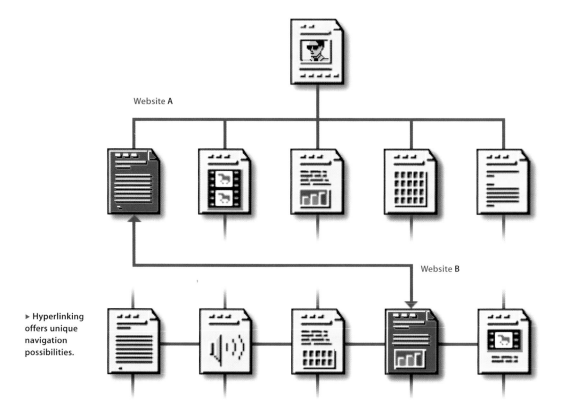

Website **A**

Website **B**

▶ Hyperlinking offers unique navigation possibilities.

The quality of content strongly determines your site's success. But what constitutes good content? For example, will a list of interesting hyperlinks that lead to other Web sites appeal to the reader? Offering a home page that serves as a sort of bridge to other sites may be sufficient reason for the visitor to come back to your site. The disadvantage of including such references is that it doesn't let you communicate much personal information. If the intention is to inform, use external hyperlinks sparingly. Create links to pages within your own Web site—this will keep visitors around longer and expose them to your message.

Of course, to achieve this objective, the quality and presentation of your information must be up to snuff. The page design must cater to your audience and simultaneously serve as a navigation instrument. If you satisfy these two core conditions effectively and consistently in your Web site design, you're on the right track.

▶ Navigating and Maneuvering

All good Web pages have a number of common elements. First of all, there's a clear "sender," or owner, of the Web site. A visitor needs to understand right away whose pages he is viewing. This sounds obvious, but many Web pages don't make this clear. If a visitor bookmarks such a page and returns to it later, he won't be able to find the origin of the page—the company or individual who placed in on the Web—and at that point the browser's Back option won't do him any good. Bookmarks should always give Web pages a clear, concise title so that the reader can see at a glance both the origin and the subject of the Web page.

You must take into account the growth of your Web site from the outset. It is not feasible to present all the information at one level. The interaction between the different pages is precisely what makes a Web site interesting. This means the pages must be linked to one another not only vertically, but also across the various layers. In the example shown on this page, only vertical "jumps" are possible.

This means the user must go all the way back to the home page before heading off in another direction. Of course, that is not the intention. By using good navigation tools such as button bars and including clickable image maps, you can steer the reader through the information.

You don't always have to use a graphic solution such as a navigation bar; a summary of the most important themes may provide a sufficient road map for your site. Keeping this summary separate from the rest of the information, preferably at the same place on every page, strengthens its value. For long pages, the preferred locations are the top and the bottom of the page.

▲ A Web site is more than text and images, it is an interactive multimedia communication medium.

Avoid a design
that's too flat ... ▶

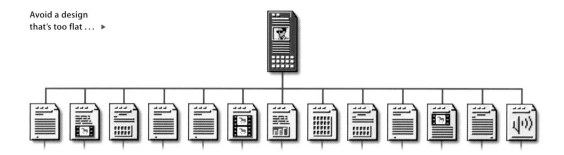

Generally an image is used for navigation bars at the top of the page. If you consistently use the same image, it can be displayed on the screen quickly, thanks to the sophisticated "cache" mechanism used in the popular browsers. An image that has already been loaded once is read from the hard disk when it is reused on another page. The browser software temporarily saves the images from the pages already loaded in a separate cache. This is cleared regularly by the software based on the preferences the user has set for his cache size *(4MB to 8MB is standard)*.

A second element each page must contain is an option for contacting the party who sent or created the Web page. This can be a reference to an e-mail address or, if possible, a hyperlink to a form where the visitor can fill to express his detailed opinion.

▶ Web Site Structure

Taking the trouble to diagram your Web site in advance can prevent many problems down the line. Such a tree structure can be created in any drawing program and serves as a kind of logbook for the designer. The advantage of this approach is that it not only provides insight into the site setup, it also clearly shows where the information is and what aspects must *(or can)* be augmented.

This overview is also handy for the users themselves; you can later create a poster showing all the pages and their links to one another. This stimulates people to visit the site and shows the visitor what information is available that cannot be seen at first glance.

In contrast to a folder or brochure the reader can page through, an interactive medium isn't transparent—it's up to the reader to discover what's behind the button. But you shouldn't let this keep visitors from viewing essential pages. The basic design for a site can also be included in visual form on the actual Web site. Called a site map, such a visual guide supports the primary navigation and, more important, serves as an overview for regular visitors.

...or too
deep. ▶

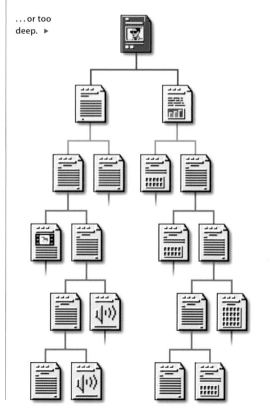

640 pixels wide x 480 pixels high

◀ The standard monitor size of 640 by 480 pixels defines the size for Web page design. If you base your layout on a bigger monitor size, a large percentage of your audience will have difficulty reading the information.

800 pixels wide x 600 pixels high

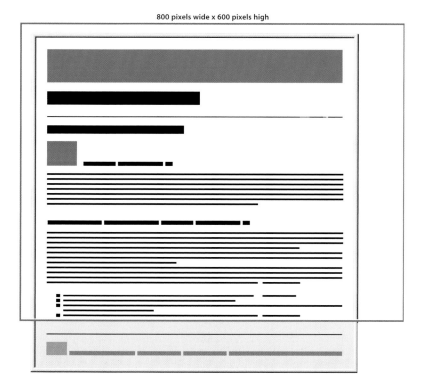

◀ Users with a 17-inch monitor have room to spare with the standard screen setting.

▶ Varying Monitors

The Web is for everyone, and that includes all screens! The various types and sizes must all be able to display all the information of your site. This is an aspect the Web designer must duly take into account. The preceding schematic shows the difference between a 14-inch monitor and a 17-inch monitor.

The size of the monitor determines the experience of the Web page. The most commonly used monitor has a diagonal width of 15 inches, but 17-inch monitors are becoming increasingly popular. This means the most commonly used screen setting has a width of 800 pixels and a height of 600 pixels. According to www.statmarket.com, over 50 percent of all Internet viewers use this size monitor.

The second-largest group of Web surfers uses 15-inch to 21-inch monitors, which have a resolution of 1024 by 768 pixels. To a large extent, these dimensions create the basis for Web page design. However, because quite a number of users, almost 15 percent, still view sites with a screen setting of 640 by

Using small banners, you can ▶ visually specify the ideal monitor settings of a Web site.

480 pixels, these monitor dimensions determine the minimum requirements. The challenge for the Web designer is developing a site that is optimally displayed on the screens used by the target group. Large commercial sites are thus constructed so that the most important content can be displayed at a width of 600 pixels.

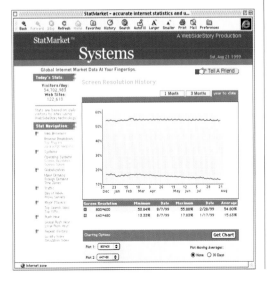

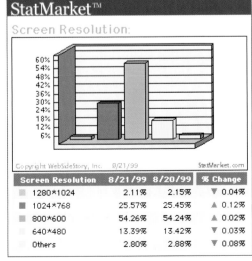

Screen Resolution	8/21/99	8/20/99	% Change
1280*1024	2.11%	2.15%	▼ 0.04%
1024*768	25.57%	25.45%	▲ 0.12%
800*600	54.26%	54.24%	▲ 0.02%
640*480	13.39%	13.42%	▼ 0.03%
Others	2.80%	2.88%	▼ 0.08%

◀ The same Web page is shown here with three different monitor settings:

- 640 x 480 pixels on the left page;
- 800 x 600 pixels at the top right;
- 1024 x 768 pixels at the bottom of the page.

The Web page is constructed such that a background pattern is visible if the page is viewed at a higher resolution. This method ensures that the viewer doesn't see much white space.
Setting the text to a fixed width using a table prevents lines from being too long.

A second aspect we cannot control is the browser width set by the user. Some users have their monitor set so as to completely fill the screen; others make the display smaller so that part of the desktop remains visible. This is a common phenomenon among users with large monitors—a page displayed across the full width of a 21-inch screen is illegible and cannot be printed efficiently.

▶ Tips for Font Size and Width

The length of the Web page is also a variable element. If the reader has his preferences set for a large font size, the page is longer than for a user who has selected a small font size or a condensed font. You can specify in the introduction to your Web page that "this page is best viewed using Times Roman c.12," for example, but there is no guarantee that users will follow this guideline. Ensure that the page is created flexibly or fix its width using tables. The reader will then have the tendency to modify his screen width to suit the contents.

You can also include a "ruler" on the home page with text such as "This page is best viewed if you adjust your screen width to that of the ruler." Of course, this is a stopgap measure and you never know how many people will pay attention to it.

▶ To Scroll or Not to Scroll

What is the correct length for a Web page? Opinions differ on this. Some designers create pages in such a way that the

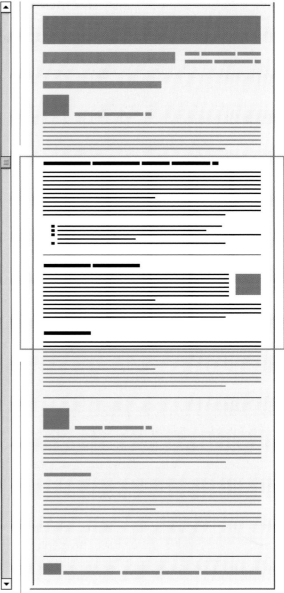

user never needs to scroll—all the information is displayed within the 600 by 400 pixel

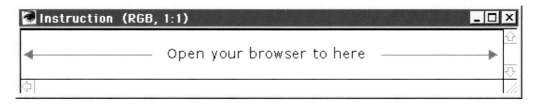

Instruction (RGB, 1:1)

Open your browser to here

▲ The screen ruler is a handy tool for specifying the width of photos and illustrations.

format or divided into fragments that fill the screen using a hyperlink. Naturally, this is not feasible for all Web sites; long pieces of text also have a place on the Web. An online manual or a press release are examples of typical long text passages that are difficult to break into small segments.

A Web site visitor shouldn't have to scroll more than four pages. When text stretches longer than that, the viewer's attention tends to fade because he no longer knows where he is in the document. Placing references in the text can make reading long text pages a more pleasant experience, but in general, reading text from a screen has its restrictions. Most people read a lot slower onscreen than on paper. That says something about the Web.

▶ Disadvantages

However, the disadvantage of short pages is that if you need to display a lot of text, it has to be divided into several subpages. This can create problems if there's a lot of traffic on the Internet, since a new connection must be made for each subpage. Thus one long page containing all the text still has certain advantages. Printing the pages plays a role here, as well. A long page can be sent to the printer as a complete document, whereas separate subpages must be read and printed one at a time. Of course, the best solution is a combination of the two—short, easy-to-read pages and a separate page with all the relevant text for printing.

The moral of the story: Examine each situation separately and take your audience into account.

▶ How Many Hyperlinks

A large number of hyperlinks and references makes it more difficult to get an overview of the page as a whole. If you also use lots of bold text and large headings, the reader gets lost with so many loud elements vying for his attention. Keep pages clean by using bold text sparingly and not marking entire text segments as hyperlinks.

Also avoid "dead ends" as much as possible. Nothing is more irritating than a hyperlink that leads nowhere and generates an error message. Always check the site offline, from the hard disk on which it is being developed, to ensure that all internal and external links work properly. And make sure each page offers a means for returning directly to the home page.

▶ Bandwidth and Images

There's no medium to which the expression "time is money" applies more than the Internet. If the visitor is connected to the Net via a 56Kbps or ISDN modem, the meter is running while the user is retrieving information. If one has a poor or slow connection, the time it takes to connect with an external server is more of an obstacle to the user than the scope of the pages themselves.

For textual information the consequences are small, but the situation is completely different if a page is filled with all sorts of images and logos. Many Web surfers don't have a 56Kbps or cable modem and will be less than thrilled with yet another cute startup image. So be cautious with the graphic information you place on the page. Superfluous embellishments are best avoided. And try to limit the number of kilobytes to about 50 for a home page and about 30 for the other pages.

If you really need to use a large image, observe the following precautions:

■ Ensure that the width and height of the image is defined in the HTML code. This extra effort will be well rewarded—the browser will display the text on the page before displaying the images, so the user has something to read and can quickly decide whether it is worthwhile to wait for the additional screen information or to click immediately on one of the hyperlinks.

■ A second efficient measure is to apply "interlacing" for GIF files. This technique ensures that the image is created in four steps, from a rough image to the final image. The illustration on the page to the right shows how this works. The image simultaneously becomes sharper and somewhat clearer. Various browsers have developed their own techniques for displaying the interlacing. Some Unix systems use a sort of Venetian blind effect. Netscape Navigator, however, creates the image by first displaying lines 1 and 9 and then, in the second pass, lines 5 and 13. Then come lines 3, 7, and 11, and the remaining lines are displayed in the last pass. The missing information in between consists of copies of the lines already displayed.

You can specify the interlace option in most drawing packages and GIF editing programs *(generally, the GIF89a version of the GIF format recognizes the interlace option)*. It is also advisable to include the file size in kilobytes for large images, so the user knows what to expect.

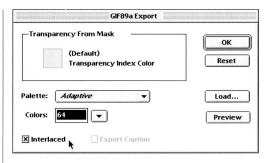

▲ Interlacing adds some heft to a GIF image but ensures that the user sees something quickly on the screen.

■ Finally, keep in mind that one large image is read and displayed faster than several small images that collectively take up the same number of kilobytes. This is because of the browser's connection technique.

The fact is, images are what give the Web its multimedia character and make it attractive. For each image, you must weigh its usefulness against its loading time. A message conveyed online needs to be accompanied by relevant illustrations, and a commercial Web site without a company logo is, of course, inconceivable.

▶ **JPEG Compression and Progression**

The JPEG file format also has a technique for building up an image in phases, or stated more rigorously, loading progressively. Once about 10 to 15 percent of the image has been read, the viewer has a reasonable impression of the complete image. Browsers that do not recognize this standard simply read from top to bottom.

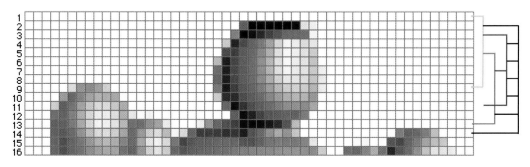

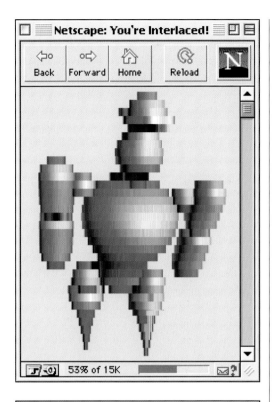

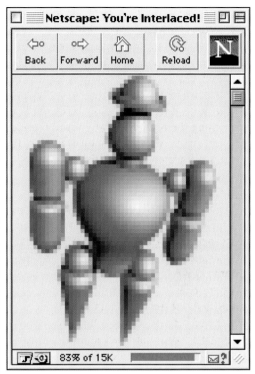

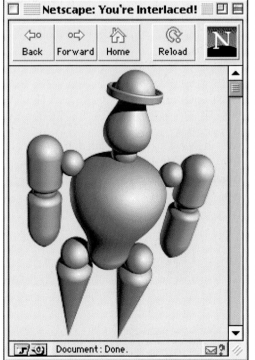

◄ Here are the three phases of loading an interlaced GIF image.

These JPEG images can be created in Adobe Photoshop, JASC Paintshop Pro, and in PhotoImpact Smartsaver.

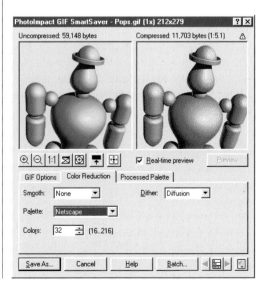

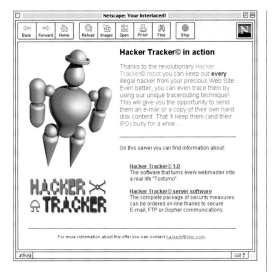

▲ A white background makes the text more legible.

▶ Background Color

Many a discussion has been conducted about the optimum background color for Web pages. Why was a neutral—but not really light—gray color adopted as the standard? The people who specified the original Web standards were looking for a compromise that would provide a pleasant background for both textual and visual information on the screen.

However, they did not take into account that people are accustomed to seeing text *(as well as images)* against a contrasting white background. Text is not as legible against the standard gray of a Web page. Luckily, HTML includes a tag that changes the background color: The code <BODY bgcolor="#FFFFFF"> produces a white page. The color is written as a hexadecimal value. You can also use the alternative <BODY bgcolor="White">.

Producing ▶
a high-quality
Web page
requires studying
the creative
possibilities that
go into the
process.

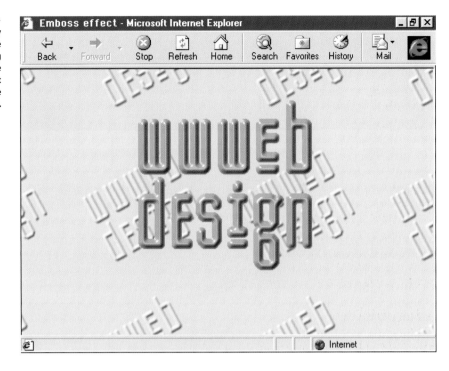

Learning HTML is a good foundation for creating and maintaining a Web site. It's like learning musical notation—you can play an instrument intuitively, but knowing the language of music means you can be trained better and faster.

Basic HTML Concepts

Learning the HTML page markup language isn't really difficult. If you read this chapter carefully and keep it handy while creating a standard Web page, you will have the lion's share of the basic concepts down pat. Embellishments such as tables and frames, as well as the more specialized HTML codes, are dealt with in other chapters. The essentials are in this chapter, beginning with an elementary explanation of HTML's text attributes and basic typographical possibilities.

Then you'll find instructions for structuring your text elements, followed by an overview of the special form codes, which constitute a separate segment within HTML. Last, you'll read an explanation of the various line versions and the image tags. As you're writing the HTML code and viewing it in one window, the results that will appear in the browser are simultaneously shown in another window next to the code.

Standard header ▸
sizes range from
<H1> to <H6>.

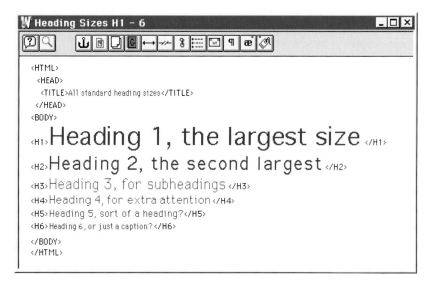

After each </Hx> ▸
close tag, the next
line automatically
falls in a new
paragraph with an
extra line space.

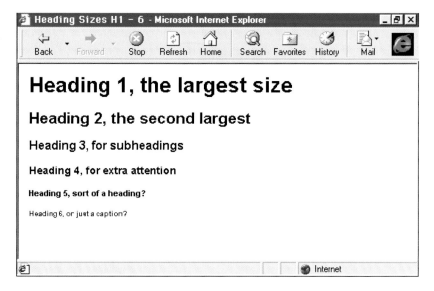

▶ Starting Point

Since virtually all Web browsers support the features in HTML 4, the current Web standard, we will begin with the codes of this version. The extensions and attributes Netscape and Microsoft have introduced will also be discussed where relevant; however, many of these are too specialized to be dealt with in this chapter and will be covered later. This book is not designed to be the ultimate summary of all the extensions currently being used. It would be impossible to write such a book in any case, since changes to the so-called standard are made every week. How to use the codes for practical Web design is more important. The main purpose of this guide is primarily to elucidate how specific codes can be applied and to explain the relationships the codes have with each other. In practice, this is what counts.

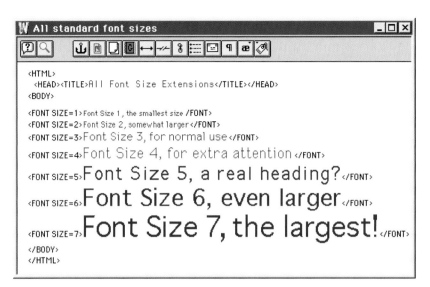

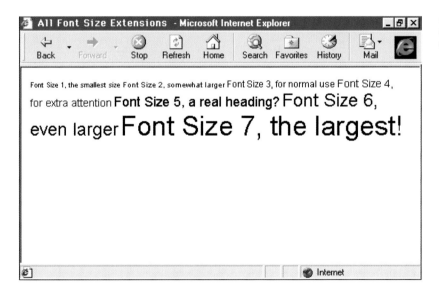

▶ **Heading and Font Size**

Even before getting started, we encounter the first controversy: the battle between the tags (*also called labels or codes*) <Hx></Hx> and their Netscape counterparts, <FONT Size="x"></FONT>. The x stands for a value. Since HTML was defined long before Netscape came into being, the <Hx> tags have seniority. As you can see from the example, there are six heading levels. The headings <H1> and <H2> are generally used as page openers. The small <H6> heading is virtually unusable, certainly if the reader has specified a font size smaller than 12 point. The tag <TITLE></TITLE> indicates the title of the page and formally belongs in the heading category. Text that follows an <Hx> heading is always placed in a new paragraph. The <FONT SIZE> tag, shown on this page, consists of a definition: "FONT" and the related attribute, size.

The <BR> tag ▶
places lines of text
on a new line.

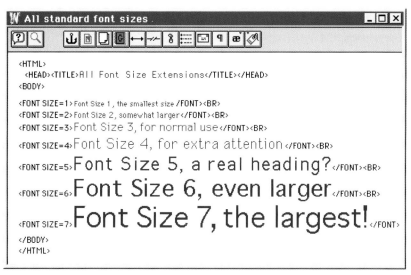

Here's what the ▶
browser displays as
a result of the HTML
code above.

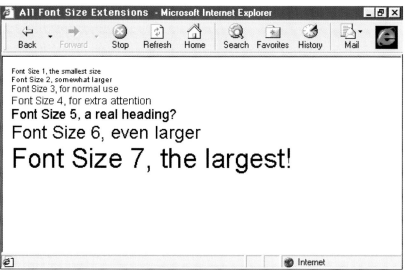

These are always used in combination and are gaining more and more popularity. The <FONT SIZE> is a number between 1 and 7. The smallest font sizes, especially size ="1", leave little to see on the screen. It is extremely important to realize that the label <FONT SIZE> does not influence the text that follows the close tag </FONT> This is handy if you want to have a particular line dominate your page. You can also create upper- and lower-case letters this way.

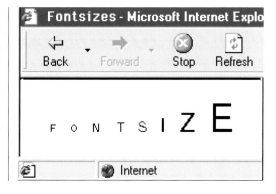

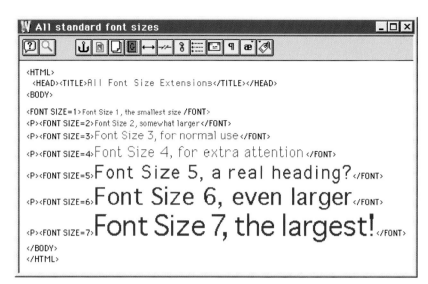

◄ The addition of
<P> to each line ...

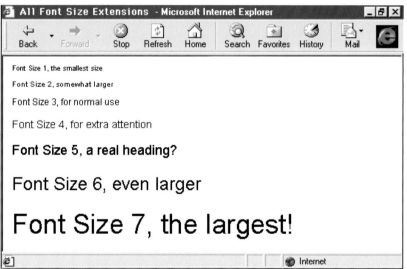

◄ ... results in a new
paragraph for each
line with a line space
in between.

A special version of the <FONT> tag is <BASEFONT>. This code can be placed immediately after the <BODY> tag and ensures that the standard font size for the fonts is modified. Normally the font size in the browser is size="3". If you specify a <BASEFONT SIZE="+1"> the value for all the subsequent fonts will be increased by one. You can also specify a negative value. <FONT SIZE="-1"> provides the same result as <FONT SIZE="2">. As you can see on these pages, There are two methods for placing text on a new line. A simple <BR> code, short for "BReak," forces a new line. The tag <P> goes a step further: It starts a new paragraph. HTML defines the close tag </P>. If you combine this tag with the attribute 'align = center' or 'align = left', the close tag is mandatory.

The tag <P align=center>text</P> centers the text on the line. The next line will start again at the left margin.

▶ **Logical and Physical Text Styles**

The codes that determine the text display can be divided into two groups—logical codes that can be generated by text-oriented browsers, and physical styles that determine precisely how specific text is displayed. The difference between these two text styles is inherent in the Internet, whose origins are textual, not graphic. The first browser versions focused totally on displaying text as accurately as possible. A text-based browser like Lynx, which cannot make formatting distinctions, simply leaves the labels out.

The disadvantage of logical codes is that different browsers interpret the tags *(and thus display the text)* differently. The tag <STRONG></STRONG> indicates that the text between these tags must be accentuated.

For one browser this means displaying the text in bold; for another it means increasing the font size. The tag <EM></EM> produces the same result.

Physical text styles define precisely how the browser must display the selected text. There is no room for interpretation. The two most well-known codes are <B></B> and <I></I>. These instruct the browser to display the code in bold and italics, respectively. Internet purists think this is heresy, but the HTML creators believe this method gives the greatest certainty as to how the various browsers ultimately interpret the code.

▼ The most commonly used styles are shown here as HTML code alongside the browser display.

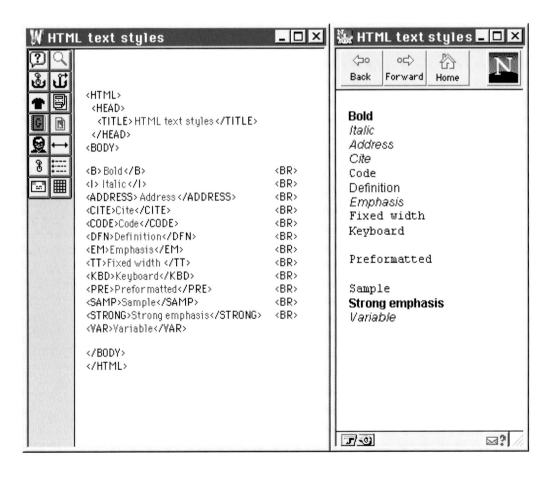

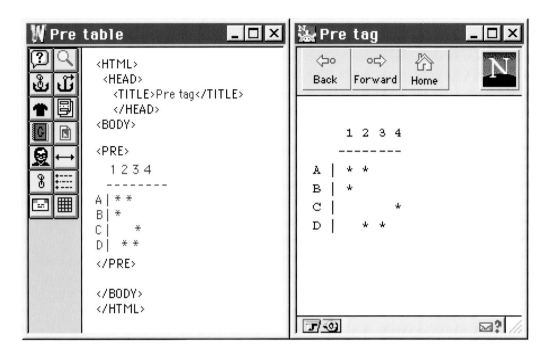

▲ Preformatted text lets you create simple tables in HTML.

▶ Preformatted Text

The reader sets the preferred screen font; usually this is a proportional font, since by default, HTML displays text in this type of font. This means, for example, that the letter *i* takes up much less space than the letter *m*. The spacing value—the exact space between letters—is stored in the font itself.

However, the user can also set the browser to display certain text in a "monospaced," or nonproportional, font. In this kind of font, the space for each letter and punctuation mark is identical; even the space takes up an equal width. Such fonts are perfect for creating a small table, for example. The table lines can be drawn with hyphens, and pipe (|) characters and spaces can be used to align the columns of text and figures. Even tabs can be used in a table, though you run the risk that some browsers won't recognize the tabs.

Monospaced fonts are a godsend for Web pages, and there are several tags that can be used to display them. One such tag combination is <PRE></PRE>. All the text between these codes is displayed based on browser prefer-

ences. In Netscape Navigator, this is called Fixed Font. Be sure you select a font that is easy to read on the screen. Courier and Letter Gothic are good choices for a standard monospaced font. The <PRE> tag can be used for lists, displaying e-mail text and the like. The tag also has an attribute: <PRE width="x">, in which the width specifies the maximum number of characters that can be placed within the tag on one line. The tag <TT></TT>, or "typewriter text," gives the text between the tags a typical typewriter-like effect. You can create interesting effects by switching between the monospaced font and the proportional font.

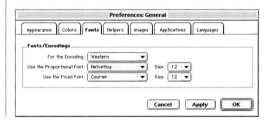

The four characters ▶ &, ", >, and < cannot be used in HTML code, so you need to use an alternative method to display them in the browser.

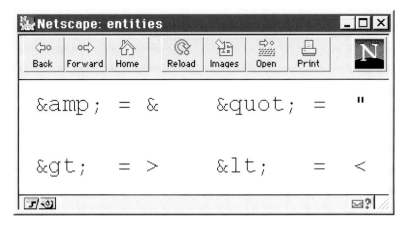

▶ Exceptions to the Rule

HTML was designed to be platform-independent. That means a special character, an *é*, for example, must be displayed identically on a PC and a Unix system. To ensure that this happens, so-called entities were invented—each character was assigned its own HTML code.

The code for the character "*é*" just mentioned is é. The HTML code for the German "*ß*" is ß. As you can see, each entity begins with an ampersand. The smaller-than *(<)* and greater-than *(>)* symbols indicate, respectively, the start and end of a tag.

The question is then what to do if you want to display the ampersand, the greater-than character, or the less-than character on your Web page. The solution is simple: These characters have also been assigned their own entity. If you want to display the text </FONT>, you must type in the HTML code </FONT> Another piece of HTML code applies to comment lines. For example, sometimes it's nice to include the name of the Web page creator in the code. Or you might want to write in a date and an e-mail address. If you enter the code <!-- before the comment text and the code --> after it, it will not be displayed on the Web page.

▶ Extensions to HTML

The W3C *(Web consortium)* is continually evaluating and making additions to the HTML markup language. After version 3.2, HTML 4.0 appeared. You can see a typical example of tags added later below. The Strikeout and Underline tags were needed to produce these typical text effects in an online display.

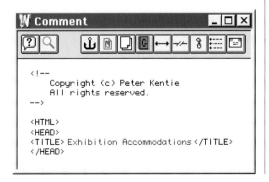

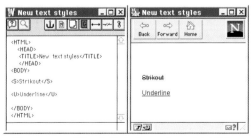

◀ These comment lines indicate the creator and rightful owner of the copyright. This text is not displayed in the browser software!

▶ List Structures

Not all text can be displayed on Web pages in paragraphs. Sometimes information is best shown in summaries or lists.

HTML can accommodate various list structures that are distinguished by using numbers or bullets. Netscape Navigator adds an extra touch by letting the user vary the shape of the bullets. The lists have one thing in common: The lines are always specified using the code <LI> This list tag also has a close tag </LI>, but it is seldom used. The description of the list type depends on the intended effect.

The standard list type is specified with the labels <UL></UL>. The abbreviation UL stands for "unnumbered list." This combination of start and end tag must completely enclose the lines separated by the <LI>tag. Each line is preceded by a round, solid bullet and is indented a number of spaces. One variant of the UL label is the start and end tag <OL></OL>, short for "ordered list." These codes produce an incrementally numbered list. Here, too, the lines are indented, and extra spacing is added between the lines to clearly separate the information.

Nesting Lists

Most text styles and headings can be combined using a technique called nesting. Be sure that codes do not overlap one another. That leads to unpredictable text results in various browsers. By nesting various items together, you can create sublists with a different look. The bullet for a sublist in an unnumbered list is a hollow circle. Take this list, for example:

My favorite Web sites:
<UL>
<LI>Adobe
<LI>Apple
<LI>Macromedia
<LI>Search-engines:

<UL>
<LI>AltaVista
<LI>Excite
<LI>HotBot
<LI>Lycos
<LI>WebCrawler
<LI>Yahoo
</UL>
</UL>

Nesting Variations

You can alternate nesting for a clearer structure:
<B>My favorite Web sites:</B>
<UL>
<LI>Hardware
<UL>
<LI>Apple
<LI>Sun
</UL>
<LI>Web Software
<UL>
<LI>Microsoft
<LI>Netscape
</UL>
<LI>Graphic Software
<UL>
<LI>Adobe
<LI>Macromedia
</UL>
</UL>

Definition Lists

A separate tag is designated for short series, or definition lists: <DL></DL>. This code indents the text, but does not insert a bullet at the beginning of the line. The tag <DT> signifies the term, while <DD> indicates the definition.

```
<B>My software Web sites:</B>
<DL>
<DT>Adobe
<DD>PageMaker
<DD>Photoshop
<DD>Illustrator
<DT>Macromedia
<DD>Director
<DD>FreeHand
<DT>MetaTools
<DD>KPT Bryce
<DD>KPT PowerTools
<DT>Fractal Design
<DD>Painter
</DL>
```

Nesting Version

Definition lists can also be nested, to make a clear distinction between levels of priorities assigned to different information. The tag <DT> causes each line to be indented separately.

```
My favorite Web sites:
<UL>
<LI>Browserwatch
<LI>C|Net
<LI>InfoWorld
<LI>Wired
<LI>Graphic tools:
<P>
<DL>
<DT>Adobe
<DT>Fractal
<DT>Macromedia
<DT>MetaTools
<DT>Quark
</DL>
</UL>
```

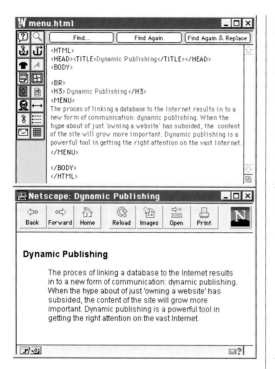

▲ The <MENU> tag behaves like the <DL> tag and indents the text on the left.

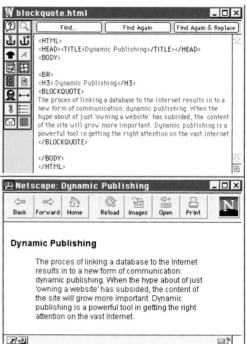

▲ The <BLOCKQUOTE> tag indents on the left and right simultaneously. This sometimes creates space problems.

▶ Alternative List Structures

The arsenal of list structures extends beyond the summary on the previous pages. List codes can also be used for short and very short items, that is:

<MENU></MENU> for short items, and
<DIR></DIR>   for very short items.

In a browser such as Netscape Navigator, it's hard to see a distinction between these two list items. The tag <MENU></MENU> is also used to indent short bits of text. A wide margin is maintained on the left-hand side so that the text is clearly distinguished from the header. This effect can also be achieved using the <DIR></DIR> tags and even with the <DL></DL> tags.

An alternative solution, sometimes better for longer pieces of text, is using the somewhat less familiar tag <BLOCKQUOTE> </BLOCKQUOTE>. This code inserts a white margin on both the left and the right side. Normally this is used for quotations—hence the name *quote*—and for indicating external sources and references.

▶ Netscape Extensions

As mentioned earlier, Netscape added a number of list tags to HTML, particularly bullet display with the following attributes:

<type=square>   for making a bullet an open square;
<type=circle>   for making a bullet an open circle;
<type=disc>   for making a bullet a solid plus sign.

You can try these out in an item list.

▶ Forms and CGI

Forms that your visitors can fill in play an important role in the communication process on the Web. Just including an e-mail address on the page gives the reader few options *(or space)* to express an opinion. Moreover, because the user must write everything out, he may be stingy with the information he gives.

When you provide the user with a clear, appropriate form, he will be more inclined to express his opinion—or, even better, place an order. The disadvantage of such a form is having to creating it first, which isn't exactly a snap. Not only does it involve quite a number of tags, it also requires a CGI script to process the data entered. CGI stands for Common Gateway Interface, the system that handles the communication between a Web server and external programs. Normally this is done using "environment variables." Creating CGI scripts and the underlying programs is a skill in itself that not many graphic designers want to master. Programmers, and certainly those who are accustomed to working in Microsoft Visual Basic, have it somewhat easier. Most CGI scripts are written in Perl, C, and C++. And of course, the use of Java for CGI is on the rise.

▶ Forms

Every form is placed between the tags <FORM></FORM>. This tag has two attributes: <action> and <method>. In the HTML code the form is linked to the script as follows: <FORM action="cgi-bin/script">.

The data on the form can be sent to the server in two ways by using the attribute <METHOD>, which distinguishes two options for sending the form: <GET> and <POST>.

The first is the default method; if you don't enter anything, this option is chosen automatically. <POST> is the most frequently used method for sending forms to the server. If you are going to create a form, first take the trouble to discuss the technical server requirements with the server manager. This will save you a great deal of unnecessary work.

▶ Form Tags

Once the processing method has been specified, you can perform the second step: entering the <INPUT> tags. The syntax for this is as follows: <INPUT [TYPE="type"] [VALUE="value"] [SIZE=x] [NAME="name"] [CHECKED] [MAXLENGTH=x] >. A brief explanation is in order here. TYPE specifies whether check boxes, text boxes, radio buttons, and so on, are used when filling in the form. SIZE determines the width of the text box, and CHECKED indicates whether the check box must be shown already filled in. The attribute VALUE specifies the standard value, and NAME is the name that must be sent to the server. The last option, MAXLENGTH, determines the number of characters that are accepted in a check box.

▶ Input Types

The attribute TYPE is also subdivided into TEXT, IMAGE, RADIO, PASSWORD, CHECK BOX, SUBMIT, RESET, and HIDDEN. In addition to these input tags, which are shown on the following pages, there are two types of input tags: the <SELECT> tag for entering a scroll-down menu and the <TEXTAREA>tag for entering multiple lines of text. This is actually a special version of the text-box attribute. You can also design the form using a WYSIWYG editor.

▶ A Sample Form

The most widely used <INPUT> attributes are displayed on this page and the following page.

```
<HTML>
  <HEAD>
    <TITLE> Form</TITLE>
  </HEAD>
<BODY>
```

Begin the form with the <FORM> tag ▷

This code marks the processing procedure as well.

```
<FORM ACTION="cgi-bin/script.cgi" METHOD="POST">
```

Tag <INPUT> type "text" ▷

This defines a standard text box in the form.

```
<INPUT TYPE="text" NAME="text field" SIZE=53
MAXLENGTH=80> input field
<P>
```

Tag <INPUT> type "checkbox" ▷

This box has only two values: on and off.

```
<INPUT TYPE="checkbox" NAME="Check"
VALUE="on" >
```

Tag <INPUT> type "radio" ▷

This is a group of round check boxes with the same name, of which only one can be selected at a time.

```
<INPUT TYPE="radio" NAME="Radio button"
VALUE="on" >
<P>
```

Tag <SELECT> ▷

With this tag you can set up a roll-down or scrolling menu, which can be displayed as a list box using the special attribute MULTIPLE. This keeps a number of fields, to be specified by the designer, constantly visible.

```
<SELECT NAME="Pop-up menu">
<OPTION> Choice 1
<OPTION> Choice 2
<OPTION> Choice 3
</SELECT>
<P>
```

Tag <TEXTAREA> ▷

This special version of the text box allows space for extra text lines. This is useful when asking for Web site visitors' opinions or reactions. Width and height are determined by the attributes rows and cols.

```
<TEXTAREA NAME="Textfield" ROWS=5 COLS=50>
</TEXTAREA>
<P>
```

Tag <INPUT> types "reset" and "submit" ▷

"Reset" is a button that sets the form back to its standard value. "Submit" is a button that ensures the form is sent to the server.

```
<INPUT TYPE="reset" VALUE="Reset" >
<INPUT TYPE="submit" VALUE="Submit" >
```

End form </FORM> ▷

The tag </FORM> indicates that the form area on the HTML page ends, and that we return to the <BODY> part of the page.

```
</FORM>



</BODY>
</HTML>
```

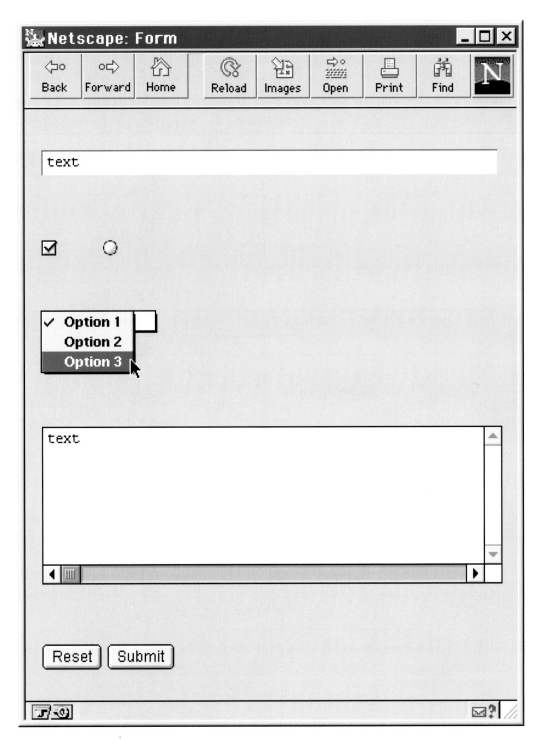

▲ Here is how the HTML code shown on the left page is displayed in the Web browser.

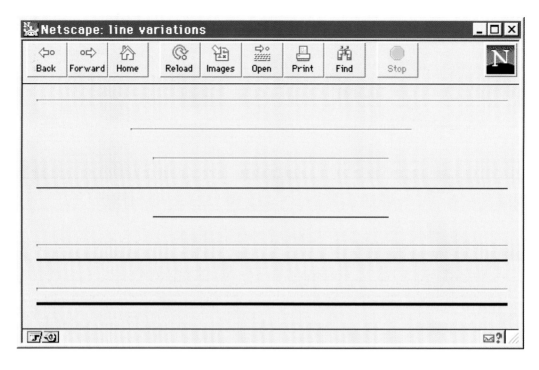

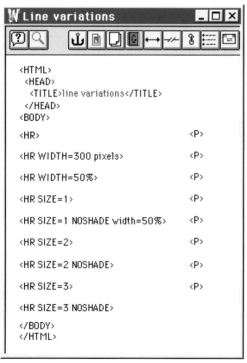

```
<HTML>
  <HEAD>
    <TITLE>line variations</TITLE>
  </HEAD>
<BODY>

<HR>                                        <P>

<HR WIDTH=300 pixels>                       <P>

<HR WIDTH=50%>                              <P>

<HR SIZE=1>                                 <P>

<HR SIZE=1 NOSHADE width=50%>               <P>

<HR SIZE=2>                                 <P>

<HR SIZE=2 NOSHADE>                         <P>

<HR SIZE=3>                                 <P>

<HR SIZE=3 NOSHADE>

</BODY>
</HTML>
```

▲ You can do a lot with standard horizontal lines using various codes.

▶ Horizontal Lines

A horizontal line can add value to a Web page by serving as a graphic element and simultaneously organizing the page. The line can even divide text and graphic information from each other.

The standard tag for a horizontal line is <HR> or, horizontal ruler. HTML code is often derived from English words, which makes it easy to memorize tags.

The <HR> code displays a horizontal line across the entire width of the page. The line normally has a thickness of two pixels, and it maintains a margin at the left and right side of the visible Web page.

▶ Line Attributes

Just as with virtually all other tags, Netscape has added a number of its own attributes to the <HR> tag. These attributes affect not only the shape of the line, but also its width.

As you can see on these two pages, there are numerous possibilities for lines. Later in

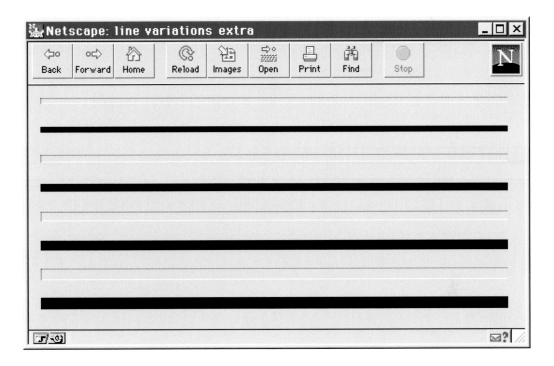

the book you will see how you can also use graphic files as separators, further adding to your creative options. Of course, displaying a Web page with coded lines takes less time to load than a page in which the lines have been added as in-line images. The term *in-line* means that the browser can display the image *(or any other addition to the page)* without having to use an auxiliary program.

The modern browser's solution of working with plug-ins is the ideal method for supporting the never-ending stream of new in-line files. The user is spared the effort of typing in multipurpose Internet mail extensions *(MIME)* types in order to view an image or animation.

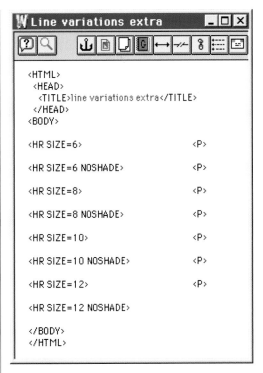

```
<HTML>
  <HEAD>
    <TITLE>line variations extra</TITLE>
  </HEAD>
<BODY>

<HR SIZE=6>                    <P>

<HR SIZE=6 NOSHADE>           <P>

<HR SIZE=8>                    <P>

<HR SIZE=8 NOSHADE>           <P>

<HR SIZE=10>                   <P>

<HR SIZE=10 NOSHADE>          <P>

<HR SIZE=12>                   <P>

<HR SIZE=12 NOSHADE>

</BODY>
</HTML>
```

▲ Using the attribute <NOSHADE>, you can display real bars in the Web browser.

▶ **Hyperlinks and Anchors**

No matter how beautiful a Web page is, if it has no link to the outside world, it is literally lost. The Web's enormous success and popularity can be attributed in large part to hyperlinks. Of course, the uniform resource locators, or URLs, are absolutely essential, because they clearly specify the server address in a fashion that is easy to recall. Everyone knows Apple's URL: http://www.apple.com, and Microsoft's Web address follows the same format: http://www.microsoft.com. In an up-to-date browser you can drop the prefix http://. The browser fills in the missing code when you press the Return key. Microsoft Internet Explorer completes the URL as you type it.

Once you've arrived at a page, the rest of the journey is determined by hyperlinks. If text or a drawing indicates that more information can be found on another page, the user only has to click on it, and the URL for the requested address appears at the bottom of the page.

When creating such a page, a hyperlink is specified in HTML code using the anchor tag. This can be recognized by the prefix <A></A>. The anchor specifies whether the document is the source or the destination of a hyperlink. When the anchor is the source of the reference, the attribute <NAME> is used. This generally results in a link to another location in the same document. This page shows an example of how this works. If you click on the link ISO 9001, the page immediately jumps to the location referred to by this name in the HTML code. This provides a wonderful navigation tool for long text pages.

It's a good idea to include a link to the top of the page at the end of every article; otherwise the user must scroll back. By placing an anchor at the top of the page as well, you can refer to it in the code. This works as follows: At the top of the page, type the text

<A NAME="top">. For the reference back to this name, you must use the second attribute for the anchor tag.

When the anchor itself is the source, HREF is placed after the <A. Thus, if you are at the end of the article, at the bottom of the Web page,

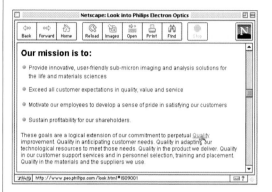

<P>

These goals are a logical extension of our commitment to perpetual <A HREF="#ISO9001">Quality</A> improvement. Quality in anticipating customer needs. Quality in adapting our technological resources to meet those needs. Quality in the product we deliver. Quality in our customer support services and in personnel selection, training, and placement. Quality in the materials and the suppliers we use.

<A NAME="ISO9001"></A>
<IMG SRC="iso.gif" ALIGN=right ALT="ISO 9000 logo">
The company's Centre of Competence at Eindhoven in the Netherlands, as well as each of its regional sales & service organizations, have been awarded the internationally acclaimed ISO 9001 certification. So global quality is a matter of fact!

and want to return to the top, the reference <A HREF="#top"> will produce the intended result. The # character specifies the name referred to. Using the HREF attribute, you can refer to another page or even to another server.

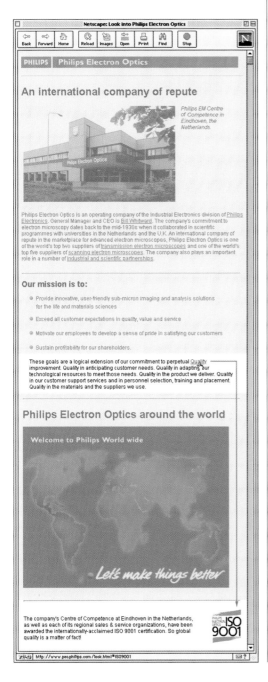

A link to a page on an external server is hard-coded as such:

<A HREF="http://www.server.nl/ref.html">hyperlink</a>.

Make sure that the quotation marks are in the correct place and that you don't forget the end tag </A> Here too, you can specify an exact location on the external page by adding the # character to the HTML code:

<A HREF="http://www.peo.philips.com/look.html#ISO9001"> hyperlink</A>.

At the bottom of the browser you will see the following reference.

▲ The browser outer window displays the URL of the link.

▶ **Hyperlinks to Images**

You can also create a direct reference to an image. It doesn't matter whether the image is a GIF or JPEG file. If you insert the code <A HREF="sign.jpg">, the browser will read this image and report its height and width in the title bar on the page. The background is always standard gray.

▼ The JPEG image is opened in a new window.

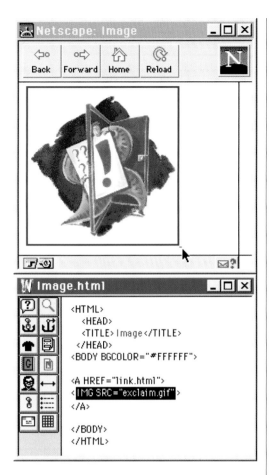

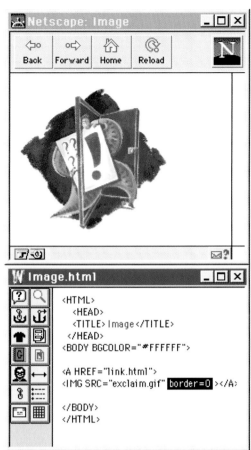

▲ If you type a hard return after the <IMG SRC> tag, an irritating horizontal line appears.

▲ If you add <BORDER=0> to the code, an invisible border is generated around the linked image.

▶ Image Tags

One of the most important HTML codes is the image tag, or <IMG>. By including an image tag in a Web page, you reference a GIF or JPEG image, which is then displayed in-line *(all Web browsers can display the JPEG file format)*. The image tag consists of the definition <IMG> and always has the code SRC="name.gif" as an attribute. The text placed between the quotation marks is the name of the GIF or JPEG image to be displayed, and it is also a URL In this case, however, the URL refers not to an HTML file but to a graphic image.

When an image refers to an HTML file using an anchor—a border, three pixels thick—is placed around the outside of image and displayed in the "Link" color. You can modify this frame with the border attribute.

When the HTML code <BORDER=0> is placed in the image tag, the colored frame will vanish. The advantage is that you remove a disturbing element, but the disadvantage is that the viewer can no longer see which of the images contains hyperlinks. If you prefer a thin visible border around the image, then use the code <BORDER=1>.

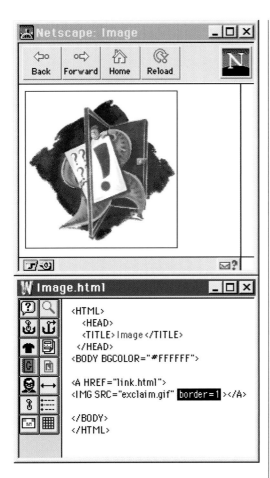

▲ The addition <BORDER=1> results in a border of one pixel around the rectangular contours of the image.

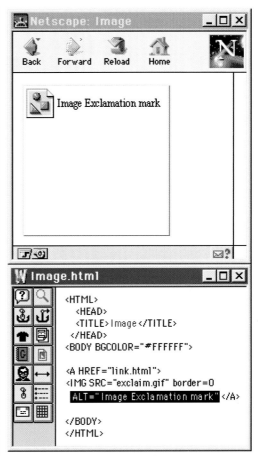

▲ The <ALT> (alternative) text is intended for browsers that cannot display images.

While an image is loading in the Netscape Communicator or Microsoft Internet Explorer browser, you can provide text indicating what the image contains by using the attribute ALT. The code looks like this: <ALT="text">. This text becomes visible if the reader moves the cursor over the image and just waits a second.

Internet Explorer supports a tag that creates an explanatory "balloon" for a textual link. The code is <A HREF="link.htm" TITLE="This link leads to product information.">External link</A>.

Using the <TITLE> attribute, you can add an informative ▶ comment to a hyperlink.

▲ The <ALT> text can be seen in Internet Explorer.

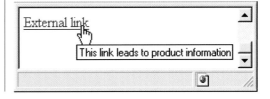

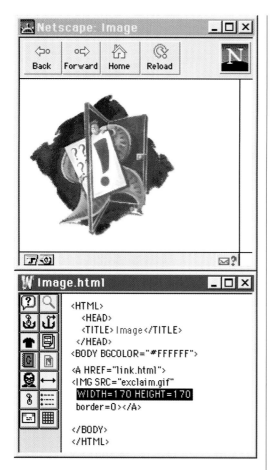

▲ An image's width and height are indispensable for the proper functioning of an HTML document.

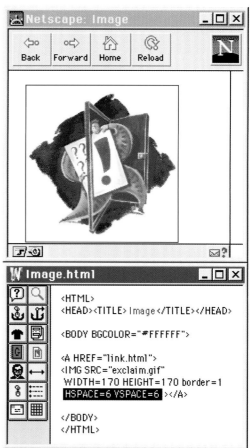

▲ <HSPACE> and <VSPACE> determine the distance around the image. The spacing is visible on both sides.

▶ Image Tags Continued

As we've seen, you can use attributes to determine the height and width of graphic information. This allows textual information to be displayed without the reader having to wait for the images to load. This is a great boon for pages that open with large images. The reader, who is otherwise unsure whether a connection has been established, immediately sees a result on his screen and knows that the graphic information is arriving. The width and height are coded *(in pixels)* as follows: <WIDTH=x HEIGHT=x>. There is also an option for specifying a percentage: <WIDTH=x% HEIGHT=x%>. However, this sometimes produces unreliable results. A second handy attribute for designers is <SPACE>. It specifies the distance around an image in its environment. The tag <HSPACE=6>, for example, places six pixels of spacing on the left and right of the image. The vertical spacing can be specified too, with the attribute <VSPACE=x> With these two attributes, you can align your image.

The special tag <ISMAP> specifies that the image contains a reference to URLs, or Web page addresses. You must use this tag to create clickable image maps—images the

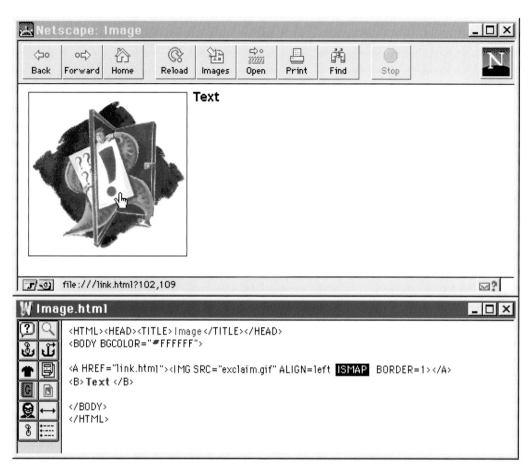

▲ The <ISMAP> tag indicates that the illustration has become a clickable map. You can see this from the x and y coordinates shown next to the little key in the browser display.

user can click on to jump to other Web pages. *(One or more URLs are linked to specific areas of the image, so when you click on that part of the image, the browser opens that particular URL.)* A separate chapter will deal extensively with the possibilities and restrictions this sort of reference offers. The advantage—that the user has to read in only one image— is negated since the map has to be consulted each time. And because the map is a separate file stored on the server, there are further delays. Luckily an extension has been developed to apply this technique in the form of a "client-side" clickable map—one that is downloaded to and stored on the user's machine so that whenever the user's browser needs it, it's available. The extension, introduced by Netscape, makes it feasible to work with a clickable map, but all the references are built directly into the HTML file, so there are no server delays. The only disadvantage of this extension is that many browsers do not support the <USEMAP> attribute. In HTML, the complete tag looks like this: <USEMAP ="#name">. The name of the map refers to the list of URLs and corresponding x and y coordinates that must be in the very same HTML document or the client-side clickable map will not work. You will find more information about this technique in the chapter "Clickable Image Maps."

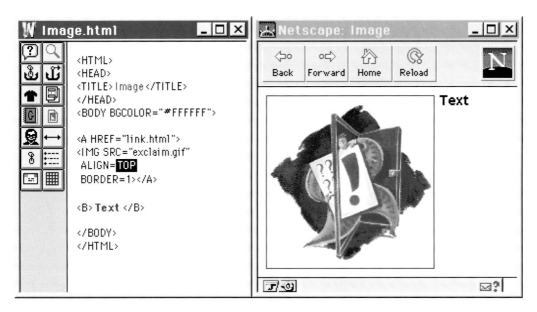

▲ The attribute <ALIGN=TOP> aligns the text that follows it with the top of the illustration.

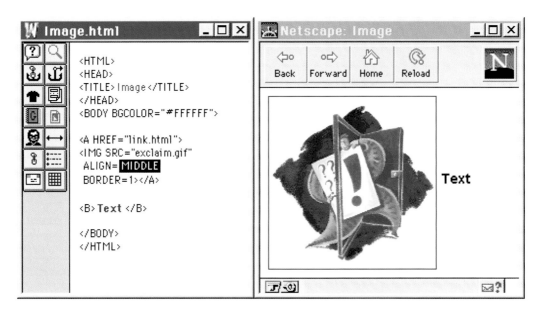

▲ <ALIGN=MIDDLE> ensures that the text that follows will be aligned with the vertical center of the illustration.

Netscape has also extended the number of <ALIGN> attributes. *(Greater control over aligning text and images was at the top of the HTML 3 specifications wish list.)* Examples of the most important <ALIGN> attributes are shown on the next three pages. However, there's much more to the complete arsenal of possible tags; the interaction between text and image has been greatly improved in HTML 4.0.

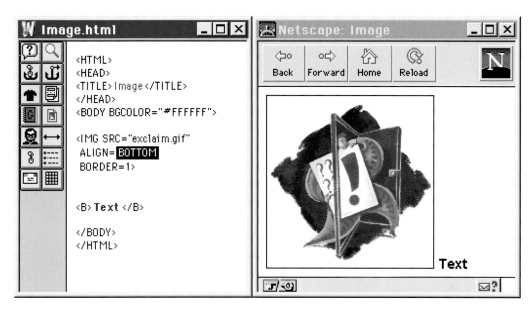

```
W Image.html                    _ □ X

<HTML>
<HEAD>
<TITLE>Image</TITLE>
</HEAD>
<BODY BGCOLOR="#FFFFFF">

<IMG SRC="exclaim.gif"
 ALIGN=BOTTOM
 BORDER=1>


<B>Text</B>

</BODY>
</HTML>
```

▲ The attribute <ALIGN=BOTTOM> aligns the text that follows with the bottom of the illustration.

The most important four attributes are <ALIGN=top>, <ALIGN=left>, <ALIGN=middle> and <ALIGN=right>. An align tag requires that you use one of these four attributes. The <ALIGN=top> attribute ensures that the top of the image aligns with the text that follows it. Note that the top left pixel is the starting point for the illustration. When viewing a clipped image, it looks as though the text starts higher.

That's true because the transparent color is probably the first pixel that serves as a reference. In this case it's often neater to give the image a border of one pixel. If the image doesn't serve as a hyperlink, you can still use the <BORDER=1> option. However, the illustration will be surrounded by a black line one pixel thick.

Using the <ALIGN=bottom> attribute, you can align text with the bottom of an image.

The <ALIGN=middle> attribute centers the text vertically. The reason the word middle is used, rather than center, is that an attribute called center is already used to center information at the paragraph level.

Variations of this are also possible; the official W3C standard method is <P ALIGN=center></P>. Netscape makes do with the tag <CENTER></CENTER>. Note that you must use the American spelling *(center)*, not the British spelling *(centre)*.

Here are other attributes you can use to position your text:

<ALIGN=texttop>	to align the longest line of text with the top
<ALIGN=absmiddle>	to align the middle of an image with the middle of the longest text line
<ALIGN=absbottom>	to align the bottom of an image with the lowest item in the line
<ALIGN=baseline>	to produce the same result as with bottom

A tag that Web designers are using more and more is <DIV>, or division. This lets you modify a paragraph or a graphic element on the page locally, no matter what the global settings of the page. The align attributes can be applied here as well. Here is an example:

<DIV ALIGN=right> to right-justify</DIV>

When this code is placed in a centered page, only this text will be different.

▶ BREAK clear=all

HTML can occasionally be very irritating. When you've been working for hours aligning a layout to make a Web page that is easy to comprehend, you suddenly come up against text that must be displayed next to an image and refuses to be positioned to the left of the image. Even worse, it completely disappears! This is a classic example of when the tag <BR clear=all> can work wonders. What does this do? Using the attribute <ALIGN=right> pushes all the subsequent information to the right side of the window. This instruction must be cancelled with another tag; otherwise the code that follows will not be displayed correctly. The instruction <clear=all> repairs the negative effects of the tag. There are also <clear=left> and <clear=right> versions, but use these tags with caution, or you may create the opposite effect you intended. The remaining HTML code will ignore the general settings. Most of the time the <DIV> tag provides a solution for this situation.

▼ The attribute <ALIGN=LEFT> pushes the illustration to the left margin of the page.

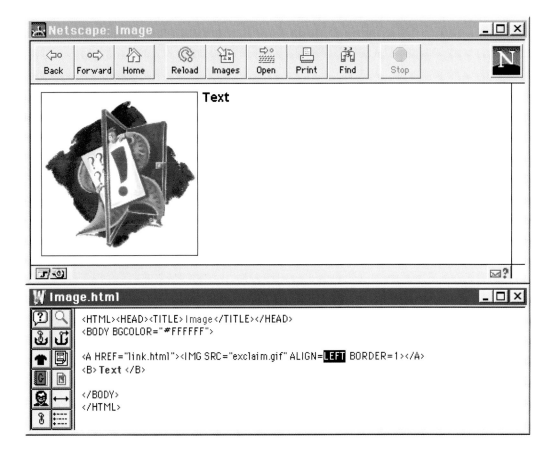

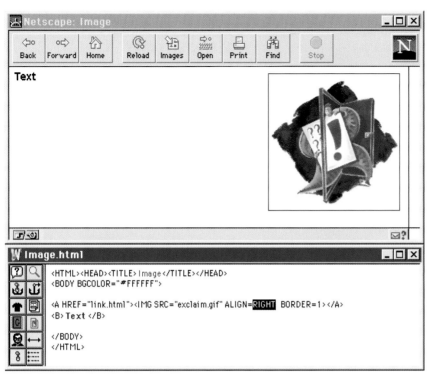

◄ The addition <ALIGN=RIGHT> pushes the illustration to the right margin of the page.

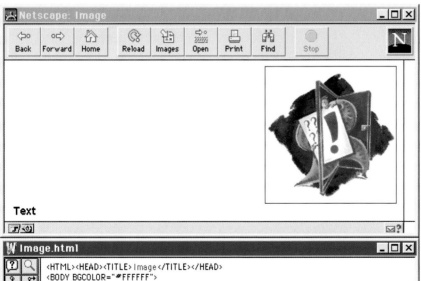

◄ The <BR clear=all> tag, which ensures that the text falls in a new paragraph, is indispensable when applying the <ALIGN=LEFT> and <ALIGN=RIGHT> attributes.

▶ Automating Layout

The sheer quantity of tags and layout codes shown on the previous pages implies that you must do a considerable amount of typing before a page is displayed correctly in the browser window. Actually this is not such a big chore—soon enough you will start using an editor or, even better, a WYSIWYG layout program. The codes then become less important because they are written for you.

Yet you might have to intervene frequently during the final stages of this semiautomated layout process—for instance, by using the <BR clear=all> tag discussed above. None of the HTML editors will add the tag <clear=all> to the page, because this is a layout decision. The program can't detect whether the designer intended to place the text next to the image. Without this tag, the creator can only wonder what went wrong.

▶ INCLUDE Tag

An HTML page is divided into three parts: The header, the body, and the footer together constitute the whole page. When you construct a large Web site, you will soon discover that 99 percent of the information that varies per page is in the body section.

Only the title of the Web page changes each time. The rest of the information, the background color, the text color, the individual or company "sending" the page, is the same everywhere. That is why these are subpages. Instead of continually adding the same header and footer to the pages, you can use the <INCLUDE> tag to automate this chore. Note that this works only when one is online and uses a server equipped to do the job. This example was created using Apache server software.

```
<HR SIZE=1 WIDTH=320 NOSHADE>
<CENTER>
<a href="var.htm">Partners, Developers &amp; VARs</a>
<a href="cases.htm">Cases</a>
<a href="products.htm">Product info</a>
```

```
<a href="r-d.htm">R &amp; D</a>
<a href="press.htm">Press info</a>
<a href="info.htm">General info and FAQ</a>
<a href="profile.htm">Company profile</a>

<FONT size=-1>Copyright &#169; Philips, All rights reserved
</FONT>

</CENTER>

</BODY>
</HTML>
```

Instead of the standard procedure in which the text is built in, save the HTML code as a separate file called footer. Then do something similar for the header: At the start of the body of the HTML page, insert the reference <!-- #include file="header"-->. At the end of the bodytext, type <!-- #include file="footer"-->.

Because the text is between comment tags, it is not displayed on the Web page. And the command #include file="file" ensures that the server places these files automatically!

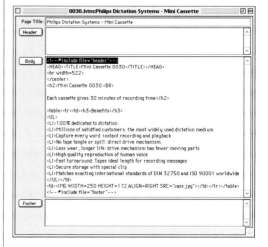

▲ The <INCLUDE> tag can automatically add a date to Web pages. The designer only needs to provide the body text.

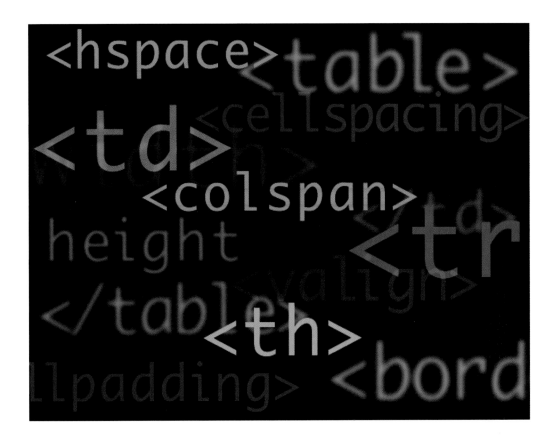

Web designers absolutely have to master the HTML technique for creating tables. A unique combination of tags allows you to create an attractive display of data and images. But you will have to sit down and make the effort to learn it.

Basic Table Design

A table is the most powerful tool a Web designer has at his disposal. This sounds like a bold assertion—what does a table have to do with structuring information on the Web? The possibilities the HTML <TABLE> extension offers are far more extensive than all the other tags and attributes in the whole markup language combined.

A table gives a designer considerable control over the positioning and alignment of the graphic and textual elements on his Web page. Table coding is part of the HTML 3 standard specification and is supported by all commercial browsers including WebTV. Tables are primarily intended for arranging large amounts of information in an orderly fashion.

By arranging data into rows and columns and using headings and subheadings, you create structure—a way to present information clearly. It sounds great, but can't you create tables with the <PRE></PRE> or <TT></TT> tags? In fact you can, but then the text is displayed in the typewriter font and the entire section must be aligned by using spaces. When these solutions aren't appropriate, you can use the <TABLE> tag.

▶ Table Tags

The main idea behind creating tables in HTML is that you specify the information row by row. The tags <TR> and </TR> mark the beginning and ending, respectively, of each table row. Within each row, the information is arranged in cells; the tags <TD> and </TD>. *("table data")* begin and complete each cell. The tag combo <TH> and <TD> creates a table header cell with its contents centered and in bold. A cell can also contain an image.

◄ This simple table is based on the HTML code shown below.

```
table basics

   Back   Forward   Home      N

   1  2  3

   4  5  6

   7  8  9
```

```
table.html

<HTML>
  <HEAD>
    <TITLE>table basics</TITLE>
  </HEAD>
  <BODY>

  <TABLE>
    <TR>
        <TD>1</TD>
        <TD>2</TD>
        <TD>3</TD>
    </TR>
    <TR>
        <TD>4</TD>
        <TD>5</TD>
        <TD>6</TD>
    </TR>
    <TR>
        <TD>7</TD>
        <TD>8</TD>
        <TD>9</TD>
    </TR>
  </TABLE>
  </BODY>
</HTML>
```

▼ These two diagrams show the basic method for constructing a table.

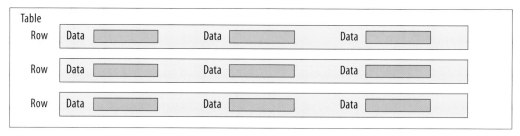

TD = Table Data   TR = Table Row

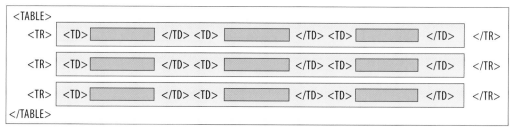

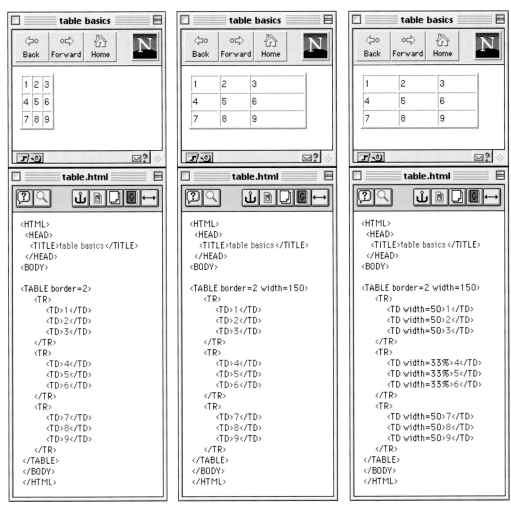

▲ In these three examples you can see that the width and height of individual table cells can be specified by adding extra code.

▶ Modifiable Code

As you can see in the example, creating a table is quite a chore—you must enter a considerable amount of code to produce a desired result on the screen. Moreover, in the example shown on this and the following pages, the HTML table codes have been arranged to provide a clear overview. If you were to place all this information in one continuous sequence, you would quickly lose track of the table structure, and making corrections would become a nightmare.

Of the <TABLE> tag's various attributes, one is <BORDER>. This lets you display a border around the table and specify its thickness. The tag <TABLE border=1> produces a table with a decorative border, one pixel thick. Other attributes that can be used with both the <TABLE> tag and the <TR>, <TH> en <TD> tags are <WIDTH> and <HEIGHT>.

The dimensions can be hard-coded in pixels or specified in percentages, provided the cells collectively add up to a width of 100 percent. In the example above you can see that a table for which only the width was defined produces unequal table widths. Setting the cell width restores the table's balance.

▶ **Caption**

A special tag used in the <TABLE> structure is the header or paragraph code <CAPTION> </CAPTION>. Text enclosed in this tag combination becomes the table title. The unique feature of this tag is that this title is placed above the table. If you wish to have the title displayed beneath the table, you must also include the attribute <ALIGN=bottom>. Only then does the caption tag really live up to its name.

▶ **ALIGN = center**

Not only can you specify the cell width and height, you can also influence the position of text in a cell using the five versions of the <ALIGN> tag.

<ALIGN=center>
<ALIGN=left>
<ALIGN=right>
<ALIGN=top>
<ALIGN=bottom>

There is also a version that specifies vertical positioning. Placing the letter "V" before the <ALIGN> tag creates the version <VALIGN>. Here are your options:

<VALIGN=top>
<VALIGN=bottom>
<VALIGN=middle>
<VALIGN=baseline>

The table example on this page—a model of clarity—contains a mix of the two versions. The tags are arranged using spaces and hard returns. The <TR> tags and the <TD> tags are on separate lines, with the latter slightly indented to accentuate a different hierarchical level. Of course the spaces are not displayed on the Web page; after all, we are still dealing with a markup language.

A space is not a code and thus has no influence on the final result; however, a hard return does. It is a disruptive element, particularly for tables in which the cell

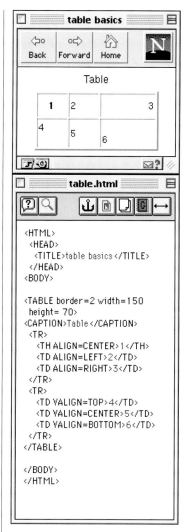

▲ You can align the text of individual cells in a number of ways by using attributes.

contains an image. You cannot place illustrations or photos right up against each other or against the border if you place each <TR> and <TD> tag on a separate line. The Web browser interprets this as deliberately specified spacing. Consequently, the cell is placed four pixels away from the line. This creates problems if you want cells to be displayed seamlessly next to one another.

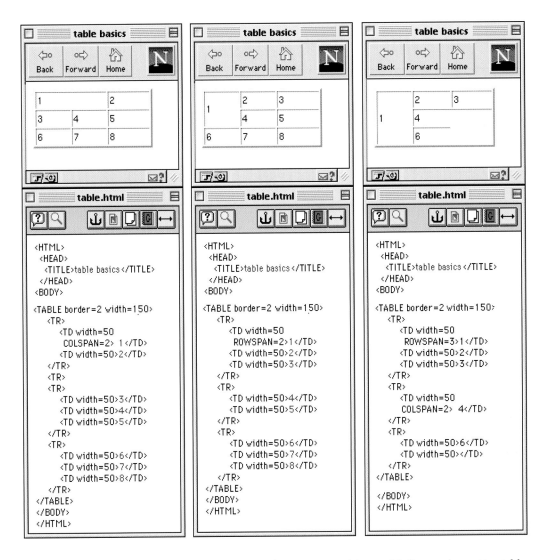

▶ Count Accurately

Sometimes you'll need one cell to cover several rows or columns. Two attributes have been invented for just that situation: <ROWSPAN> and <COLSPAN>. These can be placed only inside the <TR>, <TH> and <TD> tag combos. The tag <TD colspan=2> specifies that the cell must occupy two adjacent positions. If you have placed three cells in the rest of the rows, the row with the <TD colspan=2> tag will occupy only one more cell. The tag <TD colspan=3> would then take up the entire row. If you were to define an extra cell in the same row, this would distort the entire table structure. Thus, you need to follow this guideline: First draw the table, then code rows and cells. The tag <TD rowspan=2> produces a cell that takes up two vertical cells.

▶ Blank Cell

You can choose to leave a cell empty, as shown in the example on the right. The cell is then "closed." If you enter a <BR> tag in the cell, the frame will be displayed around the empty cell. The HTML code for a space ( ) produces the same result.

Border Version

A table border can be specified in a number of ways:

```
<TABLE cellpadding=0  cellspacing=0
  border=2 width=500 height=500>
  <TR>
    <TD width=250 COLSPAN=2>1</TD>
    <TD width=125>2</TD>
    <TD width=125>3</TD>
  </TR>
  <TR>
    <TD width=125>4</TD>
    <TD COLSPAN=2  width=250>5</TD>
    <TD ROWSPAN=2 width=125>6</TD>
  </TR>
  <TR>
    <TD width=125>7</TD>
    <TD width=125>8</TD>
    <TD width=125>9</TD>
  </TR>
</TABLE>
```

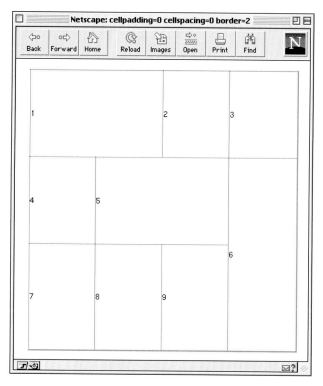

Cell Padding Version

The attribute <cellpadding> determines the margin between the cell contents and the border.

```
<TABLE cellpadding=6
  width=500 height=500>
  <TR>
    <TD width=250 COLSPAN=2>1</TD>
    <TD width=125>2</TD>
    <TD width=125>3</TD>
  </TR>
  <TR>
    <TD width=125>4</TD>
    <TD COLSPAN=2  width=250>5</TD>
    <TD ROWSPAN=2 width=125>6</TD>
  </TR>
  <TR>
    <TD width=125>7</TD>
    <TD width=125>8</TD>
    <TD width=125>9</TD>
  </TR>
</TABLE>
```

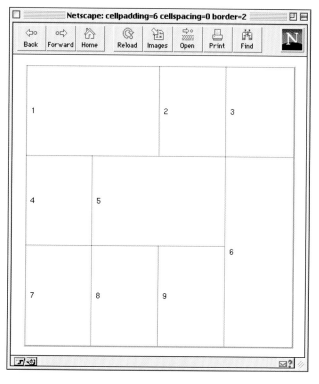

Cell Spacing Version

The <cellspacing> attribute determines the width of the cell border:

```
<TABLE cellpadding=6 cellspacing=6
  border=2 width=500 height=500>
    <TR>
      <TD width=250 COLSPAN=2>1</TD>
      <TD width=125>2</TD>
      <TD width=125>3</TD>
    </TR>
    <TR>
      <TD width=125>4</TD>
      <TD COLSPAN=2  width=250>5</TD>
      <TD ROWSPAN=2 width=125>6</TD>
    </TR>
    <TR>
      <TD width=125>7</TD>
      <TD width=125>8</TD>
      <TD width=125>9</TD>
    </TR>
</TABLE>
```

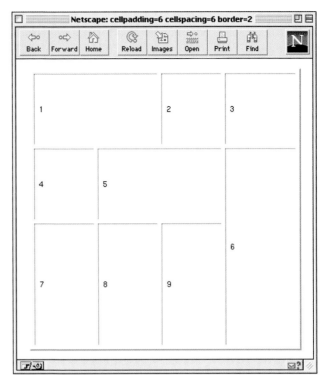

Combination

By combining the <cellpadding>, <cellspacing>, and <border> tags, you get the following:

```
<TABLE cellpadding=6 cellspacing=6
  border=6 width=500 height=500>
    <TR>
      <TD width=250 COLSPAN=2>1</TD>
      <TD width=125>2</TD>
      <TD width=125>3</TD>
    </TR>
    <TR>
      <TD width=125>4</TD>
      <TD COLSPAN=2  width=250>5</TD>
      <TD ROWSPAN=2 width=125>6</TD>
    </TR>
    <TR>
      <TD width=125>7</TD>
      <TD width=125>8</TD>
      <TD width=125>9</TD>
    </TR>
</TABLE>
```

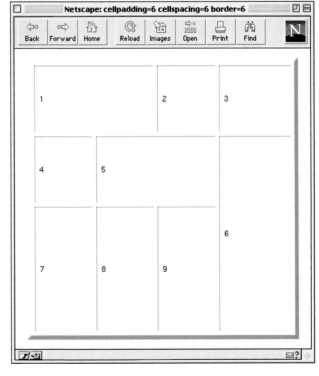

▶ **Microsoft Internet Explorer Tags**

Microsoft added a number of attributes to table tags. These attributes assign colors to the content and borders of cells. In the HTML shown here, you see what code produces what visual effect. Web designers welcome this option to assign colors to cells.

The Attribute <BORDERCOLOR> ▷

The attributes BORDERCOLOR="#x", BORDERCOLORLIGHT="#x" and BORDERCOLOR-DARK="#x" specify the border color. The "#x" represents a hexadecimal color value.

<FONT COLOR> Tag ▷

The tag <FONT color="#x"></FONT> is not a Microsoft invention, but it lends itself well to this part of our discussion. This tag colors the text based on a hexadecimal color value. You must be careful if you use this tag in combination with the <FONT size> tag. It may seem obvious that the color values should be placed inside the same brackets, but that is precisely what you must avoid doing! If you want to display the sample text in color and in a larger font, you must use the following code: <FONT size=+2><FONT color="#x">text </FONT>. The end tag </FONT> needs to be entered only once.

The Attribute <BGCOLOR> ▷

The color of one cell can be specified using the attribute <BGCOLOR="#x">. This lets you zoom in on one cell and its text contents.

In the example below you can clearly see the attractive results this can produce. The attribute <BACKGROUND="url">, which Microsoft introduced, goes one step further: With it you can apply a repeating GIF or JPEG image as a background to a table or even to a table cell.

```
<HTML><HEAD><TITLE>Warehouse</TITLE></HEAD>
<BODY BGCOLOR="#CCFFFF">


<center><IMG Align=Top SRC="warehouse.gif"><BR>
<H3><MARQUEE>Welcome to the <B>online shopping
centre</B></H3></MARQUEE><BR></center>

<TABLE cellpadding=6 cellspacing=0 border=2
BORDERCOLOR="#FFBB57" BORDERCOLORLIGHT="#F7EFAD"
BORDERCOLORDARK="#A59335" width=500 height=500>
  <TR>
    <TD width=250 COLSPAN=2 BGCOLOR="#FFFFFF">
      <IMG WIDTH=75 HEIGHT=90
        SRC="audio.gif">text</TD>
      <TD width=125 BGCOLOR=#003399><H3>
        <FONT COLOR="#FFFFFF">text</H3></FONT></TD>
      <TD width=125 BGCOLOR="#FFFFFF">
        <IMG WIDTH=75 HEIGHT=90
        SRC="smokes.gif"></TD>
  </TR>
  <TR>
    <TD width=125 BGCOLOR="#FFFFFF">
      <IMG WIDTH=75 HEIGHT=90
        SRC="living.gif"></TD>
    <TD COLSPAN=2 BGCOLOR="#FFFFFF" width=250>
      <IMG ALIGN=RIGHT WIDTH=75 HEIGHT=90
        SRC="makeup.gif">text</TD>
    <TD ROWSPAN=2 BGCOLOR="#FFEEAA"
      VALIGN=BOTTOM width=125>
      <IMG WIDTH=75 HEIGHT=72 SRC="letter.gif">text
      <P ALIGN=CENTER><I>e-mail us<I></P></TD>
  </TR>
  <TR>
    <TD width=125 VALIGN=BOTTOM
      BACKGROUND="pattern.gif" >
        <FONT COLOR="#003399">text</FONT></TD>
    <TD width=125 BGCOLOR="#FFFFFF">
      <IMG WIDTH=75 HEIGHT=90 VALIGN=TOP
        SRC="alcohol.gif">text</TD>
    <TD width=125 BGCOLOR="#FFFFFF">
      <IMG WIDTH=75 HEIGHT=90 VALIGN=BOTTOM
        SRC="autopart.gif">text</TD>
  </TR>
</TABLE>
</BODY>
</HTML>
```

Warehouse - Microsoft Internet Explorer

File　Edit　View　Go　Favorites　Help

Back　Forward　Stop　Refresh　Home　Search　Favorites　Print

Welcome to the **online shopping centre**

The **audio** department has a lot of new articles and they are extra low-priced for online shoppers!

We take all your plastic in our online store.

Make-up make-over
Beauty is only skin-deep and on the Internet: who knows you're a real woman?

If you have any questions, comments, wishes, needs or whatever you can contact us on- and offline and we'll try to accomodate your wishes.

Brown-bag deliveries
If you want to avoid customs; tell us! And we'll send you your article in an anonymous brown bag. The tax-man will never know...

Any **drink** you can imagine, we've got it in our virtual bar.

Need **spare parts** for the electronic highway?

e-mail us

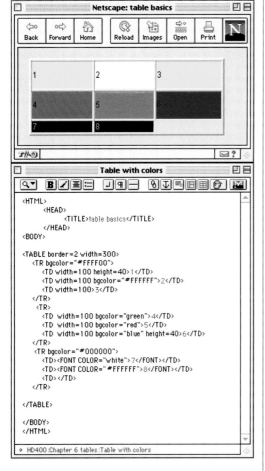

HD400 :Chapter 6 tables :Table with colors

▶ **Tips and Tricks for Tables**

Version 3.2 of HTML added a large number of options for creating tables. On the previous page you saw the effect of the use of background colors and patterns. A simple tag with which an entire row is assigned the same background color—yellow, in this case—is <TR bgcolor="#FFFF00">.

When you use one of the 16 main colors, you get the same result with the HTML code <TR bgcolor="yellow">. Remember to omit the pound sign *(#)* if you use the name of the color. Even if the entire table row is yellow, you can still assign another color to separate cells.

To set a fixed width for a table, add the tag <width="x"> to the table header. If you don't set the width, it will be adjusted to fit the browser window size. In practice, you will discover that specifying the exact table width is a difficult and unpredictable chore: Not only do the different browsers interpret the table coding differently, the results are also inconsistent across various computer platforms. The best method for forcing a table to maintain a specific width per row or cell is to include an invisible graphic element per row or cell.

The WYSIWYG editor NetObjects Fusion uses this specific technique. This method is discussed extensively in the chapter "Aligning Text and Images."

▶ **Modify Tables with a WYSIWYG HTML Editor**

Working with tables is often difficult for beginning Web designers. One error in the HTML code can mess up the entire page. And to track down the error, you must thoroughly check each line of code and meticulously count the number of rows.

Sometimes it's easier to use a WYSIWYG HTML editor such as Adobe GoLive, Macromedia Dreamweaver, Netscape Communicator, or Microsoft FrontPage 2000 for your table design.

(GoLive is a trademark of Adobe Systems, Inc.; Dreamweaver is a trademark of Macromedia, Inc.; Communicator is a trademark of Netscape; and FrontPage is a trademark of Microsoft Corp.)

▲ You can quickly and easily construct complex tables with the visual HTML assistant in FrontPage 98.

This online ▶ comic is based on a combination of frames and the <META> tag. Every 15 seconds a new drawing automatically appears in the big frame.

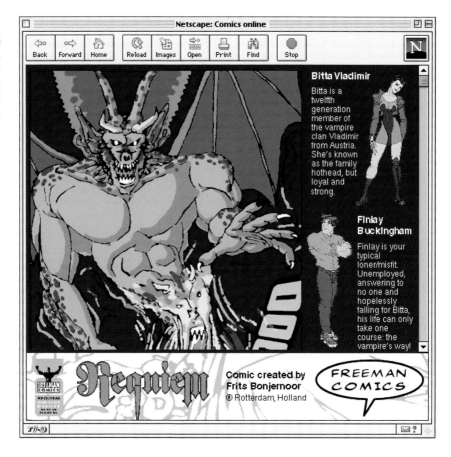

The introduction of frames has had significant consequences in Web design. Dividing a page into different compartments sometimes lets you create a better user interface. The downside is that the user and the search engines sometimes lose their way.

Frames and the Meta Tag

The relationship between Web pages is determined by the user interface *(for an in-depth discussion, read the chapter "Interactive Navigation on the Web")*. Adding menu bars and hyperlinks lets you control the navigation between pages. Your options remain limited, however, since the user has to read in new data time and again. It also means that the navigation tools have to be repeated at the same spot on each and every Web page.

Netscape's programmers have introduced a method that makes the interaction between Web pages a lot more logical. With the help of frames, a page can be divided into segments.

▶ Dividing into Frames

A Web page that is divided into frames actually displays a different page in each segment. Thus each frame has its own URL, which can be a page containing text and images, or even a PDF file or a Shockwave animation. Splitting the Web page even allows the different parts of the page to communicate with each other, though special Java scripts are needed to link the frames. Clearly, the extra options that frames offer have introduced an entirely new dimension to Web page design.

▶ Scroll Bars

Since each frame is a normal Web page, the page segments can scroll horizontally and vertically. This is logical, since each segment is a URL; if the contents are too large to fit into the space provided by the frame, the viewer must be able to scroll. However, since you can define the width and height of each frame, you can fit an identical-size image in that frame, making the horizontal and vertical scroll bars unnecessary.

Netscape's developers have introduced a number of new attributes that let you modify the frame display.

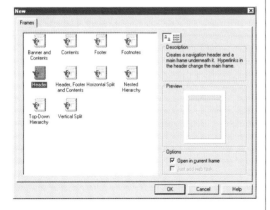

▲ Microsoft FrontPage can automatically generate the basic code for a frames-based page using the Frames Wizard.

This site is Frames Free

▶ Problems with Frames

The success of a Web page with frames depends on the percentage of browsers that recognize the HTML tags for frames. In contrast to what happens with most tags, viewing frames-based pages through an older browser can wreak havoc.

A separate tag combination in the frames code has been developed to deal with this problem: <NOFRAMES> </NOFRAMES>. The text between these tags is the only information an old browser sees! This means that you have the additional chore of placing the entire original HTML text between the <NOFRAMES> tags. For a huge Web site consisting of many pages, this would be an impossible task.

▶ Search Engines and Frames

Another disadvantage of frames is that search engines encounter problems when searching for data at deeper levels in a frames-based site. Thus it's important to have well-balanced meta data, especially on the home page. Bookmarking poses the biggest disadvantage of frames. Pages other than the home page, in which the division of the frames is defined, cannot be included in the surfer's list of favorites.

Fortunately, Internet Explorer 5.0 no longer suffers from this disadvantage: This browser can bookmark a site using frames at any level. This fix is a giant leap forward, removing one of the major objections to frames. What remains a hindrance for Web designers is creating simultaneous control of several frames, a task that requires Java scripting.

Since coding frames is a complicated job, it makes sense to use a package like Microsoft FrontPage. The package lets you rapidly and efficiently produce the complex HTML code frames on the screen.

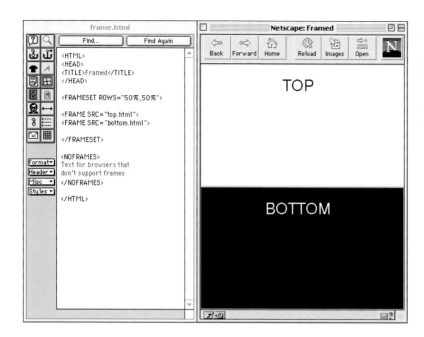

◄ The two horizontal rows are the same size because the <ROWS> attribute is set to 50 percent for both rows. The source for the top frame is the file top.html, and the file bottom.html goes in the bottom frame.

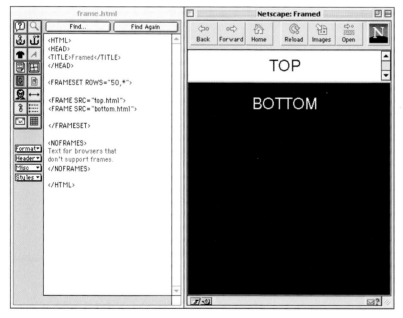

◄ Here the first frame is assigned a fixed height of 50 pixels. The rest of the screen height in the browser window is allocated to the second frame using the "*" setting.

▶ Frame Set Basics

Defining frames in HTML code is relatively simple. The frame code replaces the <BODY> tags. The basic HTML code consists of <FRAMESET ROWS="x,y"> </FRAMESET>. The <ROWS> attribute specifies the number of sections in which the screen must be divided. The relationship between the sections can be expressed in percentages or defined with a fixed setting. The wildcard "*" (see screen images) indicates that the remaining space must be added to this frame.

You can create ▸
a vertical page division
by using the <COLS>
attribute. The columns
can be expressed as
percentages with a total
of 100 percent—for
example, instead of
the 50 percent,
50 percent relationship
shown, you could specify
30 percent, 40 percent,
and 30 percent.

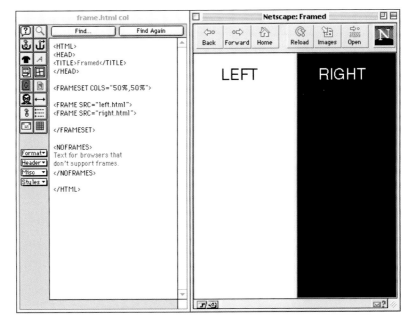

You can also express ▸
a fixed width in number
of pixels and a wildcard.

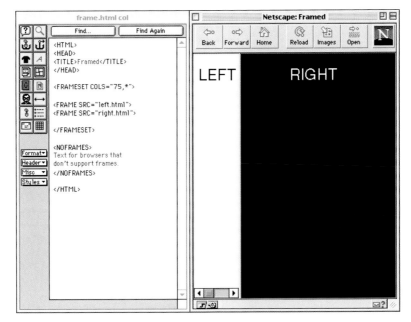

▸ References to URLs

The contents of the <FRAMESET> cannot be displayed on the same page in which the frames are specified. Only references to the URLs are specified within the frame set, using the tag <FRAME SRC="one.html"> and <FRAME SRC="two.html">. The number of URLs defined has to equal the number of frames specified in the <COL> or <ROW> attributes. The text placed between the <NOFRAME> tags is intended for browsers that do not support the frames standard.

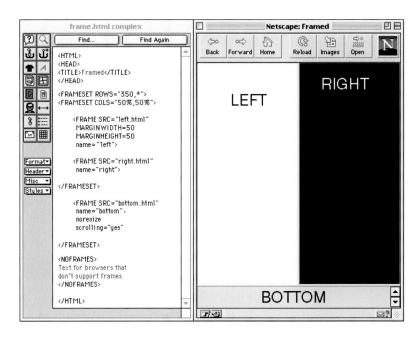

◄ The number of attributes can be expressed in <NORESIZE> so the user cannot modify the size of the frame. The location attributes <MARGINWIDTH> and <MARGINHEIGHT> produce a free margin expressed in pixels.

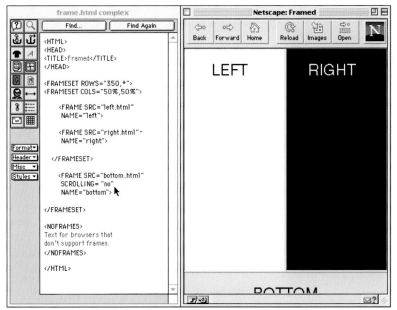

◄ The special <SCROLLING="NO"> attribute ensures that the frame is always displayed without horizontal or vertical scroll bars.

▶ **Nested Frames**

Just as with tables, a frame can be nested inside another frame. However, to do this you must modify the frame set. In the illustration shown above, the vertical frame set has been divided into two segments. In this case it is advisable to assign a name to the frames by adding the <NAME="name"> attribute to the frame source. A second attribute that comes in handy here is <SCROLLING>. The values "YES" and "NO" determine whether a scroll bar will be displayed in the subframe.

The attribute <TARGET> ▶
adds an extra dimension
to a Web page with
frames. If you specify
a particular URL as the
target, it will be displayed
only in the designated
frame.

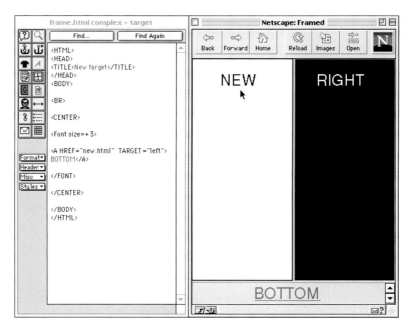

If you do not specify ▶
a <TARGET>, the browser
will open an entirely new
standard size window
and display the URL in
that window.

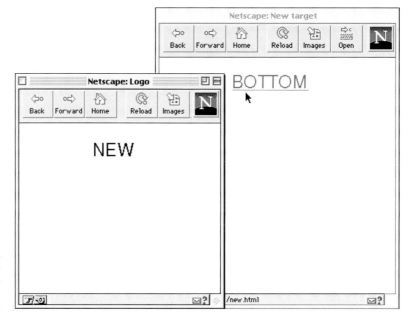

▶ Target Training

The attribute <TARGET="name.html"> is a different story: It lets you specify the frame in which a specific URL must be displayed. This is when the frame name comes in handy. Defining the name as the <TARGET> ensures that the content of a new URL is kept on the same Web page. If the frames have not been assigned names, the code <TARGET="_parent"> or <TARGET="_top"> must be added in order for the URL to stay within the frame.

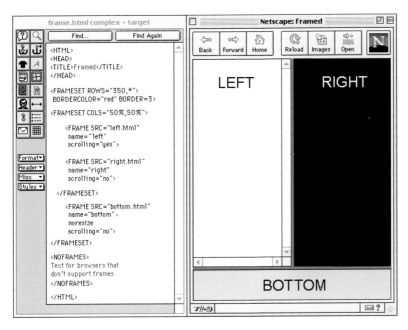

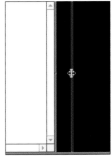

◄ The <FRAMEBORDER> attribute is normally set to YES. If the attribute is used in the <FRAMESET> tag, the setting is applied to the entire frame and all the subsets.

▲ A highlighted mark on the edge of the frame indicates that the frame size can be modified.

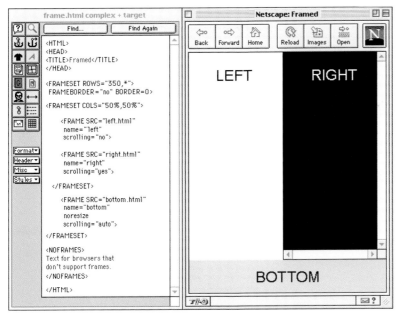

◄ The combination <FRAMEBORDER="no" BORDER=0> ensures that Netscape Navigator and Microsoft Internet Explorer do not display the borders of the frames. This specification may seem redundant, but it's necessary because the two browsers interpret the code differently.

▶ Microsoft Attributes for Frames

Since Internet Explorer also supports frames, it should come as no surprise that a number of new attributes have been introduced in the program. These attributes are <FRAMEBORDER="yes" or "no">, <BORDERCOLOR ="x"> and <FRAMESPACING=x>. The first attribute determines whether a frame has a visible border. To be sure that the border is removed in Navigator 3.0, you must add <BORDER=0> to the code. <FRAMESPACING> adds extra white space between the frames.

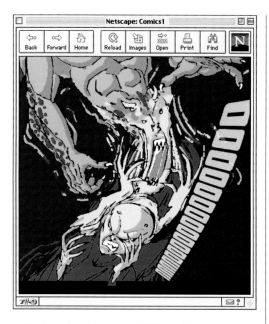

▲ The dynamic comic consists of different drawings ...

▲ ...that all have the same dimensions. The illustrations ...

▶ Frames in Combination with the Meta Tag

Because each frame refers to a specific URL, different "behavior" can be specified for each frame. This option is quite suitable for the example displayed on this and the following pages, in which a "client-pull" technique is used to create a dynamic comic.

◀ The right-hand frame displays the animated comic's main characters and a brief description of them.

▲ ... are all based on the same indexed ...

▲ ... colors, which limits the file size.

A tag in the HTML code triggers the browser to initiate downloading another HTML file after a specific period. The frame will continue to download a new image and display it on the user's screen because the <META> tag has been included in the heading at the top frame of the comic page. Of course, the time increments should not be too small, because not everyone has a fast modem—a 15-second interval is sufficient.

▼ The bottom frame, which cannot be resized, is reserved for credits and the creator's name.

▶ Automatic Update

Here is the complete HTML code to download the comic Web page after 15 seconds:

```
<META HTTP-EQUIV="refresh"
  CONTENT="15; URL= strip2.html">
```

The <HTTP-EQUIV> and <CONTENT> attributes add the client-pull feature to the HTML page. You can include a reference to a Shockwave Flash animation or to an audio or video file in a URL.

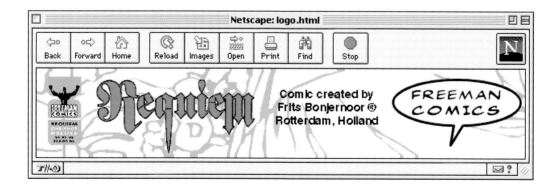

▶ The Requiem Home Page

This HTML page is displayed after typing in the URL. The page is divided into three frames:

<FRAME SRC="comic1.html"> ▷

The frame comic1.html is the first frame of the series of illustrations that make up the comic.

<FRAME SRC="right.html"> ▷

The two frame attributes <SCROLLING="YES"> and <NORESIZE> determine the settings for the right-hand frame. Here you find the legend of the comic characters.

<FRAME SRC="logo.html"> ▷

The <SCROLLING="auto"> attribute allows only the bottom frame to scroll if the reader minimizes the screen. The author's credits are displayed in this frame.

The <NOFRAMES></NOFRAMES> Tag ▷

Explanatory text must be included for viewers who do not have one of the browsers mentioned. Another option is to refer to a script at this location so that the entire HTML code for the home page does not need to be included.

```
<HTML> <HEAD><TITLE>Requiem</TITLE></HEAD>

<FRAMESET ROWS="420,*">
<FRAMESET COLS="420,*">

    <FRAME SRC="comic1.html"
        NAME=animated-comic>

    <FRAME SRC="right.html"
        SCROLLING="YES"
        NORESIZE
        NAME="right">

  </FRAMESET>

  <FRAME SRC="logo.html"
      SCROLLING="auto"
      NORESIZE
      NAME="logo">

</FRAMESET>

<NOFRAMES>
Netscape 2.0 and Microsoft Internet Explorer 3.0 or higher
can see this comic much clearer :-). Please upgrade!
</NOFRAMES>

</HTML>
```

▶ The Requiem Characters Page

The HTML code shown on the right produces the file right.html.

The <CLEAR=all> Attribute ▷

The cartoon figures are positioned alternately on the page. The <BR> tag is expanded with the <CLEAR =all>. attribute. This prevents the text of the following comic character from touching the illustration. In principle the <CLEAR =all> attribute must always be applied when the <ALIGN> tag is used.

```
<HTML>
  <HEAD>
    <TITLE>right</TITLE>
  </HEAD>
<BODY BGCOLOR="#000000" TEXT="#FFFFFF">

<IMG width=102 height=200 ALIGN=right SRC="bitta.gif">
<H3>Bitta Vladimir</H3>
Bitta is a twelfth generation member of the vampire clan
Vladimir from Austria. She&#146;s known as the family
hothead, but loyal and strong.
<BR CLEAR=all>
</BODY>
</HTML>
```

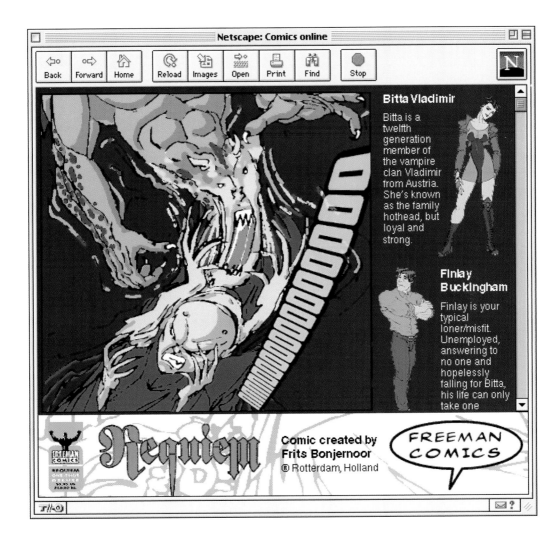

▶ The Dynamic Comic Page

The page "Comic1.html" is the first dynamic Web page from the comic series.

The <META> Tag

The dynamic comic series is created by including the <META>tag in the heading and referring to the following comic page called "comic2.html." Each following Web page refers to the following URL using the same time interval.

```
<HTML>
<HEAD>
<TITLE>animated-comic</TITLE>

<META HTTP-EQUIV="refresh"
  CONTENT="15; URL=comic2.html">
</HEAD>
<BODY bgcolor="#000000">

<CENTER>
  <IMG SRC="ill1.gif" width=400  height=400>
</CENTER>
</BODY>
</HTML>
```

▶ Meta as a Comments Tag

Not all <META>tags are client-pull codes. The tag is also used to describe the contents of a Web page or site. This information is used to indicate how a document is indexed in a search engine. Most search engines index all words in an HTML document and use the first 200 words as a summary of the contents. If you use a lot of images and not much text on your home page, your site will not score high in a search engine's results report.

You can prevent this problem by including a summary and a few key words for the search engine yourself. The <META> tag is used for this purpose. Below is an example of the HTML code for the Web site for this book:

```
<HTML>
<HEAD>
<TITLE>A real world Web design and HTML Book</TITLE>

<META Name="description" CONTENT="A Web site which
shows the graphic designs, tips and tricks and hyperlinks
featured in the book Web Design Tools and Techniques.">

<META Name="keywords" CONTENT="Web page design,
Web site design, Java, Shockwave Flash, HTML, GIF animation,
graphic design, Java script, Web content">

<META Name="ROBOTS" CONTENT="ALL">
</HEAD>
<BODY>...
```

The code is only for the search engine and is denied by the browser. There are also different <NAME> attributes; only the most important ones are displayed here. You should put careful thought into picking your keywords to be sure they're words a user would type in when using a search engine to find your page. Not all search engines use the <META> tag—some use the <ALT> information for images, so be sure to include <ALT> descriptions.

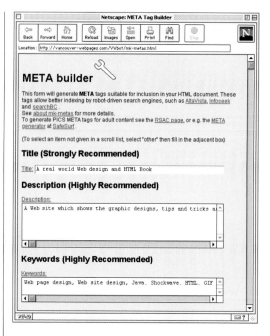

▲ You can even find automatic <META> tag builders online that create the tags for you.   ▼

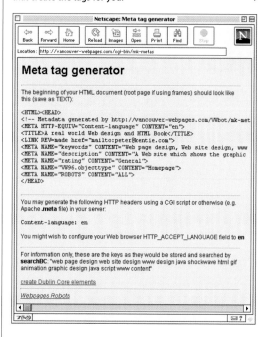

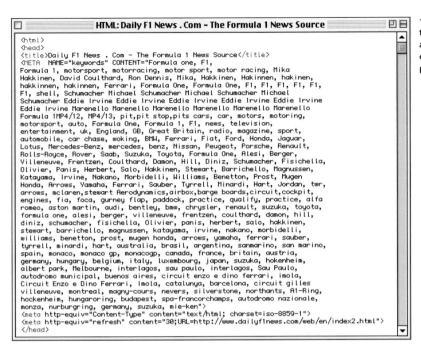

```
HTML: Daily F1 News . Com - The Formula 1 News Source
<html>
<head>
<title>Daily F1 News . Com - The Formula 1 News Source</title>
<META  NAME="keywords" CONTENT="Formula one, F1,
Formula 1, motorsport, motorracing, motor sport, motor racing, Mika
Hakkinen, David Coulthard, Ron Dennis, Mika, Hakkinen, Hakinnen, hakinen,
hakkinnen, hakinnen, Ferrari, Formula One, Formula One, F1, F1, F1, F1, F1,
F1, shell, Schumacher Michael Schumacher Michael Schumacher Michael
Schumacher Eddie Irvine Eddie Irvine Eddie Irvine Eddie Irvine Eddie Irvine
Eddie Irvine Marenello Marenello Marenello Marenello Marenello Marenello
Formula 1MP4/12, MP4/13, pit,pit stop,pits cars, car, motors, motoring,
motorsport, auto, Formula One, Formula 1, F1, news, television,
entertainment, uk, England, GB, Great Britain, radio, magazine, sport,
automobile, car chase, woking, BMW, Ferrari, Fiat, Ford, Honda, Jaguar,
Lotus, Mercedes-Benz, mercedes, benz, Nissan, Peugeot, Porsche, Renault,
Rolls-Royce, Rover, Saab, Suzuka, Toyota, Formula One, Alesi, Berger,
Villeneuve, Frentzen, Coulthard, Damon, Hill, Diniz, Schumacher, Fisichella,
Olivier, Panis, Herbert, Salo, Hakkinen, Stewart, Barrichello, Magnussen,
Katayama, Irvine, Nakano, Morbidelli, Williams, Benetton, Prost, Mugen
Honda, Arrows, Yamaha, Ferrari, Sauber, Tyrrell, Minardi, Hart, Jordan, twr,
arrows, mclaren,stewart Aerodynamics,airbox,barge boards,circuit,cockpit,
engines, fia, foca, gurney flap, paddock, practice, qualify, practice, alfa
romeo, aston martin, audi, bentley, bmw, chrysler, renault, suzuka, toyota,
formula one, alesi, berger, villeneuve, frentzen, coulthard, damon, hill,
diniz, schumacher, fisichella, Olivier, panis, herbert, salo, hakkinen,
stewart, barrichello, magnussen, katayama, irvine, nakano, morbidelli,
williams, benetton, prost, mugen honda, arrows, yamaha, ferrari, sauber,
tyrrell, minardi, hart, australia, brasil, argentina, sanmarino, san marino,
spain, monaco, monaco gp, monacogp, canada, france, britain, austria,
germany, hungary, belgium, italy, luxembourg, japan, suzuka, hokenheim,
albert park, Melbourne, interlagos, sau paulo, interlagos, Sau Paulo,
autodromo municipal, buenos aires, circuit enzo e dino ferrari, imola,
Circuit Enzo e Dino Ferrari, Imola, catalunya, barcelona, circuit gilles
villeneuve, montreal, magny-cours, nevers, silverstone, northants, A1-Ring,
hockenheim, hungaroring, budapest, spa-francorchamps, autodromo nazionale,
monza, nurburgring, germany, suzuka, mie-ken">
<meta http-equiv="Content-Type" content="text/html; charset=iso-8859-1">
<meta http-equiv="refresh" content="30;URL=http://www.dailyf1news.com/web/en/index2.html">
</head>
```

◄ Some Web sites will try anything to end up as high in the search engines results as possible.

▶ Meta Applications

<META> tags can be used to improve search engine performance, but they can also be used to include specific features in the site. If, for example, you are dealing with a Web page you don't want to be cached, you can use a <META> attribute to make sure the site will not be included in the browser's cache.

This is an ideal feature for news sites because the content is continuously updated and you wouldn't want an older page from the cache to be displayed. Since it is impossible to empty a visitor's cache remotely, you must use <META> information that performs that task.

The <Expires> attribute is the appropriate solution when using a date that has long since lapsed. The visitor's browser will classify the content as old and reload all the information without using the browser cache. Note that although the HTML is reloaded, the images are still retrieved from the cache. This is in contrast to the Shift-Reload command, which reloads all the content.

Here is the code:

```
<META HTTP-EQUIV="Expires"
  CONTENT="Mon, 06 Jan 1990 00:00:00 GMT">
```

Internet Explorer supports an alternative solution called pragma no-cache, which causes all the HTML content to be read in as new. The code is as follows:

```
<META HTTP-EQUIV="PRAGMA" CONTENT="no-cache">
```

Practical WebTIP

▶ As a Web designer, you must take the user's cache into account. For example, if you have updated your site and you check the new Web page in your browser, it may sometimes seem that something has really gone wrong. No sweat, a previous page from your cache is probably being displayed. You can see the updated

page only if you empty your cache or click on your browser's Reload button while pressing the Shift key. This is a handy tip is for your customers too!

▶ **Maximum Shelf Life**

You can also have the reverse effect of a page that must not be cached. Suppose you have a site whose content is valid up to a specific date. The <Expires> meta attribute can also be used for this purpose. You can include an expiration date and time for the page like this:

```
<META HTTP-EQUIV="Expires"
  CONTENT="Mon, 06 Jan 2010 23:59:59 GMT">
```

After the specified date, the browser will only load the HTML page if the user searches for the page again on the Web. In this example the page expires just before midnight on January 6, 2010. *(GMT stands for Greenwich Mean Time.)*

▶ **Meta and Language Versions**

The meta tag is also ideal for letting the server know what language and what character set might be used in the HTML document. In the future, the XML language will take over a part of this job, but until that time a special meta attribute can help.

For a site using the Russian character set that must be read as an HTML page, include the following command in its header:

```
<!DOCTYPE HTML PUBLIC "-//W3C//DTD HTML 3.2//RU">
```

```
<META HTTP-EQUIV="Content-type:
  CONTENT="text/html; charset=windows-1251">
```

```
<META HTTP-EQUIV="Content-language"
  CONTENT="ru-RU">
```

If the character set is missing, you'll get a screen with a bunch of question marks instead of legible text. If you're creating a multilingual Web site containing Asian languages, then you must use a "double-byte" server. Be sure to keep this in mind when purchasing Web server software and hardware.

▶ **Meta Tags and Frame Sets**

Another problem with frames-based Web sites is their score in search engine results. Many search engines are not intelligent enough to search the main frame and thus get no further than the index page. Usually in the index.html file you find only information describing the frame format, as we have seen in this chapter. So where should you store the meta information that handles the indexing for the site and the attached page?

The answer is simple: in the NOFRAMES section. If you make text links in the NOFRAMES section of the index.html document to subpages in which content can be found, the search engine will "visit" these pages and index them.

```
<NOFRAMES>
Netscape 2.0 and Microsoft Internet Explorer 3.0 or higher.
<P>
<A HREF="main.html>Introduction page.</A>
<A HREF="nav.html>Navigation links page.</A>
<A HREF="legal.html>Terms and conditions page.</A>
</BODY>
</NOFRAMES>
```

As you see, three textual links have been added to the <NOFRAMES> section. Subsequently, the search engine will include main.html, nav.html, and legal.html in its index.

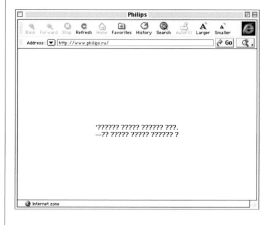

▲ If the character set is missing, you'll get a screen with illegible text. In this example the Russian content is unknown.

Typography on ▶
the World Wide
Web can be as
simple and
efficient as this
homepage.

What do concepts such as font embedding, subscript and superscript, and antialiased fonts mean for a Web designer? Answer: They are the future! A lot is happening on the Web in the field of typography, which offers a wealth of creative possibilities.

Typography and the Web

The title of this chapter seems to be a contradiction in terms. Isn't HTML just a design language describing a page structure? That's true, but that doesn't mean we shouldn't pay attention to the format and display of the text and typography.

Using an amusing font in a GIF image is not what we have in mind here. That's part of graphic design and has to do with the identity, the company's house style, and the effect of an online publication. Typography in Web pages has to do with applying structure and logic. New typographical possibilities are continuously being added to the Web designer's arsenal. This chapter describes the state of affairs in HTML and what the future has in store on the Web typography front.

▶ HTML Font Extensions

Netscape has supplied HTML with a great number of extensions, and typography has not escaped its attention. Together with the Internet Engineering Task Force and the World Wide Web Consortium *(W3C)*, a number of proposals have been launched to expand the text options. The new font attributes are correctly interpreted and displayed on the screen in Netscape Communicator and Internet Explorer.

<BIG></BIG>	The text is displayed big.
<SMALL></SMALL>	The text is displayed small.
	The text is displayed as subscript. This is used for chemical and mathematical formulas.
	The text is displayed as superscript. This is also used for chemical and mathematical formulas.

Here's a typical example of when these tags come in handy. The display of a floor area in square meters can be coded as follows:

Floor area (m²)

The browser will place the 2 figure above the level of the baseline.

▶ HTML Paragraph Extensions

Netscape has proposed a number of extensions to HTML at the paragraph level as well. The combination of the <P> and <DIV> tags with the attributes <ALIGN=center>, <ALIGN=left>, and <ALIGN=right> are interesting options for Web designers. What exactly do these paragraph tags do? The <DIV ALIGN=right> </DIV> tag combo ensures that the text placed between these codes is right-justified on the page without being followed by a blank line. The <P ALIGN=right> </P> tag creates a new paragraph along with a blank line. The <DIV> tag, short for "divisions,"

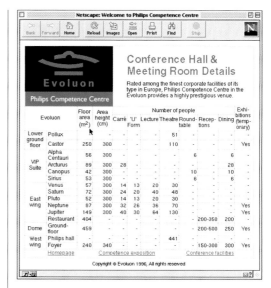

▲ The <SUP> tag is the only way to display the squared symbol in HTML.

is rarely applied but is a real godsend in some situations.

If the text is part of a table and must be aligned, the tags just mentioned are useless. You must add one of the attributes <ALIGN=left>, <ALIGN=center>, or <ALIGN=right> to the code in the table cell itself. For example, the <TD ALIGN=left> tag left-justifies the information placed in a table cell. What should your do if your entire table has to be adjusted with a larger or smaller font? That's simple—use the <BASEFONT-size="x"> option.

This lets you enlarge all the fonts on the page while maintaining their relative sizes. All <Font-size="x"> tags will be affected by this. For example, if you enter a basefont-size="+2" all the font sizes in your text that have been set using the font-size command increase by 2 points: 10-point text becomes 12, 12-point text becomes 14, and so on. You can also use negative numbers in the base-font command. This lets you increase or decrease all the fonts in your document by the same number of points using one command. Please note that the <Hx></Hx> tags are not affected by the <BASEFONT> setting.

▲ Windows and Macintosh computers display Web pages differently. ▼

▲ The user's font settings also affect the text positioning. ▼

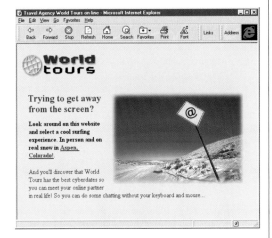

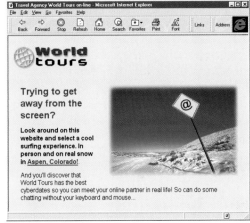

▶ **Typographic Developments**

Not only is the formatting of HTML text continuously expanding, the legibility of screen text is improving as well. The use of TrueType letters as a screen font is a step in the right direction. In the following example you will see that a PostScript font, the darling of the graphics industry, is rather disappointing as a screen font compared with Microsoft's alternative. For italicized text, TrueType fonts work considerably better.

Liberated from the restrictions of the HTML layout language, Web designers can use a special tag to specify the font in which the user must read the text.

Naturally, Microsoft offers this option in its Internet Explorer browser. The font type tag reads:

```
<FONT face="Lucidasans Roman, Arial, Helvetica">
```
Depending on the fonts the user has installed, this text is displayed in the Lucida Sans, Arial, or Helvetica font.
```
</FONT>
```

Remember that you must use the original PostScript or TrueType font specification. If you type in the font name from a font list, the <FONT FACE> tag will not work and the browser will default to its standard display font.

▶ Cascading Style Sheets

For typographically trained Web designers, cascading style sheets are a revelation compared with the cumbersome coding process that is an inevitable part of the HTML language. Moreover, style sheets are a giant step in the direction of structured layouts. Operating cascading style sheets is similar to handling style sheets in word processors and layout programs.

Accepted by the W3C, style sheets were first applied by Microsoft in Internet Explorer version 3.0. They work almost exactly like style sheets in Microsoft Word, QuarkXPress, and Adobe PageMaker. Web designers have a huge number of options at their fingertips: With style sheets they can define the font, font size, color of text and background, indentation, and line-spacing. The settings for different styles are defined at the beginning of a <BODY> text section. In the following example, the <BODY> and the heading line <H1> have been assigned a style.

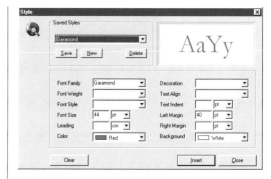

```
<HTML><HEAD><TITLE>test style</TITLE></HEAD>
<BODY BGCOLOR="white">
<STYLE>
<!--
    H1    { font-size: 24pt; font-family: Arial; font-weight: bold;
            line-height: 36pt; text-indent: 6pt; margin-left: 6pt;
            color: Silver; background: Maroon; }
    BODY  { font-size: 18pt; font-family: Century Schoolbook;
            font-weight: normal; line-height: 20pt; color: Purple; }
-->
</STYLE>
<H1> This is styled text </H1>
The body copy is styled<BR>
<SPAN STYLE="font-size: 44pt; font-family: Garamond;
        margin-left: 40pt; color: Red;">Garamond text</SPAN>
</BODY>
</HTML>
```

The styles in ▶ this example were created with the HTML editor HomeSite 2.5.

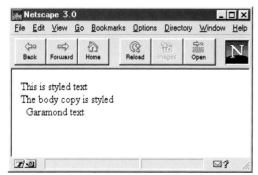

▲ Be careful with older browsers. Netscape Navigator 3.0, for example, does not support style sheets.

▶ Browser Compatibility

If the <H1> tag is subsequently applied to the Web page, a compatible browser will display the heading with the setting of the style sheet. Internet Explorer versions 3.0 and higher and Netscape Navigator 4.0 display the text as intended by the Web designer. But keep in mind that older browsers, such as Netscape Navigator 3.0 and Internet Explorer 2.0, cannot handle style sheets; instead, the user's default settings determine how the text is displayed.

If you want the display text in the various browsers to be as similar as possible, use the <FONT-SIZE="X" COLOR="#XXXXX"> tag. *(You cannot specify the vertical alignment, however.)*

▶ SPAN and LINK Tag

You do not need to include all the codes for style sheets at the beginning of an HTML document. The <SPAN></SPAN> tag combination allows you to assign another style to part of your text. *(Be sure to close this text using </SPAN>; otherwise the rest of the text will be displayed in that style as well.)*

You can also define style sheets in an external HTML file and refer to that file from the document using a <LINK> tag in the document heading.

Here is an example of how this works:

<TITLE>External link with style sheet</TITLE><HEAD>
<LINK REL=stylesheet HREF="style.css" TYPE="text/css">
</HEAD>

▲ The tag <LINK REL=stylesheet> opens an external file that enables an entire site to use a style sheet. That makes changing the style easier. Following is the code for an external style sheet:

Copyright (c) Macaw New Media NV, Hoofddorp, www.macaw.nl

```
<HTML>
<STYLE TYPE="text/css">
<!--
BODY      { background: "#FEFFCD"
            color: black;
            font-size: 80%; }

P         { color: black;
            font-size: 100%;
            margin-left: 12%;
            margin-right: 0%;
            font-family: Times, Times New Roman; }

H3, H4    { font-size: 100%;
            margin-left: 12%;
            margin-right: 0%;
            font-weight: bold;
            color: black;
            font-family: Arial, Helvetica, helv, Verdana, sans-serif; }

A:link    { color: "#0000DF";
            font-weight: bold;
            text-decoration: none; }

A:visited { color: "#DC5A5A";
            font-weight: bold;
            text-decoration: none; }

A:active  { color: "#FF0000";
            font-weight: bold;
            text-decoration: none; }
-->
</STYLE>
<BODY>
 
</BODY>
</HTML>
```

▶ W3C Style Sheets Example

On this page is an annotated example of the code for a Web page using style sheets; on the facing page you'll see the Web page as displayed by Internet Explorer 4.0.

The <STYLE> Tag ▷

The <STYLE> tag defines the beginning of a style sheet. The various components of the style sheet have been arranged vertically.

Between Brackets ▷

To prevent the contents of the <STYLE> tag from being displayed as normal text, the code is placed between comments brackets (<!-- and -->). Browsers that recognize the W3C style sheet specifications will not display the comments that are marked this way.

The <SPAN> Tag ▷

The <SPAN> tag lets you assign another style to part of the text. The font size (the height of the font) code can expressed absolutely in points or relatively in percentages.

The <STYLE> Attribute ▷

The code <SPAN STYLE="color: Black; background: White"> displays text in black on a white bar. The   code allows for extra space on the left and right side of the bar.

The <A STYLE> Tag ▷

The <A STYLE="font-size:9pt; color:lime" HREF="index.htm" TARGET="_top"> overwrites the settings of the <A> tag that were specified at the beginning of the document. So there are two ways to replace a style.

```
<HTML>
   <HEAD>
      <TITLE>Styles Example</TITLE>
   </HEAD>

<STYLE>
<!--
   BODY {font: 9pt/18pt Arial; color: white}
   H1 {font: 24pt Garamond; color: yellow}
   H3 {font: 18pt Arial; font-weight: bold; color: white}
   B {font-size: 18pt; font-family: Courier; font-weight: bold;
      color: Teal; background: Silver}
   A:link {font: 12pt helv; font-weight: bold; color: aqua}
-->
</STYLE>

<BODY TOPMARGIN=20 LEFTMARGIN=1
   BGCOLOR=maroon LINK=white VLINK=white>

<H1>Style Sheets</H1>
This page shows a superb technique which enables
<SPAN STYLE="font-size: 18pt; font-family: Arial; font-weight:
bold; line-height: 36pt; color: Silver; background: Maroon">
authors</SPAN> to create web pages with <SPAN STYLE="color:
Black; background: White">style sheets</SPAN>. A bit like
producing a document with <A HREF="http://www.quark.com/">
Quark XPress&reg; </A>, with the same versatility and
ease-of-use. <SPAN STYLE="color: Black; background: White">
Style sheets</SPAN> were created at the W3C consortium
and introduced to the browserwars by <A HREF=
"http://www.microsoft.com/">Microsoft&reg;</A>. Webdesign
will benefit enormously from these options.
<P>

<H3>Tags</H3>
The <SPAN STYLE="color: Black; background: White">  
style sheet   </SPAN> tags are not easily learned, but
once mastered you'll appreciate the versatility of this technique.
Webdesign has gained a key concept of page design. The last
two letters of the word <A STYLE="Font-size:9pt; color:lime"
HREF="index.htm" TARGET="_top">H</SPAN>TML</A>, the
abbreviation of Hyper Text Mark-up Language, is being
transformed into <B>M</B>ultiple <B>L</B>ayout.

</BODY>
</HTML>
```

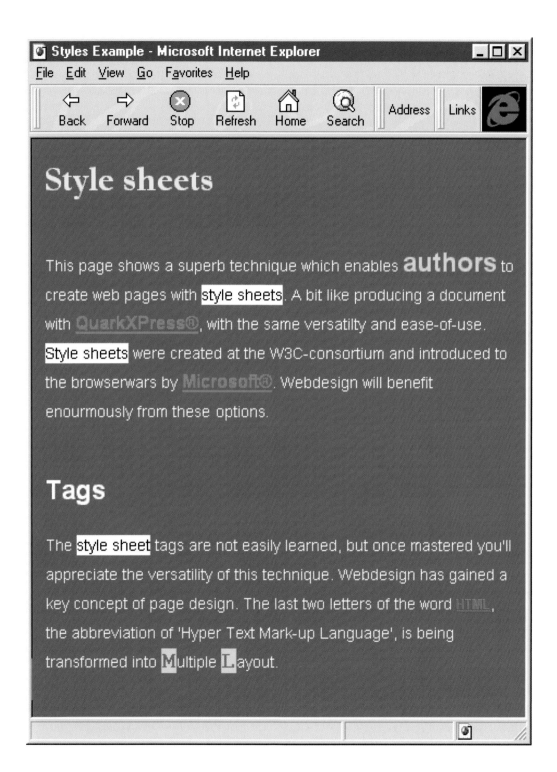

▲ HTML code using style sheets can produce a colorful Web page.

▶ Font Size in Pixels

If the design of a Web page has to fit exactly on a displayed page, you'll find that there are considerable differences in terms of display among the browsers and operating systems. The font size between a Macintosh and a Windows PC, for example, sometimes varies more than 30 percent. The use of cascading style sheets neutralizes this problem. A font size can be specified in pixels *(px)*, which neutralizes the differences between the browsers and computer systems almost completely. In the style sheet the code is the following: {font-family: Verdana, Arial, Helvetica; font-size: 26px} Although this technique is useful, it has two disadvantages: Users can no longer modify the font size, and they may encounter some printing problems.

▲ In Macromedia Dreamweaver two new style sheets called .sizes and .sizes2 are created.

◀ The font size of .sizes is set at 26 pixels and saved as a style sheet.

This HTML code ▶ shows that we are comparing three font size descriptions:

<font size = "6">

and two style sheet variations: .sizes in pixels .sizes2 in points.

The illustrations on the adjacent page show variations in platform and browser types. The displays of the fixed font size expressed as size 6 or 26 points differs dramatically among the browsers, whereas those expressed as 26 pixels is more or less constant.

```
<html>
<head>
<title>Always use pixels</title>
<style type="text/css">
<!--
  .sizes { font-family: Verdana, Arial, Helvetica, sans-serif; font-size: 26px}
  .sizes2 { font-family: Verdana, Arial, Helvetica, sans-serif; font-size: 26pt}
-->
</style>
</head>
<body bgcolor="#FFFFFF">
<p>
<font size="6" face="Verdana, Arial, Helvetica, sans-serif">Font size = 6</font></p>
<p class="sizes">
<font face="Verdana, Arial, Helvetica, sans-serif" class="sizes">Font size = 26 pixels</font></p>
<p class="sizes2">
<font face="Verdana, Arial, Helvetica, sans-serif" class="sizes2">
   Font size = 26 points</font></p>
</body>
</html>
```

■ Font size differences

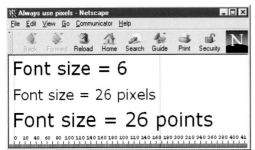

▲ The font size expressed in pixels produces a somewhat different display with Netscape Communicator on a Windows PC than it does with Microsoft Internet Explorer.

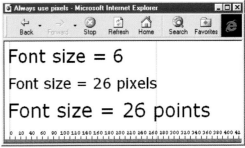

▲ Microsoft Internet Explorer on a Windows PC is more consistent in its display than a Mac. ▼

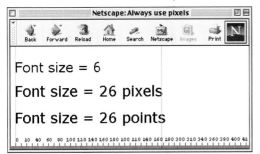

▲ Netscape Communicator on a Macintosh displays an extremely small letter for font size and the style sheet .sizes2.

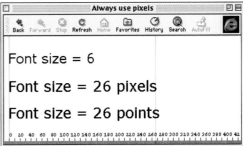

▲ Microsoft Explorer on a Macintosh produces an effect comparable to what you get using Netscape. There's a big difference from the results you get using Explorer on a Windows PC!

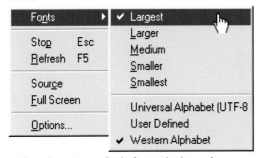

▲ If you choose Largest for the font setting in your browser, . . .

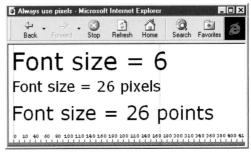

▲ . . . the font sizes changes dramatically. Font sizes expressed in pixels remain unchanged.

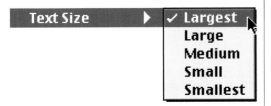

▲ Changing the text size in the browser produces a big change in the font size on the Macintosh, too.

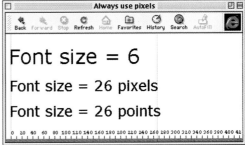

▲ Here, too, the size in pixels remains more or less constant no matter what type of browser or computer is used.

▶ Dynamic Fonts

The quality and the interactive options of the Web have been approaching the CD-ROM level. Dynamic HTML, for example, lets the Web designer add dynamic features to Web pages.

Developments are also under way in the typography domain that considerably enhance the display of images and text—namely, by means of dynamic font technology. This addresses one of the primary deficiencies of the HTML markup language: control over fonts. Normally, in HTML we can only marginally influence the font display. Because HTML is a page-layout markup language with coded descriptions indicating how a text fragment must be displayed (in bold or italics, for example), what the user sees depends on the font he has defined on his computer. This means that if we want the text on a Web page to be displayed in Gill Sans font, that font has to be available on the reader's hard disk. If the font is not available, the browser will display the default font in the user's browser preferences.

In principle, this is a thorn in the flesh for midsize and larger companies because they prefer to present as consistent an image of their company as possible, and frequently that means the use of a specific font—the corporate typeface. The fact that a Web page does not allow control over the typography forces designers to create header text in a graphics file. Unfortunately, this greatly increases the file size of the page—each new GIF adds many extra kilobytes that must be sent over the modem.

Dynamic font technology addresses this situation by sending the font information with the HTML document. The TrueDoc system, invented by Bitstream, is the basis of this development and is supported by Navigator 4.0 and higher. Internet Explorer can also employ this technology, but only with a separate ActiveX control. The reason is that Netscape is not the only company that wants to establish a standard for Web typography. Together with Adobe, Microsoft has come up with a solution called WEFT, Web Embedding Fonts Tool. The design of this font distribution system is comparable to

▼ A page that uses the TrueDoc format cannot simply be reproduced on your own PC with the same quality—there's a protection feature at the server level.

Netscape's and Bitstream's competing methods. Of course, the W3C is not happy about these developments. We will see which system wins in the near future. However, this does not change the fact that the TrueDoc system is already used in a great many sites and that it gives the Web designer a multitude of creative options.

▶ Portable Font Resource

The TrueDoc technique automatically uploads font data from the server where the Web page resides to the computer of the viewer loading the Web page. The TrueDoc file format uses the display information hidden in a PostScript Type 1 or TrueType font. In fact, the computer language instructions for displaying the font are included as part of the file. This information is saved in the Portable Font Resource *(PFR)* file. The browser has a character shape player *(CSP)* built in so that the PFR data can be uncompressed, antialiased, and presented. A CSP for Internet Explorer is available in the form of an ActiveX control.

The font file size is minimal. For example, the Gill Sans PFR that was created especially for this chapter is only 17K. Since this is additional data that the user must read in with a modem connection, the browser will use "progressive rendering." Netscape Communicator first displays the data in the browser's default font, then as soon as the PFR file is loaded, the text is displayed in the TrueDoc font. The text remains legible even with smaller font sizes because the system also uses antialiasing.

Clearly, this is a technology that begs to be more widely used. So why isn't it? The reason is probably more technical than creative. Creating a PFR font isn't hard, but the whole security concept designed to protect the font designer's rights raises many complications. Obviously, the person viewing the Web page is sent a complete font type. This means that this data could be converted into a font that could be reused in the user's system. For a font type manufacturer like Bitstream this scenario is a nightmare, and the TrueDoc system has been developed so that the PFR font works only on a specific server referred to in the PFR file. This protection is adequate, but it's not easy for the Web designer to implement.

▶ A Server on Your Own Hard Disk

Usually, a Web designer first creates a test version of a site that is placed on a local test or staging server. How can you test the TrueDoc system testing if it is not on the public server yet? One way to check the intended effect on your own system is to install the server software on your computer. However, one condition is that the MIME type can be modified in the server software. There are lots of options here for Windows users; for Macintosh fans, there is a solution in the form of the freeware program QuidProQuo. This Web server, which is as simple as it is effective, can be installed in no time on a Mac. And the great advantage of QuidProQuo 2.0 is that the configuration can easily be modified. This also applies to the suffix *(.pfr)* and the related MIME type *(application/font-tdpfr)*. By creating a separate PFR font with the IP address of your own computer, you can test locally to your heart's content. As you can see on the adjacent page, the dynamic font produces a nice typeface display on your Web page.

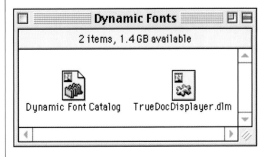

▲ The dynamic font icons of Netscape.

▶ Color in Text

Working with text color is another way to draw attention to a specific part of the page. HTML offers a number of options for determining text color—at the local level or for an entire page *(generally a combination of the two is the ideal approach)*.

Not only are the background's pattern and/or color specified in the <BODY> of the HTML document; the colors of the text and the hyperlinks are also specified there. The color values are specified as hexadecimals.

Here are text attributes with a color value:

<TEXT="#X">	The color of the page text.
< LINK="#X">	The color of the hyperlink.
<VLINK="#X">	The color of a hyperlink that has been used *(Visited)*.
< ALINK="#X">	The color of a hyperlink the moment it is activated *(Active)*.

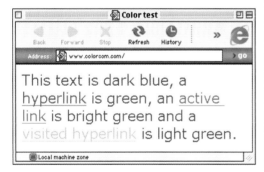

```
<HTML>
  <HEAD>
    <TITLE>colortest</TITLE>
  </HEAD>
<BODY BGCOLOR="#FFFFFF" TEXT="#003399"
LINK="#007000" VLINK="#94CA99" ALINK="#00FF00">
<FONT size=+3>This text is dark blue, a
<A HREF="link1.html">hyperlink</A> is green, an
<A HREF="link2.html">active link</A> is bright green
and a <A HREF="link3.html">visted hyperlink </A> is
light green.</FONT>
</BODY>
</HTML>
```

The example clearly shows the result of the settings in the <BODY> of the document. You can also work with color at the local level: A sentence, word, or even a letter can be colored using the <FONT COLOR="#X"></FONT> tag. Naturally you need to use this option with restraint; otherwise it loses its effectiveness. The same restrictions apply to the color selections as for the GIF images and backgrounds. The 216 colors Netscape has defined are the safest ones to use in an HTML page. This prevents the text from being dithered, an effect that can make the text illegible at the customer end.

▶ Improving Legibility Through Layout

A Web page's accessibility doesn't depend only on the size and color of the text. The page layout and the use of blank space, illustrations, buttons, and icons also determine the navigability of the document. The graphic design of a Web page also contributes to the page's attractiveness—and thus its success—as well as the accessibility of the information. To create a good layout, there are a number of criteria you should take into account: First, the layout should be consistent throughout the site. Make sure you leave enough white space on the page, particularly between the text elements. Use lines and indents to arrange the data. Restrict the length of one page to a maximum of three screens.

◀ With the help of an ASCII editor, you can leave a unique "originator" in the HTML code. This is an ideal feature for curious servers who want to sniff around in the source code. Be sure to place the drawing between comment tags!

▲ The www.zefer.com site has put all its textual content in GIF files to guarantee the proper display of a complex layout.

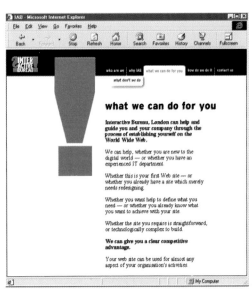

▲ Interactive Bureau is an advocate of large, clear typography, with ample spacing around the text.

▶ Improving Legibility with Fonts

You don't need to let the settings of your page layout program determine the font of your Web page. Usually you're given the fonts Arial or Times New Roman, but both Georgia and Verdana are more legible onscreen, and they're installed on standard Windows PCs. Ideal is online customization.

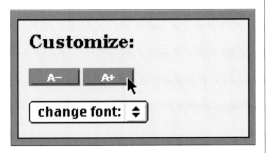

▶ The legibility of the Georgia and Verdana fonts is unquestionable.

▼ Macromedia Dreamweaver includes a number of standard fonts. Geneva was added to the list as a favor to Macintosh users. Unix users will favor "SunSans-Regular" as well.

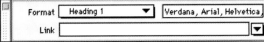

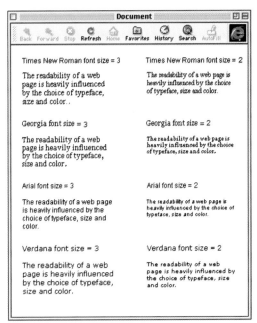

▶ **Special Characters**

The list below, based on the ISO standard, contains an overview of the most commonly used special characters. The first column shows the syntax as it must be entered in HTML. The second column gives a description, and third shows the letter itself.

Syntax	Description	Letter	Syntax	Description	Letter
&Aacute;	Capital A, acute accent	Á	&aacute;	Lowercase a, acute accent	á
&Agrave;	Capital A, grave accent	À	&agrave;	Lowercase a, grave accent	à
&Acirc;	Capital A, circumflex	Â	&acirc;	Lowercase a, circumflex	â
&Atilde;	Capital A, tilde	Ã	&atilde;	Lowercase a, tilde	ã
&Aring;	Capital A, ring	Å	&auml;	Lowercase a, umlaut	ä
&Auml;	Capital A, umlaut	Ä	&aelig;	Lowercase ae, ligature	æ
&AElig;	Capital ÂE, ligature	Æ	&ccedil;	Lowercase c, cedilla	ç
&Ccedil;	Capital C, cedilla	Ç	&eacute;	Lowercase e, acute accent	é
&Eacute;	Capital E, acute accent	É	&egrave;	Lowercase e, grave accent	è
&Egrave;	Capital E, grave accent	È	&ecirc;	Lowercase e, circumflex	ê
&Ecirc;	Capital E, circumflex	Ê	&euml;	Lowercase e, umlaut	ë
&Euml;	Capital E, umlaut	Ë	&iacute;	Lowercase i, acute accent	í
&Iacute;	Capital I, acute accent	Í	&igrave;	Lowercase i, grave accent	ì
&Igrave;	Capital I, grave accent	Ì	&icirc;	Lowercase i, circumflex	î
&Icirc;	Capital I, circumflex	Î	&iuml;	Lowercase i, umlaut	ï
&Iuml;	Capital I, umlaut	Ï	&ntilde;	Lowercase n, tilde	ñ
&Ntilde;	Capital N, tilde	Ñ	&oacute;	Lowercase o, acute accent	ó
&Oacute;	Capital O, acute accent	Ó	&ograve;	Lowercase o, grave accent	ò
&Ograve;	Capital O, grave accent	Ò	&ocirc;	Lowercase o, circumflex	ô
&Ocirc;	Capital O, circumflex	Ô	&otilde;	Lowercase o, tilde	õ
&Otilde;	Capital O, tilde	Õ	&ouml;	Lowercase o, umlaut	ö
&Ouml;	Capital O, umlaut	Ö	&oslash;	Lowercase o, slash	ø
&Oslash;	Capital O, slash	Ø	&uacute;	Lowercase u, acute accent	ú
&Uacute;	Capital U, acute accent	Ú	&ugrave;	Lowercase u, grave accent	ù
&Ugrave;	Capital U, grave accent	Ù	&ucirc;	Lowercase u, circumflex	û
&Ucirc;	Capital U, circumflex	Ù	&uuml;	Lowercase u, umlaut	ü
&Uuml;	Capital U, umlaut	Ü	&#146;	Plus/minus sign	±
&Yacute;	Capital Y, acute accent	†	© of ©	Copyright symbol	©
	Space		® of ®	Registered trademark symbol	®
&szlig;	German 'S'	ß	&euro;	Euro symbol	€

▶ **Typing Errors**

Dead links—pages that have been "under construction" for months and contain sloppy errors in the HTML text—cause much of the annoyance people have with the Web. These mistakes are frequently the result of a nonchalant cut-and-paste design. Designers should know that some symbols cannot be translated into HTML and always check the site in a browser before it is launched.

◀ In this example, there was probably a stray apostrophe in the text file. HTML did not recognize the code and replaced it with an unrecognizable character that detracts from the page and must be corrected.

The title of this chapter could be "From Your Desktop to the Web" or "How to Convert Copy from Your Word Processor or Page Layout Program to HTML with the Least Possible Effort."
This chapter covers a number of options to do just that—from a Microsoft Word translator to HTML editors—and introduces a dedicated QuarkXPress XTension.

From Copy to HTML

Web pages are not all created from scratch, not by a long shot. Existing copy is usually the basis of the information on a Web page. The text has already been entered into the computer in some form, such as a Microsoft Word text file. If copy in print must be placed on the Net, chances are it's in a QuarkXPress file or an Adobe InDesign document. *(InDesign is a trademark of Adobe Systems Inc.)*

Obviously it makes no sense to retype the copy into an HTML editor. There are a number of standard solutions that simplify the "Web-top publishing" process. A minimum of HTML knowledge is required to create an HTML document this way, but maintaining a site requires more extensive knowledge of the language.

▶ **Microsoft Word 2000**

A good starting point for creating a Web page is Microsoft Office 2000. The editor in Microsoft Word is logically designed and supports the most important HTML tags. Also, tables are clearly displayed in the correct manner—a decided advantage. The typographical options are limited to the standard HTML tags, but changing text with the help of an editor is considerably simpler and more intuitive than writing code. You simply select the text and choose the corresponding style from the button bar at the top of the Microsoft Word screen. The standard Word facilities are used to create lists and forms. The integration is quite extensive. To create external links you select the HyperLink command, and to position an image you simply use the Insert Picture command.

▶ **Microsoft FrontPage 2000**

Microsoft acquired the HTML editor FrontPage in an expensive buyout deal. The program, especially popular in office

This Web page ▶ of Merck | Vel was designed completely in Microsoft Word.

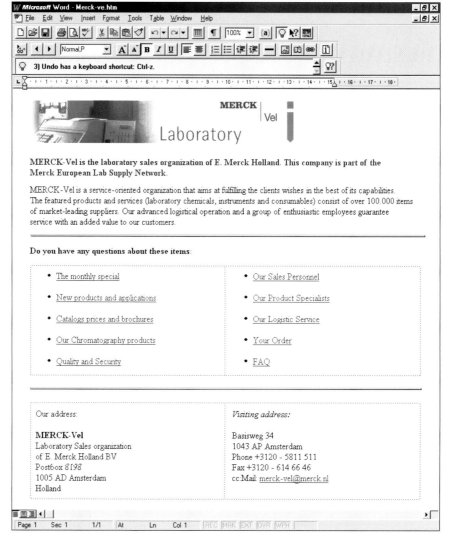

environments, is exceptionally well suited for creating complex pages, with functions such as nested tables, frames, and extensive form and selection fields. The work method in this top-class editor is so logical that most users will see little reason for learning HTML.

FrontPage's list of options is virtually infinite, and troublesome Web functions such as search engines and database links can be automated using "bots," which are designed to search data based on your instructions. Even dynamic HTML is included in the program, as well as style sheets and page transitions based on ActiveX controls. It is easy to maintain your site by creating standard pages in Microsoft FrontPage 2000.

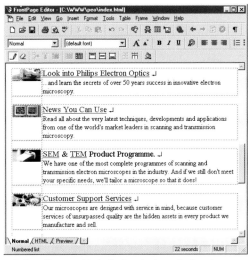

▲ In FrontPage a table is displayed schematically using dotted lines to indicate cells. The break is indicated by a "new line" symbol.

▶ Adobe PageMaker and HTML Export

As of version 6.5, the Adobe PageMaker page layout program includes an extensive HTML export filter. By setting a number of standard parameters per document, you can meticulously convert text into an HTML document by linking style sheets to HTML styles. Generally you must then do a bit of final touch-up work using a real HTML editor. But you still need to know something about HTML to make sure you get all the results you want.

▲ Microsoft FrontPage offers "themes" with which even the user who has little creativity and no background in Web site design can create a neat, appealing site.

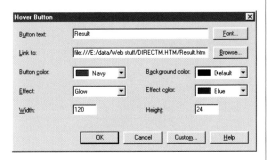

▲ With Microsoft FrontPage you can create interactive navigation elements without any knowledge of the Java programming language.

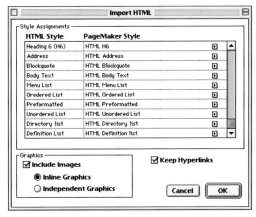

▲ In Adobe PageMaker you can set preferences to make all text styles correspond to HTML text sizes.

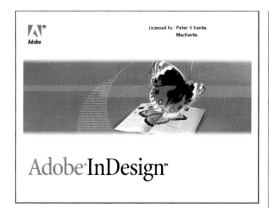

▲ The complex layout in Adobe InDesign consists of layers.

▲ The conversion of the design is successful.   ▼

▶ **Adobe InDesign and HTML Export**

The page layout program Adobe InDesign boasts impressive export features. The core technologies of the program are PostScript and PDF, both Adobe inventions. Thus it goes without saying that InDesign has good PDF export options. You cannot open and edit PDF files in InDesign, but you can position and mask them.

The program has an HTML export option that you can tailor to suit your needs. By specifying a difference between the editability of the site generated and its appearance, you produce either an HTML document that makes the legibility of the Web page its first priority or one that attempts to accurately display the original InDesign file. However, the latter doesn't always produce usable results.

▶ **Exporting Layers**

The Web site shown on this page has few text elements and a great deal of graphic material. In this case, InDesign's Appearance option can produce a very detailed result in which the HTML is identical to the original.

InDesign uses "layers" to ensure that all image elements appear in the correct position. That works extremely well, and the quality and positioning of the HTML is also quite neat. If you also convert the accompanying text using this setting, you get a screen dump of the text—handsome, but usually illegible and therefore unusable.

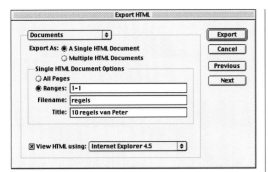

▲ A larger InDesign file can be converted as a single Web page or as a mini site.

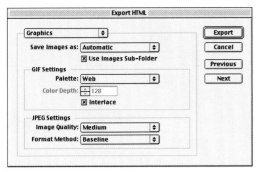

▲ InDesign offers graphic settings for conversion to the Web.

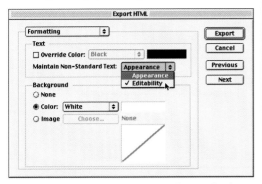

▲ InDesign's export settings for an HTML file must be chosen with care.

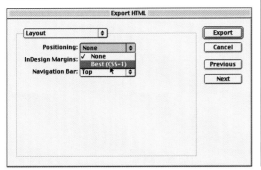

▲ Here is the sample file as laid out in InDesign.

In the example on this page, the Editability option was selected. This is how the InDesign text was converted to HTML text coding rather than to a static image. The text length therefore depends on your browser settings.

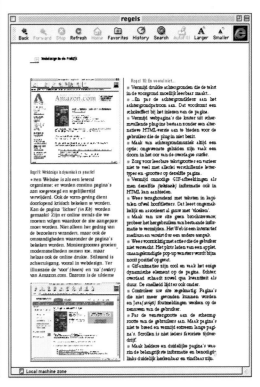

▶ **QuarkXPress: BeyondPress XTension**

The original developers of Extensis's BeyondPress worked at Quark, where they helped develop the market-leading page-layout program QuarkXPress. The experience served them well; the integration between the XTension and QuarkXPress is virtually perfect. Even the preferences in BeyondPress give the impression that they are standard Quark-XPress options. The power of this XTension lies primarily in the integration between the online and offline versions of the Quark-XPress document. BeyondPress lets you attune the style sheets in the Quark document to the styles in the HTML headers. In the overview window shown here, you can see that the heading "The first Gameboy in Holland" was created as Headline 1 from the Quark document. That means the tags <H1></H1> were placed before and after the heading text.

The way BeyondPress handles image information is also impressive. A drawing or photo in Quark is generally imported in a somewhat larger image frame. For conversion to a GIF or JPEG file, this normally means that extra white space is converted as well—at least that's how the competition does it. BeyondPress is more clever: You can cut out the frame in the Image Settings window! This is ideal if the Web page has a color background. GIF images can be prepared completely in Quark. You can set the indexed color palette and specify the transparency color. The file can be scaled too, but it is better not to do that since it degrades the quality. A JPEG image can be reduced; the JPEG

compression algorithm can take it. Thanks to AppleScript, BeyondPress can also be automated. This lets you convert catalogues to the Web.

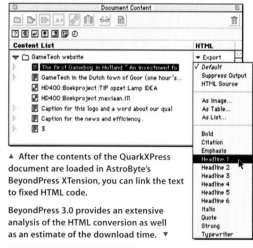

▲ After the contents of the QuarkXPress document are loaded in AstroByte's BeyondPress XTension, you can link the text to fixed HTML code.

BeyondPress 3.0 provides an extensive analysis of the HTML conversion as well as an estimate of the download time. ▼

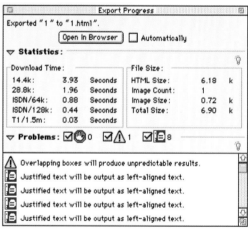

▼ In BeyondPress the margin around an image can be adjusted before conversion.

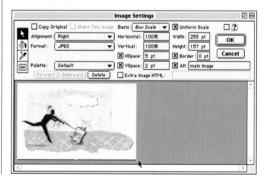

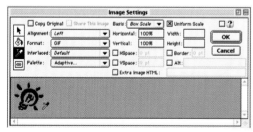

▲ You can make a GIF file transparent and interlaced.

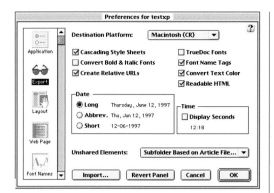

▲ The Preferences settings in BeyondPress let you avoid the notorious carriage return/line feed problem by entering this option. This XTension also supports cascading style sheets, which let you convert style sheets into HTML.

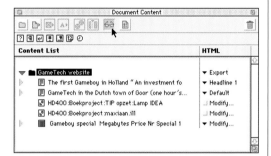

▲ If the QuarkXPress page contains a table, you can mark it separately in BeyondPress's style list.

▶ Table Support

It makes sense that BeyondPress 3.0 would support the standard HTML tags. But this is by no means the full extent of its options; BeyondPress has also made it possible to automatically convert tables in the Quark document into HTML table code! Not only is this handy for the conversion process; it also offers considerable potential for those who need to create entire complex tables in HTML. It is probably quicker to create the tables in Quark and "export" them to HTML code with BeyondPress.

It is clear that BeyondPress is not really intended for converting single Quark pages. However, if you have to place a large brochure or even a catalogue on the Web, this product is absolutely worth the trouble. If the work is already laid out in Quark, the software pays for itself after just a few pages.

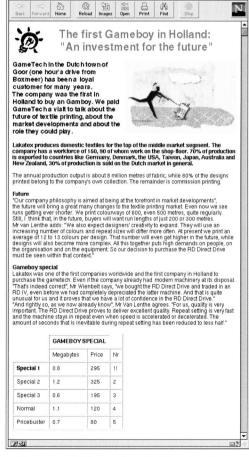

▲ The converted Web page shows that the automatic conversion has gone perfectly.

▶ Professional HTML Editors: HotMetal Pro

The first HTML editors were created as public-domain programs. Most of the original developers are still trying to improve them. Meanwhile, a few makers of WYSIWYG HTML editors have earned good money selling their work to Adobe and Microsoft. They introduced improvements and made the programs commercial products.

Creating a graphic design based on dry computer code is, and always will be, an unnatural process. You can control the codes better, but you must continually check to make sure that what you intended to create is actually what shows up in the browser. Hybrid editors simplify this process by displaying the HTML code clearly. SoftQuad HotMetal Pro is a good example of this type of software.

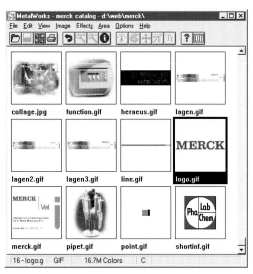

▲ Here is a visual overview of all the images in a site design.

The list of ▶ HotMetal Pro HTML extensions is perfect as a reference for all HTML tags and corresponding attributes.

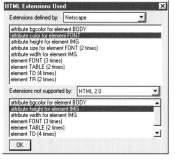

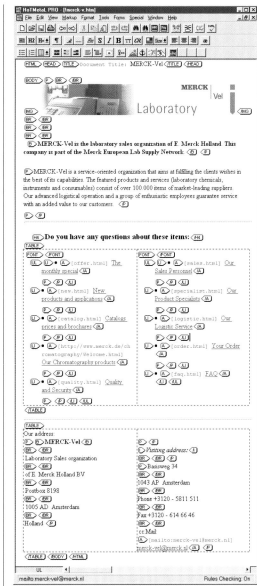

▲ HotMetal Pro displays the Merck home page as a jumble of HTML codes and WYSIWYG images. The program can also display a clean image of the page.

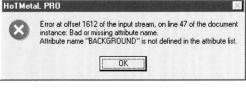

▲ Just like other HTML editors, HotMetal Pro checks the tags in an open document.

▶ BBEdit, the Code Editor

Bare Bones Software's BBEdit, a text-editing program for the Macintosh, is a non-WYSI-WYG HTML editor that cleverly evades this problem. This program lets you undo multiple changes and is thus ideal for Web designers. Using BBEdit, you can view your pages as you work on different browsers. This is a handy function, since it makes no sense to create a Web page for just one type of browser. Microsoft dominates the market, but Netscape still has a substantial market share.

The home pages shown on the previous page are displayed using HotMetal Pro. This program combines a WYSIWYG display with HTML codes. BBEdit is the opposite of this sort of program. Many professional Web designers use the Macintosh BBEdit program because it gives them total control over the HTML coding. Manual coding is labor intensive, but ultimately it produces the best result.

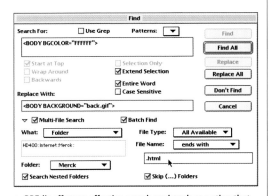

▲ BBEdit offers an effective search-and-replace option that lets you make changes for an entire site all at once.

The results of a search are shown in a separate window, so you can check the text replaced. ▶

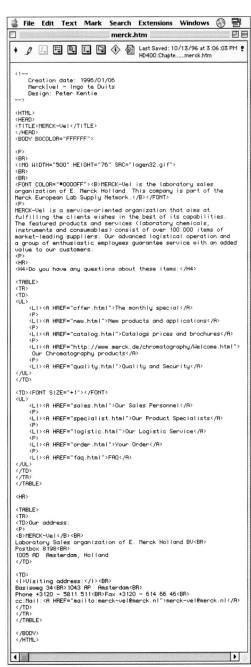

▲ BBEdit is a leader among non-WYSIWYG programs and is used by most professional Web designers.

► Macromedia Homesite

Macromedia Homesite is an editor created for and by Web developers who want to have complete control over how a page is put together. No WYSIWYG–you simply have to know your stuff and code manually. Fortunately, Homesite offers a number of handy wizards and standard settings that enable you to write code for complex tables, JavaScript, and Active Server Pages *(ASP)* quickly.

In addition, Homesite contains an extensive help system, a cascading style sheet editor. The program also has a simple method for navigating through your Web project. And last but not least: Homesite can preview the results of the WYSIWYG code by making the Microsoft Internet Explorer browser appear in the program window. This allows you to switch back and forth between the tabs for the code display and the page preview in a flash.

▲ BBEdit's CodeSweeper checks and corrects the HTML.

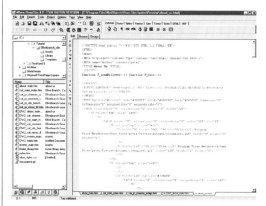

▲ The HTML code is displayed in color code.

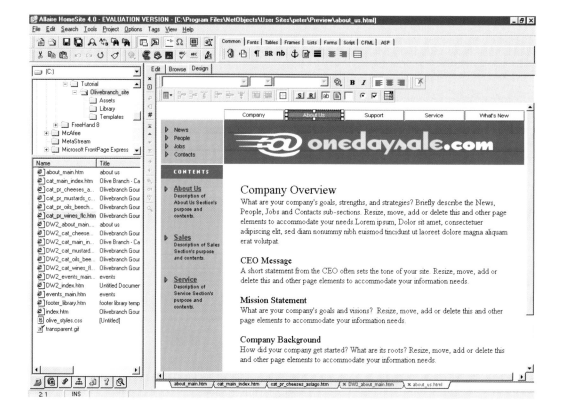

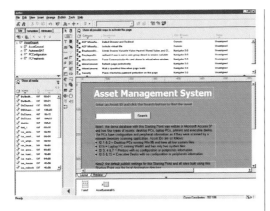

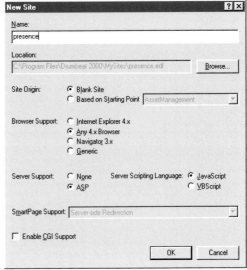

▶ **Macromedia UltraDev**

Macromedia UltraDev is the Visual Basic of HTML editors. It is suitable for people with little programming knowledge who want to create dynamic Web sites *(including database links)* relatively simply. The program creates automatic ASP code for Microsoft's Web server, but can also handle Java Server Pages *(JSP)*, a Sun initiative, comparable to ASP but based on the Java language. A popular solution for dynamic Web sites.

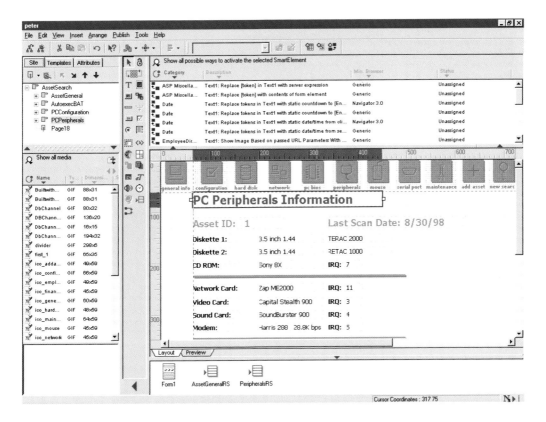

▶ NetObjects Fusion

To develop a successful site, a Web designer must be a jack-of-all-trades. However, design tools are not specifically designed for artistic purposes.

Thankfully, Clement Mok, a guru from the graphics world, has developed a program for Web design that is as easy to use as a DTP program. That program, NetObjects Fusion, is the ultimate tool for Web design. It offers not only WYSIWYG functionality, but also the ability to meticulously determine the position of text and image elements.

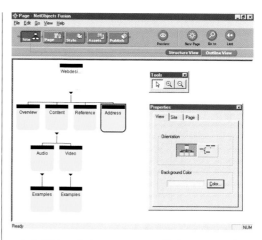

▲ In NetObjects Fusion users can specify the structure of a Web site in advance. The program uses the names of the pages for titles and buttons.

Thanks to the WYSIWYG design environment of NetObjects Fusion, it's easy to add a graphic element. ▼

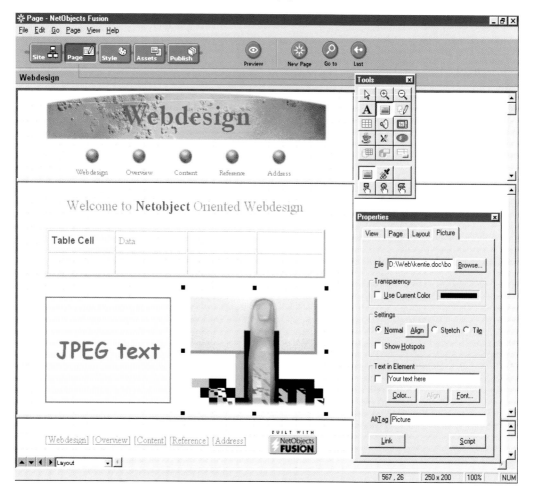

▶ Creating Web Sites with Fusion

NetObjects Fusion lives up to its name: It combines the functionality of database links with the structured layout of Web pages. With Fusion, a designer can create pages by adding his own graphic elements to a fixed structure. He can also use previously defined styles. You can see a number of examples of this on this page.

The quality of the templates is exceptionally high. Fusion is ideal for Web sites that must be updated regularly; the program can even automatically generate the graphic files for heading lines and button bars.

▲ NetObjects Fusion has several standard styles ...

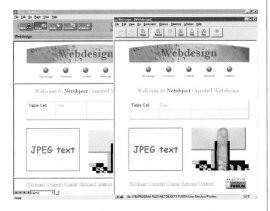

▲ The browser precisely reproduced the text and image elements in a Fusion page. All the image elements have fixed positions. This was done using a 1-by-1-pixel transparent GIF file.

▲ ... of which this is a representative selection. ▼

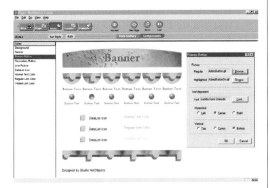

▲ You can create an attractive Web site based on a standard style in NetObjects Fusion. ▶

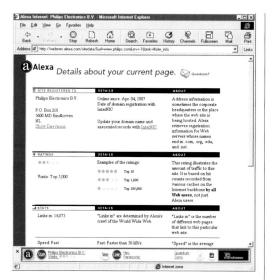

▲ Alexa provides an extra window with relevant information about a site, its visitors, and comparable content.

▶ Community of Editors

There is yet another group of "editors" busy on the Web. No, not the code writers and technicians who communicate in hexadecimals, but externally operating editors and opinion leaders who express their opinions about sites in public. They come in all shapes and sizes, but two stand out: Alexa and ThirdVoice—the difference between organized and anarchistic expressions of opinion. Just as in real life, there are decent people and rebels. The Web is merely a digital mirror of this situation.

The power of the Web is its unlimited accessibility. This cannot be restricted by any person or entity. ThirdVoice is an open venue for third parties to express their opinions about a site, its products, and so on. Anyone who registers with ThirdVoice can type his opinion or reaction in the window that floats above the actual Web page. Naturally, the remarks vary from playful to libelous. The discussion rages in public, which is always difficult for the owner of site. The only thing he can do is to take a criticism to heart if it is relevant to the performance of his Web site.

Alexa is much more serious. Here, too, the client must install an application that adds an extra field to the browser window. This displays information that Alexa has gathered thanks to its artificial intelligence software. This is combined with information regarding the surfing and clicking patterns of all the members connected and thereby generates a profile and ranking for the site.

Undoubtedly, other similar initiatives will appear on the Internet. They only serve to underscore the original fundamental principles of the Web as a medium. We must live with them and make the best of them.

▲ ThirdVoice users openly discuss IBM on its own Web site!

The visitor is ▶ faced with unraveling the Gordian knot— a scenario that Web designers should avoid.

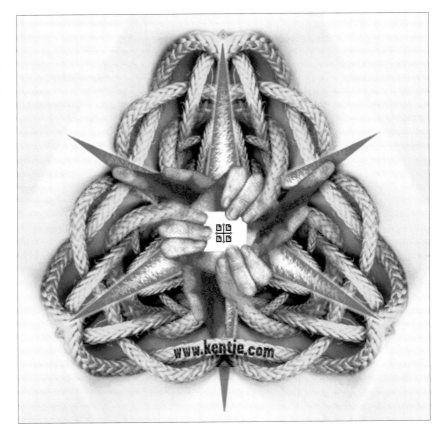

Human-Computer Interaction, or HCI, is the science describing the relationship between the computer and its users. A good Web designer is also an HCI expert since he deals with ergonomics, social science, and interface and interaction design.

Usability Design

The Web is a very democratic medium; to say it more emphatically, on the Web the user is in control. Not only is the customer always right, he is all-powerful. This shift in power from manufacturer to consumer is having major social consequences. At the same time the number of Web sites is growing faster than the number of surfers, Web content providers are becoming even more dependent on users' judgment. In order to guarantee that people will continue to visit a site in the long run, a site's layout and presentation must be tailored to users' desires and behavior. User- and consumer-oriented Web design requires a specific knowledge and anticipation of visitors' desires.

▶ Online Usability Testing

Practically speaking, this means we should listen very carefully to what customers need and want. Clear navigation is important, but entertaining navigation is not what surfers are looking for. What they want is valuable and significant content. Well-thought-out navigation is a prerequisite, not a luxury! Of course, this brings up the question of how the site builder can facilitate the user's experience in the best possible way, so the user will spend more time at the site. The ultimate goal is that the visitor will return to the site again because of a pleasant experience the first time. To achieve this we have to ask ourselves what the user is looking for. A useful answer to this question requires research; for example, research with statistics on a particular site is important for qualitative input.

On the Web, too, we can find an abundance of usability information. The Web site of the usability guru Jakob Nielsen, www.useit.com, is a must. His provocative viewpoint and the arguments he presents with considerable

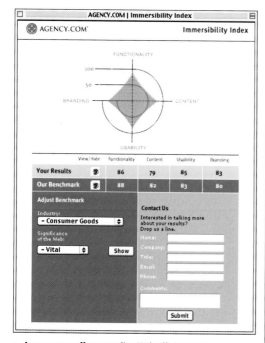

▲ Agency.com offers an online Web efficiency test.

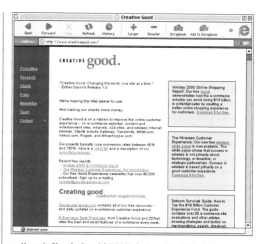

▲ Keep It Simple Stupid (KISS) design. The Web design agency Creative Good based its Ease of Use design on balanced composition and simple typography.

skill are more than merely instructive. In cooperation with one of the biggest Web design agencies in the world, Agency.com, Nielsen's company has developed a usability test that can be performed online.

▶ User Testing and Focus Groups

The second method for obtaining input from the user is to ask him for his opinion. A user test is an outstanding and proven way to find out precisely whether your target group appreciates a new design style or navigation structure. A user test can also help you find out in advance what criteria the site has to satisfy in order to achieve the desired level of appreciation.

Experience has shown us what the user really wants. And yet these minimum criteria frequently turn out to be a surprise for many Web developers. This is especially true when a large company's site is tested against these criteria. Here are the primary factors that make a visitor return:

- qualitative and unique content
- up-to-date content that is revised frequently
- minimum download time through the use of light Web pages
- optimal user-friendliness tailored to the visitor of the site.

▶ The Web As a Linear Medium

Admittedly, a number of these factors are impossible to translate into specific instructions. Still, these criteria are crucial for a site's success. Simply converting existing information into data to be used on the Web has long been an unsatisfactory approach. The value of the content aside, this kind of information was created for media that are linearly oriented: A brochure reads from beginning to end in a continuous stream of information. In contrast, the Web is not linearly oriented; hyperlinks produce an associative way of processing data that jumps from one thing to another.

▶ Converting Content

When converting existing content to the Web, the added value lies in establishing the relationships between the documents. Naturally this requires some editorial effort, but the visitor will appreciate it. Besides, if the site can be used to replace traditional sources of information such as help desks, the investment is quickly earned back.

▲ A search engine is a must for larger Web sites.

▶ One-to-One Communication

The distinctive difference between the Web and other media is the Web's interactive possibilities. A dialogue can be established with the user, even on a one-to-one basis. This direct form of communication between the supplier and the consumer of the information results in a wealth of data about the consumer's preferences, his actions on the Web and, if applicable, his purchasing behavior.

All this information can be used in the further development of the site. If people fail to anticipate these developments and continue to conduct one-way communication, they're letting the advantages of the dialogue go to waste.

In the long run, the site that is sensitive to the user will have a competitive advantage, because it offers more chances for anticipating the consumer's desires. It must be emphasized here that in spite of the repeated use of the words *consumer* and *user*, we should not forget that we are dealing with people!

▲ A splash page must always be functional—to provide a plug-in option, for example, or to request information.

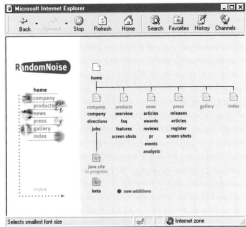

▲ A good site map need not be complicated to help point a visitor in the right direction.

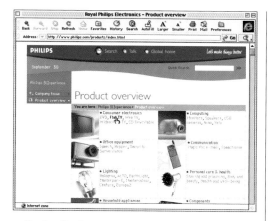

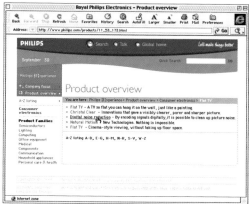

▶ Design for Trust

Specific instructions can be given for making a site as user-friendly as possible and for constructing Web pages correctly. Note that the word *instructions* has not been chosen carelessly. The Web and the Web design profession are still too young and too dynamic to apply definitive rules and laws. Techniques advance rapidly and continuously, and these changes constantly affect conventions and criteria.

The Web is becoming the most important medium in the world and is decisively affecting all other media. With its role in business continuing to grow, the Web will revolutionize economic conventions. At the same time, the criteria will shift from communication-oriented information to content that is geared toward relationship marketing and sales.

One thing is certain: The accessibility of information and the ease with which desired data can be found are important criteria for Web site designers—at least as important as the graphical appearance. A wise balance between a professional graphic design and a clear, consistent structure, along with easy navigation will give the visitor confidence in the brand behind the site. In the world of e-commerce after the advent of companies like Amazon.com, confidence will become the paramount feature—confidence not so much in the brand itself, but its reputation. The site will not only embody the brand

▲ A trail of crumbs is left for the visitor at www.philips.com. The You Are Here bar indicates precisely where the visitor is and what options he has.

image, but will also be the customer's avenue of contact with the company.

▶ Abandoned Shopping Carts

When you want to create a Web site with easy navigation, an important question to ask is "Can I see on every page where I am, where I came from, and where I am going?" This seems to be very basic, but just try it out when you are surfing on the Web. Many sites don't even have a Home button or other means of returning to the home page.

Adding trails of crumbs is a technique applied in many e-commerce sites. Remember the fairy tale about Hansel and Gretel, who

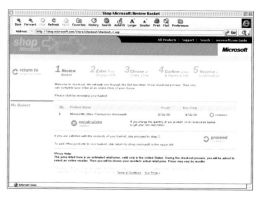

▲ In this example from Microsoft Webshop, the visual information tells the customer exactly how many steps the purchasing and registration process requires.

found their way back through the dark woods by leaving behind a trail of crumbs? This method comes in handy in Web designing, by showing the path that has been followed step-by-step at the top of the page so the visitor knows where he is in the structure. If the steps are active hyperlinks, however, the user can always go back to another category to continue surfing from there.

▶ E-commerce Design

This example is found in sites that attempt to make online purchasing processes more accessible. The steps the customer has to take are clearly indicated so it is always clear how much more effort is required to complete the purchase. This technique helps reduce the number of abandoned shopping carts.

■ **User testing in practice. Navigation and semantic options are tested for www.philips.com**

▲ **The home page at www.philips.com offers the focus group different solutions.** ▼

▲ **The testers could choose from a variety of search fields and descriptions of the various sections.** ▼

▶ Continuous and Consistent Navigation Display

Finding information is just as important as the information itself. This means that the fewer clicks needed to get to the information, the more effective the navigation. A Web site's information architecture determines both the organization of the content and the relationship between the various parts of the site. The navigation bar is thus an important part of the site. This bar can be used both horizontally and vertically. Where you place it on the page is not that important, but it should be located at a consistent position on all the relevant pages. For the user to become familiar with the navigation tools, the tools must be easy to learn.

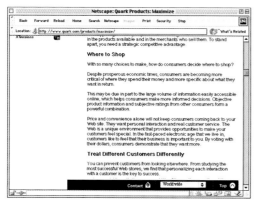

▲ Quark has a navigation bar that scrolls with the Web page, so the basic options are always visible. The bar is a separate layer that runs on Java code.

▶ Constant Feedback Everywhere

The most potent weapon is often also the most dangerous one. This also holds true for direct communication with the user. If the customer doesn't get what she wants or if she thinks she's not being served adequately or fast enough, you will be inundated by irate e-mails. However, there are alternative ways for letting customers contact you. Callback options allowing for personal contact or limited online questionnaires are methods for letting the visitor give her opinion in a friendly, and, above all, interactive manner.

▲ An option such as Click2Talk is ideal for assisting a customer who requires immediate attention.

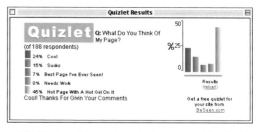

▲ A Quizlet is a mini questionnaire that can provide valuable input for the site manager.

Of course, this kind of communication is invaluable: You get the user's opinion firsthand, simply by opening yourself up on your site. Interactivity is two-way communication!

Developing a Web site seems to be a time-consuming and somewhat irrational process. With the help of special tags, or codes, pages must be designed and laid out simultaneously. This chapter describes an easier way: creating a Web site with the help of the popular WYSIWYG layout programs Adobe GoLive, Macromedia Fireworks, and Macromedia Dreamweaver.

WYSIWYG Web Design

The main function of a Web page is to communicate a message in both word and image to users over the Internet. The Web has a much broader reach than publications on paper. That makes it a fascinating challenge to create a site with which you can potentially reach the world.

Time was when building a Web site was the domain of programmers and network managers. Thanks to the introduction of "what you see is what you get"*(WYSIWYG)* software, it is possible to work in real time and design pages without the hurdle of dealing with dry computer code. However, the quality of the WYSIWYG package is what determines the final result. No matter how beautiful the page looks in preview mode, the real test is how it appears on the Web using a large variety of browsers and operating systems.

▶ **Custom Web Design**

Graphic software supplier Adobe Systems offers a complete Web design program called GoLive, with which a Web site can be created using the proven work method of a page layout program. For instance, positioning a GIF image in GoLive is as simple as dragging and dropping it onto the page. The corresponding HTML code is added automatically:

```
<IMG align=left SRC="file.gif" border=0 width=100
height=100 ALT="image">.
```

This intuitive work method makes manual programming in HTML partly superfluous. The WYSIWYG HTML-editors change the creative process into a visual affair rather than an exercise in typing in obscure HTML codes. Although a thorough knowledge of HTML markup language is always useful for site production, Adobe GoLive makes it easier by offering professional designers all the requisite functionality needed in the Web design process.

At the same time, GoLive offers two options for correcting page code. It includes a purely textual display of HTML, as well as a display of the imported images together with the code in the page hierarchy. This makes it possible to visually search the code for an incorrect tag. The visual presentation method of GoLive—and the fact that the program operates seamlessly with the rest of Adobe's suite of graphic software—make GoLive a welcome choice for Web designers who are not obsessed with code.

The interface is user friendly, and the program integrates extremely well with the other Adobe products such as Photoshop and Illustrator.

▶ **Creating in a Drawing Program**

We use Adobe Photoshop as the starting point for designing the home page for a fictitious online wig salesman whose name is, appropriately, "Wysiwig." By using a bitmap-oriented drawing program, the designer can focus on the layout of the Web page without worrying about any technical details at this point. Of course, the basic laws of Web design must be taken into account.

A design with multiple text and image layers cannot be created in HTML —unless, of course, it is being designed for use with a browser that supports layers. A site for the masses cannot afford this kind of technique. When deciding on the form of the site, the target group's desires must be considered, as well as the environment in which the site will be viewed. Designing a page in a Web editor is almost impossible; a large blank screen really doesn't inspire creativity. A hand-drawn sketch is a much better way to start the creative process. Get the idea and the concept on paper, and then you can proceed to the computer screen!

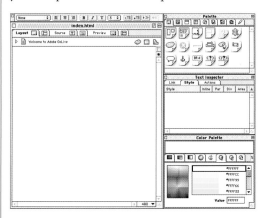

▲ The basic screen of a wysiwyg editor is not an inspiring start for a creative process.

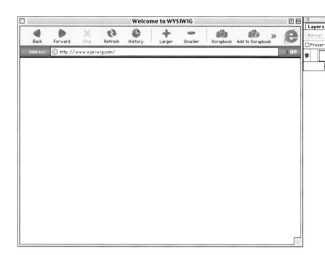

◄ Get WYSIWYG Web design in Adobe Photoshop! You create the layout for the wysiwig.com Web site by placing a screen dump of an empty Web page in the background.

◄ Then you add the content layer by layer.

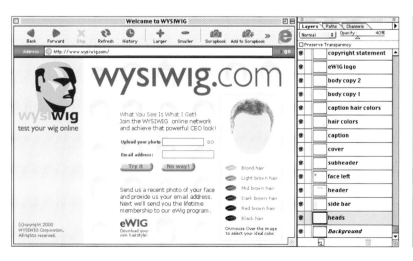

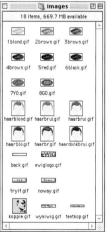

So first make a sketch and work it out in a drawing program you are familiar with. In order to make the experience of the page as real as possible, Photoshop simulates the Web page by placing a screen dump of an empty Web page on the bottom layer in Photoshop. Then the design can be constructed progressively, layer by layer, until all the image and text elements are in the right place. This method of construction is ideal for migration to the Web.

From Layers to Files

The next step is to convert the Photoshop layered image into file formats that Adobe GoLive recognizes. There are several options for this. Because layers were used, the graphic elements can simply be converted into GIF and JPEG files. Just select an image in a layer, copy it, and open a new file with the same background as the original. Paste the copied image and save the file as a GIF or JPEG document. The rule is still valid: Graphic files such as logos are best saved as GIF files, while photographs should be saved as JPEG files.

The reason the corresponding background color must be used is that otherwise problems will arise with clipped images that are conver-

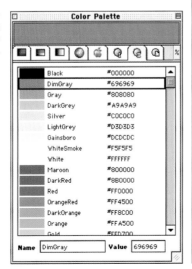

GoLive offers ▶ more than the standard 216 Web colors.

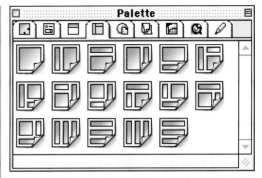

▲ Setting up a site using frames requires only one action. The most commonly used versions are standard options.

ted into transparent GIFs, if the colors are very different. The antialiasing effect works well only if the colors fit together. A light-colored aura around an image will look peculiar if it is placed on a dark background on the Web page.

White is by far the simplest background color for clipping images (this explains why there are so many white Web pages). This is not simply because the greater contrast makes the text more legible. When the layered file has been converted to separate GIF and JPEG images, you can start the layout. GoLive actually behaves just like a WYSIWYG page layout program. You position the graphic files in their proper place using drag and drop or by importing separate images. This can be done in GoLive if you use a page grid. Using fixed coordinates, each file can be placed precisely at its proper position on the page. Even though this works only in versions 4 or higher of Microsoft Internet Explorer or Netscape Navigator , absolute positioning is a giant step forward in Web design development. And it opens the world of Web design to many more designers. The excuse that complex code makes it impossible to see the forest for the trees has been eliminated!

Harmonizing Background Color and Pattern

After opening a new document in GoLive, first the background color is specified. We use white because it corresponds with the

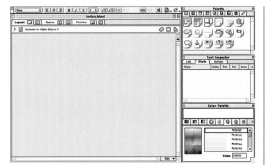

▲ We start with a new document in GoLive.

▲ The title is entered as well as the background color.

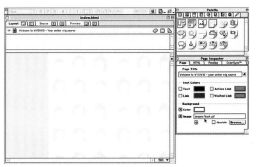

▲ The background pattern is then added.

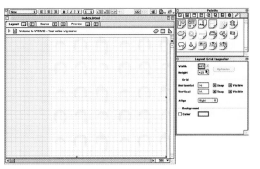

▲ Since the design has to fit exactly, the grid is put to use.

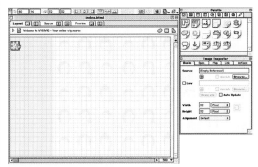

▲ A blank image symbol is positioned on the grid.

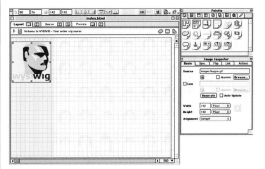

▲ The corresponding image is set.

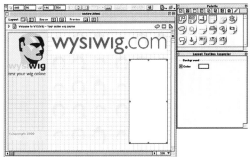

▲ The frame for the wig colors is created.

◀ The page is continually viewed in a real browser.

background drawing we used in the drawing program. This makes the visual change less jarring after loading the background image.

▶ Making Rollovers

On the Web everything is about interactivity and dynamics. These key words play a role on wysiwig.com as follows: Moving the mouse across various still images of hair samples changes the color of the wig in the frame. This type of effect is known as a rollover, and it's an ideal assignment for GoLive. To create such a dynamic effect you have to use a button image. These are in the Palette window near the green icons; simply drag the icon to the correct position in the frame. Using a question mark, GoLive indicates that the corresponding image must be specified.

You can specify the image for the first, or Main, position in the Button Inspector window, and create a special icon indicating the hair color for this purpose. You can load the second position, or Over, by clicking on Browse and retrieving the image. The third position, the actual Click, requests the third image. Repeat this procedure for all six hair colors. Then link the interaction to the wig colors—all without typing a single line of JavaScript. Simply select the button with the right hair color and choose Action, then

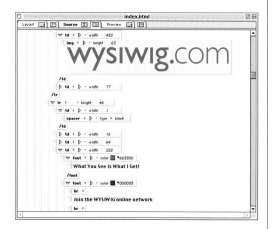

▲ GoLive can display a preview of the site in a site structure. This falls somewhere between WYSIWYG and HTML.

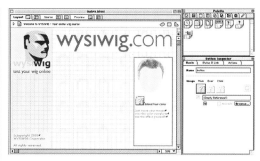

▲ A separate palette is used for dynamic buttons.

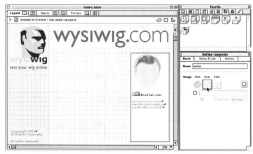

▲ The rollovers are created with the Button Inspector. ▼

◀ All the images used for wig colors are in the Images folder. ▼

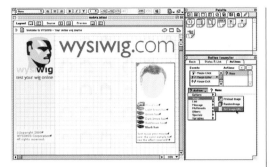

select Mouse Enter in the Button Inspector window.

A drop-down list of possible actions appears in the lower part of the window. Now select the correct wig color button from the numbered list and repeat this step for all the buttons. You can preview the interaction in GoLive's preview mode or in your Web browser. You will see that the effect works fine and has been achieved in record time. Compare that with manually entering the requisite code!

▶ Site Overview

The site presentation and the corresponding images and subpages are a WYSIWYG affair. Link Inspector displays the entire site along with its interrelated pages. You can also add

◀ By assigning an action to the rollover, the corresponding wig can be displayed.

◀ The three rollover modes with their corresponding interactions are ready.

pages or entire sections in this window. When you use templates, all the necessary files and links are generated. In addition, GoLive places the imported files in a separate folder called Images. That is quite a neat feature and ensures an orderly hard disk.

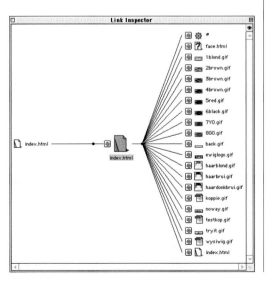

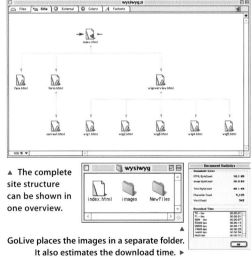

▲ The complete site structure can be shown in one overview.

GoLive places the images in a separate folder. It also estimates the download time. ▶

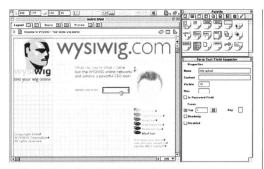

▲ Simply drag a Form Text Field to the page.

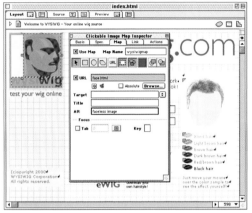

▲ Clickable image maps are standard in GoLive.

▲ All the colors chosen are neatly recorded.

▶ **WYSIWYG Forms**

Coding a form is a thing of the past too, thanks to GoLive's Form Text Field Inspector. The various types of buttons, input fields, and pop-up menus can be positioned without coding. GoLive also supports more recent HTML 4.0 codes such as the Password input field *(only black dots are shown where text is entered)*.

However, the corresponding CGI scripts must be linked to the form in consultation with your Internet service provider. There are considerable variations in these scripts.

▶ **Clickable Image Map**

GoLive also lets you create a clickable map, or a drawing—parts of which refer to various hyperlinks—thanks to the built-in tools. Select the Map option in the Inspector window, and a floating window appears onscreen with a number of drawing options. The image map can now be drawn on the images in real time.

GoLive then asks which URLs you wish to refer to. Dragging the reference document titles over the images creates the hyperlinks. The last step is to select the button Use Map in the Inspector window. Now you can check the clickable map in GoLive offline.

▶ **Finishing the Web Site**

You can publish the site on your ISP's server using GoLive. There's no longer any need to upload separate files using FTP programs such as Fetch for the Mac or WS-FTP for Windows.

The WYSIWYG program can handle all the site management. As you have seen in our example, the entire procedure is simple and requires little coding. However, a good design and a smart *(layered)* Photoshop file are big time-savers. Long live the wysiWIGs!

◀ The finalized homepage of wysiwig.com. Hopefully it will sell a lot of wigs...

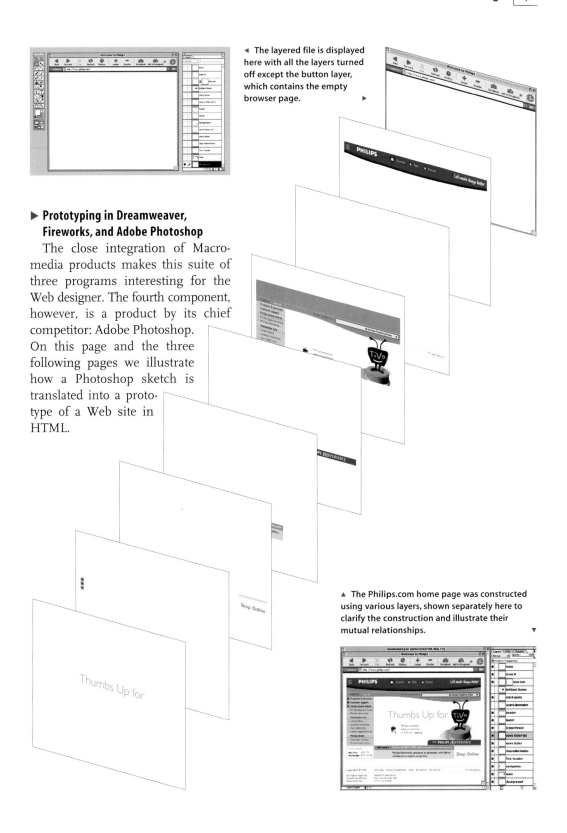

◀ The layered file is displayed here with all the layers turned off except the button layer, which contains the empty browser page. ▶

▶ Prototyping in Dreamweaver, Fireworks, and Adobe Photoshop

The close integration of Macromedia products makes this suite of three programs interesting for the Web designer. The fourth component, however, is a product by its chief competitor: Adobe Photoshop. On this page and the three following pages we illustrate how a Photoshop sketch is translated into a prototype of a Web site in HTML.

▲ The Philips.com home page was constructed using various layers, shown separately here to clarify the construction and illustrate their mutual relationships. ▼

▲ Guides are pulled down from the rulers.

▲ The surfaces that will later be sliced are drawn on the guide intersections.

▲ The green guides have been temporarily removed.

▲ Select the slice symbol and use a striking color to accentuate the zones. A check is performed per zone to see whether the image is to be exported as a GIF or JPEG file. ▼

▲ In the Export preview, specific colors can be locked in.

▶ **Slicing in Fireworks**

Macromedia Fireworks can read a Photoshop file layer by layer. However, you can also import a flattened version. This is the option we use for this example because the design is "sliced" for a prototype page. Moreover, in Fireworks interaction is added by using rollovers.

◀ Choose the option Use Slice Objects in the export window when slicing. You can set the HTML to Generic or Dreamweaver. The Location (where the GIF files are) is one level higher.

▼ An interim preview in the Web browser is always useful.

Slicing is an attractive option for creating a design prototype in Fireworks. It can transform a flat design into an HTML version. By publishing this prototype, the design can be viewed in the browser itself and can already have a realistic look.

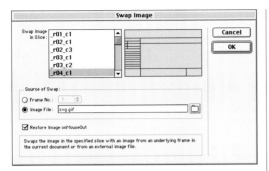

▲ In Macromedia Fireworks you can create a rollover with the option Swap Image. The second image, which lets you create the rollover, is selected from the window. ▼

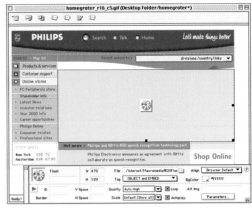

▲ In Macromedia Dreamweaver you can add functionality such as a Flash version of the central illustration. This can be drawn quickly using Flashwriter.

▶ Finishing in Dreamweaver

The completely drawn Web page, including all JavaScript code and corresponding images, can be opened in Macromedia Dreamweaver without adjustment. The page can be further developed in Dreamweaver. Adding a Flash animation is one option; to do this, you replace the central illustration with an SWF file of the same size.

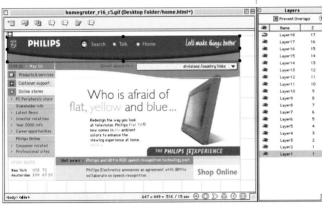

▲ The separate table cells are converted to layers.

Another, even more creative, possibility is to convert the table cells to layers *(this is a standard option in Dreamweaver)*. Then layers can be animated by letting them fly on the Web page, for instance. This works as follows: Select a layer and choose Add to Timeline. Then the object can be assigned a Behavior. The possibilities are endless.

▲ After the layer is added to the time line, the movement can be recorded using Record Path.

▲ The placement of key frames determines the start and end point for the animation in the animation window.

▲ Thanks to Autoplay, the horizontal identification bar appears automatically on the screen while loading the Web page.

▶ The Prototype As Presentation Design

The end result of this design exercise is an animated Web page with a high degree of interactivity and dynamics. Yet it is still a prototype, because we took the original Photoshop design as our starting point. That means that all text has been converted into images.

This prototyping technique is extremely suitable for an initial presentation to a group of live customers on the Web. It simulates the real Web site just enough to communicate the interactive principles of the site's concept. That makes it much easier to judge the virtues of the concept. A last tip for Mac users: Install Windows emulation software such as Virtual PC so you can check what the customer sees.

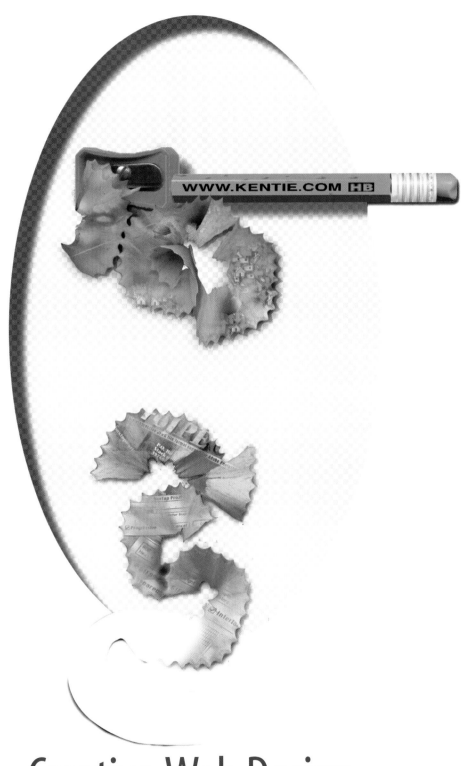

Creative Web Design

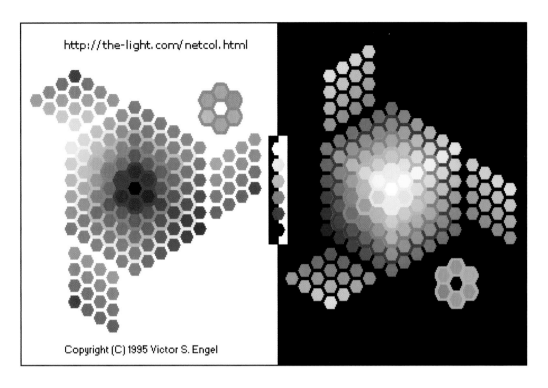

http://the-light.com/netcol.html

The display quality of images on the Web is not determined solely by which scanning and drawing programs the designer uses to create the images. The color quality also depends on the Web surfer's own computer platform and video card. This chapter attempts to shed some light on how the Netscape Navigator browser deals with color.

Adjusting Colors for the Web

The phenomenon is quite familiar: A normally high-quality image looks unacceptable when viewed in Navigator. The reason can be difficult to trace, and the situation becomes even more complicated when the same Web image is viewed on different computer systems. For example, an image displayed on a Macintosh set for 256 colors looks worse than on a Windows PC configured for the same number of colors. But on a Mac that is set for thousands or millions of colors, that same image appears brilliant and clear in Navigator.

To keep your images as legible as possible regardless of which computer platform is displaying them, it helps to know the logic *(or lack thereof)* behind such visual variations. A good understanding of the "Web-safe" color system is essential if you want your Web images to look good across platforms and on the widest range of displays, browsers and Web appliances.

▶ Color Look-Up Tables

Navigator uses its own 216-color palette, known as a CLUT *(color look-up table)*. But the standard RGB palette offers 256 colors, so how do you get the remaining 40 colors? Simple: A color that is not represented in the CLUT is replaced by an existing color that most closely resembles it—or, in some cases, is substituted with two colors from the CLUT that, when combined, approximate the desired color—a process called dithering.

Dithering behavior varies depending on the computer system being used. On Macs, for example, dithering is not always an option.

▶ 216 Colors

Web browsers use a color model in which each primary color is built up based on the hexadecimal values 00, 33, 66, 99, CC and FF. *(The corresponding decimal values are 0, 51, 102, 153, 204, and 255.)* Thus the color <color="#cc3300">, for example, will never dither on either a PC or a Macintosh.

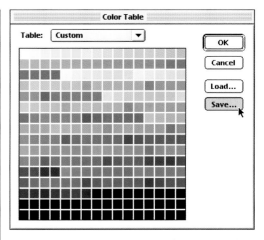

▲ Using Victor Engel's or Douglas R. Jacobson's color card, you can create your own Web-safe CLUT—or simply download one from Peter Kentie's site (http://www.kentie.com/download/webclut.gif)

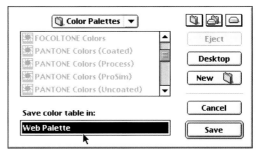

▲ By indexing the colors, you can save the 216-color palette separately. If you store the CLUT in Photoshop's Color Palette folder as "Web colors," you can reload it for every Photoshop operation.

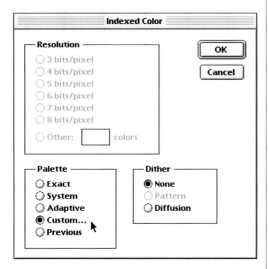

▲ When you select Custom from the Palette options in Photoshop, you'll see the window shown here. If you then load the correct color palette, you can recalibrate a GIF photo or illustration to the proper colors. The result is a "Web-safe" image that looks equally good on a Windows PC or a Mac.

▲ Adobe Photoshop 5.5 has its own built-in Web Palette.

FFFFFF	FFCCFF	FF99FF	FF66FF	FF33FF	FF00FF
FFFFCC	FFCCCC	FF99CC	FF66CC	FF33CC	FF00CC
FFFF99	FFCC99	FF9999	FF6699	FF3399	FF0099
FFFF66	FFCC66	FF9966	FF6666	FF3366	FF0066
FFFF33	FFCC33	FF9933	FF6633	FF3333	FF0033
FFFF00	FFCC00	FF9900	FF6600	FF3300	FF0000
CCFFFF	CCCCFF	CC99FF	CC66FF	CC33FF	CC00FF
CCFFCC	CCCCCC	CC99CC	CC66CC	CC33CC	CC00CC
CCFF99	CCCC99	CC9999	CC6699	CC3399	CC0099
CCFF66	CCCC66	CC9966	CC6666	CC3366	CC0066
CCFF33	CCCC33	CC9933	CC6633	CC3333	CC0033
CCFF00	CCCC00	CC9900	CC6600	CC3300	CC0000
99FFFF	99CCFF	9999FF	9966FF	9933FF	9900FF
99FFCC	99CCCC	9999CC	9966CC	9933CC	9900CC
99FF99	99CC99	999999	996699	993399	990099
99FF66	99CC66	999966	996666	993366	990066
99FF33	99CC33	999933	996633	993333	990033
99FF00	99CC00	999900	996600	993300	990000
66FFFF	66CCFF	6699FF	6666FF	6633FF	6600FF
66FFCC	66CCCC	6699CC	6666CC	6633CC	6600CC
66FF99	66CC99	669999	666699	663399	660099
66FF66	66CC66	669966	666666	663366	660066
66FF33	66CC33	669933	666633	663333	660033
66FF00	66CC00	669900	666600	663300	660000
33FFFF	33CCFF	3399FF	3366FF	3333FF	3300FF
33FFCC	33CCCC	3399CC	3366CC	3333CC	3300CC
33FF99	33CC99	339999	336699	333399	330099
33FF66	33CC66	339966	336666	333366	330066
33FF33	33CC33	339933	336633	333333	330033
33FF00	33CC00	339900	336600	333300	330000
00FFFF	00CCFF	0099FF	0066FF	0033FF	0000FF
00FFCC	00CCCC	0099CC	0066CC	0033CC	0000CC
00FF99	00CC99	009999	006699	003399	000099
00FF66	00CC66	009966	006666	003366	000066
00FF33	00CC33	009933	006633	003333	000033
00FF00	00CC00	009900	006600	003300	000000

◄ This chart shows the 216 colors from the Web Palette.

© Douglas R. Jacobson

▶ Basic Palette

The chart on the previous page illustrates all the colors in the CLUT, along with their corresponding hexadecimal values. The basic palette consists of combinations of 00, 33, 66, 99, cc, and FF that represent every red, green, and blue element of the color description, for a total of 216 *(6x6x6)* specific colors. But Navigator also uses the pure RGB colors; these have numbers such as #000000 *(better known as black)* and #FFFFFF *(white)*. Note that this theory applies to foreground colors. Where, you may ask, can I find a complete "color card"? A number of Web sites offer charts that display all the Web-safe colors, along with their corresponding numerical values. An example of such a color card is shown *[on the right-hand page]*.

▶ Custom Palette

Once you're armed with a good color card, you can create your own Navigator CLUT to use in a pixel-oriented image-editing program such as Adobe Photoshop *(for the Macintosh and PC)* or Equilibrium DeBabelizer for the Mac.

To create your own CLUT in Photoshop, first open your color card and save it as an 8-bit GIF file. *(Make sure the Dithering option is turned off.)* If you select the Color Table option from the Mode menu, all 256 colors from the table will be displayed. Next, select the Save option to create and name your CLUT.

By repeatedly reading this table and then applying it to a selected image, you can make every illustration or photograph suitable to work with your custom Navigator color palette.

▶ The Unix Niche

The Unix version of Navigator is usually based on a matrix of 5x5x5 *(125)* colors. The hexadecimal values for the RGB colors are 00, 40, 80, BF, and FE *(corresponding to decimal values 0, 64, 128, 191, and 255)*.

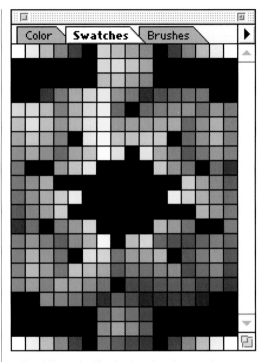

▲ The VisiBone classification, based on the 216-color Web-safe palette, is set up according to color group. This simplifies the process of looking up a color or related colors.

VISIBONE Colors

◀ The VisiBone color swatch, which you install in Photoshop's Goodies folder, can be found at VisiBone's site (www.visibone.com).

▶ Colors by Name

The specifications for hypertext markup language *(HTML)* include an extension for defining colors; 16 color names are currently standardized. The two most popular Web browsers, Netscape Navigator and Microsoft Internet Explorer, recognize these names and apply the colors automatically. HTML's 16 basic colors also correspond to the standard colors supported by the Windows VGA palette.

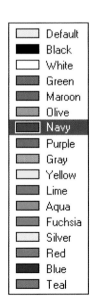

Default
Black
White
Green
Maroon
Olive
Navy
Purple
Gray
Yellow
Lime
Aqua
Fuchsia
Silver
Red
Blue
Teal

Before you can optimize your Web images for Unix systems, you need to create a different color look-up table than the one used for the standard Windows and Mac versions of Navigator. Unfortunately, the two tables are incompatible, so make sure to carefully consider which platform your images should be optimized for. Generally, it's best to take the biggest group of users as your starting point—currently, of course, Windows users make up the largest numbers of Web surfers—but your specific needs may vary.

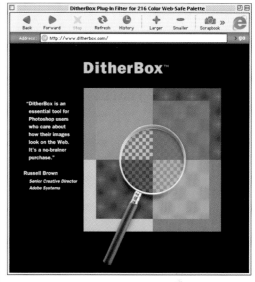

▲ DitherBox is as simple to use as it is effective: It nicely approximates your "hybrid" color by combining two colors from the 216-color set. Because the new color is based on the Web-safe palette, dithering problems do not occur.

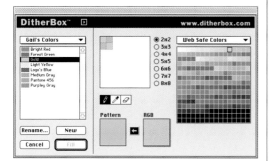

▶ The DitherBox Alternative

Until Web users have access to better video cards with more colors, we are best served by intelligent alternatives such as DitherBox. This feature, available with ImageReady, enables you to generate your own "hybrid" colors that are compatible across all Web platforms. DitherBox simply converts your chosen color to a two-color, four-pixel rendition based on Navigator's 216-color Web-safe palette. The results look surprisingly good, and you can be assured that no further dithering will occur, because the hybrid color is based on a combination of two Web-safe colors. DitherBox can also save combinations of hybrid colors in a library.

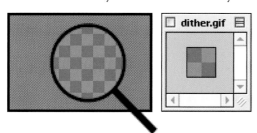

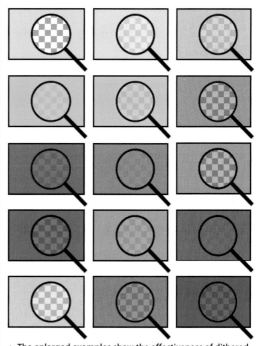

▲ The enlarged examples show the effectiveness of dithered colors—provided that the color saturation does not deviate
◄ too much and lead to unappealing results.

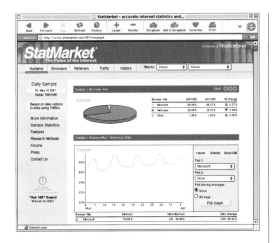

▲ WebSideStory's StatMarket provides reliable aggregate profiles of millions of Web users worldwide.

▶ Where Do We Go from Here?

The adage "You can't please everybody" is certainly true when it comes to designing for the Web. If you had to prepare every image for a large Web site using the methods described above, you would have a lot of work in store. Are the results worth all that trouble?

Increasingly, Web designers are electing not to limit themselves to only 216 or 256 colors—and current statistics lend credence to this trend. According to WebSideStory's StatMarket, which culls data on global Internet-usage trends *(www.statmarket.com)*, nearly 90 percent of Web surfers now have access to computers that can display 65,000 or more colors. Therefore, it no longer makes sense for Web designers to restrict their creative options just to serve the relatively small number of users still limited to 256 colors. *(If you do decide to go beyond the Web-safe palette, select colors that do not appear too garish on a monitor with limited color options when the closest alternatives are chosen from the 216-color set.)*

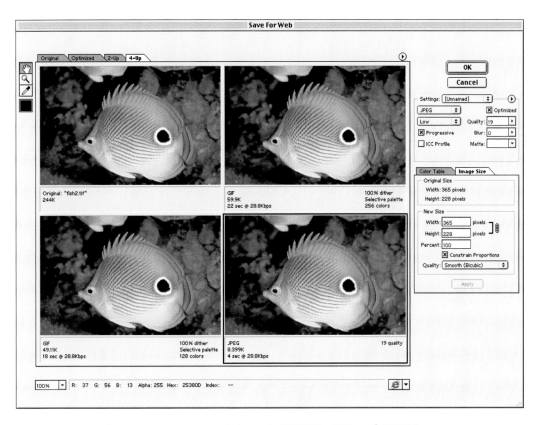

Images are an essential component of Web pages. This chapter uses numerous illustrations and examples to explain how to take advantage of all the possibilities they offer and how to use the appropriate file formats.

GIF and JPEG Images

The Web is a visual medium. The images and logos complement the text, creating an appealing experience for the reader. Logos are important because they identify the company, but they can also take a long time to load, which may discourage visitors to the site. The trick is to find the right balance between file size and image quality. New software such as Adobe ImageReady, a component of Photoshop, and Macromedia Fireworks provide a solution. Currently there are two standard file formats that can be recognized and displayed by all browsers: GIF and JPEG. The choice of format depends on the type of image and how it will be used on the Web page. In the near future more flexible graphical formats like PNG, JPEG 2000 and especially SVG, Scalable Vector Graphics, will be accepted by the browsers.

▶ GIF Compression

When the conventions for Web design were created, GIF was the only file format that could be displayed on the Web. Thanks to the introduction of the JPEG format and CompuServe's plug-in technology, several different formats are available. Still, the Graphics Interchange Format, or GIF, is the most commonly used option.

Compuserve, GIF's creator, intended the format to be universally applicable; indeed, it has not been necessary to adjust the GIF format to the various operating systems, so the format can be regarded as "universal." The only restrictions on the format's performance come from the monitor quality *(color or black and white)* and the computer's color card. The color card determines how much of the full range of 256 colors can be displayed.

The GIF format supports indexed bitmap images with a color depth up to 8 bits or 256

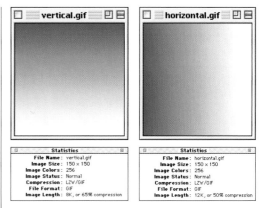

▲ A horizontal gradient results in better GIF image compression.

colors. You can't use more than 256 colors, but if you use fewer colors, the GIF file can be stored more compactly. As shown in the example above, the compression works horizontally.

▼ Macromedia Fireworks has an Export to Size Wizard that enables you to specify a particular file size.

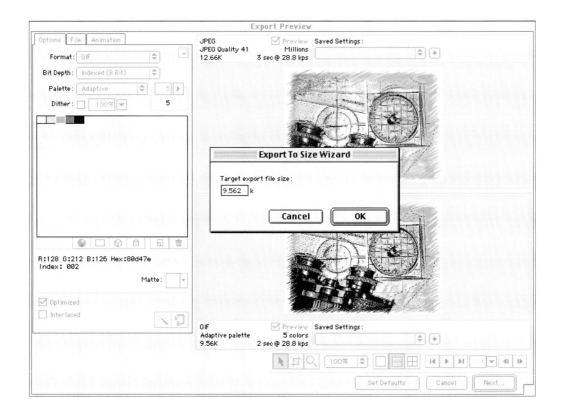

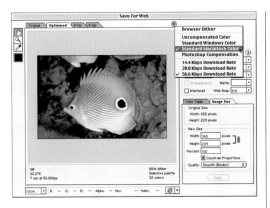

▲ The display on a Mac differs considerably from that on a Windows PC.

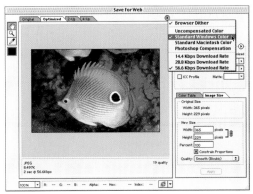

▲ In Adobe ImageReady this can be previewed on the screen.

Equivalent pixels, or graphic elements with the same color value, can be described as a unit by the algorithm in a horizontal direction. The familiar LZW compression method is used for this. The TIFF format, familiar from the printing world, also uses this method. The GIF format is best suited for logos and images that do not have to be reproduced precisely. It is less suitable for the level of detail that photos display. A range of 256 colors is insufficient, and the compression is not optimal.

A GIF file always compresses photos less efficiently than JPEG. The dot patterns in halftone images prevent the GIF compression algorithm from achieving a small file size. However, for purely graphic images, such as logos or texts that must be displayed in a particular font, GIF is unbeatable.

▶ Interlacing and Transparency

The quality of the LZW algorithm was not the only reason for adopting GIF as the standard on the Web. The GIF file format has other features that make it the compression format of choice: It can be read "in steps," saving time because the viewer quickly gets an impression of the ultimate results.

With transparency, one color in the GIF image can be rendered literally transparent, which allows the background to "show

through." This option is a blessing for Web designers, because it offers enormous creative possibilities. Images can be placed so that they appear to be free standing against a background.

And a transparent image of 1 by 1 pixel, for example, can be used to define a specific distance in the HTML layout. This trick is often used by professional Web designers and in page-layout programs such as NetObjects Fusion.

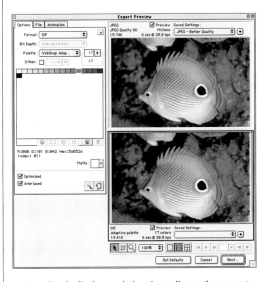

▲ ImageReady displays variations in quality on the screen to facilitate the selection process.

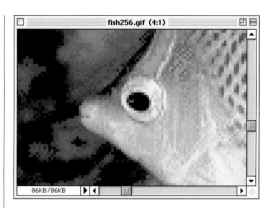

▶ File Size and Quality

The unique LZW compression technique —named after its creators, Lempel, Ziv, and Welch—is the basis of the GIF file format. Since it can describe "repeated" patterns and pixels *(short for "picture elements")*, this has consequences for the number of colors used in an image.

A dithered photo whose colors are built up of pixels that collectively create the illusion of color will be compressed much more poorly than a nondithered photo. And the fewer colors an image contains, the greater the chance that the LZW compression will find horizontal rows of pixels with the same color value.

This means the file size in kilobytes becomes increasingly smaller, while the file size in horizontal and vertical pixels remains the same. Unfortunately, this convenience comes at a price: The fewer colors used to display a detailed photo, the poorer the image quality.

Compare the enlargement of a 256-color file with that of an 8-color version. These are the two extremes between which you must find a compromise. The 1-bit version of the fish is only 18K; the 8-bit version takes up 59K of space. This means it will take more than three times as long to send this image by modem or cable to the user. Quite a waste of time and bandwidth!

fish16.gif

Image Colors: 16   Image Length: 21K, or 51% compression

◄ The GIF images shown on this page, which range from 256 to 8 indexed colors, not only become increasingly smaller, but the quality deteriorates proportionately as well.

▼ In GIF Converter you can include a comment with every file in the document. This is handy for specifying copyright information.

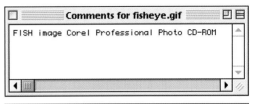

Comments for fisheye.gif

FISH image Corel Professional Photo CD-ROM

fish8.gif

Image Colors: 8   Image Length: 18K, or 45% compression

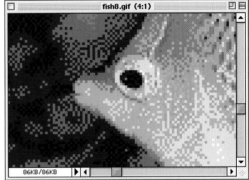

fish8.gif (4:1)

86KB/86KB

▶ Adjusted Colors in Photoshop

If you want to have more control over the discarding of colors during the color-reduction process, you can use an interesting option in Adobe Photoshop: Select an important area, and then specify Indexed Colors.

The program will attempt to use as many colors as possible from the selected area. Frequently this produces a much better result.

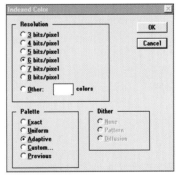

Indexed Color

Resolution
- ○ 3 bits/pixel
- ○ 4 bits/pixel
- ○ 5 bits/pixel
- ◉ 6 bits/pixel
- ○ 7 bits/pixel
- ○ 8 bits/pixel
- ○ Other: ___ colors

Palette
- ○ Exact
- ○ Uniform
- ◉ Adaptive
- ○ Custom...
- ○ Previous

Dither
- ○ None
- ○ Pattern
- ○ Diffusion

OK   Cancel

▲ A detail enlargement shows the dithered pixel pattern. If you select an area before indexing and then select Adaptive, these colors are given preference. ▼

fish (RGB, 1:1)

258KB/258KB

fish16.gif na selectie

Image Colors: 16   Image Length: 21K, or 51% compression

▶ **JPEG Compression**

The JPEG compression format was created by the Joint Photographic Experts Group and also has roots in the graphics industry. As stated earlier, this file format has not been in use on the World Wide Web for very long. Netscape was the first to support JPEG in its Web browser.

When designers started using JPEG, Navigator was the only browser that could display this file inline. Mosaic *(version 1.x)*, the most commonly used browser at that time, had problems with this new file format. The image could only be displayed on the screen by using a separate help program. JPEG view was used for this on the Macintosh.

Now all the important Web browsers support the JPEG format. This is a good development, because JPEG is the file format of choice for high-quality display of detailed photographic images.

▶ Image Quality from Highest to Lowest

Given that each pixel has a different color value in a photo, the GIF format is not nearly as effective as JPEG for rendering photographs. This is because the JPEG compression algorithm does not search for groups of pixels, but rather for variations between the pixels in a group.

Since the compression level in a JPEG file can be set by the user, the algorithm will accept larger or smaller variations. To get an acceptably small result, the compression must discard some of the information in the image. Of course, this reduces the quality.

▶ Spots Before Your Eyes

Obviously the file size depends on the quality you select. In the example of the fish, the highest quality image is 46K, while the lowest quality image is only 13K. That is 5K less than the coarsest *(and unusable for most purposes)* GIF version.

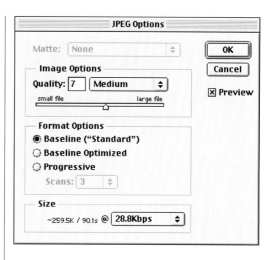

▲ Photoshop has standardized the image quality by providing four standard settings, but also offers a sliding scale.

▶ Warning for Photoshoppers

If you use Adobe Photoshop, versions 4 and 5, to save the images as JPEG files, be careful—Photoshop does not offer an option for displaying the compression loss on the monitor. This means that if the file is saved as JPEG, it will look just like it did before. Only after the file is closed and then reopened will the loss of quality be visible. If the file is opened for a second time, edited, and resaved, the damage becomes even greater. So be sure to save the original! Adobe Photoshop 6.0 has a "live" JPEG preview!

▼ The JPEG compression algorithm can be set from 0 to 100 percent without intermediate steps.

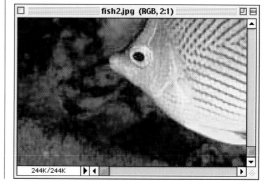

fish.jpg highest
Image Colors: Millions   Image Length: 46K, or 5:1 compression

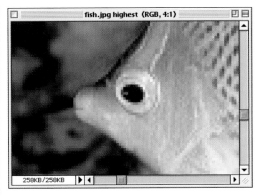

fish.jpg highest (RGB, 4:1)
258KB/258KB

fish.jpg high
Image Colors: Millions   Image Length: 28K, or 9:1 compression

▶ Further Editing

Since JPEG compression is based on pixel variations *(expressed in sine curves)*, there is no such thing as a 256-color JPEG photo. That also means that the quality of a JPEG file that is opened and edited in LView Pro, Photoshop, or GIF Converter will deteriorate further

Thus, always save the original version in PICT or TIFF format to use for any corrections that may be necessary. If a JPEG file is saved for the second or third time, you will note increasing degradation of the image quality.

So save the original! The JPEG format can also be read in phases, thanks to Progressive JPEG compression. Netscape Navigator and Internet Explorer support this option, which produces a recognizable image in the browser after about 10 percent of the data has been imported.

fish.jpg medium
Image Colors: Millions   Image Length: 17K, or 15:1 compression

fish.jpg low
Image Colors: Millions   Image Length: 13K, or 21:1 compression

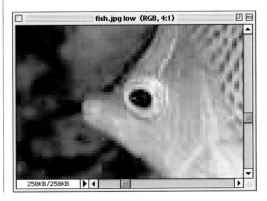

fish.jpg low (RGB, 4:1)
258KB/258KB

▲ With its sharp lines and very small file size, a graphic image is perfectly suited to the GIF file format.

▲ JPEG compression is unsuitable for a graphic file—it produces poor quality and is unnecessarily large.

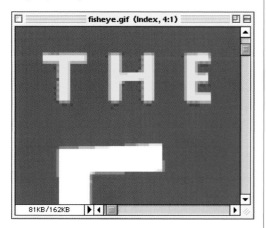

▶ GIF for Graphic Images

Logos and lettering are perfect candidates for the GIF compression technique. Long, repetitive rows of pixels lend themselves perfectly to this format. Graphic images often employ a minimum number of colors, which increases the compression still further. Instead of four or five different shades of green, you can use one shade of green for a larger area.

The GIF version of the logo shown here only uses 5K. The figures demonstrate not only that the JPEG version is larger *(10K),* but also that the quality is quite a bit poorer. The spot pattern is annoyingly visible in evenly colored areas. Also, JPEG has no transparency option.

▲ The characteristic JPEG effect is clearly visible in the enlargement, making this the wrong method for logos and graphic art. It also has no transparency option, so sharp edges are impossible. ▼

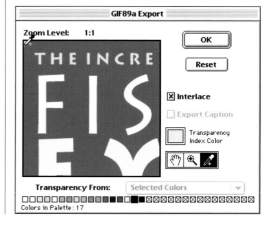

▲ A combined image is a special case, and success usually comes with trial and error. Sometimes you can achieve good results with the GIF file format …

▲ … and sometimes JPEG compression produces the best balance between quality and file size. Remember not to edit the same JPEG file more than once.

▶ Combined Images

It is quite difficult to combine text information and a halftone image in one file. You can avoid this combination by dividing the image into sections or placing it in a table.

This stores the graphic information in a different cell from the photographic image. If this solution is impossible, you can create a file in which you keep the quality at an acceptable level by not selecting extreme compression.

In the examples shown here, the quality of the logo's GIF version is comparable to that of the JPEG version. The file size will then determine your format choice; in that case, the JPEG compression is frequently the better choice.

▶ SVGA and XVGA Monitors

The enormous increase in availability of computers that can display thousands of colors has considerably widened the Web designer's playing field. You can achieve a good balance between file size and image quality by using the GIF format and an "adaptive color palette." On some monitors

with 65,000 colors, an image rendered this way looks perfect!

◀ Always keep a copy of the original Photoshop image when saving a file in JPEG format. Then you will always be able to return to it if necessary.

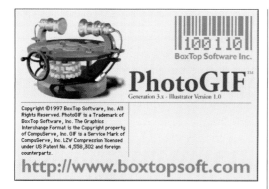

▶ Plug-ins and Other Tools

Of course, there are other methods that achieve good results. The PhotoGIF filter, from BoxTop Software, is an outstanding product that can make a GIF image transparent using a layer mask.

Compared with the standard method, in which a specific color is chosen, the Photo-GIF method is easier to manage because you don't have to worry about whether the color selected for the transparency appears somewhere else in the file and will create unintended areas of transparency. In the example shown here, the airplane tail is the same color as the background against which it must stand out, but thanks to PhotoGIF, this is not a problem.

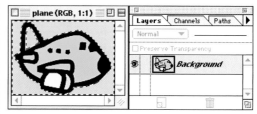

▲ Select the image background, but deselect the unwanted mask color in the tail.

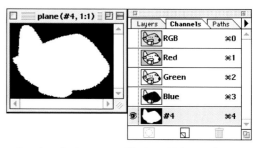

▲ Save the selection as a masking layer. Make sure that no pixels can be seen in the clipped image. The airplane's mask must be completely white.

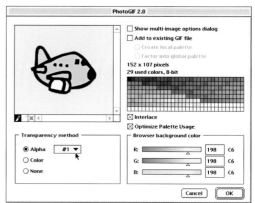

▲ Select the correct color palette and the alpha channel in the PhotoGIF window, and the transparent GIF is ready. ▼

◄ In the browser you can clearly see that the clipped airplane does not have transparent pixels.

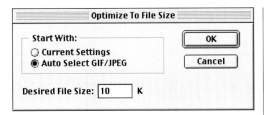

◀ For images whose background is difficult to isolate with a simple selection, the Extensis plug-in Mask Pro is an ideal solution.

▶ File-Size Perils

The fewer pixels an image has, the better. However, the eye wants interesting detail as well, right? Finding the correct balance is a tiresome chore. However, the graphics software manufacturers are continuing to offer better solutions for this problem.

One of the best complete graphics packages is Macromedia Fireworks. In addition to all sorts of intelligent wizards, Fireworks also has a function whereby the user specifies the ideal file size and the program then creates the best possible illustration. The program's Auto Select feature ensures that Fireworks chooses the most suitable option: JPEG or GIF.

Checking the correct file size is a whole other story. Many sites—the graphic design and the prototype in particular—are developed on a Macintosh. However, Macs have a feature that makes it difficult to check the actual file size: The icon and the preview image are included in the size, but in actuality the file is much smaller.

▲ The background is removed step-by-step based on the color range until only the foreground image is left. Troublesome details such as hair have been removed from the busy background. ▶

▲ A GIF image including preview and Photoshop icon is 12K too large.

▲ Without the preview and icon, the number of kilobytes falls to 3. The value is visible at the bottom of the browser window while loading.

▶ Deleting Complex Backgrounds

Some images require more skill to clip than others. Portraits in which hair is visible are especially problematic for the average graphic designer. Retouching and editing images is an art in itself. Luckily, software has been developed for this as well. A fine example is Extensis Mask Pro.

This Photoshop filter enables you to use color selection to remove the background from complex images step-by-step. You can use the eyedropper tool to remove the background without tedious channel and masking operations.

▶ PNG File Format

PNG *(Portable Network Graphics)* is a new file format that combines the best features of GIF and JPEG. PNG is already supported by a few graphics programs such as Adobe Photoshop. In Macromedia Fireworks, PNG has even become the standard format for all image processing. The most important advantage of the PNG compression method is that it supports 48-bit color storage, in contrast to GIF's maximum of 8 bits, while still achieving an enormous compression ratio. PNG files are 30% smaller than comparable TIFF files. In addition, PNG has adopted the most important advantage of TIFF-document compression with no loss of data. PNG is an important improvement over both the GIF and JPEG formats.

▶ Scalable Vector Graphics and JPEG 2000

Besides the PNG format, there are other potential competitors of GIF and JPEG. SVG has a good chance, and there is also an ISO initiative called JPEG 2000. Not much can be said yet about the latter file format, but plenty can be said about SVG, which could become the officially recognized norm for the World Wide Web Consortium. SVG is actually one of Macromedia Flash's competitors, because it also uses vectors to describe a form. Its biggest distinction from Flash is that SVG is based on XML. That guarantees the uniformity of the images on media and various types of screens. The continual growth of the Web means that Web pages must be appropriate for display on other media, such as television screens and handheld computers. This last group may well become the largest platform. If the anticipated integration between portable telephones and handheld devices materializes, the Web will be liberated from the bonds of cables and plugs. SVG and XML anticipate this revolution because SVG can be displayed optimally on all media at lightning speed. SVG files are completely text based, so the illustrations can also be indexed *(textually)*. Moreover, high-resolution prints can be made of the images, and they offer all the other Macromedia Flash advantages.

SVG Plugin

▼ Photoshop 5.0 offers a number of (puzzling) options for viewing a PNG image.

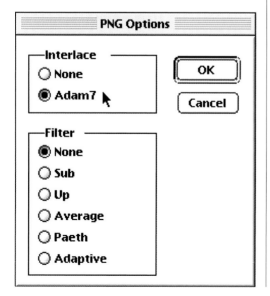

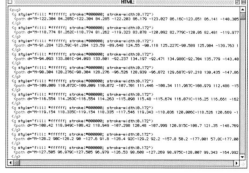

▲ The Mozilla browsers natively reads .svg files.

▲ SVG code, which is based on XML, can be indexed.

A wide variety ▶
of different
patterns are used
in Web pages to
enhance visual
appeal.

From the moment Netscape introduced the <background> tag, which allows a small image to be repeated across an entire page, Web designers all over the world started using tiled backgrounds. This chapter shows how to create these patterns.

Tiled Background Patterns

Some Web designers and HTML programmers prefer to have an interesting pattern in the background, rather than a plain surface. However, creating a pattern is challenging, as the seams must be invisible. The basis of the pattern, the so-called tile, is repeated by the browser infinitely so that the background is completely covered with the pattern.

Of course, this affects the Web page's loading time. Thus it is important to keep the file size of the background illustration as small as possible—ideally, under 10K. It's also a good idea to apply the same background to subsequent pages; the browser will then retrieve the background image from the cache of the viewer's computer. An alternating background will mean additional loading time.

► Seamless Connection

A tile has to be repeatable without visible transitions. This means that an image is not usable as a background tile unless it has been adapted through the use of special techniques and/or illustration programs that can create seamless drawings.

This chapter shows how to make a pattern in Corel Painter. Later in this chapter we'll examine the possibilities of the Specular TextureScape program, as well as two handy plug-ins—Terrazzo and KPT Seamless Welder. The chapters "Background Color and Pattern" and "Painter: Image Hose and Patterns" describe handy techniques for creating background patterns.

► Painter Standard Patterns

When it comes to producing seamless repeating patterns, Painter has no peer. The package not only boasts a considerable number of handy tools that enormously simplify pattern creation; it also comes with an enormous number of standard patterns and backgrounds that can be further modified by the user. A paper structure called Eggscape is the basis for the pattern.

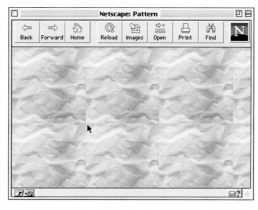

▲ A pattern that does not repeat properly is very unattractive; its effect is lost. The "infinite," seamless background below is better. ▼

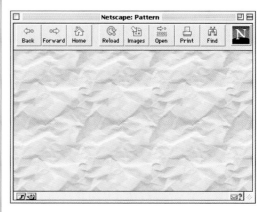

This pattern is 200 by 200 pixels, and Corel Painter has already made it repetitive. Then we create a new illustration of the same size and select Apply Surface Texture. By varying the light angle we can generate an interesting 3D pattern. Then we brighten it a little, change the color to light blue, and save the illustration as a GIF file with 16 indexed colors. When seen as a whole in the browser, it is clearly an appealing pattern.

◄ The individual pattern as created by Painter.

Practical Web **TIP**

► Of course, the best place to look for backgrounds is on the Web itself. A number of Web sites offer basic material for backgrounds without copyright. You click on the image, keep the mouse button pressed, and then specify a location on the hard drive where you want to save the GIF file. First retrieve the source code from the Web page. Then look for the tag <BODY background = "x.gif">. Copy the background GIF's text code, and paste it after the last slash in this URL: http://www.site.com/x.gif. Press Enter (Windows) or

Return (Mac), and there's your GIF. Don't forget to ask for permission to use the GIF. In Navigator 2.0 and higher you can select Document Info to retrieve the file.

The first step in ▶ creating a repeating tile in Corel Painter is to select a paper structure.

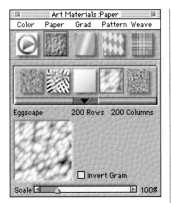

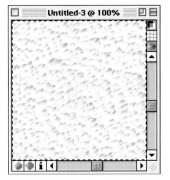

◀ The lighter color setting is an improvement. Now we add some color.

Then a surface ▶ structure is created using Apply Surface Texture. The Inverted option results in an attractive effect.

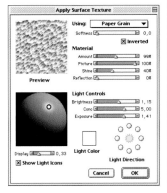

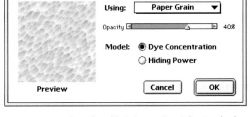

▲ A pattern can be colored in Painter using Color Overlay by adding a second color layer over it and making it transparent.

The 200-by- ▶ 200-pixel pattern now looks like this. It is still a little too dark for a background pattern.

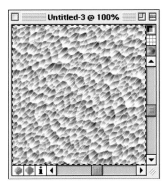

▲ When the pattern is ready, the GIF file is saved in 16 indexed colors without the Interlacing option turned on.

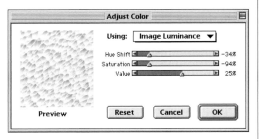

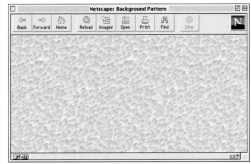

▲ By selecting Adjust Color, we can adjust the HSV values in Painter using a preview.

▶ KPT Seamless Welder

Also very helpful for creating tiled backgrounds is KPT Seamless Welder, one of the Corel KPT image filters for Photoshop. This filter enables you to produce very creative patterns from any photo or illustration.

KPT Seamless Welder works quite simply: You select part of a photo and then choose Seamless Welder from the KPT filters menu. In the window that appears, you can set up the mode, opacity, and the "Glue."

This plug-in creates a repeatable tile by repeating parts of the selected area. Even though these parts are displayed a bit blurred, the result is very effective. The only condition KPT Seamless Welder imposes is that enough free image space must be selected around the framed image.

In the example shown here, you can see that the sweater and necklace are repeated at

KPT Help...
KPT Gradient Designer 3.0...
KPT Interform 3.0...
KPT Spheroid Designer 3.0...
KPT Texture Explorer 3.0...
KPT 3D Stereo Noise 3.0...
KPT Edge f/x 3.0...
KPT Gaussian f/x 3.0...
KPT Glass Lens 3.0...
KPT Intensity f/x 3.0...
KPT Noise f/x 3.0...
KPT Page Curl 3.0...
KPT Pixel f/x 3.0...
KPT Planar Tiling 3.0...
KPT Seamless Welder 3.0...
KPT Smudge f/x 3.0...
KPT Twirl 3.0...
KPT Video Feedback 3.0...
KPT Vortex Tiling 3.0...

◀ KPT Seamless Welder is one of the most creative filters in Kai Krause's extensive collection.

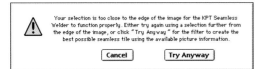

Your selection is too close to the edge of the image for the KPT Seamless Welder to function properly. Either try again using a selection further from the edge of the image, or click "Try Anyway" for the filter to create the best possible seamless tile using the available picture information.

[Cancel]   [Try Anyway]

The results of the various settings and variations are ▶ displayed in the preview window. When you click the green button, the filter is applied.

▲ The image selection requires a generous margin.

▲ The result of the KPT Seamless Welder filter.

the top of the pattern. As this image is monochrome, it can be saved as either a GIF or a JPEG file. In this case we have chosen the GIF format, because browsers can process this better as a background.

A setting of 128 Indexed colors is sufficient to safeguard enough detail in the image. When the pattern is viewed in the browser, one image element appears to flow seamlessly into the next. The result looks similar to that of a fixe retouche but is in reality made with the click of a button in KPT Seamless Welder. So, when you want to surprise a loved one with a personal Web page, you know what to do ...

When the pattern is completed, it must be saved in a file format that can be placed between the <body> tags. ▸ ▾

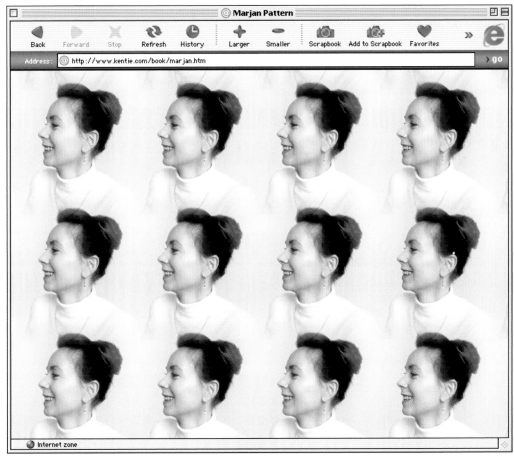

▶ Testing Patterns

You can use an option in Adobe Photoshop to see if a repeating pattern is displayed without seams. Open the document in Photoshop, select the desired area, and choose Define Pattern from the Edit menu. Then create a new document with generous dimensions, such as 500 by 500 pixels. Now open the Fill window from the

Edit menu, and select the option Use: Pattern in the Contents pane. The whole area will now be filled with the previous selection. This allows you to see the effect without using a separate Web page and a GIF or JPEG image.

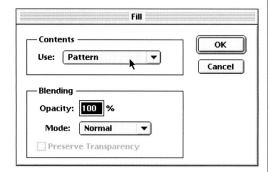

▲ A repetitive background pattern can be checked quickly with Photoshop's Use: Pattern option.

The schoolbook- ▶
like character of
this Web site is
achieved primarily
by using the ring-
binder image in
the background.
The images in the
foreground also
contribute to this
effect.

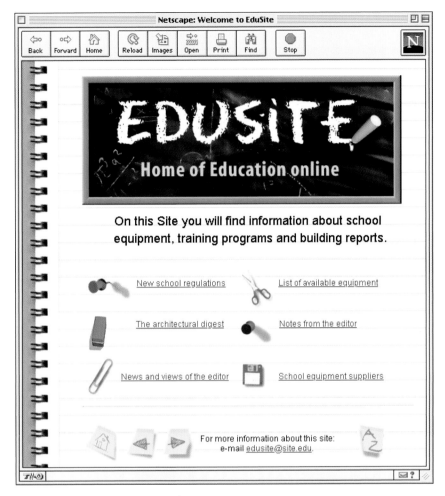

By creatively employing the options HTML offers, you can create original and unexpected Web pages. Typical examples of this are pages on which a repetitive background pattern creates an optical illusion.

Background Lines and Patterns

Some patterns are especially suitable for a Web page background. The ring binder pattern prominently displayed on this page gives the impression that one large GIF image was placed in the background. In reality, a thin strip with one ring is repeated by the browser to create a seamless whole. The application of this kind of background image has a number of important advantages: The GIF file is very small—just a few kilobytes—and will not affect the page's loading time. There's also a visual benefit: The Web page acquires a special "signature" that makes it stand out from run-of-the-mill pages.

▶ Efficient Design

If you were to temporarily remove the foreground information from the Edusite page, the page would still be appealing. The pattern is particularly suitable for a Web site that must convey a clear theme. Six examples of recognizable background patterns created from a strong basic visual element are shown on the following two pages. The background illustrations were all created by Jay Boersma.

The common element in these GIF illustrations is the restricted use of color and the deceptive simplicity of the drawings. These GIF files are models of efficient design even though some of the illustrations were created from scanned photos.

Sometimes it is necessary to edit a GIF image pixel by pixel and to fiddle with it until you are satisfied with it. Try to limit the number of colors. If you can manage to have a number of adjacent horizontal pixels with the same color values, the compression factor for the GIF becomes higher and the file size even smaller.

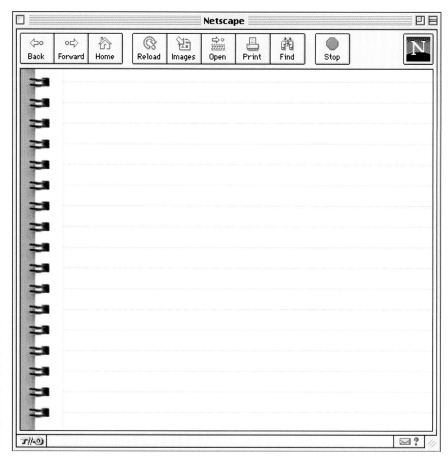

The illusion of ▶ a school notebook is created by the browser's repetition of the pattern. The GIF image defined in the <BODY> as background is shown below. ▼

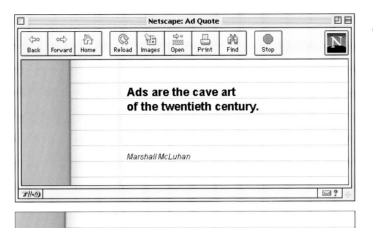

◀ This repeating background is called "exam_book."

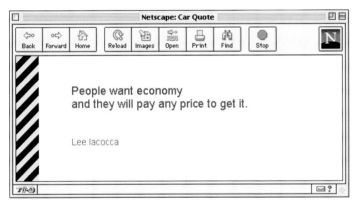

◀ This background, called "caution_stripe," is ideal for pages that are under construction.

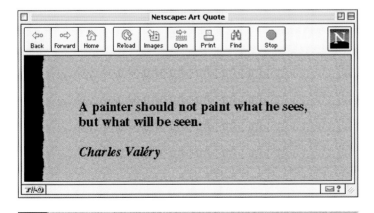

◀ This paper structure with its torn edge is called "torn_brown_kraft."

This background design is ▶
called "bound_pages_blk."

The "music_paper" pattern is▶
ideal for musical Web sites.

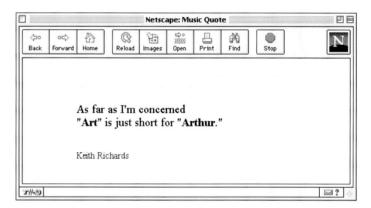

This wavy background is used ▶
in the Hacker Tracker page and
is simply called "back.gif."

▶ Margins for Web Browsers

If you use creative demarcation lines and repeating background patterns, you will soon discover that different browsers display them differently. The extent of deviation between the background pattern, the foreground text, and images depends on the platform. Microsoft introduced a new set of tags in Internet Explorer 2.0 for Windows and Macintosh to solve this problem: LEFTMARGIN, TOPMARGIN and RIGHTMARGIN.

The new tags are included in the <BODY> of the document. If these tags are not used, the browser applies the standard margin of 8 pixels. If you want to place the foreground information close to the edge of the browser window, as shown in the example on the left, you must add the following tags: TOPMARGIN=0 LEFTMARGIN=0. The page is then divided into three columns to separate the data.

▲ Pay close attention to the differences in the width of the text fields. ▼

```
<HTML>
<HEAD><TITLE>Info page</TITLE></HEAD>
<BODY BGCOLOR="#FFFFFF" LINK="#FF0000"
   VLINK="#006600" BACKGROUND="back.gif"
   TOPMARGIN=8 LEFTMARGIN=8>
<TABLE BORDER=1 WIDTH=560>
   <TR>
      <TD WIDTH=110 VALIGN=top> </TD>
      <TD WIDTH=60> </td>
      <TD WIDTH=390><IMG SRC="hack.gif"
      WIDTH=342 HEIGHT=172></TD>
   </TR>
</TABLE><BR>
<TABLE border=0 width=560>
   <TR>
      <TD WIDTH=110 VALIGN=top>Text and Images</TD>
      <TD WIDTH=60> </td>
      <TD WIDTH=390>Text and Images</TD>
   </TR></TABLE>
</BODY>
</HTML>
```

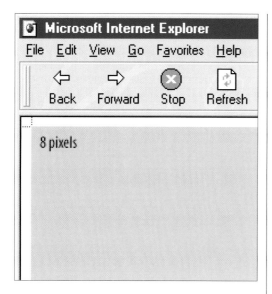

▶ Varying Margins for Different Web Browsers

In spite of all attempts at standardization, the browsers interpret margin distances differently. If you have a layout that requires precise positioning of the foreground and background, this will certainly cause you problems.

Even though the differences are relatively small—a maximum of 5 pixels—the eye will ruthlessly detect this, and the intended effect goes down the drain. Actually, the only remedy for this is to use a JavaScript that detects browsers, which lets you offer each browser a customized background image.

Browser	Version	OS	Horizontal Distance	Vertical Distance
Navigator	3.0	WIN	10 pixels	15 pixels
Navigator	4.0	WIN	10 pixels	15 pixels
Navigator	3.0	MAC	8 pixels	8 pixels
Navigator	4.0	MAC	8 pixels	8 pixels
Internet Explorer	3.0	WIN	10 pixels	16 pixels
Internet Explorer	4.0	WIN	10 pixels	16 pixels
Internet Explorer	3.0	MAC	8 pixels	8 pixels
Internet Explorer	4.0	MAC	8 pixels	8 pixels

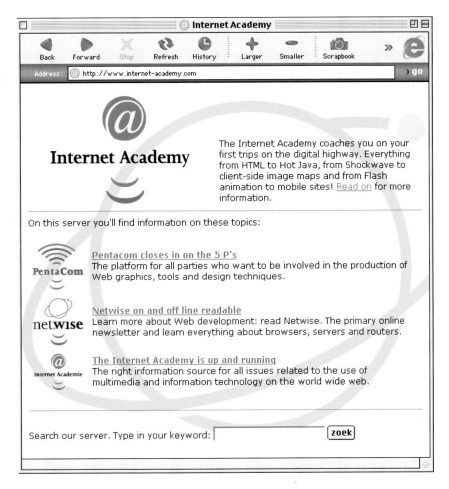

Thanks to one ▶ large GIF file, this page acquires a distinct identity without disrupting the transfer of information.

A single GIF image can produce surprising results when placed on the background of a Web page. However, this procedure requires good planning. This chapter shows the method you can use for a home page and a subpage.

Large Background Pattern

The repetitive effect of a background pattern offers a multitude of creative possibilities. The Web designer can fill up the background by repeating a single row horizontally or vertically. In previous chapters, you have read how this offers the Web designer an attractive option for embellishing a page. Now we will go a step further—using a large GIF image as a graphic element on the background of the home page and the derived pages. Of course, this imposes requirements on the illustration, since you'll need to avoid letting the GIF image greatly increase page-loading time or reduce text legibility.

▶ How Big Is Big?

The concept of size has two interpretations —and in this case, both are important. Size expressed in pixels depends on the result you wish to achieve. If the GIF image is applied repetitively using an even hue, you need not concern yourself much with the width and height.

The adjacent example shows a GIF image of 662 by 533 pixels, a size that is equal to a surface area of 9 by 7.5 inches. The drawing was created in Adobe Illustrator and then copied and pasted into Adobe Photoshop. The definitive image from this program was saved as a GIF file.

Since the graphical image contains a limited number of colors, the GIF file *(called globe.gif)* is relatively small—only 6K! Because the surface consists largely of one even color, the GIF algorithm can compress the file a great deal and the browser can load it quickly. A large GIF image will cause problems if the user's computer has too little RAM memory.

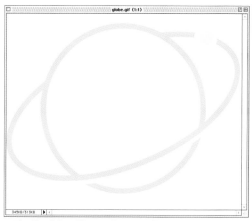

▲ The file globe.gif is saved as a GIF file with only eight indexed colors.

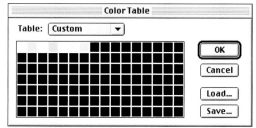

▲ The color table in the GIF file can be changed in Photoshop by clicking on individual colors.

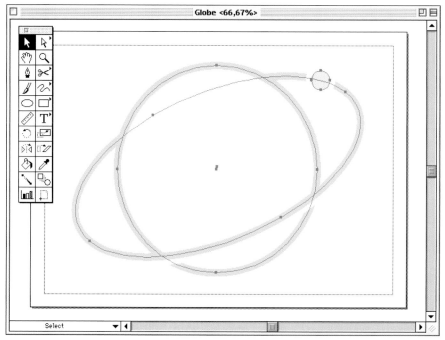

◀ The original logo drawing was designed and laid out in Adobe Ilustrator.

▲ The logo for the Internet Academy is clipped against a white background.

▲ Any disturbing transitions between the image and the background GIF are eliminated.

▶ Transparent Images

In Web page construction, a repetitive background pattern has consequences primarily related to the use of transparent images. When a Web page is loaded, the browser will display the background file last. The text and the images in the foreground show up first. As you can imagine, this loading sequence causes problems for darker Web pages that contain transparent GIF files. The light text and images become legible only after the background GIF has been completely loaded.

Luckily there is a remedy for this problem: Define both a background color and a background illustration in the HTML code.

The body line will then look like this:

```
<BODY bgcolor="#FFFFFF" background="globe.gif">
```

The sequence of bgcolor and background is not important. As an alternative to "#FFFFFF" you can also specify "white" without the pound (#) sign.

▲ By saving a copy of the GIF image as GIF89a ...

... it is displayed transparently in the background. ▶

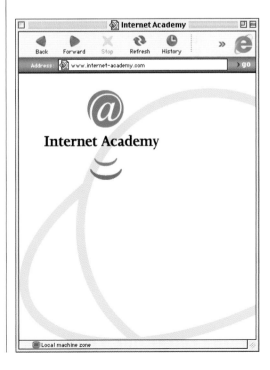

▶ **Background GIF Animation**

The arrival of fourth-generation browsers introduced an option that adds a new dimension to working with background images: Netscape Navigator and Microsoft Internet Explorer support GIF animations as a background image!

In the example on this page, a ball is made to appear to orbit the globe by changing its position in several steps. The motion can be created in a GIF animation drawing program. *(The technique is explained in the chapter called "Optimal GIF Animations.")*

The end result is an intriguing image. However, there are limits to this application. First, continuous movement in the background makes it more difficult for the reader to concentrate on the text. Furthermore, older browsers do not support this option and display an empty background, so it is advisable to run a "browser check"—a JavaScript with which you can identify various browsers. Version 4 or higher of a browser will display the background animation, while an older browser will display static GIF images. In the chapter "Programming with JavaScript" you will find more information about this important scripting technology.

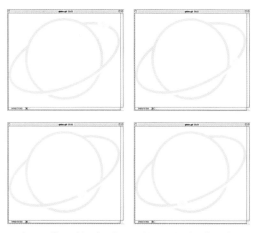

▲ The satellite orbits the planet. This is a simple effect that is not too distracting for the reader.

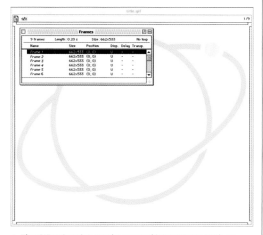

▲ The GIF animation can be created in programs such as GifBuilder or GIF Construction Set.

chipcard site (Chapter 17 Clickable maps/chipcard.html*)

Chipcardwise

Project status   Suppliers info
Standards   Calender
Helpdesk   News

<body> <img>

603 x 412 ▾   1K / 1 sec

Image, 20K	W	501	Src	wafer.gif		Align	Browser Default ▾	?
		H	301	Link			Alt	
	V Space		Target		▾	Border		Map...
	H Space		Low Src				Refresh	Edit

An alternative to standard text and graphic hyperlinks, clickable image maps allow Web designers to combine multiple links into a single image. In this chapter, you'll learn step by step how to create these maps and hear about the demands they place on Web servers.

Clickable Image Maps

When explaining to Web novices how to move from one site or page to another, you would normally tell them to click on the underlined blue text. This is the simplest and most common method of indicating hyperlinks. In practice, however, the linked text can appear in any conceivable color—and, in fact, many hyperlinks are activated by clicking on images rather than text. Some graphic links are recognizable because of their colored borders; with others, the cursor changes into a hand shape when the viewer moves the mouse over them.

And then there is a special type of graphic link called a clickable image map, a navigation tool whereby coordinates—or even an accompanying text—appear along the bottom of the browser window. Using clickable maps, Web designers can combine multiple hyperlinks into one image. This also reduces download times considerably.

▶ Standard Clickable Image Maps

A conventional clickable map consists of three components, to be installed on the server: an illustration, an <ISMAP> tag, and a map file. An HTML page contains the <ISMAP> tag, which indicates that the image is a sort of map pointing to hyperlinks based on coordinates. The map file is a separate ASCII document containing the coordinates and their corresponding URLs.

When a viewer clicks on the clickable map, a client-side program *(generally a cgi-bin interface)* sends the x and y coordinates to the server, where another program converts the coordinates to a URL. This hyperlink is then sent back to the viewer via the client program. The process may sound complex, but in fact it is quite simple. However, the conversion step can take time, and it's even slower if the viewer has a slow Internet connection.

Clickable image maps also mean extra work for Web designers: You not only must divide up the image, but also need to create the accompanying map. As the examples show, different programs can handle this task. Corel Painter, for example, allows you to generate URLs in the form of "Floaters" so that you can easily change them at any time.

▲ In Corel Painter, you can indicate a "Floater" as a clickable region and save it as an image map. ▼

In the program, you must choose between a CERN map and an NCSA map, depending on your server type and software *(see example figures)*; your service provider can determine which one is right for you. Also, note that you cannot test a standard clickable image map offline—that is, on your own computer.

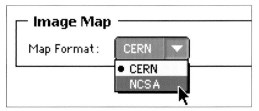

▼ Using Map This, a Windows-based freeware program, you can easily create a clickable map based on an image.

▲ In a conventional clickable map, only the coordinates are given, not the URL.

```
# Created by WebMap 1.0.1
# Format: CERN

default
rect (414,160) (493,189)  project.html
rect (393,124) (493,158)  standard.html
rect (356,91) (493,123)   help.html
rect (12,157) (174,192)   supply.html
rect (12,125) (174,154)   calender.html
rect (12,91) (174,123)    news.html
```

▲ The structure of a CERN illustration map clearly differs from that of an NCSA map. For both types you must send the text file to the server without using hard carriage returns. The latter is especially important for Macintosh users. ▼

```
# Created by WebMap 1.0.1
# Format: NCSA

default
rect project.html     12,91 174,123
rect standard.html    12,125 174,154
rect help.html        12,157 174,192
rect supply.html      356,91 493,123
rect calender.html    393,124 493,158
rect news.html        414,160 493,189
```

Adobe GoLive generates all required HTML code and presents it in a clear and comprehensible manner. The program uses different colors for the tag, the attribute, and the actual text, making manual adjustment to the code easier. ▶

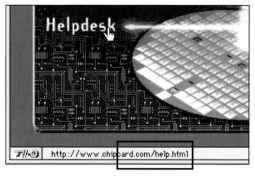

▲ The "hot spot" indicates where the user is going in a client-side clickable map using text.

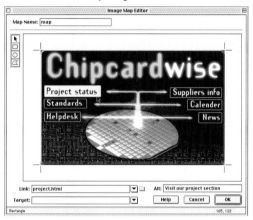

▲ Macromedia Dreamweaver's Image Map Editor is an ideal tool for creating clickable image maps.

▶ Client-Side Image Maps

Most modern browsers support *client-side* image maps, an alternative solution in which the x and y coordinates, normally contained in the map file on the server, are defined in the HTML page using the tag <USEMAP="name">, where *name* refers to an anchor containing the corresponding coordinates and URLs.

▶ Combination of Standard and Client-Side Image Maps

Not all browsers recognize or support client-side image maps, whereas Navigator gives them priority over standard image maps. In the examples shown, both solutions are used.

Combination of <ISMAP> and <USEMAP> ▶

The image wafer.gif is coded as a clickable image map by using the <ISMAP> and <USEMAP> tags.

The <MAP NAME="wafer"> ▶

The <USEMAP> tag is accompanied by a map in which the coordinates are determined by the COORDS attribute. The standard position —0,0—is the starting point, originating at the upper left corner of the image, so "10,93" means that the first coordinate series begins 10 horizontal pixels and 93 vertical pixels from the starting position. The next set of numbers, "201,123", indicates the width and height coordinates <AREA SHAPE> comes in three varieties: rect (for rectangle), poly (for polygon), and circle.
Note that all of these different coordinate types can be combined in one clickable map.

Text-Only Hyperlinks ▶

In this example, viewers can click on the text hyperlinks along the bottom of the Web page if the clickable image map does not appear or when server activity is slow. If your site uses clickable image maps, I highly recommend giving viewers this option.

```
<HTML>
   <HEAD>
      <TITLE>Welcome to Chipcardwise</TITLE>
   </HEAD>

<BODY bgcolor="green" text="#ffffff"
  vlink="#ffcc66" vlink="#ffcc33">

<BR>

<CENTER>
<a href="/cgi-bin/map">
<IMG SRC="wafer.gif" border=0 WIDTH=500 HEIGHT=300
ISMAP  USEMAP="#wafer"></a>

<map name="wafer">
<area shape="rect" coords="10,93,201,123"
  href="project.html">
<area shape="rect" coords="10,127,201,155"
  href="standard.html">
<area shape="rect" coords="10,159,201,191"
  href="help.html">
<area shape="rect" coords="317,91,497,124"
  href="suppliers.html">
<area shape="rect" coords="317,128,497,158"
  href="calendar.html">
<area shape="rect" coords="317,162,498,194"
  href="news.html">
</map>

<br>
<strong><font SIZE=+3>
<tt>All information about Chipcards</tt></font></strong>
<br>

<a href="project.html">Project Status</a> |
<a href="standard.html">Standards</a> |
<a href="help.html">Help desk</a> |
<a href="supplier.html">Suppliers info</a> |
<a href="calendar.html">Calendar</a> |
<a href="news.html">News</a>

</CENTER>

</BODY>
</HTML>
```

▲ In this design, the clickable map is successfully integrated. With client-side clickable maps, URLs can be tested locally on the HTML developer's computer, and Web sites can be viewed offline at fairs or exhibitions, for example. By contrast, a standard clickable map would give the viewer nothing to click on that produces a result.

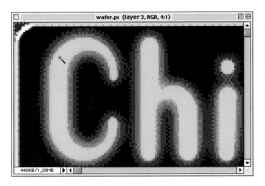

◄ You can achieve a clipped -corner effect by choosing strongly contrasting colors to make the image transparent. Here the effect can be seen quite clearly. ►

► The "digit GIFs" in a hit counter typically resemble the numerals on a car odometer, but the images here look like the LEDs that the Centre Pompidou in Paris uses to count visitors. The typeface is Futura Light. Each letter is placed in a separate layer and rendered semi-transparent by reducing the opacity to 35 percent. The glowing numeral has an opacity of 100 percent.

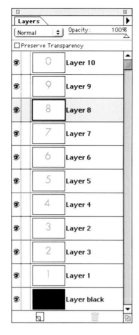

▼ Here the digit "8" is clear. The other numerals have been made semi-transparent.

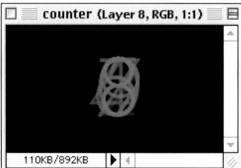

▲ In the digitdir folder, we replaced the old digit GIFs with LED-style images we created ourselves.

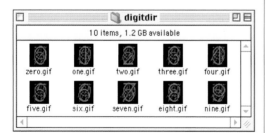

▲ This text on the home page lets you see how many visitors the site has had.

► Building in a Counter

To gauge the number of visitors to your Web site, you can of course use the server statistics. However, such information is too detailed and unmanageable for public viewing. A better method is to add a "hit counter," which increases the current page-hit count by 1 each time a viewer opens your home page. This provides a general impression of how many people have visited the site, without showing explicit usage data. If hit counts are low, however, this approach can be risky: The message "You are visitor number 12" makes a distinctly negative statement about a commercial site's popularity.

◄ Typical standard counter.

► Adjusting Graphics

The standard method for adding a hit counter to your Web site involves a few steps. First you need to find out the computer platform used for the site's server *(in most cases it will be a Unix or Windows NT system)*, then simply search the Internet for a suitable counter program. These are generally cgi-bin programs or PERL scripts that must be placed on the server. That will notify the server that you are signing up your Web page and that any hits will be counted by a service.

A set of "digit GIFs" usually comes with the software, but these images can be replaced by your own, as shown in the example. Include the following in the HTML code to define where the counter is displayed on your page:

```
<IMG SRC="counter.acgi?index.html" ALT="access counter">
```

Each time the page is visited *(or reloaded)*, the counter software automatically increments and displays the new number using the digit GIFs.

This page ▶
from the Dutch
multimedia
design agency
WDS was created
completely in
Flash. The
navigation is
enhanced with
emotion.

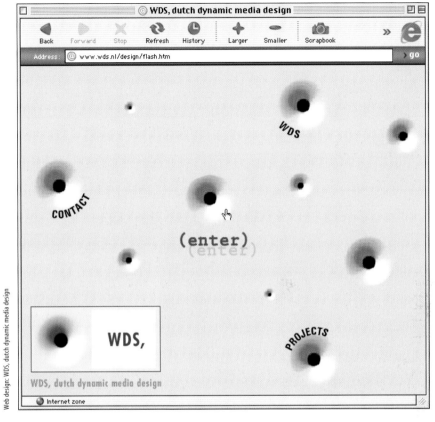

Web design: WDS, dutch dynamic media design

Surfing the World Wide Web is like trying to find a needle in the proverbial haystack. Even within a Web site one can lose track. Well-designed button bars, a clear structure, and clear navigation improve communication with the user.

Interactive Navigation on the Web

The image above shows how Web surfing sometimes leads to unpredictable results. Each button represents a hyperlink, which is a surprise to the first-time visitor. This element of surprise is used effectively by the design firm WDS in its experimental Web site.

A "normal" Web site, however, must be organized so that the visitor never loses track and can find his or her objective with as few mouse clicks as possible. For optimal management of this process, a button bar is an ideal tool for smooth navigation. After all, the electronic highway also needs some traffic cops. Well-thought-out design and clearly drawn button bars are the road signs on a Web site. And they deserve special attention during the design process.

▶ Standard Buttons and Plug-Ins

Button bars are an ideal navigational tool on a Web site. Not only do they simplify navigation between the pages, they also add a graphic element, making it feasible to add color and an individual style to the pages. Of course, the style and appearance of the buttons must fit in with the general graphic "signature" of the site. Consistent application of the button bar reinforces the Web site's identity, even when the user sends screen information to the printer. The creation of buttons thus depends on the design and imagery used in the site. If you have some freedom in this field, you can use a number of standard solutions to produce buttons. The plug-ins from Kai's Power Tools, offer virtually infinite possibilities for creating buttons of all types and sizes. These filters, which perform their creative magic in Adobe Photoshop and Fractal Design Painter, are tailor-made for creating cool buttons and navigation bars.

The facing page shows how a three-dimensional "NEW" button is created in Corel KPT Spheroid Designer, step-by-step.

▲ Corel KPT Shapeshifter offers many options for creating buttons that can compete with 3D programs.
▼ The final result is quite lifelike.

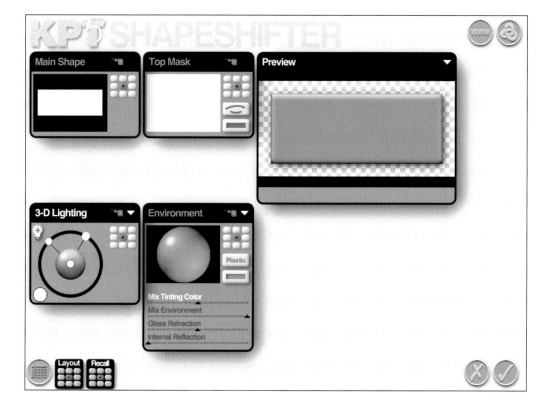

1 Using the MetaTools Sphere, a sphere is created with a somewhat lighter color range for more contrast with the ground shadow.

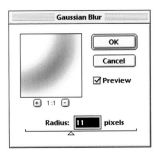

2 Once KPT Spheroid Designer has done its job, it is wise to save the selection in a separate channel and then copy it using the Option key. Fill in the selection with white …

3 … and assign to the information in Channel #4 an 11-pixel Gaussian blur.

4 Adding the ground shadow under the KPT sphere creates the desired effect.

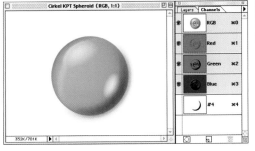

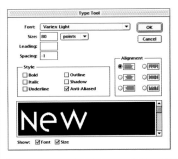

5 The word "New" is created in the Emigré font Variex Light.

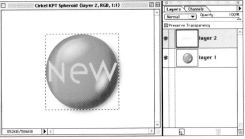

6 The text is sized to fit and placed in a separate layer.

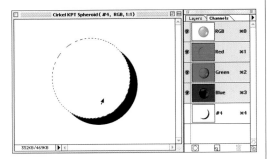

7 Editing the text layer with the Photoshop filter Spherize gives the lettering the desired three-dimensional effect.

8 The position of the text can be shifted if necessary.

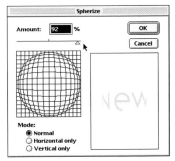

9 Then the layers are joined, and the entire creation can be reduced. This is simpler if you express the value as a percentage.

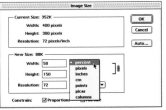

▶ Buttons That Appear to Be On or Off

By giving a button a three-dimensional appearance, you can create a typical multimedia effect similar to that in Macromedia Director CD-ROM productions. This technique is not only applied for its visual effect; the button's "position" also functions as a signal. In the image to the right you can see at a glance that the Help button is pressed in.

This method can be applied in Web pages just as effectively as in multimedia productions. With the help of Java or Macromedia Shockwave techniques you can even add sound and animation to the push button. Later in this book you will find more about this subject.

The "Glass design" buttons are based on a Letraset Phototone scan and are transformed into different color variations with the help of the KPT Convolver filter. Compared with the standard operations in Photoshop, this plug-in has the advantage that multiple variables can be displayed simultaneously in preview mode. For instance, you can sharpen a selection and change the color simultaneously.

And all of it is displayed in 15 simultaneous versions alongside the original, all in one window. This makes selecting the right choice much easier.

▲ The Help button is clearly activated. This sort of visual indicator is enormously helpful when navigating a Web site.

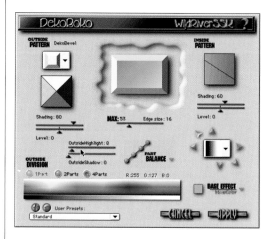

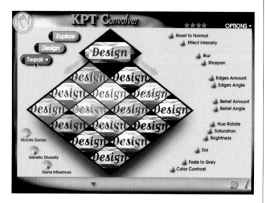

▲ The KPT Convolver filter offers a virtually endless number of variations on a theme. You can adjust the settings to view 15 variations at a time and work quite intuitively without missing any possible variations.

▲ By placing the text in a separate layer, you can create the individual buttons.

Text-Based Buttons

The process of creating the button can include the use of lettering. To illustrate this, we will create a real "forward" button. From the image elements that Painter offers, we select a flat gray button. We achieve a realistic text effect by using the Eye Candy 3.0 Cutout and Inner Bevel filters *(in that sequence)*.

The resulting text looks as though it has been gouged into the surface. A realistic 3D push button is created by adding a ground shadow as well. Combining this technique with JavaScript code, one can achieve a true rollover effect like the one the user is accustomed to seeing in CD-ROM titles. For the user this is a functional addition; the button provides feedback, which encourages more interaction.

If you wish to work with text that is white or another light color, it is advisable to place an extra text layer above the original and give this an opacity of 40%. The reason is that a single white or light-colored text layer does not come across as such—the background color seems to shine through. This effect is strongest when a light text style or a thin typeface is used. Placing a duplicate of the original layer with less opacity on top of it makes the text clear again.

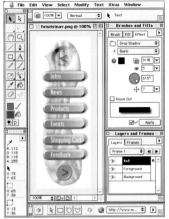

◄ Macromedia Fireworks is truly ideal for creating buttons and navigation bars. The program can create lettering that appears three-dimensional, complete with ground shadows, and you can still edit the text.

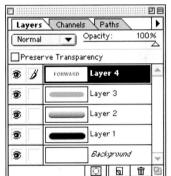

◄ Placing the designs in separate layers allows you to make changes and create alternatives efficiently. It's a good practice to always save a copy of the original.

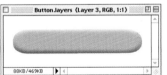

◄ The text is placed on the standard button from Painter.

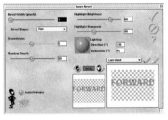

◄ Eye Candy is a filter set that makes it much simpler to create 3D effects.

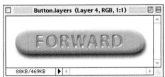

◄ With the Alien Skin filters Cutout and Inner Bevel you can achieve a realistic effect.

▲ A duplicate of the original layer clearly enhances the clarity of the text. ▼

▶ Button Bar Versus Separate Buttons

When multiple buttons have to be lined up, one is faced with a dilemma: Should this be realized in a single design, or does one make a separate GIF for each button? In the first case, a CGI bin command has to be placed behind the button row because a clickable map must be used with the corresponding X and Y coordinates.

Fortunately, the number of browsers that support client-side clickable maps is increasing, but when it comes to faster download times they cannot compete with separate buttons. And if the same buttons are used throughout all the pages on the Web site, the advantage is even greater.

The buttons are then retrieved from the cache and displayed on the screen at maximum speed. The difference in speed is clear because a uniform button row is not generally applied to the entire site. In some cases, however, you are forced to create a button bar as one complete unit.

The example on these pages shows what is possible when one really goes all the way artistically and creatively. This Web site was designed by Christopher Thomas, Eric Mathews and Simon Knight of the Bitmap Brothers for a renowned English computer game developer.

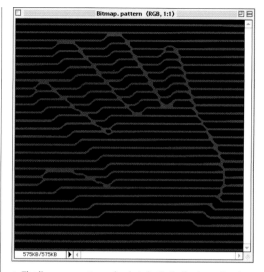

▲ The lines connect seamlessly in both the horizontal and vertical directions, creating a quite distinctive background pattern.

▶ Integration of Foreground and Background Information

Making the button bar semitransparent creates an intriguing effect on the Bitmap Brothers Web site. The buttons are strung together by a kind of "light thread," necessitating a clickable map. However, the result is impressive and gives the site a distinctive character. The integration with the line pattern in the background is the finishing touch on this attractive Web site.

The button bar ▶ changes on each page because the selected subjects are displayed dimmed. All button bars are drawn in 3D Studio.

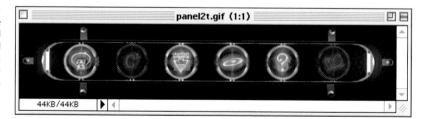

The black color is ▶ rendered transparent using the Transparency program. This creates the semi-transparent effect.

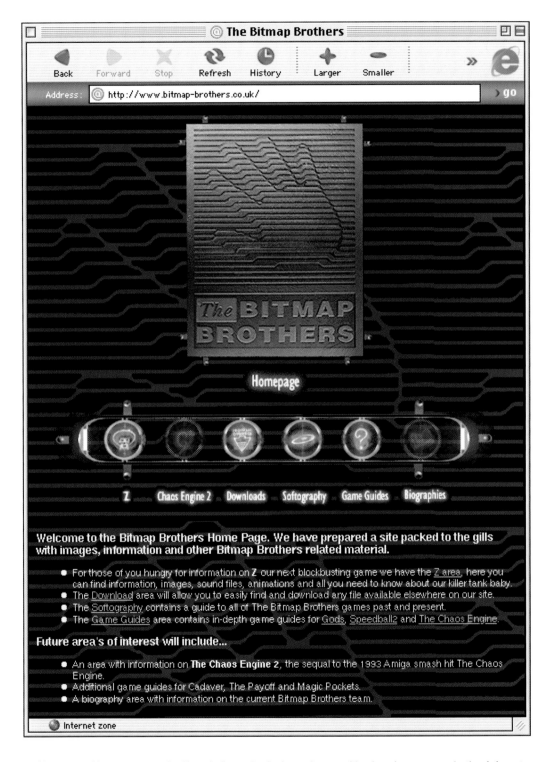

Welcome to the Bitmap Brothers Home Page. We have prepared a site packed to the gills with images, information and other Bitmap Brothers related material.

- For those of you hungry for information on Z our next blockbusting game we have the Z area, here you can find information, images, sound files, animations and all you need to know about our killer tank baby.
- The Download area will allow you to easily find and download any file available elsewhere on our site.
- The Softography contains a guide to all of The Bitmap Brothers games past and present.
- The Game Guides area contains in-depth game guides for Gods, Speedball2 and The Chaos Engine.

Future area's of interest will include...

- An area with information on The Chaos Engine 2, the sequal to the 1993 Amiga smash hit The Chaos Engine.
- Additional game guides for Cadaver, The Payoff and Magic Pockets.
- A biography area with information on the current Bitmap Brothers team.

▲ This page provides a great example of how the button bar both can play a graphic role and serve as a navigational element.

▶ Programming Languages and Navigation

Internet technology is developing at lightning speed. With the introduction of the World Wide Web and programming languages such as JavaScript, Sun's Java and Microsoft's ActiveX, a great deal of interaction between pages and page elements is now possible.

Moving buttons, highlights, windows, and scroll menus are all possible thanks to applets and scripts that can be added to HTML pages. The creative process of the future will demand ever more technical knowledge from the designer. The Internet public wants more and more interaction, which places increasingly stringent technical demands on the design.

The designers of the future will have to cater to these demands. The line separating creativity and technique is becoming less and less clear.

▲ Using a JavaScript script you can add a control panel to a Web site. The control panel is a separate browser window that opens automatically and functions as a sort of remote control. A Java applet ensures that the navigation buttons light up when the mouse pointer is placed on them.

"What a poser." ▶
This program
helps you to create
realistic-looking
figures. They can
play a striking
role in Web sites.

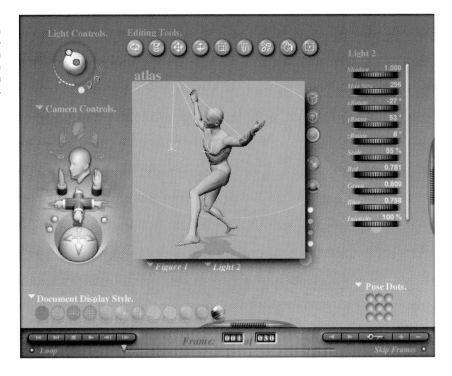

Suppose you want to place a few lines of HTML text at a specific location on a Web page—for instance, near the left hand in the illustration above. How do you do this? Simply by reading this chapter, which describes a special application of a transparent GIF image.

Aligning Text and Images

Despite the fact that HTML is a markup language, designers still want to be able to determine the exact positions of their page elements. In previous chapters you learned that a large number of environmental factors make this impossible, such as the Web browser's fixed width, the monitor resolution, and the standard font size. The only real alternative for determining the exact form of the page seems to be Acrobat's PDF.

However, you can also fix the location of text and graphic elements with HTML, by using tables wisely. This method is a bit more laborious and requires some knowledge of tables and their possibilities. The work method in itself is easy to explain: Place invisible GIF images in the layout so that the positions of all page parts and graphic elements are precisely specified. You will discover that this method offers many creative options.

▶What a Poser...

A 3D illustration of the famous Atlas figure has been created as a starting

point for a Web site in which the precise text position is crucial. To realize this drawing, we used a program that is tailor-made for this task: Curious Lab Poser.

The Atlas figure is one of the poses in this software's standard package. This means that the figure's pose—the position of arms and legs and even the curve of the fingers—is already specified in a model. Of course, the pose can be modified to your own taste, but as we want to reproduce the original figure as closely as possible, this will not be necessary.

The color of the figure and the surrounding light are more important in this case. The camera position—in other words, the point from which the figure is rendered—is also important for the composition. Since there is a red filament-like model of the earth in the program's library of stock illustrations, a "red Atlas" is an interesting option. When the model is lit with three variations of red lamps, the desired image emerges by itself. Poser has a clear preview window that quickly and efficiently displays the new spotlight colors.

The lighting accentuates the model's virtual muscles. Once you are satisfied with the pose, the model can be rendered. Then, in a montage in Adobe Photoshop, the Atlas figure and the globe are merged into one unit. To do this, you use a feature called a "layer mask." This prevents you from having to erase the original information—you create a layer mask in which the excess information is simply covered.

The layer mask is ▶ deactivated by clicking it while pressing the Command key.

◄ The Atlas is a standard figure from Poser's program library. The mask was made during the rendering process.

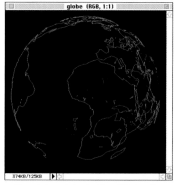

▲ The globe originated in a 3D-drawing collection.

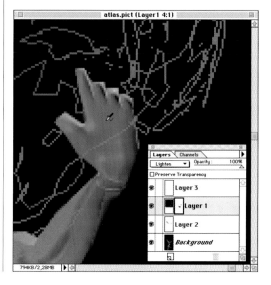

▶ Positioning Text and Image

The designer's intention here is to position the text, which also functions as a hyperlink, within the globe. The word "here" must be placed exactly next to the Atlas figure's right index finger.

Normally this is an impossible task in HTML—and yet it can be done! The trick is to create a GIF file that is only 1 by 1 pixel in size. Use a color that corresponds to the surrounding color—in this case, black. Then make the GIF image transparent, and save it with a simple name, such as "dot.gif."

You might be wondering, what do I need this GIF image for? Well, by using the <hspace> and <vspace> attributes, you can specify the horizontal and vertical spacing around the image. For example, if you want to have 50 pixels of spacing before a text line, the HTML code is as follows:

<IMG hspace=50 vspace=0 SRC="dot.gif">.

▶ Spacing Using Pixels

Now, by assigning each text line a specific amount of white space, you can position the lines exactly where you want them in the globe. You can structure the entire Web page by placing all the page elements in a table with specific column widths.

The rest of the logos are also saved as transparent GIFs and included in the HTML code. Under normal circumstances, the browser will display all this correctly and smoothly in one go. The 1-by-1-pixel GIF image goes immediately into the cache and will load extremely fast. If necessary, reloading the page will resolve all display problems.

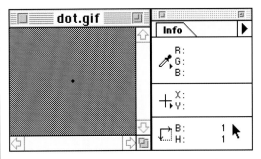

▲ The graphic is 1 by 1 pixel and has been rendered transparent.

▲ Thanks to the <hspace> value and the 1 by 1 GIF, you can place the text precisely within the globe's contours.

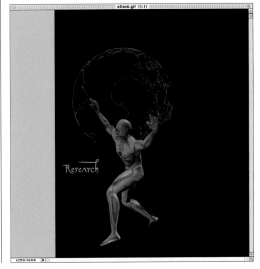

▶ **Invisible Alignment in HTML**

The HTML code on this page results in the image on the facing page.

Tag <BR clear=all> ▷

This left-aligns all the text again.

Displaying the Table Border ▷

The command <TABLE border=2> (temporarily) displays the border, making it easier to calculate the width and height. The <width=600> attribute determines the width of the entire table. The text column on the left side of the Web page is specified first. The tag <TD width=120> specifies the width of that column. The remaining 480 pixels are reserved for the second (text) column.

Aligning with "dot.gif" ▷

The vertical and horizontal space around the text lines is specified using the <hspace> and <vspace> attributes. The first text line in our example Web page requires the greatest amount of spacing on the left side; the bottom line needs the least spacing.

You can also assign a value to the GIF image by modifying the width:

<IMG SRC="dot.gif" width=16 height=80>

Because the width is only assigned to the image, the value is twice as great as with the <hspace> and <vspace> option. The reason is that the tag <hspace> places equal spacing to the left and right of the image. That makes the value twice as great.

```
<HTML><HEAD>
<TITLE>Corporate Intelligence on Multimedia</TITLE>
</HEAD>
<BODY background="atlas6.gif" text="#000000"
link="#ffffff" alink="#ffffff" vlink="#ffffff">

<IMG SRC="logo.gif">
<IMG SRC="corpkop.gif" hspace=12 vspace=2>
<br clear=all>

<TABLE border=2 width=600>
<TR>
<TD width=120>
<B>Seeing is believing</B><P>tekst

<A HREF="cim2.htm">
<IMG WIDTH=8 border=0 HEIGHT=14 ALT="arrow"
ALIGN=RIGHT SRC="arrow.gif"></a>
</TD>

<TD valign=top>
<IMG vspace=1 hspace=71 SRC="dot.gif">
<A HREF="cim2.htm">There are employees</A><BR>
<IMG vspace=8 hspace=57 SRC="dot.gif">
<A HREF="cim2.htm">within your
organisation</A><BR>
<IMG vspace=8 hspace=45 SRC="dot.gif">
<A HREF="cim2.htm">who are busy charting the
developments</A><BR>
<IMG vspace=8 hspace=40 SRC="dot.gif">
<A HREF="cim2.htm">and making plans to use
multimedia within</A><BR>
<IMG vspace=8 hspace=33 SRC="dot.gif">
<A HREF="cim2.htm">your business organization and
commercial oulet.</A><BR>
<IMG vspace=8 hspace=29 SRC="dot.gif">
<A HREF="cim2.htm">But how can you asses their big
plans and ideas?</A><BR>
<IMG vspace=8 hspace=25 SRC="dot.gif">
<A HREF="cim2.htm">Click <BLINK>here</BLINK>
for more information on the CIM meeting!</A><BR>
</TD></TR>
</TABLE>

</BODY>
</HTML>
```

Corporate Intelligence on Multimedia

Seeing is believing
Information technology shouldn't be a paper tiger. It can have immense impact on a commercial outfit, but results are hard to achieve if every staff-member starts its own virtual target group. Because the developments in this industry are ongoing and at the staggering pace, it is difficult to keep in touch with the latest online craze.

The program strives to keep the information accessible without all the mambo jambo full of techno speak and hard to follow high-tech nerds trying to communicate their wildest thoughts and technologies.

The CIM meetings
Next November the first CIM meeting will be held. Prominent speakers will give you insight in their thought process and will give you an idea of what the future has in hold for your company or organization.

Click on the arrow and go to the next page if you want to attend.

Multi Media Research Institute

Corporate Intelligence on Multimedia

There are employees
within your large organization
who are busy charting the developments
and making plans to use multimedia within
your business organization or commercial outfit.
But how can you assess their big plans and ideas?
Click here for more information on the CIM meeting!

Research

▶ Alternatives?

Instead of the <hspace=x> attribute, you could use <width=x>.However, this alternative has a negative consequence: A 1-by-1-pixel image will be interpreted by the <width=50> tag as a 50-by-50-pixel GIF file. That means that unwanted extra vertical space will be added. You can eliminate this problem by adding the attributes <width=50 height=1>. Conveniently, spacing is created only on one side of the image.

Keep in mind that the attribute <hspace=50> places 50 pixels of space on both sides of the GIF image. If you want use this trick to position an image or text precisely, you will have to find out how much space you need on the sides by trial and error.

In the example below, the next page of the "human figures" Web site, the text has been grouped next to the noble head of the thinker!

▶ Spacer Tag

With Navigator 3.0, Netscape introduced a special tag for setting horizontal and vertical

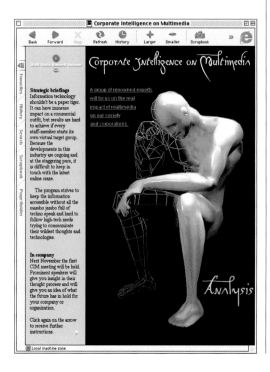

spacing. The tag is called "Spacer" and has attributes that create invisible blocks of spacing on an HTML page. The tag has a number of attributes that can best be explained using an HTML example:

```
<SPACER TYPE=horizontal SIZE=71>
<A HREF="cim2.htm">Within your organization</A><BR>
```

This HTML code creates a spacing of 71 pixels. The spacer tag is ideal for indenting text, because the alternative, the fixed space code ( ), specifies a relative value that is dependent on the typeface being used.

▶ Spacer Attributes

As you can see in the preceding example, Netscape used the <TYPE> and <SIZE> attributes. <WIDTH>, <HEIGHT> and <ALIGN>attributes can also be used. For instance:

```
<SPACER TYPE=vertical SIZE=10>
```

This results in a vertical white space 10 pixels high. This coding method can be used to create extra spacing between paragraphs. However, keep in mind that not all browsers support this HTML tag. To be certain, it is better to use the method with the 1-by-1 GIF image. Please note that many WYSIWYG HTML editors also use this technique to position the elements on the page—for example, Adobe GoLive and NetObjects Fusion.

Of course, with the help of style sheets you can also specify the exact distances. In the chapter "Dynamic HTML and TV browsers" this subject is covered extensively.

In an earlier chapter we discussed the fundamental concepts and work methods for tables (see "Basic Table Design"). We indicated that HTML code for tables is ideal for graphic applications because it gives the Web designer control over the page as well as the text and graphic elements it contains.

Seamless Tables

The image shown on this page can be created only by using table tags in HTML. Originally these tags were intended for organizing text, but they are also extremely well suited for positioning graphic elements.

These tags are not a generally accepted standard; Netscape has introduced a number of tags and Microsoft has also added extensions and applications to the table codes. In spite of the multitude of additional tags for tables, there is a basic set of table codes that most browsers support. The application shown in this chapter can be reproduced with these browsers without problems.

▶ Tags and Tabs

To illustrate the graphic possibilities a table offers, we created a Web site for a fictional electronic magazine, or e-zine, called Net New. The concept of the Web site is based on the metaphor of a virtual card file.

By clicking on the tabs, the user jumps to the selected subpage. To make the card-file effect as realistic as possible, five drawings were created whose tabs alternately appear in the foreground. These drawings were created in a PostScript program, Adobe Illustrator. The artwork for the five drawings can be quickly and efficiently by selecting and moving the individual tabs.

The drawings are then copied one by one and pasted directly into Adobe Photoshop.

The tab drawings are created in Adobe Illustrator in order to produce the five versions as simply as possible. ▼

If you first create a new document, Photoshop ensures that it has exactly the same dimensions as the PostScript drawing in the computer's memory.

If you select the Paste command, the program asks whether the information should be pasted as pixels or as paths. Select the first option, then choose the Anti-Alias option to avoid hard edges so that all five tab lines end up the same height and width.

First create a new document and then paste the copied
▼ information into it.

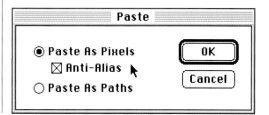

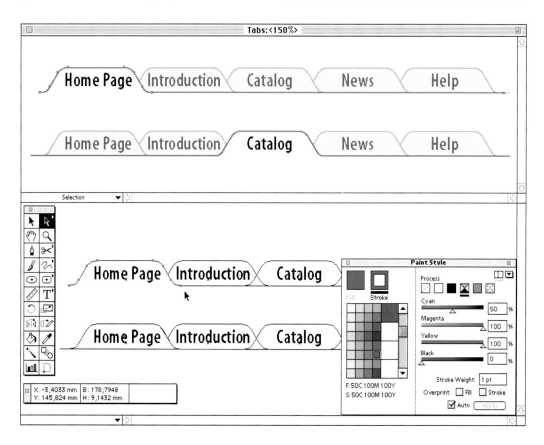

▲ Using the eyedropper tool, select each pixel that needs to be removed from the background pattern one at a time.

▲ The selected pixels are given the specified RGB value, resulting in an even tonal field.

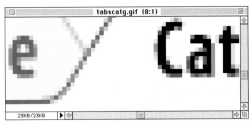

▲ An even tonal field is ideal for GIF compression.

◄ Choosing Similar from the "Select" menu causes all pixels with the same RGB value to be selected.

▼ Mind the Magic Wand tool settings to avoid mistakes.

▶ Color Correction

The next step consists of converting the Photoshop document to a GIF image. Save the GIF files to keep them small, first converting to Indexed Color and choosing 16 colors in the Indexed Color dialog box. However, disruptive patterns may arise in the background. Because the drawings are later made transparent, the background color must be even. To correct this, reopen the GIF files in Photoshop. *(Alternatively, you can do all this in one step, using the Save for Web command.)*

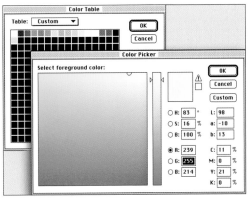

Now decide which color you want use for the background of your Web page. When you click on the colored area in the GIF, the correct RGB value is displayed. Jot down the value and select the magic wand tool. Then click on a pixel with the color you wish to eliminate. Be sure the tolerance is set to 0 and the Anti-Alias option is turned off. Choose the Similar option from the menu to select all the incorrect background colors. Then assign the correct RGB value to the pixels and you will

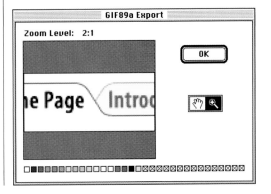

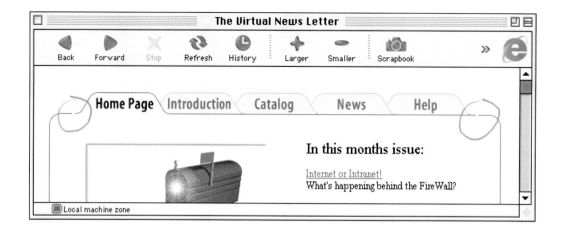

```
<HTML><HEAD><TITLE>*Net News* summer edition</TITLE>
</HEAD> <BODY BGCOLOR="#EFFFEF"><BR>
<TABLE border=2 cellpadding=0 cellspacing=0>
<TR valign=top>
<TD rowspan=3><IMG SRC="vertli.gif">
</TD>
<TD height=44 valign=top>
<IMG ISMAP border=0 SRC="tabscatg.gif">
</TD>
```

The two vertical ▶ borders are equal in height to the total table height. Jot these dimensions down in advance so you can include them later in the table code.

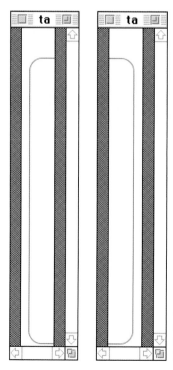

▶ Table Composition

As you can see in the example on the right-hand page, the Web page consists of five parts—five clickable image maps with the actual tabs, two vertical lines and a horizontal line connecting them. By creatively using various table tags, you can create a seamless whole. The manner in which the tags are specified in the HTML code is very important here.

If you type line spaces or hard returns in the table data, troublesome alignment problems arise. If the two <TD> tags are not on the same line, one or more pixels of white space will appear in the table between the table elements. Since we want to link the various table components seamlessly, we must make sure this does not happen.

It is also important that the height of the GIF files be included in the <TD> tags. This ensures that the central area *(No. 4 in the image above)* can be fully utilized. The attributes <border=0 cellspacing=0 cellpadding=0> must be included in the table tag if you want to be sure no seams are visible.

The Table function processes the table row by row. The attributes <rowspan> and <colspan> must thus be entered in this sequence as well. It helps to draw the table prior to coding. Tables demand a sound, well-considered approach!

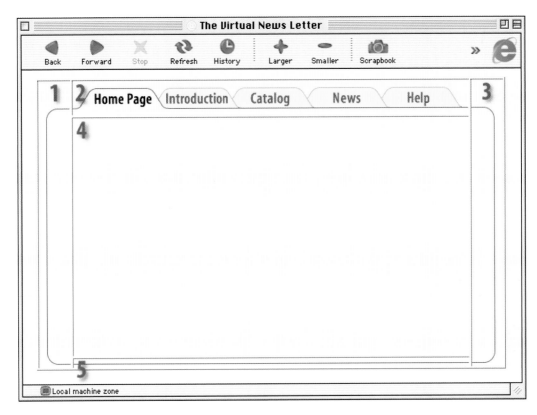

▶ Table Diagram

In this example the border is expressly assigned a value of 2 to make the page design clearer.

Tag <TD valign=top, bottom>

The attributes must include alignment instructions in the Table Data tag. These attributes may not be placed in the <TABLE> tag; otherwise the alignment does not work. The Table Data lines are typed in without extra spaces or hard returns to avoid "gaps."

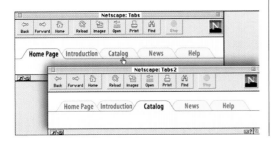

```
<HTML> <HEAD> <TITLE>Table</TITLE> </HEAD>
<BODY BGCOLOR="#EFFFEF">  <CENTER> <BR>
<TABLE border=2 cellpadding=0 cellspacing=0>
  <TR valign=top>
    <TD rowspan= 3><IMG SRC="vertli.gif"> 1 </TD>
    <TD height= 44 valign=top>
    <IMG ISMAP border=0 SRC="tabscatg.gif"> 2 </TD>
    <TD rowspan=3><IMG SRC="vertre.gif"> 3 </TD>
  </TR>
  <TR>
    <TD height= 240 valign=top> 4 </TD>
  </TR>
  <TR>
    <TD height=3 valign=bottom>
    <IMG SRC="bot.gif">5 </TD>
  </TR>
</TABLE>
</CENTER>
 </BODY> </HTML>
```

◀ You get real interaction between Web pages.

▶ Table with Fixed Widths

The Web site shown in this chapter will not encounter any problems when displayed in the various browsers. The reason is that each table cell has a fixed width because an image the same width as the cell is placed in the cell. It is more difficult if you want to specify a table cell without using an illustration. The following code is an obvious solution for this problem:

```
<TABLE width=600 cellpadding=0 cellspacing=0>
  <TR>
    <TD width=100> </TD>
    <TD width=400> </TD>
    <TD width=100> </TD>
  </TR>
</TABLE>
```

In practice, it turns out that a number of browsers will not conform to this display. The effect is unpredictable and, moreover, it differs depending on the computer platform!
A better method is to insert a copy of the transparent 1-by-1 pixel GIF image in each row and to assign this the width of the table cell. This forces every browser to honor the table and will not cause any negative effects when modifying the browser window. The new code is thus as follows:

```
<TABLE width=600 cellpadding=0 cellspacing=0>
<TR>
  <TD><IMG SRC="dot.gif" width=100 height=1></TD>
  <TD><IMG SRC="dot.gif" width=400 height=1></TD>
  <TD><IMG SRC="dot.gif" width=100 height=1></TD>
</TR>
<TR>
  <TD> </TD>
  <TD> </TD>
  <TD> </TD>
</TR>
</TABLE>
```

This PhotoDisc ▶ image served as the basis for the Web site shown in this chapter.

Placing a GIF or JPEG file in the background of the page can produce quite attractive results, especially if it is related to the content in the foreground.
The EyeSite Web site demonstrates how the two information layers in a Web page can be successfully synthesized.

Foreground and Background Integration

Anyone who surfs the World Wide Web occasionally sees Web sites in which the pattern in the background makes the textual information in the foreground illegible. In some cases the HTML programmer has done this deliberately; in other situations it is entirely due to the creator's lack of skill. The drawback is that many people start to doubt the usefulness of a background pattern or design. That is unfortunate, because placing a repetitive graphic image behind the information on a Web page offers many creative possibilities. Harmonizing the color and/or the pattern of the two levels enhances the value of the page. If this is done with discretion, it need not slow down the loading of the page. The result is a Web site with a distinctive character.

▶ Everything in Sight

The graphic concept of the EyeSite, an online optical center, was achieved by creatively utilizing the two information layers on the Web page. By displaying a specific pattern in the glasses' lenses sharply and at the same time keeping the repetitive background blurry, an appealing and intriguing image was created. The method used to accomplish this is explained step-by-step in the next few pages.

A stock photo from PhotoDisc was used for the image of the glasses. This extensive, good-quality image bank has a photo in its collection that was perfectly suited for this design: It is a digital photo of two eyeglasses frames, photographed against an even, beige background. The glasses will be used as clipped images, so we must first create a mask. Since the background pattern does not have an even structure, it is difficult to use the magic wand tool to create the mask based on a specific color selection.

Therefore, we will use the Quick Mask option in Adobe Photoshop. This tool is near the bottom of the Toolbox. Click the solid circle to activate Quick Mask mode. Alternatively, you can use the Q key on the keyboard *(Photoshop has shortcut key combinations for all its primary functions)*. Then select the paintbrush tool, and draw a mask over the glasses image. Photoshop displays the mask's

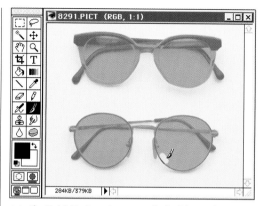

▲ In the Quick Mask mode, you can "paint" the mask over the original photo using the paintbrush tool. Varying the brush size will help you work more quickly. ▼

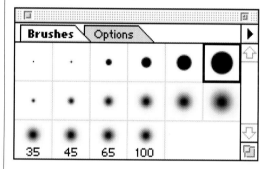

contours in the familiar red mask color. Vary the thickness of the brush stroke, drawing the edges of the contour with a fine line and then shading the large areas with a thick brush stroke. Each time you press the "]" key, the brush-stroke thickness is increased; the "[" key does the opposite.

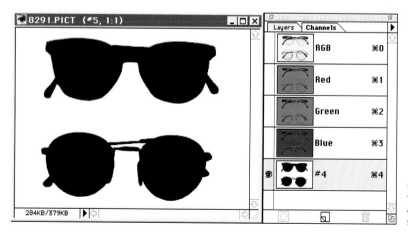

◀ Clicking the left-hand symbol at the bottom of the Channels palette automatically converts the selection to a mask.

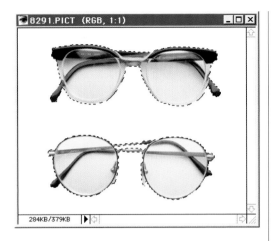

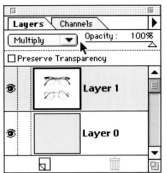

◄ By placing the clipped glasses in a separate layer above the background, you can use the Multiply mode to create a complete image in which the background becomes visible through the lenses.

◄ The background can be removed from the masked glasses by filling the inverted selection with white.

▶ Mask Plus Background

You can make corrections by inverting the paintbrush tool's color setting. If you place the white color in the foreground, the paintbrush tool functions as an eraser. You can select the color using the mouse or simply press the "X" key. Once the mask is ready, exit Quick Mask mode; the contours of the mask will be indicated by the marching ants. Then save this mask in a separate layer.

The background is created using a Painter pattern that starts off as blue. By applying the Color/Saturation option in Photoshop you can create a beige color while maintaining the original pattern structure. With the pattern file open, Select All *(command/Ctrl-A)* and choose Define Pattern from the Edit menu; name the pattern if you so desire and click OK.

Working in the main file, create a new layer beneath the glasses layer and fill it with the pattern *(Edit > Fill)*. Choose Multiply as the Blending Mode for the eyeglasses layer, and the intended effect is achieved— the pattern of letters is visible behind the glasses.

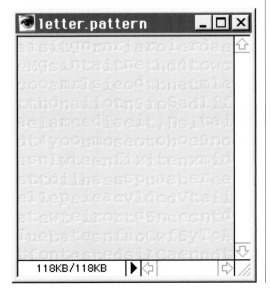

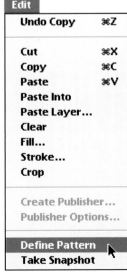

◄ Coloring the original Painter pattern beige creates the basis for the background of the Web site. To place this seamless pattern under the glasses as a background, select Define Pattern. You can then fill a separate layer with this pattern by choosing the appropriate Fill option.

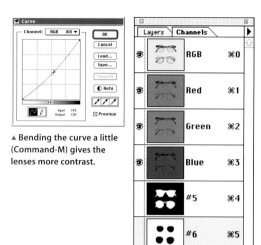

▲ Bending the curve a little (Command-M) gives the lenses more contrast.

Save a separate mask for ▶ the glasses in Channel #6.

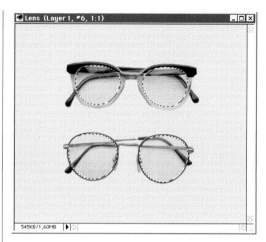

▲ Once the lenses are selected, they can be modified without having any impact on the frames.

▶ Adjusting Sharpness and Contrast

To enhance the effect, you can emphasize the pattern area visible behind the glasses. To do this, create a second mask in the exact form of the glasses. You can then use this mask to increase the contrast of the lenses.

The background must be edited in reverse order. In order to give the letter pattern a vague, somewhat blurry appearance, we are applying the Lens F/X filter of Corel's KPT 6.0 filterset. The unique feature of this Gaussian F/X filter is that it allows you to continually modify the lens setting and displays the result on the screen almost simultaneously.

You can then repeat the filter setting on the separately saved letter pattern, and create the blurry but seamlessly repetitive background.

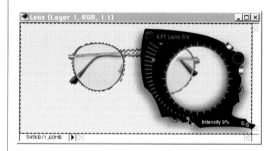

▲ Using the KPT Lens F/X filter, you can see the effects that Gaussian Blur creates.

▼ The two pairs of glasses are each saved as a JPEG file.

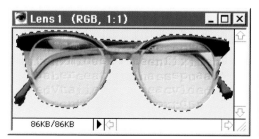

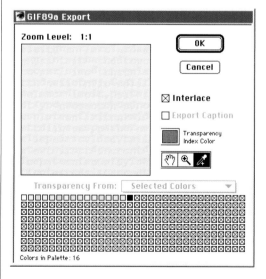

▲ The background pattern is exported in GIF format.

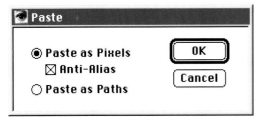

▲ The original PostScript lettering can be copied and pasted directly into Photoshop via the clipboard. ▼

importing the EPS file, you can also import the PostScript image via the clipboard. If you open a new file in Photoshop, the correct dimensions will have already been derived from the imported file.

Be sure the PostScript lettering is converted to Create Outlines. Otherwise, the letters will be deformed. ▼

▶ From PostScript to Pixels

Because the Web is based on styled documents, your typographic options are limited. Still, you can give pages character by displaying lettering as GIF files. The name EyeSite serves well as an example. The typography was done in Illustrator using the Emigré font Matrix Script. By specifying the image in pixels in Illustrator, you can switch between the programs to work on corresponding pixels. Once the lettering has been completed and selected as a font, the conversion to pixels in Photoshop can create considerable problems. It is much better to convert the lettering to Create Outlines first, and then export it. As an alternative to

▶ Seamless Montage

Since the lettering will be transparent on the page, it is important that the background color of the mask be the same as the color of the blurry pattern.

The reason is this: If the mask color is white, the lettering will always have an irritating white edge. If the mask color is beige, the edge will naturally be beige, but this will not be noticeable because the background pattern is also beige.

Saving the lettering as a 3-bit GIF-format file takes up the least disk space. It also keeps the loading time on the Web relatively brief. This image, with eight different colors, only takes up 2K of space.

◄ When the lettering is rendered transparent against white, an irritating white edge becomes visible around the characters.

◄ It is better to harmonize the masking color with the background color. This produces a seamless transition between foreground information and background structure.

▶ The Completely Laid-Out Page

In combination with the images on the previous pages, the HTML code in the adjacent column produces the result shown on the facing page in Netscape Navigator.

Colored Background <BGCOLOR=#> ▷

Adding the tag <BGCOLOR=CCCC33> to the <BODY> gives the page a beige hue immediately after the HTML file has been downloaded. Then the browser downloads the foreground information, and as a final step the beige background GIF is also displayed.

Table for Intro Text ▷

The introductory text with the two eyes on either side is placed in a 400-pixel-wide table. This prevents the text from appearing too stretched out if the reader's browser is set to the full screen width on a 17-inch monitor. The table also has a setting for displaying the borders.

Specifying Width and Height in <IMG> ▷

If width and height are expressed in pixels in the <IMG> tag, the browser will know how much space the image needs, which will enable it to immediately start displaying the additional information while in the process of downloading the image. Visitors will thus be able to read the Web page's text while the image is still being built in the space reserved for it by the browser.

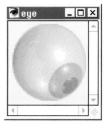

▲ The eye illustration was clipped and rendered transparent in a single action using the PhotoGIF plug-in.

```
<!--Copyright (c) Peter Kentie, peter@kentie.com-->

<HTML>
  <HEAD>
    <TITLE>EyeSite: Come and See us</TITLE>
  </HEAD>
<BODY BACKGROUND="letblur.gif"  BGCOLOR="CCCC33" >

<BR>
<CENTER>
<TABLE WIDTH=400 cellspacing=4 cellpadding=4
  BORDER=2>
<TR>
<TD ALIGN=CENTER >
<IMG WIDTH=60 HEIGHT=59 ALIGN=LEFT SRC="eyeli.gif">
<IMG WIDTH=60 HEIGHT=59 ALIGN=RIGHT SRC="eyere.gif">
<FONT SIZE=+1>
<B>Welcome at EyeSite</B><BR>
The website for people who spend more time in front of
their monitors than with their families...</FONT>
</TD></TR>
</TABLE>
<BR>

<IMG WIDTH=316 HEIGHT=92  SRC="eyesite.gif">
<BR>
<TABLE WIDTH=400 BORDER=0>
<TR><TD  ALIGN=CENTER>
Check out our models especially created for webmasters &amp;
HTML-programmers with an average workday of 10 hours.
</TD></TR></TABLE>
<BR><BR>
<IMG WIDTH=274 HEIGHT=106  SRC="bril.jpg"><BR>

Eyesite&copy; <B>Online Special</B> &#177;
<I>25 cyberbucks</I>
<BR><P>

<IMG WIDTH=274 HEIGHT=106  SRC="bril2.jpg">
<BR>
Eyesite&copy; <B>Geek look</B> &#177;
<I>55  cyberbucks</I><BR><P>
</CENTER>

</BODY>
</HTML>
```

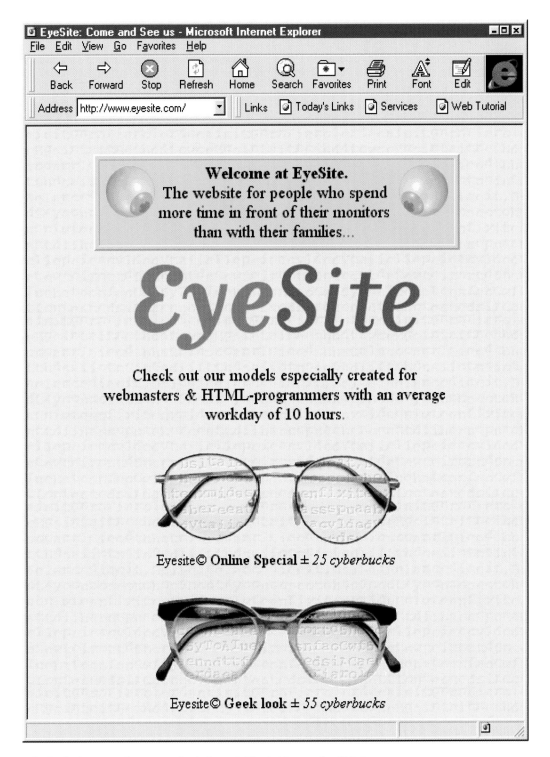

▲ The EyeSite home page has an attractive design and still only takes up a few kilobytes.

▶ Removing the Edge in Adobe Photoshop

If you use a colored background pattern, ensure that the logos in the foreground are made transparent with the same color. If the logo is clipped while on a white background, the illustration program will place a one pixel wide border around the image. This will look unattractive against the colored background—the background color must harmonize completely with the mask color of the foreground illustration. Fortunately, if this situation cannot be avoided or if you are using existing material that was created for different background, Photoshop has a remedy.

The procedure for deleting the edge with the "incorrect" color is as follows: Make a selection that comes as close to the pixel edge as possible. Since the background has an even color, the magic wand tool can be set to 1 pixel.

▲ When a setting of 1 pixel is selected, the magic wand tool can be used to select the background all at once. Then the selection has to be reversed to select the logo.

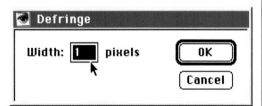

▼ After the logo is modified in Photoshop, the white pixel edge has vanished without affecting the rest of the illustration.

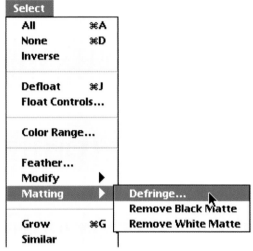

▲ Make sure the inside portions of all the e's are added to the selection. Then you can select the Defringe option from the Matting submenu.

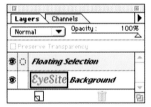

◀ If the Matting menu bar is displayed in gray, you must first float the selection by typing Command-J. A floating selection appears in the Layers palette.

Invert the selection, and select the inside of all the e's in the text. It is important to let the selection float by selecting Command-J. Choose Remove Edge from the Select menu. Give this a value of 1 pixel and click OK. The disturbing edge has now vanished!

A picture is worth a thousand words. This saying also applies to the World Wide Web, if in a somewhat watered-down version: the pixel size of an image can be a hundred times larger than that of a text file. And yet, both page elements can be combined perfectly on the same Web page.

Integration of Text and Image

The fact that the hypertext markup language is "only" a markup language is experienced by aspiring Web designers as a considerable disadvantage. The control one has over the images and the typography is still extremely limited. One can simply give up, or find a way—within the limits of the medium—to search for a sound graphic solution. Such a solution will never be the truly definitive method; the Internet is continually changing, and meanwhile the "big boys" in the graphics industry have become involved in expanding its possibilities. Until there is a definitive method, one must make do with the techniques that are currently available.

Cuisine

▶ Cuisine

This chapter demonstrates that a Web site can also be designed by carefully combining GIF and JPEG images. On some pages the typography is pure HTML code, and on others it consists of a GIF image. By consistently applying this method, you can create a very attractive Web site. Three GIF files are combined on the home page; the second page shows how a graphic element such as an initial can be simultaneously functional and appealing on a Web page.

The design is based on illustrations from the Top Drawers Art Library. These are high-quality drawings that are scanned in high resolution and are freely available for anyone's use. The product photos also come from a stock collection. PhotoAlto has tastefully photographed food items, and the photographs are available on a CD-ROM.

The image material is combined with striking typography. The headings are set in

▲ Remedy Double Extras is a very distinctive font.

the Remedy Double Extras font. This is a version of the Remedy font in which the letters are enhanced with decorative elements. By displaying the images and text in the same (green) hues, we can keep the GIF files relatively small because only a limited number of indexed colors are used. On the facing page is a test for finding the correct balance between quality and size.

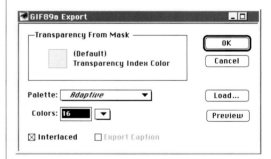

▲ The GIF export plug-in shows that 16 colors is sufficient.

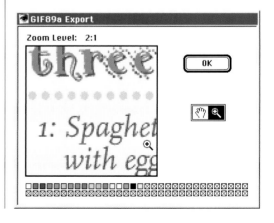

▲ Placing the lettering in layers makes correction simple.

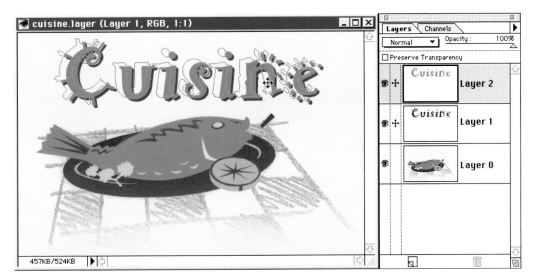

▲ The color-adjusted Top Drawers illustration is placed in the lowest layer. The typography is based on the same colors.

▲ The main illustration on the homepage, shown in 8 colors …

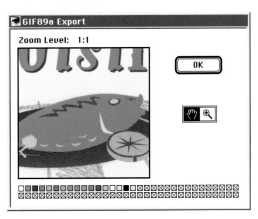

▲ … in 16 indexed 4-bit colors …

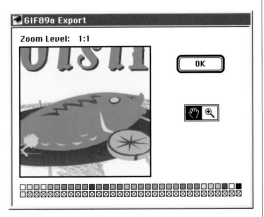

▲ … in 32 indexed 5-bit colors …

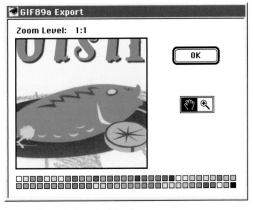

▲ … and in 64 indexed 6-bit colors.

▶ Layout with Table

The Web page consists of four parts:
- the large illustration, titled cuisine.gif,
- the two smaller illustrations, waiter.gif and text.gif, which are placed in a table,
- the footer with a hairline and contact links.

Tag <center> ▷

The tag <CENTER></CENTER> ensures that the complete page is always centered on the screen. Since the horizontal lines <HR> have a fixed width, the lines will always be neatly centered.

Tag <TD width=50%> ▷

The tag <TD WIDTH=50%> ensures that there are two cells in one row of the table, and each cell is half the width of the table.

Tag <FONT size=-1> ▷

The address line is displayed in a slightly smaller font size because the tag <FONT size=-1></FONT> is used. The closing tag <A HREF = MAILTO: "peter@pasta.com"></A> ensures that the browser can invoke the sender's e-mail address directly.

```
<HTML>
  <HEAD>
    <TITLE>Cuisine</TITLE>
  </HEAD>
<BODY BGCOLOR="#DEFFE7" LINK="#8A2A49"
  VLINK="#196A3E">

<center>
<IMG  SRC="cuisine.gif"  WIDTH=499 HEIGHT=312>
<BR><HR size=1 width=502 noshade><BR>
<TABLE cellpadding=0  cellspacing=0 border=0>
  <TR>
    <TD width=50%><A HREF="service.html">
    <IMG WIDTH=250 HEIGHT=300 border=0
      SRC="waiter.gif"></TD>
      <TD width=50%><A HREF="initial.html">
      <IMG border=0 WIDTH=250 HEIGHT=300
        SRC="text.gif"></A></TD>
  </TR>
</TABLE>
<BR><HR size=1 width=500 noshade><BR>

<FONT size="-1"><i>
For help<a href="help.html">click here</a>.
For feedback<a href="feedback.html">click here</a>.
For your comments:
<A HREF="MAILTO:peter@pasta.com">
anti@pasta.com</a>
</i></FONT>
</center>
</BODY>
</HTML>
```

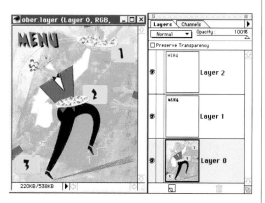

▲ The menu options are placed in separate layers.

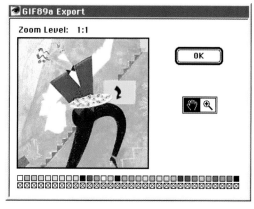

▲ The complete page has a distinctive character, and the file sizes of the images have still been kept to a minimum.

▶ Thin Initial

The second page of the Cuisine Web site is a combination of HTML text and a typographical GIF image. To build in a link between these two Web design extremes, we use an initial. The first letter of the body text is N. This is also displayed in the Remedy font. The version used for the initial, however, is Remedy Single, which is not as bold as the basic font.

Since the initial only consists of eight indexed colors, the GIF file can be loaded quite quickly. When the height and width of the image are included in the HTML code, the online visitor can start reading the text before the image is fully downloaded. The image of the basket comes from the PhotoAlto CD collection. To give the image an authentic Italian flavor, a special border has been used.

The image, called Photo/Graphic Edges Volume I, came from an Auto F/X clip-art CD-ROM and includes its own masking

◀ The decorative N in the Remedy Single font is created in a large font size …

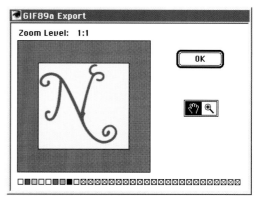

▲ … and saved as a GIF file in eight indexed colors.

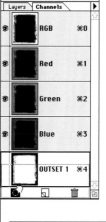

channel. Channel 4 is activated by selecting Load Selection from the Select menu or by dragging the channel to the Load Channel as Selection button in the Channels palette. After the selection is activated, the photo of the basket can be positioned.

▲ To activate the selection, drag Channel 4 in the Channels palette to the symbol on the left.

▲ You can achieve interesting effects with quotation marks if you save them in a separate GIF file.

▲ The original
PhotoAlto shot is a
1177-by-1552-pixel
CMYK file, scanned at 260 dpi. For the Web page the file is
reduced to 260 by 297 pixels at 72 dpi, the screen resolution.

▲ The selection is still active in the Photoframe file. The
reduced vegetable-basket image is pasted into the active
selection using the Photoshop option Paste Within. This
selection must remain active …

▼ …because the area around the edge must be converted
to the background color using the Select Inverse option.

▶ Paste Within

Before the photo of the Italian vegetable basket can be pasted into the Web page, its size *(and possibly its proportions)* must be adjusted to fit the open frame. The image, including the frame, will have a width of 250 pixels on the Web page. Consequently, the high-resolution PhotoAlto file must first be set to the correct proportions in Photoshop using the Image Size command.

Once that has been done, the entire selection is copied and the Photoframe file is again moved to the foreground. The selection is still active. It is extremely important at this point that you select the option Paste Within from the Change menu in Photoshop. The photo is now pasted in the active selection. By then selecting Select Inverse, you can modify the color of the area around the frame to match the page background.

▶ **Layout with <MENU>**

The second page of the Cuisine Web site is somewhat more complicated than the home page because it is a combination of HTML text and GIF and JPEG images.

Menu-Command ▷

The text is shifted away from the margin a bit by using the (appropriately named) <MENU> command. This distance has no influence on the initial drawing, which is specified in the code as initial.gif. As a precaution, all the file names adhere to the DOS 8.3 convention.

Good Beginning ▷

Remember to omit the first letter N from the text; otherwise the initial makes no sense.

**The Entity ** ▷

The   entity is used to indent the text in the second paragraph. In HTML this abbreviation stands for "nonbreaking space."

.

The <BR clear=all> Tag ▷

To be certain that the text is displayed below the horizontal line <HR>, the tag <BR CLEAR=ALL> is added. The width and thickness of the line are specified by the attributes <SIZE=1 NOSHADE>. The end result of the HTML code and the artwork discussed in the last few pages is shown on the facing page. Bon appetit!

```
<HTML>
  <HEAD>
    <TITLE>Cuisine: Italian cooking</TITLE>
  </HEAD>
<BODY BGCOLOR="#DEFFE7" LINK="8E2323">

<IMG SRC="cuisine2.gif" WIDTH=550 HEIGHT=242>
<MENU>
<BR>
<IMG SRC="initial.gif" WIDTH=130 HEIGHT=124
  ALIGN=left>
<IMG SRC="ingredient.jpg" WIDTH=255 HEIGHT=297
  hspace=8 ALIGN=right>

<FONT size=4>
ow look at our menu, the first thought that comes to your
mind will be: 'just another Italian restaurant on the world
wide web'. But that is not the whole truth; we at Cuisine
on-line have a good selection of fine Italian foods and
beverages you can order on-line with your credit card.
Keep it near by for your administration.
<BR>
    All our recepies are unique,
especially our world famous pasta sauces in which we put
original ingredients, not factory-made sauces and chemi-
cals... So <A HREF="order.html">make your choice</A>
and we will <A HREF="deliver.html"> deliver</A> your
Cuisine order anywhere on this planet right on your
doorstep! Would you believe that?
<P>

</FONT>
<HR size=1  noshade>
<BR clear=all>

<FONT size=-1><i>
For help<a href="help.html">click here</a>.
For feedback<a href="feedback.html">click here</a>.
For your comments:
<A HREF="MAILTO:peter@pasta.com">
anti@pasta.com</a>
</FONT>
</menu>

</BODY>
</HTML>
```

CLASSIC ITALIAN COOKING

For those of you who think Italian cooking is just pizza, pasta and tomatos here's a surprise: Cuisine Restaurant not only offers the ordinary but also a choice of highly appreciated specials!

ow look at our menu; your first thought will probably be: just another Italian restaurant on the Web. But you would be wrong. We at Cuisine On-line have a wide selection of fine Italian foods and beverages you can order on-line with your credit card. Keep it close at hand for your records.

All our recipes are unique, especially our world-famous pasta sauces, which only contain natural ingredients, no factory-made sauces or chemicals... So make your choice and we will deliver your Cuisine order anywhere on this planet, right to your doorstep. Would you believe that!

For help click here. For feedback click here. For your comments anti@pasta.com

▲ The Cuisine pasta Web site is ready. Now all they have to do is organize the worldwide distribution....

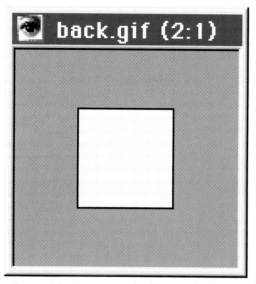

▲ A separate background image is added to each Web page.

▶ Background Image

To ensure that the background color is identical on all computer platforms, you can add a separate background file. In some browsers a hexadecimal color is frequently changed to a more appropriate color value. This creates differences between the colors of imported images and the background color of the Web page. These color deviations can be avoided by adding a background file with the same color value as the other images.

Look closely.... ▶
Where does the
background
pattern end and
the foreground
illustrations
begin?

Normally, combining the foreground and background information on a Web page is not a problem. However, it is more of a chore if you want to use a shadow in the foreground and a pattern in the background on the same page.

Shadow and Pattern in HTML

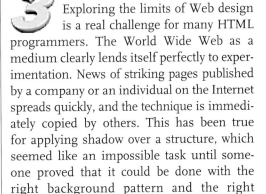

Exploring the limits of Web design is a real challenge for many HTML programmers. The World Wide Web as a medium clearly lends itself perfectly to experimentation. News of striking pages published by a company or an individual on the Internet spreads quickly, and the technique is immediately copied by others. This has been true for applying shadow over a structure, which seemed like an impossible task until someone proved that it could be done with the right background pattern and the right image-editing skills.

The trick is to do it effectively without visible seams and disturbing transitions. The combination of the correct background structure and a bit of craftsmanship in the area of image editing produces the result.

◀ Corel Painter has all the functionality the Web designer needs.

Corel Painter is used ▶ for this chapter. First, a background color and corresponding paper background pattern are specified.

▶ 3D Lettering in Painter

Corel Painter is an ideal package for achieving the intended effect when applying shadow over a structure. This program offers a large number of standard patterns and structures, varying from paper to Scotch plaid patterns. For this Web site design we chose a simple paper structure and a mauve background color. Painter contains quite an extensive library of backgrounds. The accompanying CD-ROM contains even more versions. However, Painter is also an ideal program for creating realistic three-dimensional text effects.

The basis of the illustration is lettering created in the Chelsea Bold font. This font comes from the Fontshop's beautiful Fontfonts collection. Click the A symbol to select the text tool. Painter displays a floating window in which the font type and size as well as the spacing can be specified.

The text can now be typed directly on the background pattern; it is in the familiar marching ants display.

▶ Masking the Text

Now we come to an important phase: specifying the mask. With the text selection active, choose the Shape Selection tool and select the text outlines. Then use Shapes > Convert to Selection in order to use commands like Feather and Apply Surface Texture. Choose a feathering of approximately 6 to 7 pixels using Select > Feather.

The program calculates a feather radius of the specified number of pixels for each letter selected. Keeping the selection active, select Surface Control > Apply Surface Texture from the Effects menu in the main menu bar. This option offers a multitude of possibilities. You simply have to try them all out at some point. To create the 3D effect, select Mask in

The words are typed in ▶ Chelsea Bold on the paper background pattern in a large font size. A feathering of 5.7 pixels is set in the Path Adjuster window. Painter then calculates the soft contour around the letters. The selection must be kept active.

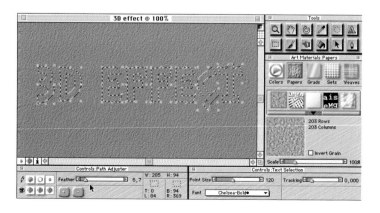

the Using pull-down menu. In the Preview window you immediately see the consequences of this action:

The text appears to rise from the background, creating a sort of raised effect. The degree of this effect is determined by the Material and Light Controls settings. After a bit of experimentation, you will be able to produce the illusion of depth with a clear contour and sufficient contrast. Click OK, and Painter returns to the main window.

▶ Background Shadow

The selection must remain active because we are going to separate the lettering from the background pattern. Before doing this we must undo the feathering. This is extremely important, since the value set earlier still applies and thus will influence the copy process later. So drag the sliding bar in the Controls: Path Adjuster back to zero, and copy the selection.

For the Web page, we use a neutral background against which the 3D lettering will stand out best, both literally and figuratively. Paste the copied lettering in the new drawing area, but keep the selection active because we will add yet another shadow under the lettering to further enhance the illusion of three dimensions. Painter has a special filter for this called Drop Shadow. Select a 5-pixel offset and a coverage of 100 percent, and then witness the perfect illusion: floating three-dimensional lettering.

Of course, this method offers an infinite variety of possibilities, since you have other interesting filters at your disposal as well, such as the one for lighting effects. Illustrators who are more comfortable with Adobe Photoshop can easily switch to this competing painting package while retaining all the layers and mask information from Painter. To do this, save your drawing in Painter as a Photoshop file. The floating selection is displayed in the Photoshop Layers palette as Floater.

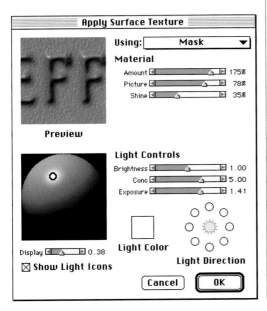

◀ The text appears raised, as it were, thanks to the Mask option.

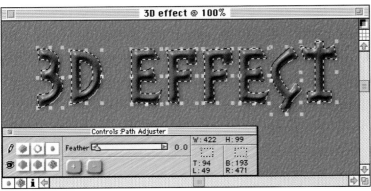

◀ It is important to set the feathering back to 0.0; otherwise, the blurry edge is copied. We want the background shadow to be applied only to the three-dimensional lettering.

A shadow is ▶ applied to the copied selection in Painter by selecting the standard Drop Shadow function.

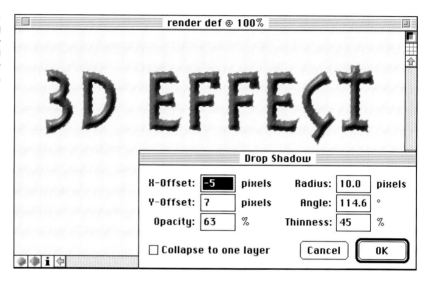

The result is ▶ "lifelike" 3D lettering with an exceptionally realistic shadow.

If the Painter file is ▶ opened in Photoshop, the layers are read separately. However, the naming convention is different from that used in Photoshop.

▶ Unusual Patterns

If you combine the GIF image of the shadowed lettering with the corresponding background GIF, this can produce surprising results in the Web browser. If you use a fine pattern for the background pattern, the tran-sition between the lettering and the pattern will be virtually invisible. This makes the illusion complete.

However, if you use a rough pattern, it is much more difficult to avoid a visible tran-sition. In the upper example on the right,

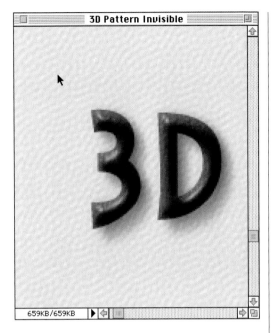

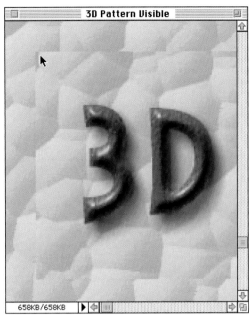

the foreground illustration clearly stands out from the background. That is not very appealing. Another disadvantage of using a pattern that contains too many colors is that the GIF colors in the foreground and background are difficult to harmonize with one another. Only by using a special color table can you contain the damage. One way to harmonize the color tables is to use DeBabelizer or Adobe Photoshop.

▲ A pattern that is too rough is more likely to reveal disruptive seams.

▶ **Image Resolution and Size**

The exact position of the GIF image depends on external circumstances: the size of the user's font, the width of the screen, and the monitor resolution. This is especially important for Windows computers. Since a 17-inch monitor can operate in a variety of

▲ The digital photo is selected with a generous margin.

▲ Then the desired Quick Mask is selected, and the filter is applied.

resolution modes, the Web page can be displayed in different sizes. In the example on this page you can see that it is possible to position an illustration seamlessly against a comparable background. The image contour is barely visible where the cursor is pointing in the following image.

▶ **Editing Images**

Perhaps fitting a 3D text against a background seamlessly does not seem all that difficult, but what happens when we place an image against a structured background pattern?

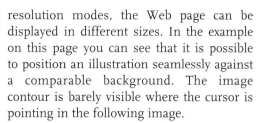

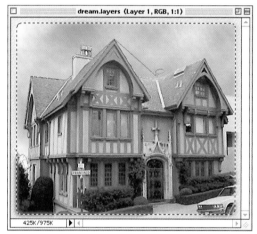

▲ The lasso tool from the work set is used to reduce the image selection.

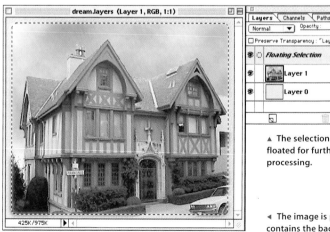

▲ The selection is floated for further processing.

▲ If you deselect the selection, you can undo the mask by adding pixels with the brush tool.

◀ The image is pasted into a new image that already contains the background pattern.

▲ If the excess area selected is removed …

▲ … a bit of correction is still required. The final photo is saved as a 6-bit dithered GIF file. ▼

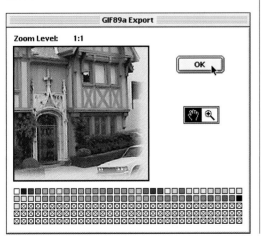

The answer to this problem is not hard to guess. It requires a bit of fiddling in Photoshop and the use of a Quick Mask, but as you can see on this and the following page, the result is impressive.

This example uses a photo of a house in San Francisco. Because the photo's edges must melt into the background, we use a Gaussian Blur of 5 pixels to make the image's contours invisible.

▲ The text is edited using the same method.

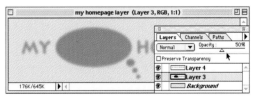

▲ The shadow is created by reducing the opacity of the original black image by 50 percent.

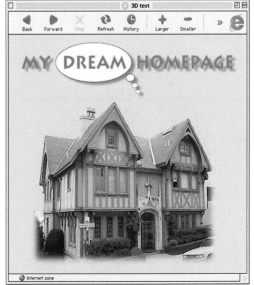

▶ Image Editing

While the Quick Mask option is still active, copy the image and paste it in a new document that is already filled with the background pattern. Now you can delete extra pixels from the photo using the lasso tool. If you simultaneously keep the Option *(Mac)*/Alt *(Windows)* key pressed, the lasso is easier to control. Click along the contours of the house, and the image will be separated from the selection. Once you are satisfied with the result, select the option Flatten Image, and the montage is complete.

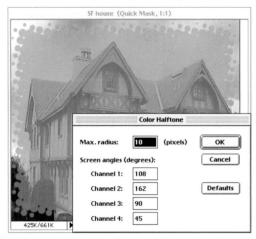

▲ The Quick Mask is used in reverse for the Color Halftone filter. A radius of 10 pixels produces a good result. The total effect is convincing when displayed in the browser. ▼

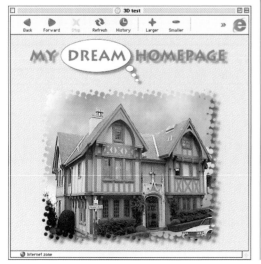

The Children's Zoo ▶ Web site is an ideal subject for demonstrating Corel Painter's creative possibilities.

Corel Painter is the undisputed king of creative image-editing programs. You can also use this program to create backgrounds. The end results are as distinctive as the method used to create them.

Corel Painter: Image Hose and Patterns

Painter distinguishes itself from other creative drawing applications not only in terms of its interface, but also in terms of the impressive speed with which its capacities are expanded. Nowadays it is even possible for multiple users to work on the same drawing in Corel Painter over the Internet. That is truly creativity without borders!

In this chapter we focus on two of the program's strong points. First we create a pattern based on a cartoon figure. Then we show how to create a background based on the various animal drawings, using the Image Hose technique. The result is shown on this page.

▶ Random Color Replacement

Six animal drawings serve as the basis for the background patterns. These are all drawn in Macromedia FreeHand using PostScript vectors. The line drawings are based on original pencil sketches that were converted into outline in FreeHand. However, these basic drawings are created in black and white. That is not suitable for a Web page, and a children's zoo certainly demands a more colorful approach.

Rather than manually coloring each illustration, you can automate this process. An ideal tool has been created for this: the Random Color Replace module in Extensis DrawTools. I love using this filter because it was developed at my personal request by the programmers at Scarlett Graphexx. The version that currently comes with DrawTools can be used to color the entire document or only selected objects.

Since each animal figure in our example is colored separately, Random Color Replace is a welcome addition for tasks such as this. If the Random Color Replace filter does not

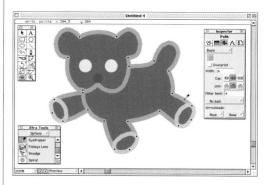

▲ DrawTools can also color parts of a drawing.

produce optimum results the first time, you can simply apply it again to the selected outlines. Once you are satisfied with the color selection, you can edit other similar elements in the drawing as shown above.

▲ The FreeHand illustration ready for the application of DrawTools.

▲ The final result of the Random Color Replace filter.

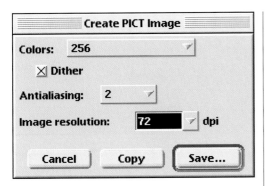

▲ FreeHand can convert a vectorized PostScript drawing to a dithered PICT file at a screen resolution of 72 dpi.

In the Fill window you can specify the transparency of the ▶ pattern in precise percentages in the Fill window.

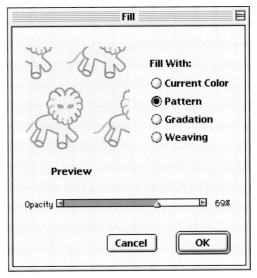

▶ Rasterizing PostScript

Macromedia FreeHand allows you to save the PostScript drawings you created in the program as bitmaps. Since the animal drawings have been edited in Painter, we select the PICT format for the export file. The drawing is rasterized at 72 dpi. A new 200-by-200-pixel file is created in Painter. The rasterized drawing is then opened in Painter and one of the animals is selected.

The frame around the lion can be drawn randomly. If we use the Capture Texture technique in Painter, the distance around the actual drawing will not affect the pattern ultimately made from it. This is thus an ideal method for generating a pattern quickly. The pattern can also be saved as a background file. You need not worry about making the tile seamless. Painter handles that for you!

▲ Once the pattern is created, you can specify and adjust the relationships between the image elements separately.

◀ The pattern is visualized in the floating palette.

▶ Creating Patterns

Once a pattern is created and stored under an appropriate name, you can select the Pattern option. The pattern you just saved appears in the Art Materials: Pattern window with the name and the size. Since the sample pattern has been considerably reduced, the size is 22 rows by 24 columns. The Offset and Scale settings can still be modified, after which Painter again calculates seamless tile elements.

After the pattern has been saved, you can also use the separate Apply Surface Texture filter in combination with the pattern. By selecting the light source and manipulating the material settings, you can create quite distinctive effects. The final result is a seamless repetitive pattern, which can contribute greatly to a Web page's attractiveness.

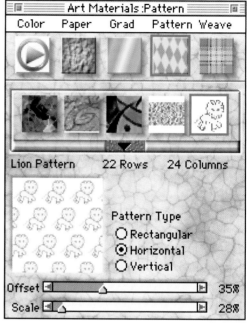

▲ The settings appear when the pattern with the Lion icon is selected.

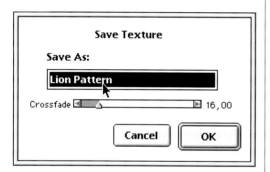

▲ The pattern must be saved with a unique name.

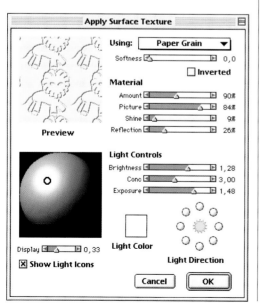

▲ The test pattern clearly displays the possibilities.

The individual ▶ drawing elements must be clipped one by one and then masked.

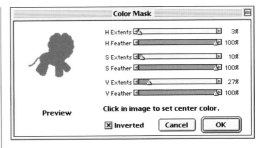

▲ You can also draw masks in Painter based on the colors used in the drawing element and the background. Add or remove colors from the mask by moving the slide controls.

The addition of ▶ shape options in Painter greatly expanded the Tools palette.

▶ Producing an Image Hose

One unique drawing option in the Painter program is the so-called Image Hose. This allows different drawing elements to be positioned in the illustration using a pressure-sensitive brush. With this technique you can create patterns that cannot be created in any other manner. However, the Image Hose has

one disadvantage: It is fairly difficult to use. Therefore, this chapter describes the technique step-by-step, so that you not only get an idea of the possibilities, but can also apply them to your own pattern or background structure.

Separate drawing elements are the basis of each Image Hose. In our example, the individual animal drawings are used to produce one Image Hose setting. One condition for this is that all graphic elements must first be masked and converted into floaters.

Once the six ▶ animal figures have been masked, they can be placed in the list as numbered floaters.

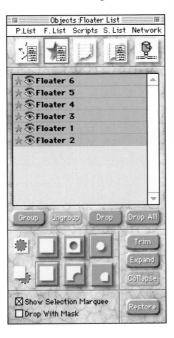

◀ To create your own Image Hose, you must group the floaters.

▶ Grouping

An Image Hose can only function if the individual drawing elements are first grouped in the Floater List. You do this by selecting all the floaters using the Shift key, and then clicking Group in the Objects: Floater List window. The designation Group 1 now appears above the floater names. Be sure this text is selected and then open the Brushes: Image Hose window. The third submenu is called Nozzle; click it and hold down the mouse button until the Nozzles menu appears. Select Make Nozzle From Group, and Painter immediately calculates the Image Hose. Painter uses both Nozzle and Image Hose for exactly the same technique.

To apply the Image Hose, it must first be saved under its own name. We have chosen Animal Nozzle and now we save the new Image Hose as a RIFF file. This is Painter's native file format. The file can still be edited or modified before the Image Hose is applied.

The extent to which the Nozzle is used depends on factors such as pressure sensitivity and the angle at which the Brush Control is set. Select the Nozzle option, and the basic settings for our Animal Nozzle are shown in a separate window. You can specify the order of the different effects.

▼ Painter uses its own file format called RIFF for the nozzle.

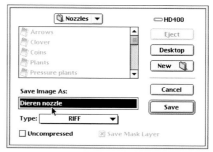

▲ Convert the grouped floaters to a Nozzle with the Make Nozzle From Group option.

▲ The Nozzle is saved with a preview of the drawing elements and can easily be modified.　▶

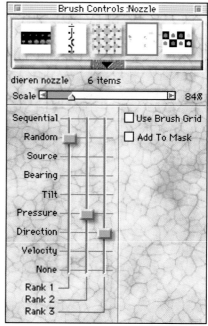

◄ The first attempt with the new Animal Nozzle cannot be called a success; it is too crowded and too dark.

The Image ► Hose has a characteristic icon.

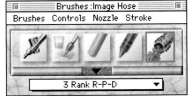

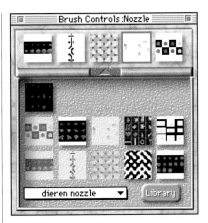

► Pressure Sensitivity

Your first cautious attempts with the new Image Hose may well result in a chaotic jumble of cartoon figures on the screen. It is clear that the Nozzle settings must be adjusted and the pressure sensitivity must be greatly reduced.

▲ Painter displays the various Nozzles using miniature icons, which makes them easier to select.

▶ Reducing Colors and Pressure

Reducing the settings for the Nozzle and adding a white layer on top of the drawing makes the image much more manageable. In a new 200-by-200-pixel window you can experiment to your heart's content. By defining this area as a Pattern, you can create a repetitive tile from it and save it as an indexed GIF file.

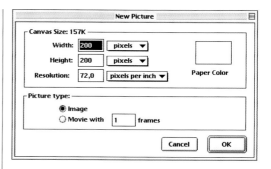

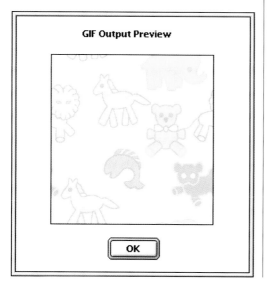

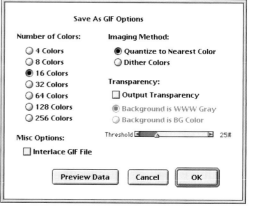

▲ The definitive tile is saved as a GIF file with 16 indexed colors. Be sure to turn off the Interlace GIF File option. The tile pattern is used in the <BODY> section of the Web page, so it is better not to interlace it.

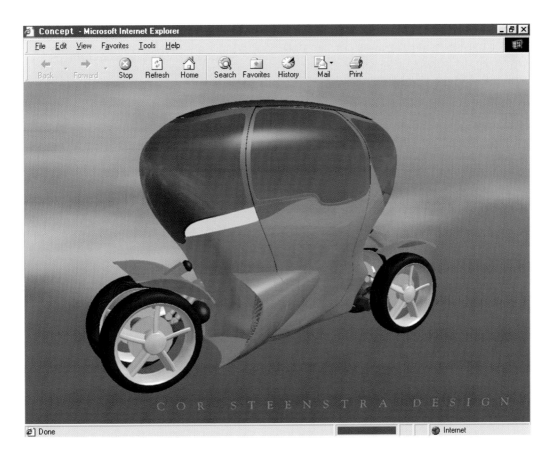

This chapter describes an alternative method for enhancing Web pages using picture frames. Realistic slide frames make the photos more attractive.

Creative Picture Frames

A Web site completely devoted to "concept cars" requires pages with a distinctive and attractive appearance. To accomplish this, one can use interesting photos of creations on wheels. However, if these images are placed on the page without any enhancement, the intended effect is not entirely achieved. The whimsical shapes of the autos demand something extra—a frame that not only accentuates the image, but also indicates that these are models.

Cor Steenstra's models may never be seen on the road. Thus their place on the digital highway deserves a different approach. Decorating the images with typical photo and slide frames makes the models appear a bit more realistic. For the site visitor, this increases the company's professional aura.

▶ **Polaroid Frame**

The first image displayed on the Concept Cars Web site home page is a creation by Cor Steenstra Design called Quad. The idea for the design was to create a vehicle that is a hybrid between a car and a motorbike.

The driver enjoys the comfort and protection of a conventional car. The name Quad refers to the fact that the model has four wheels and is thus more stable than a regular motorbike. To emphasize the futuristic character, we have elected to create a sort of Polaroid photo—a "snapshot" from the future.

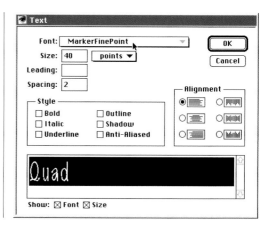

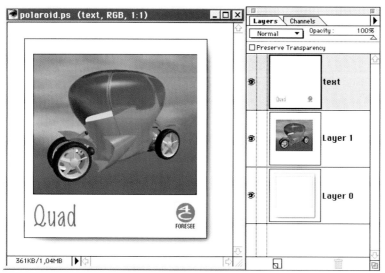

▲ The text and the 4C logo, short for Foresee, are placed
◀ in a separate text layer.

▼ Using the Curves command, you can increase the contrast.

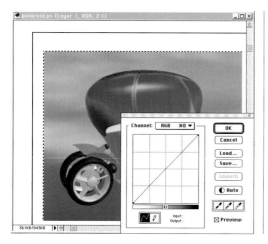

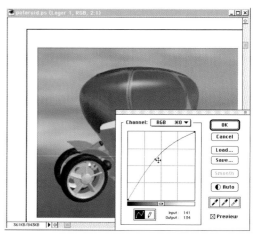

polaroid.jpg

Quad

FORESEE

Compression: JPEG
Image Length: 12K

▲ The final result of the montage is a deceptively realistic Polaroid photo.

An Adobe Illustrator drawing of a photo with two black frames serves as the basis. The dimensions are taken from a Polaroid photo.

The Illustrator file is imported into Adobe Photoshop. The Quad rendering is then imported and placed in a separate layer. You achieve these results by simply clicking the icon at the bottom left of the layer window while the selection is active. Photoshop then displays a window asking if you wish to open a new layer.

▶ **Script Lettering**

The model name is placed on the Polaroid photo in a suitable font. The Marker FinePoint font is the most appropriate choice. Then a shadow is placed under the image to give it more depth. We can create this effect by filling in a copy of the Polaroid frame with black, and then blurring it with the Gaussian Blur filter. The rendering is enlivened a bit by increasing the contrast to counterbalance the shadow. Once the entire image is finished, you can combine all the layers using the "Make one layer" command, and the illustration is complete!

▶ Photo-CD Source Material

The second model that will grace the home page is a Corel stock photo. This model is considerably more realistic than the Quad and is thus also placed in a suitable frame. A large-scale slide frame is quite appropriate to make the photo appear more real.

A Photo-CD from the gigantic Corel collection serves as the basis. To display the image on the screen in its full glory and definition, it is advisable to install the official Kodak Photo-CD Acquire Module. This plug-in allows you to import and sharpen the photo at the correct resolution in one action. For multimedia purposes, Base/4 is more than adequate. If a Web page is no wider than 600 pixels, an image of 256 by 384 pixels is quite sufficient.

▶ Creating Masks

Again, the photo frame itself is created in Illustrator. Note that the text is placed in the frame itself; this strengthens the illusion that this is a real slide frame. The frame is imported and the masks are assigned in Photoshop. The innermost frame is placed in its own mask layer so that the photo can be placed inside it.

Then reduce the Photo-CD photo to the width of the innermost frame, and select the entire image.

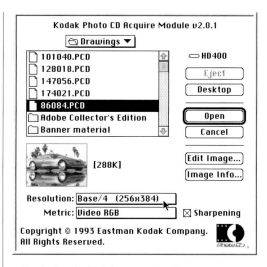

▲ Use the Acquire Module to open Base/4.

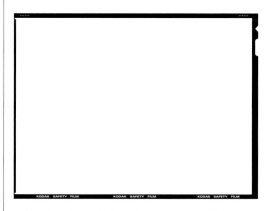

▲ The photo frame of a large-format slide is faithfully reproduced in Illustrator.

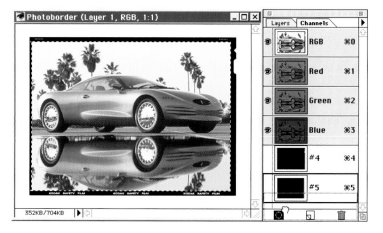

◄ The photo is positioned using the Paste Into option.

▲ To make a shadow, we select the exterior dimensions of the large-format slide frame.

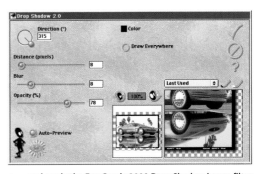

▲ …and apply the Eye Candy 3000 Drop Shadow image filter to the selection.

Now go to the photo frame file and select the innermost frame. Paste the selection using the Paste Into option, and the photo will be positioned precisely. Now we add a shadow to this photo. This time we use the Alien Skin Drop Shadow filter. The advantage of this plug-in is its preview option. The last phase consists of rotating the collage. Note that you do not select the image before applying the

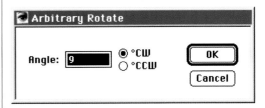

▲ Ensure that nothing is selected before the Rotate option is applied. Otherwise you lose valuable image material— the corners of the image!

Rotate effect. If you do Photoshop crops the image and deletes (!) the pixels outside the image. A nonselected image is automatically enlarged when it is rotated.

The final result is stored as a GIF file and only takes 15K of space, including the photo frame and the shadow. ▶

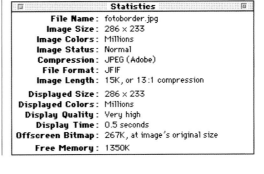

▶ **HTML for the Concept Cars Web Page**

Alternating the positions of the images creates a more appealing page.

Text Color in <BODY>   ▷

Making the text color in the <BODY> tag a striking green and then making all the text on the page black creates an interesting effect. The bullets in the list take on the color set in the <BODY>. Remember to neutralize all other text using the code <FONT COLOR= "#000000">.

Listing Without the <UL> Start Tag   ▷

If you want to use a list with no indentation, you do not have to use the <UL> start and </UL> end code. The browser will then display a normal list along the margin. You must include an extra <BR> or <P> because no paragraph is created.

<onMouseOver> JavaScript   ▷

Using a simple bit of JavaScript, the visitor is shown extra text information when the mouse is placed on the image. The text "Click here for more information about this vehicle" appears at the bottom of the browser window.

| Click here for more information on this futuristic vehicle |

With the JavaScript code onMouseOver you activate the window.status, and the text is displayed between single quotation marks. The closing code, return true, ensures that the text disappears when the mouse pointer is no longer on the image.

```
<HTML>
<HEAD>
<TITLE>Concept cars online</TITLE>
</HEAD>
<BODY BGCOLOR="WHITE" TEXT="#339966">
<CENTER>
<IMG SRC="concept.gif" WIDTH=300 HEIGHT=114
  ALIGN=LEFT>
<MARQUEE>
<FONT size=+2 COLOR="#000000">Welcome to the online
presentation of concept cars</FONT>
</MARQUEE>
<BR clear=all><BR></CENTER>
<IMG SRC="photobord.jpg" WIDTH=286 HEIGHT=233
  VSPACE=2 HSPACE=4 ALIGN=right >
<FONT size=+1 color="#000000">
On this Web site you'll find lots of information about concept
cars and studies of famous cars and design studios. Plus:
</FONT>
<BR><FONT color="#000000">
<LI>New models and studies from Italy
<LI>A virtual tour in a VR concept car
<LI>News and gossip from the industry
<LI>Computers and 3D-modelling
<LI>What about the cost?
<LI>Academic studies
<LI>Trainees abroad
<LI>Schools and education facilities for car design
</FONT>
<BR clear=right>
<A HREF="info.html" onMouseOver="window.status='Click
here for more information about this vehicle.'; return true">
<IMG SRC="polaroid.jpg" ALIGN=left WIDTH=352
HEIGHT=350 BORDER=0></A>
<BR>
<FONT size=+1 color="#000000">The featured artist of
this month's special is the head of Foresee, Cor Steenstra from
Holland.</FONT>
<BR><FONT color="#000000">
In our magazine you'll find an interview with Cor Steenstra,
the designer of the famous Quad motorbikecar. This Web site
features real 3D-models of the study in Alias designer and a
virtual tour of the concept car. Keep your VR-helmets ready
and enjoy the third dimension in car design.</FONT>
</BODY>
</HTML>
```

Concept cars online - Microsoft Internet Explorer

File   Edit   View   Favorites   Tools   Help

Back   Forward   Stop   Refresh   Home   Search   Favorites   History   Mail   Print

concept
___cars

Welcome to the
online presentation of
concept cars

On this Web site you'll find lots of
information about concept cars and
studies of famous cars and
design studios. Plus:

- New models and studies from Italy
- A virtual tour in a VR concept car
- News and gossip from the industry
- Computers and 3D-modelling
- What about the cost?
- Academic studies
- Trainees abroad
- Schools and education facilities for
  car design

The featured artist of this
month's special is the
head of Foresee, Cor
Steenstra from Holland.

In our magazine you'll find an
interview with Cor Steenstra,
the designer of the famous
Quad motorbikecar. This
Web site features real
3D-models of the study in
Alias designer and a virtual
tour of the concept car. Keep
your VR-helmets ready and
enjoy the third dimension in
car design

Quad

FORESEE

Click here for more information about this vehicle.   Internet

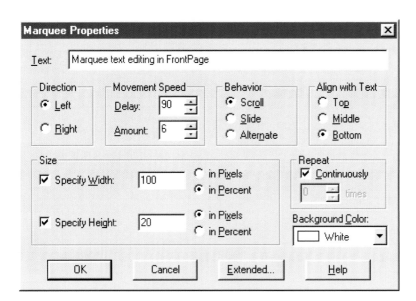

◄ In Microsoft FrontPage, you use a Marquee editor to create the desired HTML code.

▶ Standing Still Is Moving Backward

On the Internet, changes sometimes occur faster than the speed of light. The HTML standard is continually changing, primarily as a result of the competition between Microsoft and Netscape for hegemony in the browser market. After Netscape took the lead, Microsoft started gaining ground with Internet Explorer. A Web-page designer might object to the speed with which new options and tags are being added to HTML; just imagine how the author felt during the production of this book. Nonetheless, the competition benefits everyone.

More and more, HTML is becoming a markup language that offers designers complete control over the final product. Simultaneously, the World Wide Web Consortium is being forced to establish rules for an HTML standard.

It is impossible to design a Web page that is displayed the same on every viewer's computer. The number of environmental variables is simply too large. It is the Web designer's task to find the golden mean: a Web page whose tags do not cause problems for the user.

One such tag is Microsoft's Marquee. In Internet Explorer, text that is coded

```
<MARQUEE bgcolor="#x" direction=right behavior=scroll scrollamount=10 scrolldelay=200>Text</MARQUEE>
```

is displayed as scrolling text on the Web page. This produces an interesting effect; it attracts attention in a discreet way, certainly compared with the <BLINK> tag, and it does not cause any problems because a browser that does not recognize the <MARQUEE> tag simply treats the text as normal ASCII text.

This illustration ▶ created for a suntan studio is used as the main graphic for a visually striking Web page.

Combining a visually strong graphic image and monospaced font can result in an impressive-looking Web site. In this chapter, I demonstrate the creation of a large scale GIF image with a limited color table.

Graphic Web Pages

Sleep In the multitude of sites on the World Wide Web, only a few really stand out. The ones that do usually combine a consistent design with clear and memorable visual elements. The disadvantage of using such elements, however, is that the size of the graphic files involved usually results in download times that drive all but the most patient Web surfer away.

Still, if you are disciplined, you can make a big impression without incurring increased download times. After all, a graphic file's size does not depend on width and height alone, but also on number of colors. The rules that apply to designing an effective background pattern also apply to the main foreground image. Thus, you can create a Web page with maximum impact using a GIF illustration that uses a limited number of indexed colors.

▶ Painting in PostScript

The starting point for this Web site is a drawing of a female face. This image was created in Adobe Illustrator using a pressure-sensitive graphic tablet and the Brush tool. You can display the settings of the pressure-sensitive drawing stroke by double-clicking the brush icon in the toolbar of the Toolbox window.

Set the width to Variable and restrict the size of the hand-drawn line by limiting the Minimum and Maximum settings. I also recommend that you select the Caps and Joins options as shown in the illustration on the right. This will better suit the playful character of the illustration.

▶ Defining Colors

The illustration is first drawn in black and white, then colored. When the drawing is finished, select and copy all of it, and then paste it into a new document in Photoshop with the Anti-Aliased option selected. Then save the image as a 4-bit GIF with 16 indexed colors.

To check for unwanted dithering, reopen the image in Photoshop. In this case, the nose has been dithered; to correct it, simply replace the color with the adjacent color.

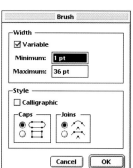

▲ The color version was created after the black-and-white version.

◀ You can achieve a realistic hand-drawn effect by defining the settings of the brush tool correctly.

◀ To keep the GIF file small, use the same colors for the face and all the other graphic elements.

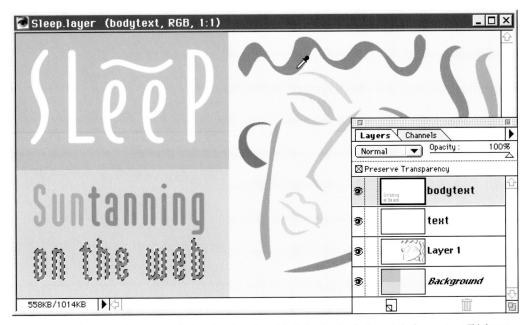

▲ Using the Eyedropper tool, you can apply the colors from the original drawing to all elements in the montage. This keeps the number of indexed colors to a minimum.

▶ Applying the Color Palette

Because some text and color is added to the illustration after its drawn, you have to set the GIF file to RGB color mode. Otherwise the lettering will have rough edges. Place all tonal fields and text in separate layers. The colors are all based on the tones found in the face, keeping the original color palette intact. Save the finished drawing using the same 4-bit indexed palette. The file size takes only 20KB of disk space!

◄ The file size of the final GIF image is only 20KB, even though the drawing is 600 by 317 pixels! For file size, do not look at the Size on disk value because it depends on the partition size. A 2GB disk uses 64KB partitions as a minimum.

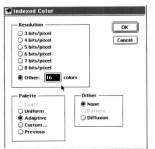

◄ The complete montage is saved as indexed colors with the same 16 colors that were used in the face.

◄ Using the same colors consistently creates a homogenous design, and the final file can be compressed considerably in the GIF file format.

▶ Compact

In the final layout in HTML, a 1 x 1-pixel GIF image is used to align the texts. By varying the <HSPACE> value, you can place the lines at different distances from the margin.

The <BASEFONT SIZE=> Tag ▷

You can enlarge or reduce all <FONT SIZE> tags by including the <BASEFONT=x> tag at the beginning of the HTML code. Mind you, this only works if you include a <FONT SIZE> tag in the following headings or if they are not formatted at all. However, if one applies the heading tags <HX></HX>, the base font tag will have no effect on the typography whatsoever.

The <TT></TT> tags ensure that the text placed between them is displayed in the monospaced typeface. This produces a distinctive effect, as is clearly visible in the example on the facing page.

```
<HTML>
  <HEAD>
    <TITLE>Sleep</TITLE>
  </HEAD>
<BODY BGCOLOR="#F7EFBD">

<BR>
<IMG width=600 height=317 ALT="sleep logo"
SRC="sleep.gif">

<BASEFONT size=+1><BR>

<TT>
<IMG hspace=35 SRC="dot.gif">
<FONT size=+1><B>Get a Suntan online!<B/>
<I>Check out this offer!</I> </FONT>
<BR>

<IMG vspace=9 hspace=78 SRC="dot.gif">
<FONT size=+1><B>Now all you palefaced
computer geeks</B></FONT>
<BR>

<IMG vspace=9 hspace=2 SRC="dot.gif">
<FONT size=+3>can get a<B>real</B>
<I>surfer-look.</I> </FONT><BR>

<IMG vspace=22 hspace=30 SRC="dot.gif">
<FONT size=+1>Just hold your face <B>close</B>
to the screen...</FONT>
<BR>

<IMG vspace=14 hspace=70 SRC="dot.gif">
<FONT size=+1><B>...and keep your eyes firmly closed
</B></FONT>
<BR>

<IMG vspace=22 hspace=60 SRC="dot.gif">
When you wake up your<FONT size=+2><I>face</I>
</FONT>looks like a Californian websurfer!
<BR>
<CENTER><HR width=120 size=1 noshade><BR>
<FONT size=-2>&copy; Sleep Suntanners in
Cyberspace</FONT></CENTER></TT>
</BODY>
</HTML>
```

▲ The combination of a strong graphic image and a monospaced typeface results in an intriguing Web page.

▲ A browser uses a fixed sequential order when downloading foreground and background information. ▼

▶ Colors in Stereo

The "Sleep Suntanning" home page employs both a background color and a background image. There are two reasons for this. First of all, color deviations are prevented, as explained in the chapter "Text and Image Integration." Second, this separately defined background color is used to improve the sequence in which browsers display the information on a Web page. Some browsers start with the background color, then load the foreground text and images, and finally the background image.

In this sequence, if you do not include a background color between the <BODY> tags of the HTML document, the page is first shown with a standard gray background with the images already visible in the foreground. This does not look very pretty, and it can be prevented simply by adding the hexadecimal color code for the background color of the GIF.

The Cosmos ▶
Automation
home page offers
a neat first
impression, and
not at the expense
of download time!

The ideal Web site combines great appeal and timeliness. The first impression must grab and hold the viewer's attention. However, download time also plays a role—an image must load quickly in addition to being appealing and functional. The example of the Cosmos Automation site shows how Corel Bryce and Macromedia Fireworks help achieve the ideal balance.

Corel Bryce Splash Page

The user's first impression of a Web page determines his subsequent surfing behavior. Of course, viewers' criteria vary, but one thing is always true: Everyone is looking for specific information, not just surfing for fun. To create a lasting impression, a site's design plays a major role. A professional and well-thought -out site inspires confidence that the information supplier values the visitor.

The user simultaneously finds the information and becomes acquainted with the company's image. To combine these values we can apply programs that generate beautiful and functional images, and also limit the loading time. Corel Bryce was used for the Cosmos site to create an impressive initial image, which simultaneously serves as a navigation element.

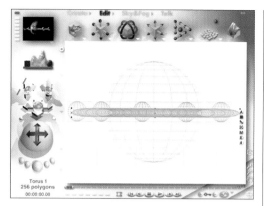

▲ The basic shapes are placed in frontal view.

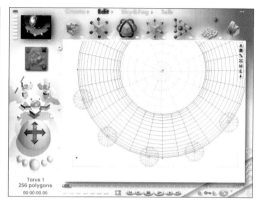

▲ Positions can be specified precisely in the view from above.

▶ Virtual World in Corel Bryce

The final concept for this site is the idea of creating a planetary system in which Cosmos' various services orbit like little planets. The individual planets are used on the subpages as navigation elements as well. The 3D program Corel Bryce is ideal for constructing this virtual world, allowing the user to experiment freely with forms and structures.

The design of the illustration itself is simple. In the view from above, a globe is drawn and given a structure. Corel Bryce contains an infinite number of options and variations in this area. It lets us create an aura around the central planet, for which a cylinder—one of Bryce's standard shapes—serves as a basis. The image is then flattened. The six planets are now added in the frontal view, each with its own distinct structure. In the view from

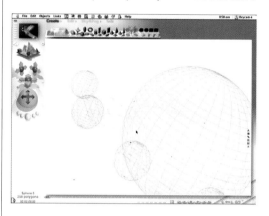

above, the final position is determined and we can specify a view in perspective. The background is specified in the Sky Lab, but merely provides lighting and shadows.

We use Bryce's alpha channel as a mask and later combine it with a repetitive background pattern. By experimenting with the

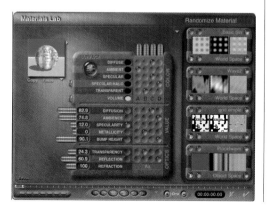

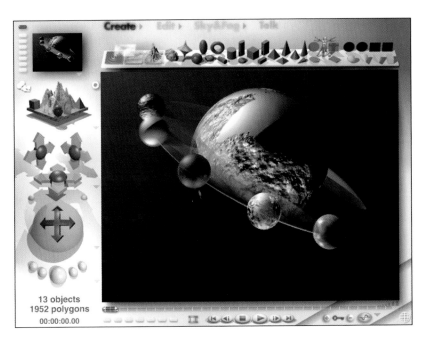

◄ View a rendered version of the previously determined perspective.

▼ Rendering time in screen resolution is minimal, not even two minutes.

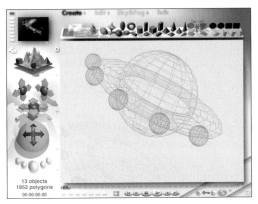

lighting and the background color, we can create various versions of the rendering. The position and color setup shown above are used. Be sure not to make the rendering too dark, especially on a Macintosh. On a Windows PC the clarity is poorer—correcting in Photoshop is a must.

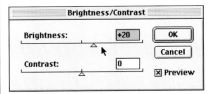

◄ The brightness setting is boosted.

▲ The position chosen is extensively highlighted and tested. ▼

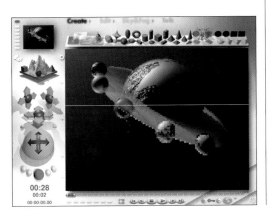

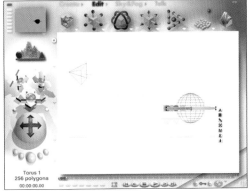

▲ The rendering is clipped and combined with the separately created background pattern backgr.jpeg. ▼

▲ The combined front and background images.

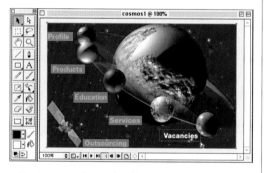

▼ The image map is completed in Fireworks.

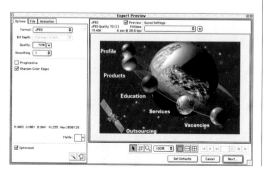

▶ Final Processing in Macromedia Fireworks

As we will work with a repetitive background pattern, the final version will be clipped using a mask. A background created earlier, called backgr.jpg, is used as a pattern.

The structure is set up in such a way that it is no problem if the repeating background overlaps the illustration placed in the foreground of the Web page. A haphazard pattern is created by randomly placing some stars with varying degrees of brightness. We use the same backgr.jpg file as a background pattern for the Web page.

The final illustration is saved as a PICT file and imported in Macromedia Fireworks. In this program we add the text near the planets. One big advantage of Fireworks is its unique PNG file format. By saving the combined illustration in this format, text corrections can still be made at a later stage, in keeping with the previously specified typography. The precise conversion method is saved in the file format as well, so managing the illustration is a lot simpler and more consistent.

▶ Adding an Image Map

The text indicating the primary navigation directions such as Profile, Products, and Education are marked as clickable regions. In Fireworks they are linked to the underlying subpages and scripts in the image map. This entire process does not require a single line of HTML coding.

The image is then exported, giving the correct balance between file size and image quality priority. Fireworks shows the various options in its Export Preview window. GIF and JPEG are compared with one another. The final JPEG version is still under 20KB and is saved as such. In the editor, the image is combined with the background pattern. The end result is the start page as displayed on the first page of this chapter. So much beauty in so few bytes!

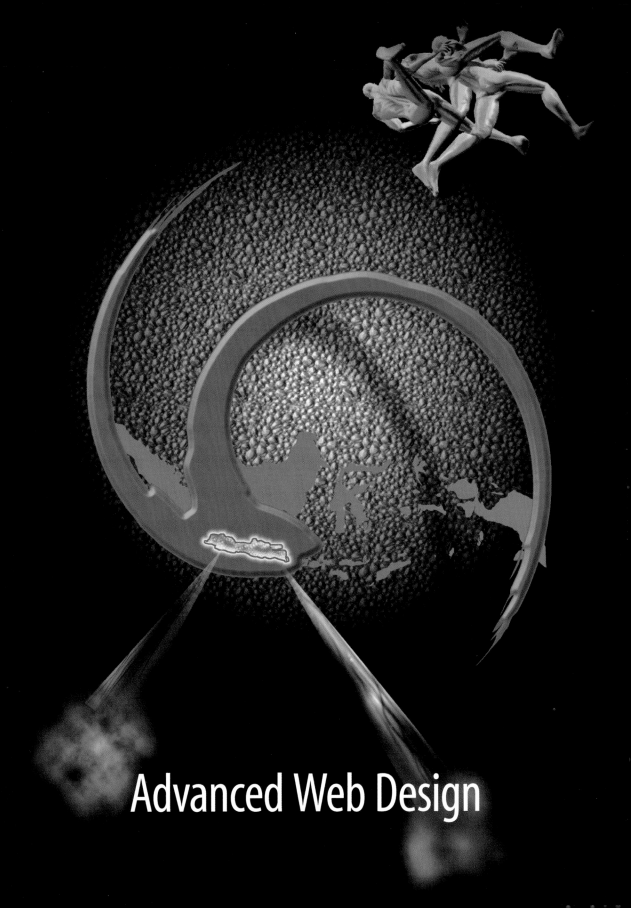

Advanced Web Design

It is an established fact that moving images add an extra dimension to a Web page. The challenge is: How does one create an animation that is really effective but does not slow down the connection too much? This chapter teaches you all about GIF animations.

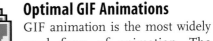

Optimal GIF Animations

GIF animation is the most widely used form of animation. The reason for its popularity is simple: Any browser can handle GIF animations. They require neither plug-ins nor installations—in short, they are simplicity itself! Yet from a creative standpoint, Web designers can do a lot with GIF animations. The most commonly used software programs come with options for creating animations. Adobe ImageReady, which is bundled with Adobe Photoshop, is a fine example. Specific programs such as Ulead GIF Animator also provide tools with which anyone can create attractive and technically correct GIF animations without a lot of graphics knowledge.

▶ Stand-Alone Animation

A typical Web page consists of multiple parts: text, logos, illustrations, and photos. However, extras such as sound, moving images, and virtual reality are gaining popularity because they allow the Web designer to use multimedia techniques to get the message across. Unfortunately, it is precisely these elements that require specialized knowledge the Web designer generally does not have. Animations based on the GIF89a file format are an exception.

A GIF89a animation is in fact a collection of drawings stored in one document. With the animated GIF technique, the drawings are quickly "played" one after another. You can create and set up these animations with the help of freely available software. All the other options the GIF89a format offers, such as transparency, interlacing, and GIF compression techniques, can also be applied to animations. To give you an idea of the possibilities, we will look at how to create a GIF animation from eight drawings.

▶ Limited Colors

Coordinating the colors is a simple task because the eight images are stored in separate layers in one Photoshop file. Each separate drawing is saved as a GIF89a file in only eight indexed colors. The same set of basic colors is used for all the illustrations.

In order to prevent problems with the sequence, the files are numbered 01.gif to 08.gif. In the animation, number 08 is immediately followed by number 01. This series of images is continually repeated, creating an endless animation that simulates fluid movement. Once you are finished with the preparatory work, you can start creating the GIF animation.

▶ GifBuilder

To illustrate this method, we are using the Macintosh program GifBuilder, by Yves Piguet. The procedure is identical to that used

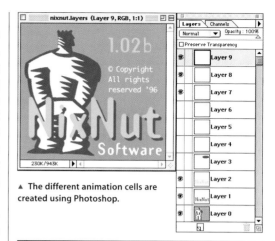

▲ The different animation cells are created using Photoshop.

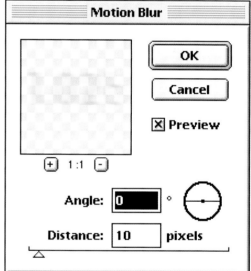

▲ The Photoshop filter Motion Blur creates the impression of speed.

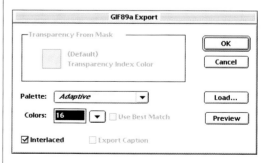

▲ The basic illustration is exported in eight different animation cells. These are saved with the same set of indexed colors.

◄ The basic illustration is divided into eight different animation cells, which collectively make up the GIF animation once they are brought together.

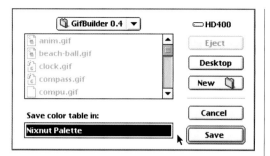

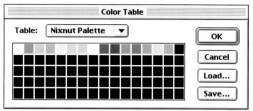

▲ The Color Table is stored separately by GifBuilder. This results in a consistent and dither-free color animation.

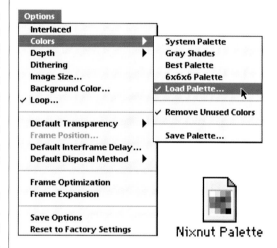

with the Windows program GIF Construction Set, by Alchemy Mindworks. This program will be described later in this chapter. Before you start using GifBuilder, check that all basic files for the animation have the same width and height. If all files are based on the same color table, the information can be stored separately so that GifBuilder can reuse the same color information. You then open the Frames window and import the eight GIF images in the correct sequence.

In GifBuilder you must enter the time interval between the frames in milliseconds. Do not make the time interval too short; otherwise the animation will not appear fluid. An interval of 50 milliseconds is sufficient. The Loop option is the second important setting. Select this option to ensure continual animation.

▶ Interlacing and Color Indexing

Although interlacing is useful, you must not use it for a GIF animation. The reason is simple: Once the GIF animation has been completely loaded on the user's computer, the interlacing will start suddenly at frame 1 but will not continue with frames 2 to 7. You can view the animation in the program, and if desired add extra cells by copying drawings and pasting them in the desired locations. Once you are done, select Frame Optimization in the Options menu. This reduces the size of the GIF file considerably. Once everything has been set up correctly, select Save As. The result is a GIF file of only 27KB.

▲ The option Load Palette is selected in GifBuilder, and then the special Nixnut Palette is created.

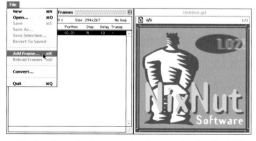

▲ The first frame in the animation is created using the Add Frame option in GifBuilder's File menu.

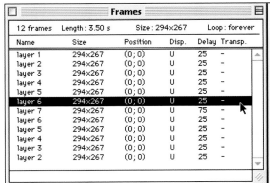

▲ The first six layers are repeated in reverse sequence. To achieve the desired effect, two new images must be added to create the illusion of a moving serial number.

◄ In the Interframe delay window you can specify the time interval between the display of two consecutive cells.

◄ When you select the Loop option, the animation is repeated continuously. Do not use the Interlaced option for this.

▲ The lettering is applied and manually corrected to remove disturbing jerkiness from the animation.

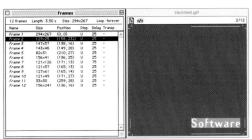

▲ After applying the Frame Optimization option, the files are much smaller.

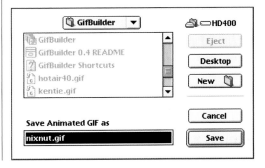

▶ Racing GIF Animations

The creative possibilities for GIF animations are unlimited. Moving buttons, logos, titles—anything is possible. Once the GIF animation has been loaded, it keeps moving. To illustrate this, a special GIF animation of a moving car is displayed on this page. The technique for creating such an animation is rather simple: A car is placed at ten different locations in the background of a drawing with a width of approximately 600 pixels. The drawings are saved as ten different files, all based on the same color palette. Select the option Disposal Method > Restore to Background in GifBuilder, and set the background color to Transparent. Save the illustration, and view the surprising results in a real Web page.

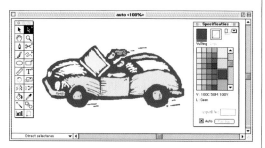

▲ The drawing is created in Adobe Illustrator and exported to Photoshop, where ten different drawings are created at the same size.

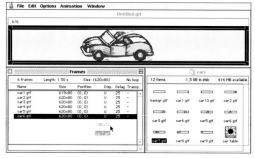

▲ The frames are positioned by dragging and dropping them.

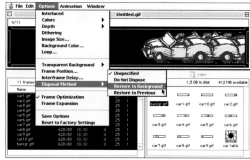

▲ The settings of the Disposal Method are extremely important for the GIF animation. The option Restore to Background is selected because the drawing has to be transparent. The background color is made transparent using the Based on First Pixel option. ▼

▲ By using a table with empty cells, the GIF animation creates the illusion of a car driving through the landscape. The table coding is relatively simple but very effective. ▶

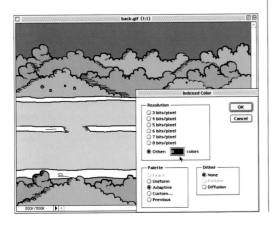

```
<HTML><HEAD><TITLE>Let's Move</TITLE></HEAD>
<BODY BACKGROUND="BACK.GIF">
<TABLE ALIGN=CENTER BORDER=0 WIDTH=620>
<TR><TD HEIGHT=40 ALIGN=CENTER>
<FONT SIZE=5 COLOR="BLUE">We present:</FONT></TD>
</TR><TR>
<TD HEIGHT=120> </TD>
</TR><TR>
<TD><IMG SRC="caranim.gif" HEIGHT=80 WIDTH=620></TD>
</TR><TR>
<TD HEIGHT=30> </TD>
</TR><TR>
<TD><IMG SRC="runner.gif" HEIGHT=64 WIDTH=510></TD>
</TR>
</TABLE>
</BODY>
</HTML>
```

▶ GIF Construction Set

The Windows 98-, 2000- and NT-compatible program GIF Construction Set Professional, by Alchemy Mindworks (*www.mindworkshop.com*), has options comparable to GifBuilder for the Mac.

GIF Construction Set Professional offers an additional advantage: the ability to stack parts of a drawing. Then the entire stack can be saved as a GIF animation. In the Web site displayed on the facing page, this option is very handy. The idea behind the illustration is clear: A clock runs 24 hours a day. It symbolizes that the company is continuously working hard to deliver top-of-the-line results for its customers. As the drawing is rather large, the normal method for creating GIF animations would result in too large a file. Because a drawing must be made for each hour, 12 drawings must be stacked on top of one another.

◀ The first "Image" is 500 by 370 pixels. That is the basic layer. The additional layers only measure 86 by 74 pixels.

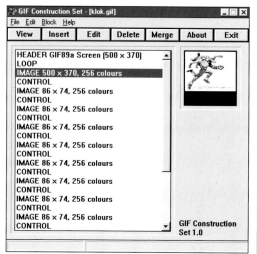

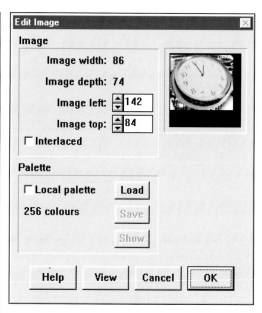

▲ The 12 layers in which only the clock information changes—the hands jump an hour each time—are precisely positioned in GIF Construction Set Professional on the coordinates of the basic layer.

▼ The 12 clocks, shown here in the correct sequence.

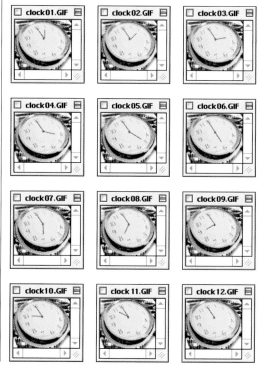

▲ Figure 1: The high source is loaded.

▲ Figure 2: The complete home page for the advertising studio.

▶ High Source After Low Source

The end result of this stacking will not be appreciated by any Web surfer, no matter how beautiful the effect. Fortunately there is GIF Construction Set. Placing the complete illustration in the bottom layer and the new clock's adjusted pointer positions in the 11 subsequent layers creates a compact GIF animation in spite of the file size and the 12 steps the animation runs through.

By using the x and y coordinates, you can position the clock exactly above the original spot in the bottom layer. This requires some calculation, but when the value for one

drawing has been determined, the ten remaining GIFs can be made in a snap. A low source version *(Figure 1)* of the illustration is used, to make the load time bearable.

The text "One moment please for great graphics..." indicates that something is yet to come *(Figure 2)*. GIF Construction Set allows you to modify all the layers after opening an animation that has already been created and saved. Thus you can easily make a correction or extend an animation with multiple GIFs.

GIF Construction Set can be found under the name GIFCON.exe at the well-known FTP sites on the Internet.

```
<HTML>
<HEAD>
<TITLE>DIP!</TITLE>
</HEAD>
<BODY BGCOLOR="white">
<H1>Heading</H1>
<IMG LOWSRC="personlo.gif" SRC="personhi.gif"
    WIDTH=500 HEIGHT=370>
    Text
</BODY>
</HTML>
```

▲ The source code of the DI&P home page.

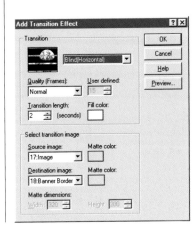

◀ The newest trend in GIF animation is the addition of transitional effects. A program like Ulead GIF Animator is a good choice.

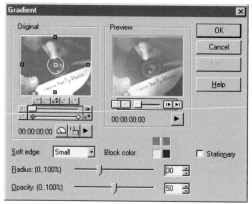

▲ An image can be modified in Ulead GIF Animator ...

▶ Ulead GIF Animator

The developers at Ulead have a number of handy and productivity-enhancing drawing programs to their name. They have developed a special application for creating GIF animations as well, which makes it possible to integrate cinematic effects in your Web design. This product, Ulead GIF Animator, can calculate transitions between two files, which makes for very different GIF animations.

The effects look like the transitions Microsoft PowerPoint uses to move to the next "slide." These effects are intended to hold the viewer's attention, and they are successful.

The way Ulead GIF Animator works is simple. You indicate a start and an end image, and then select the desired effect from the long options list. The program calculates the intermediate transitions and generates the requisite GIF files automatically. The result can be previewed in GIF Animator and edited if necessary. This simple procedure creates impressive effects and simultaneously handles the file size economically—the resulting file is only 22KB.

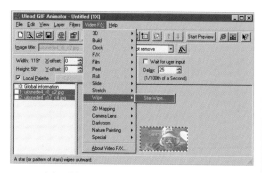

▲ ... and then blended into another image. GIF Animator creates the intermediate steps. ▼

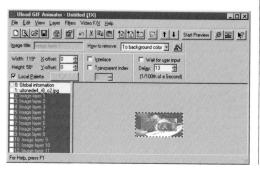

Joop's Web site ▶
is a fine example
of Flash's creative
and interactive
possibilities.
Take a look at
www.joop.com.

Webdesign: LUNA MEDIA

Macromedia Flash is rapidly changing the look of the Web, both literally and figuratively. The Web has become a much livelier medium because of the animation techniques Flash makes possible, and now it can compete even better with other media. This chapter shows a blueprint of the creative potential that Flash offers designers.

Shockwave Flash Animations

The Web is now moving, thanks to Macromedia Flash. The possibilities this drawing and animation program offers are endless, limited only by the user's creativity. If we are not careful, Flash will replace HTML-based sites because almost all the interactive possibilities of JavaScript, Java, and Dynamic HTML can be achieved using Flash.

Shockwave had better keep an eye out as well, because with each new release Flash is gaining headway on its programming possibilities. Flash can do everything, but one has to learn it, and that is not so simple. In itself, the package is not difficult, but working with a Timeline and the related cinematic way of thinking does not come naturally to everyone. Hopefully the next 21 pages will give you just the nudge you need to create a "Flashy" site yourself.

Movie Properties

Frame Rate:	12 fps	OK
	Width Height	Cancel
Dimensions:	484 px X 400 px	Save Default
Match:	Printer Contents	
Grid	18 px ☐ Show grid	
	Grid Background	
Colors:		
Ruler Units:	Pixels ▼	Help

▲ The characteristics of the movie are specified in the Movie Properties. These can always be changed.

▶ Macromedia Flash

It began long ago as SmartSketch; later it was rechristened CellAnimator, but the program became familiar to a larger audience as FutureSplash Animator. And ever since the takeover of FutureWave by Macromedia, the product has been called Flash.

Flash lets you create extremely compact files. The quality of the images is especially good because Flash is vector based and uses an antialiasing technique. That means that *(scalable)* animations of any size are displayed with optimum image quality, bringing the image quality of CD-ROM productions to the Web!

▶ Inline Publishing

The combination of quality and compactness makes a Flash animation perfectly suitable for the World Wide Web. And indeed, a number of prominent Web sites including Microsoft Network *(www.msn.com)* and the Web site for one of the Batman films, make creative use of this standard. In order to enjoy these animations, you must install the current Shockwave plug-in, which can read both Shockwave and Flash files. And Flash also supports sound. The familiar .wav and .aiff file formats can be included in a Flash animation, as can MP3 files. The main differences between Director *(Shockwave)* movies and Flash movies are:

Flash movies are vector-based, whereas Shockwave movies are based on bitmap graphics, so Shockwave movies are usually bigger.

▶ Extensive Drawing Options

Users with Director experience will find it easy to learn how to create Flash animations. The typical Timeline, used in programs such as Adobe Premiere and in many a 3D animation package, is also the basis for Flash.

Moreover, the program contains an extensive arsenal of drawing options that would be an asset to Adobe Illustrator and Macromedia FreeHand. For example, the program has an eraser tool to erase surplus image information. And in brilliant antialiased image quality. The drawings are *(almost)* infinitely scalable and are displayed on the monitor at lightning speed, thanks to this program's design.

PICT images can be included or converted to vectors, thanks to the built-in Trace Bitmap command in Flash.

Flash uses so-called symbols, which are comparable to Director's cast members. By reusing the same image elements as much as possible, you can create extremely compact animations. This is the advantage of vector-based drawings: The scaling size is not related to the file size. For instance, an

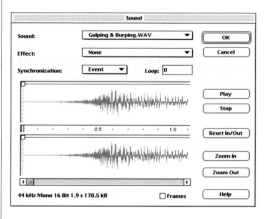

▲ Macromedia Flash allows you to include (stereo) sound and sound effects in your Flash movie.

animation in which 30 identical symbols are applied in different sizes is hardly any larger than an animation in which only one symbol is used!

You can take this into account when developing a Flash animation. Complex gradients take up hardly any space, since they are vector descriptions, and the smaller the ultimate file, the more quickly it can be sent.

▶ Animated Rollovers

In Flash you can create buttons that display different images, depending on the mouse position. So when you move the pointer *(or hand in Flash)* over the button or click the button, different images are produced.

A large number of sample buttons, which can be used freely, are a standard part of the

▼ An animated button has a maximum of four positions in Flash. Of course, fewer positions are also possible.

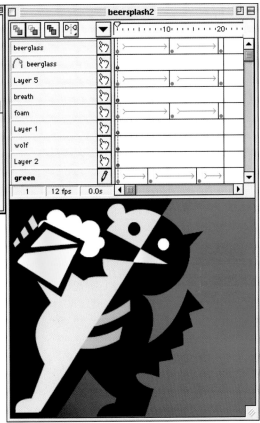

▲ At first sight, Flash's user interface appears complex, but thanks to the built-in lessons, one can quickly learn how to create a professional animation.

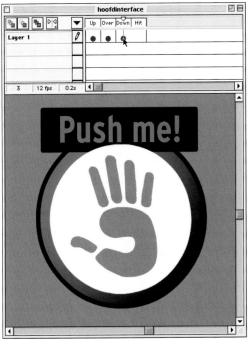

program. A button can have a maximum of four modes: Up, Over, Down, and Hit. And a specific action can be linked to each button mode, such as "Stop," "Go to position X," or "Link to the URL: http://www.example.com."

It is easy to create a simple animation. The Timeline you set is the determining factor. First, place an element at the start position.

Then position the playhead at Frame 10 and choose Insert > Frame. Now you can specify the final position for the animation. Click OK or Press Enter and the animation runs to the last position on the Timeline. Then you must move the element to the final position, where you can enlarge or reduce its size.

▲ Here, the Over position of the animated button has been selected. The familiar hand makes it visible.

▲ Interactivity is added to the button in Instance Properties —for instance, a link to a URL.

Now choose Insert > Keyframe, select the time scale, and you can then set the "tweening." Tweening means calculating the intermediate steps. Choose Insert > Create Motion Tweening and the requisite images are calculated automatically. The animation can now be viewed. It looks much better when you add another layer with a path along which the animation can move. If you make this layer invisible, the line will only be used

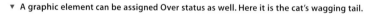

▼ A graphic element can be assigned Over status as well. Here it is the cat's wagging tail.

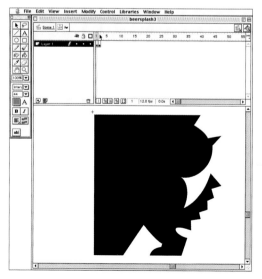

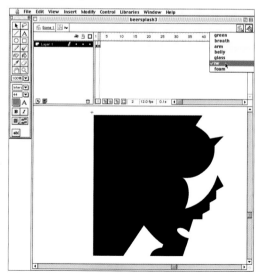

as a "motion guide." All the positions of the animation can be previewed by temporarily switching on the Onion Skin option, providing a visual overview of the result. The actions are clarified in the illustrations shown. Learning Flash well requires a great deal of practice!

▶ Export Options

One interesting Flash option is the ability to export animations in various file formats—for example, as a GIF animation or as separate Illustrator files. The compactness of the Flash file proves its worth here. The .swf file is only 5500 KB (!), while the GIF animation takes 485KB. With the help of a program such as GifBuilder, perhaps some 6KB can be removed, but the difference is still impressive. Plus the quality is much better, thanks to the Flash file's antialiased display of the image contours.

This is expressed in the treatment of text, as well. Even though the text is set in a special typeface, this does not have to be sent separately. Flash converts the information into "contours." And even then, the text can still be corrected. Nor does the use of gradients create any negative effects. Gradients can be displayed beautifully in the browser without

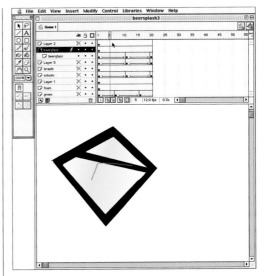

▲ Drawing a path and linking it to the glass ...

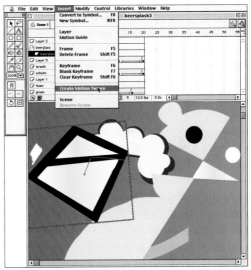

▲ ... creates the effect of a drinking cat. The option Orient to path direction must be selected.

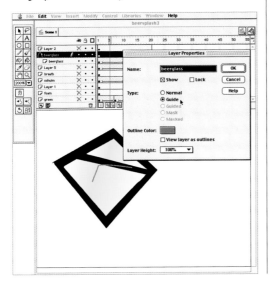

  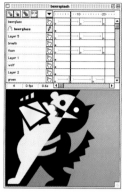 

▲ A time-scale indicator moves along while the animation is played. The background gradient changes color …

▲ … while the "Beerwolf" empties its glass, making its belly swell. All this in only 5.5K.

unnecessarily enlarging the file. Compare that with a GIF animation that includes a gradient. The quality is poor, and the download time will not be acceptable to any Web surfer.

The <EMBED> tag is used to place the Flash file in a Web page. A number of specific

Flash attributes influence the screen display. <SCALE=EXACTFIT> is one, as is <QUALITY=HIGH>. In combination with <WIDTH=100%> and <HEIGHT=100%>, these attributes ensure that the Web page that contains the Flash movie adjusts itself to the size of the user's monitor.

▼ Placing text in the animation is simple. First, select a new layer and click the text tool. Then type in the copy. It is important to know that the text can be modified in the original document afterward.

▼ Flash's text quality is very good. Even zooming in to 1600 percent, no jagged edge is visible. That is the advantage of PostScript!

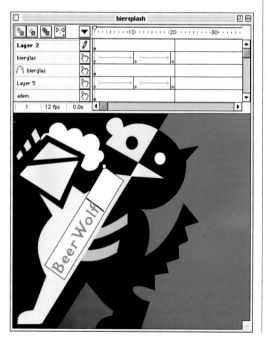

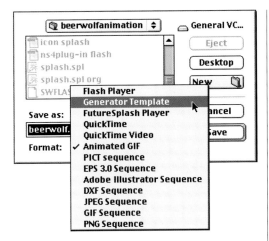

▲ The choice of export options is surprising. In spite of this variety, no other program can compete with Macromedia Flash in terms of compact file size.

Besides, an exported Flash file cannot be reopened in the original program. This is a plus for copyright reasons, but it means that one always has to keep two versions of the animation: the original and the copy saved as a .swf file.

Perhaps Macromedia Flash is the Web's long-awaited "killer app." It's an impressive program, satisfying virtually all desires and requirements without drowning in too complex an interface.

▲ The exported Flash document can be equipped with streaming audio in a variety of qualities.

■ Flash 'embedding' in HTML-code:

```
<HTML>
<HEAD>

<TITLE>Beerwolf Splash page</TITLE>
</HEAD>

<BODY BGCOLOR="YELLOW">
<CENTER>

<EMBED src="beerbest.swf" width="100%" height="100%"
loop="true" play="true" quality="high" scale=exactfit>

</CENTER>

</BODY>
</HTML>
```

▲ Once the animation has been placed in a Web page, the true power of Flash is revealed: a high-resolution, screen size–independent, streaming animation that can be used as a hyperlink to refer to other URLs on the same or an external site.

◀ A dream come true for all interactive-site designers …

▶ Text Animation in Flash

One of Flash's strengths is that the program has an infinite number of typographical options. And as the texts are based on vectors, they hardly add any kilobytes to the Flash animation. For the designer it is wonderful that the quality of the lettering is maintained. This is certainly noticeable when Flash adjusts itself to the screen's proportions. The antialiasing is extremely good; even small font sizes are clearly legible *(including in the browser window)*.

The production of a text intro in Flash is the subject of these pages. In this example a textual header is animated in a Macromedia Flash movie. The first step requires positioning the text. Flash supports all installed PostScript Type 1 and TrueType typefaces. The text "Crazy Beerwolf" has been purposely placed outside Flash's work area because we want the text to come "flying in" from right to left. During this animation the text also shifts from blurry to sharp, and the size is modified. This looks like a complex animation, but that is not the case at all. Each part of the production process will be explained step-by-step in this chapter.

Once you understand the basics of Flash— and the fantastic built-in explanations offer more than sufficient basic information —any creative person can start working with Flash. The method shown in this example can be completed in a few minutes. The final result looks brilliant, and as more and more browsers, and consequently more surfers, use Flash, it becomes more and more rewarding to apply this technique to Web design.

Flash's advantages are evident: minimal download time *(this example is not even 3KB)* and maximum image quality, under almost all circumstances. A Flash movie encounters no problems with browser dithering and even scales itself to the screen used.

The first keyframe is added at frame 25. ▶

▲ The text is set in the Interstate typeface.

▲ The first word is colored blue.

▲ The text is converted into a (library) symbol...

▲ ...and the name "heading" is added.

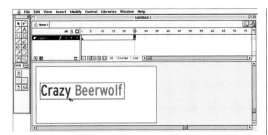

▲ In keyframe 25 the text is positioned …

▲ … and enlarged so that it fits into the frame.

▲ In frame 1, the text is still outside the screen.

▲ The color alpha is set from 100 back to 0.

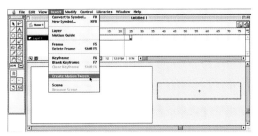

▲ Set the Timeline between 1 and 25, and select Create Motion Tween.

▲ All intermediate steps are created immediately.

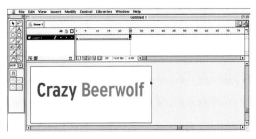

▲ In frame 25, the text is seen in all its glory!

▲ Hit F12 to view the result in a browser. The requisite Flash and HTML code is automatically generated by the program.

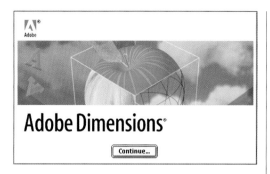

▶ Vector-Based 3D Illustrations

The program Adobe Dimensions is excellently suited for creating 3D animations for Flash, thanks to Dimensions' ability to save vector files in Illustrator's *(.ai)* file format. The procedure is logical and works on both Mac and Windows platforms.

We start with a text in Dimensions set in the Myriad typeface. The text is spaced correctly and then put into perspective by Adobe Dimensions.

▲ The text is entered and converted to outlines.   ▼

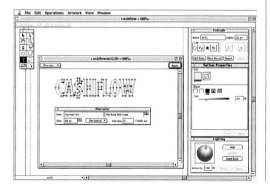

▲ The flat text is displayed in perspective.

▲ Extrude gives 20-point depth to the text.

▲ After coloring the text, select PostScript from the pull-down menu.   ▼

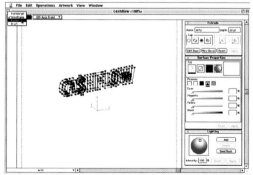

▲ The dollar sign is enlarged for extra accentuation.

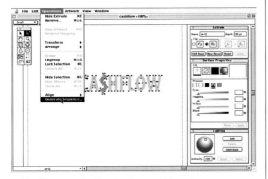

▲ The "Sequence" animation is started from the menu.

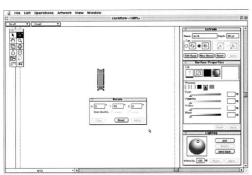

▲ The text is rotated 90 degrees. Then the sequence must be ended.

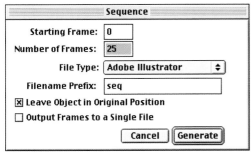

▲ Twenty-five frames are sufficient for Flash.

In this perspective view, it is simple to see the consequences of an "extrude." That is the name for the action that transforms the flat text into a spatial, three-dimensional form.

For this purpose, Dimensions has an Extrude window in which you can specify the depth of the object and the "bevel," the border shape. In our example, we give the bevel a thickness of 20 points. Dimensions extrudes the object in such a way that it creates a spatial typography. Then we assign a color to the form.

At the same time, we take advantage of the possibility of assigning a specific light source to the drawing. The $ symbol, which occupies a special position in the word CA$HFLOW, is assigned a different hue.

▶ Generating a Sequence

As we want an animation for later use in Flash, it is clear that the lettering must move. Dimensions offers a number of options for achieving that. You can manually move an image step by step and then save each progression as an Illustrator file. You can also automate this process by using a "Sequence."

If you select Generate Sequence in the Operations menu, Dimensions will ask you to indicate a final position. Choosing the Rotate menu option, we enter a rotation of 90 degrees on the Y axis. Click Apply, and the program starts spinning the lettering around its axis. Then go back to the Operations menu and select End Sequence.

This specifies that the animation ends. A Sequence menu then appears, in which the number of frames is set. We choose 25 because the animation has to last 1 second in Flash, at 25 frames per second. We save the files in Adobe Illustrator format so that we can edit the files further.

▶ Dimensions has saved 25 separate files. These can be opened in Flash.

▶ Finishing in Adobe Illustrator

We open the 25 files generated in Adobe Illustrator. On the one hand, Illustrator allows you to check that they really are PostScript drawings and not PICT previews. If they are the latter, you will have to return to

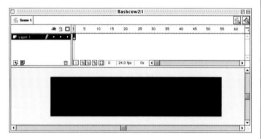

▲ Open Flash and give the movie the right settings.

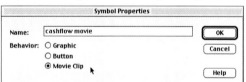

▲ Generate a new symbol after opening Flash.

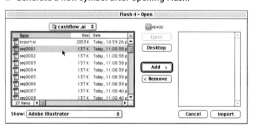

▲ Import the first file, and Flash does the rest.   ▼

Adobe Dimensions and change the display setting in the left top corner of the screen to PostScript. In all other cases, Dimensions calculates PICT previews.

OK, now that we are over this hurdle, we can check whether we can remove unnecessary points or paths from the files. Illustrator has an option *(Object > Path > Cleanup)* suitable for this purpose. In our example we used fine gradients in the lettering. Watch out that these are not set too fine, otherwise our Flash movie will become too large later on.

The number of gradient steps must be entered in the Dimensions preferences. However, it is also possible to adjust the file in Illustrator. When all 25 files are "clean," we can start creating the animation in Flash.

▶ Importing as a Movie Clip

Objects can appear in Flash in three different ways: as a button, as a graphic, or as a movie clip. In principle, it does not matter how an object is included in the library. It can still be modified later. However, our animation is quite suitable for saving as a movie clip.

The reason is that we can use the movie several times in the Flash work area without increasing the file size. In addition, we can modify the movie's presentation along the time axis. For instance, the animation starts bright and slowly becomes darker, until it moves out of sight.

This is not possible when we put the animation in the "Scene." So we import the images into a movie-clip "symbol" and not into the scene itself.

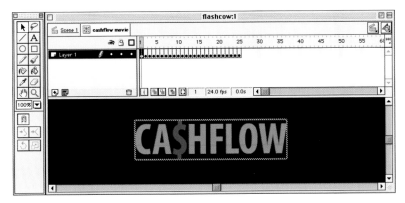

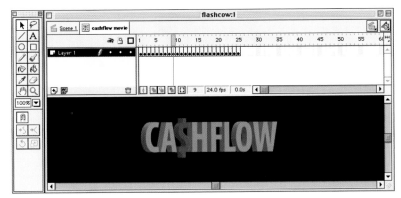

▲ After all sequences have been imported, the animation is ready! The preview is included in the library.

◄ The animation is played by moving the Timeline.

▶ Placing the Movie on the Work Area

When the Import window opens, you look up the folder in which the rendered Illustrator images were saved. They have been neatly numbered by Dimensions in a series that starts with Seq001 and ends with Seq0025. Of course, we import Seq001 first, and then something surprising happens. Flash is so intelligent that it recognizes images when they are an element in an animation series. The program asks us whether it should import the rest of the images as well. We say yes, and the entire series is imported into the object "cashflow movie." The animation is now ready. Press Enter/Return, and a preview of the animation is shown.

The last step is to import the "cashflow movie" by dragging the icon from the library to the work area. Then the movie clip can be further edited as specified earlier and shown below.

▼ Drag the movie from the library, and you can get to work.

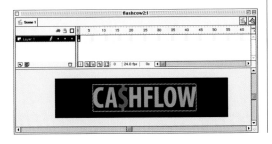

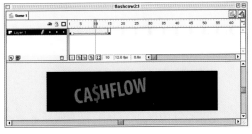

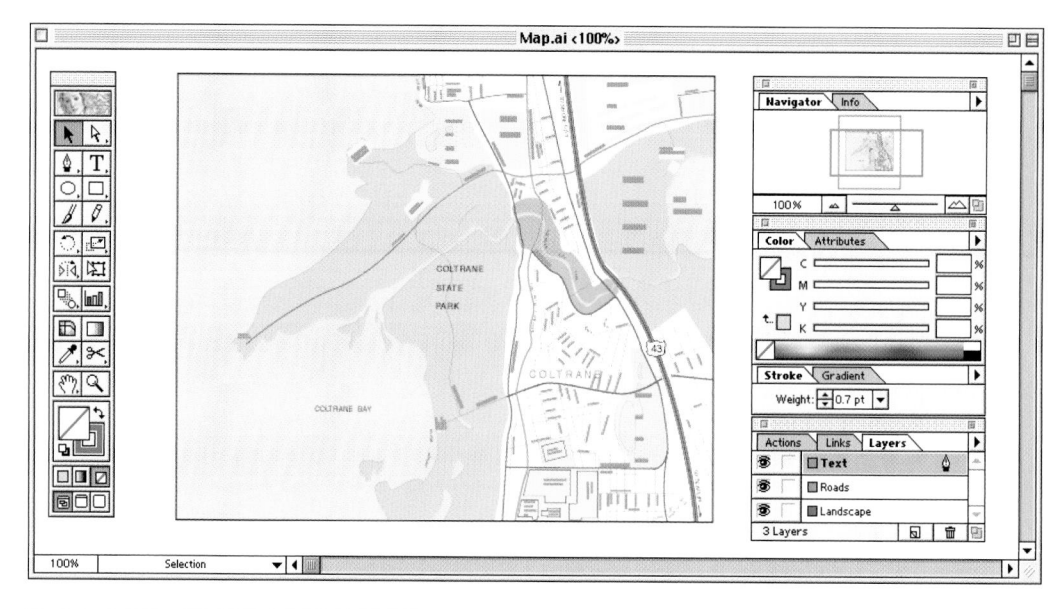

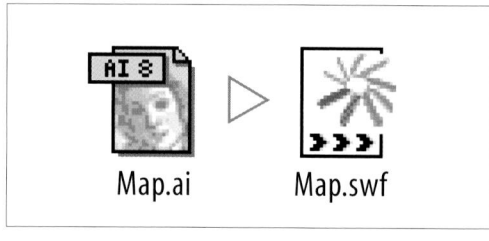

Map.ai   Map.swf

▶ Exporting Flash Files from Illustrator

Illustrator can now save illustrations in Flash format. This has lowered the threshold for creating a Flash movie even further, because the possibilities offered by this export option are virtually infinite.

The procedure for converting an Illustrator file to a Flash SWF document is as follows: Choose the Export command from the File menu and select the Flash SWF option as its file format. Then the Format Options dialog box appears in which the details can be entered. In this example we have also applied the All Layers to SWF Files option.

This enables each separate drawing layer to be saved as a separate Flash file, offering new possibilities in the continued editing in Flash 5. In our example, the text layer can appear slowly, varying from completely dimmed to entirely visible.

▲ The map has been drawn in Adobe Illustrator and is constructed in several layers. These layers can be exported as separate Flash files.

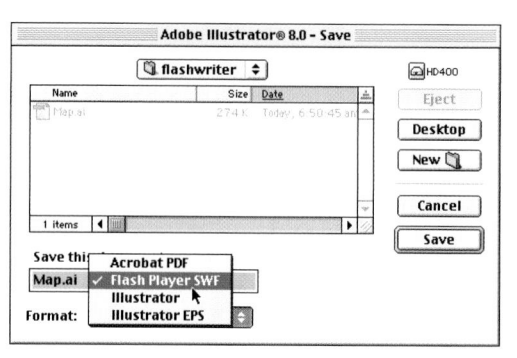

▲ The Illustrator file is saved in Flash Player SWF format. The settings are entered in a separate window. Be sure that gradients and patterns are saved as well. ▼

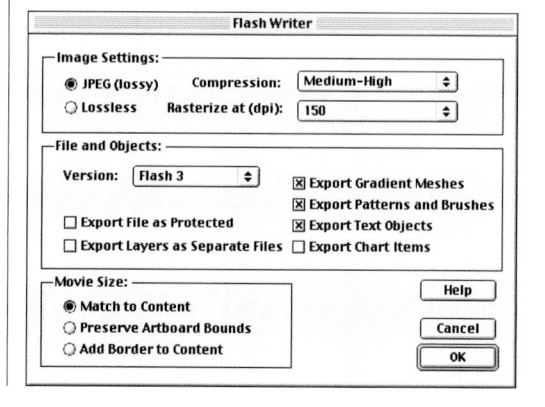

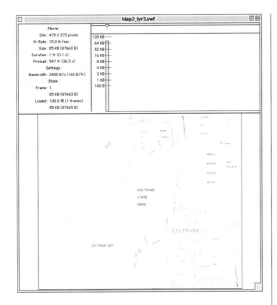

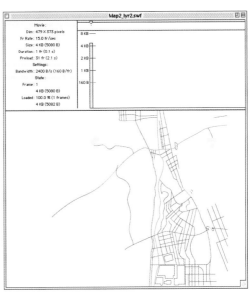

▶ Importing into Flash

Adobe Illustrator exports Flash files in the SWF format, which allows no further editing, so the only way to enhance the file further is to import it into Flash, where it will occupy its own layer. Then you can use it as one component of a more complex Flash movie.

In the accompanying example, an interface has been included in the Flash movie that enables the user to zoom in on the map.

▲ These two Flash movies have been opened in Flash Player and feature the unique option of exporting each layer separately as a Flash movie from Illustrator.

Since all data consists of vectors, this can be done very rapidly while maintaining the superior Flash text quality. The whole production is based on the original Adobe Illustrator drawing and a number of icons from the Flash library.

▲ The Flash Movie in its standard position …

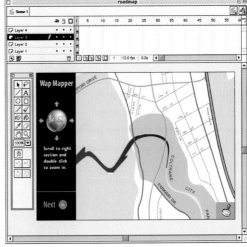

▲ … and zoomed in on the map.

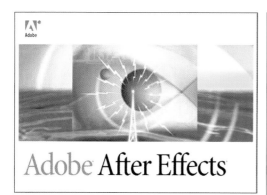

◄ The original movie clip as recorded with a webcam.

▶ Cinematic Effects in Flash

Although Flash is a strongly vector-oriented program, it can still include moving images. This seems to be a contradiction, because aren't film images always pixel based? That is the whole point! We are going to convert the film into individual images drawn in vectors. Alternatively, you can just import a QuickTime movie directly into the Flash document.

For this conversion we need an appropriate original file, preferably a QuickTime movie (.mov). In addition, you need to have access to Adobe After Effects and Adobe Streamline. Of course, there are alternative products for the individual actions, but Adobe's components interconnect very well.

We start in Adobe After Effects by importing a so-called Footage File. That is the movie with the filename original.mov. Then we create a new composition, which determines the work area in After Effects. The program is used to remove as many shades and hues from the movie as possible. This creates a highly graphic effect, which lends itself very well to conversion into vectors. For that purpose, we set the filter Threshold to rough. You will see the movie image change. Now the film can be rendered, and we are done with After Effects.

The movie is opened again in the QuickTime Player, evaluated, and saved as an "image sequence" of individual PICT images. This is our basic digital material.

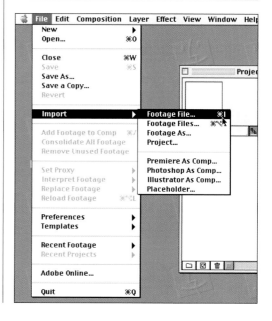

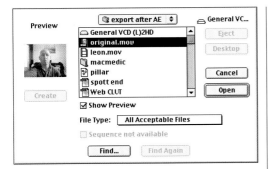

▲ The QuickTime file is placed in After Effects.

▲ A new composition is created in After Effects.

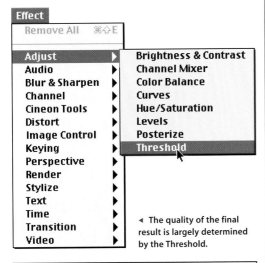

◄ The quality of the final result is largely determined by the Threshold.

▶ **Manual Work or Automation**

If you don't have Adobe Streamline, you can make the conversion to vectors yourself in Flash. However, you will have to go from image to image.

▲ The converted movie is reopened in QuickTime Player for a check.

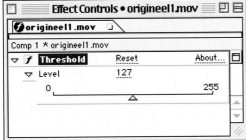

◄ The important Threshold window.

◄ The movie is "blurred" to avoid sharp edges.

◄ We export the PICT files from QuickTime.

▶ Automatic Conversion in Adobe Streamline

The conversion must first be set in Adobe Streamline. Here the Threshold is important as well. Perform the batch conversion, and then save the files as Illustrator documents. The film is now an image sequence consisting of vectorized files.

The Batch Select ▶ option enables us to import and process a series of files in Adobe Streamline.

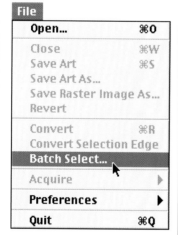

The original ▶ image is in black and white. That is why we chose these settings in Setup.

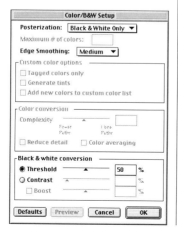

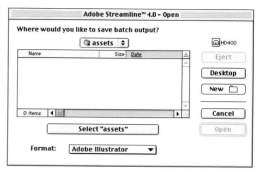

▲ A separate map called "assets" is assigned.

Next, you can clean the individual Illustrator files. Unfortunately, this is manual work. Then you import the images into Flash. To do this, proceed as described in the Dimensions example. Thus, you don't want to import directly, but in the format of a movie symbol. If you did not use Streamline, import the PICT image sequence files now. If you used Streamline, import the Illustrator sequence.

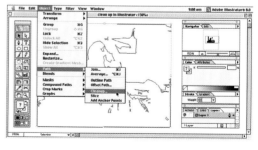

▲ If you have enough time, you can finish the traced images one by one in Illustrator. This will enhance the quality and file size of the final result in Flash. The disadvantage, of course, is the time it takes to do this. A 10-second movie clip with 25 images per second requires about 250 manual editing actions…

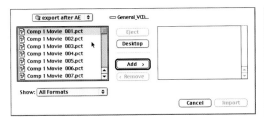

▲ The image sequence is imported in Flash ...

Once the sequence is imported, the Timeline is filled with frames. Now it is important to optimize the frames by removing separate and superfluous anchor points. This may result in a 60 percent saving in file size!

▲ ... and is displayed in a long sequence in the "movie" element.

▲ A layer mask is used to "isolate" the image of the figure.

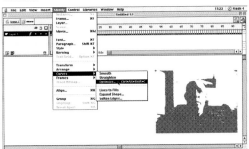

▲ The masked image is displayed in Flash.

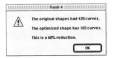

▲ A 60 percent gain through optimization!

▼ Once the PICTs are imported, they must first be "traced."

In principle, the Flash animation is now complete. If you are not yet satisfied, you can remove some of the superfluous image information using a layer mask. If Streamline has not been used, you first want to execute Trace Bitmap frame by frame in order to get vectors. Unfortunately, you will lose the audio track in this process. However, these procedures can always be performed separately. Export the audio track, and dub it into the Flash movie.

▶ Flash Considerations

After the beautiful story on the previous pages, you may be wondering why Web pages are still created in HTML. Isn't Flash the ideal solution? It combines fantastic image quality, a high degree of interactivity, and minimal download times. OK, I have no objection to that. However, one disadvantage of Flash is that not all browsers are equipped with this plug-in. In itself that is no big deal, since the newest browsers come with Flash as a standard feature. And Microsoft's and Apple's operating systems install the requisite Flash plug-in software as well, which means that the percentage of browsers that do not have the correct plug-in is diminishing considerably.

However, the troubles start when the Web page itself has to ascertain whether the user has installed the plug-in. Since there is more than one version of Flash in circulation, each with its own plug-ins, the automatic detection scripts tend to make a little mistake now and then. And things become hopeless when the browser leaves the developers in the lurch. Many a browser detection script fails to detect Microsoft Internet Explorer version 4.5 for the Macintosh, with all the attendant consequences.

Of course, smart Web designers have come up with all kinds of solutions. Planet Internet, for example, displays the error messages in the same color as the page's background itself. Thus, the user does not see them. Very clever!

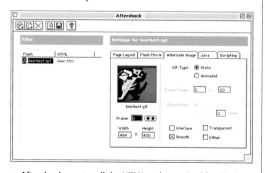

▲ Aftershock creates all the HTML code required for Flash.

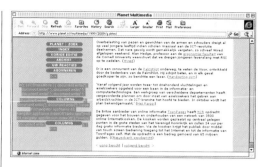

▲ The faulty Flash code is hidden on www.pi.net.

▶ Flash Embed Time

Macromedia has fully automated the publishing of Flash movies. However, be sure to remember that an "embed" and an "object" description have been created. These items are (sorely) needed for Netscape Navigator and Microsoft Internet Explorer, respectively.

```
<HTML>
<HEAD>
<TITLE>flashcow</TITLE>
</HEAD>
<BODY bgcolor="black">

<OBJECT classid="clsid:D27CDB6E-AE6D-11cf-96B8-540000"
   codebase="http://active.macromedia.com/flash2/cabs/
   swflash.cab#version=4,0,0,0"
   ID=flashcow WIDTH=500 HEIGHT=110>
   <PARAM NAME=movie VALUE="flashcow.swf">
   <PARAM NAME=quality VALUE=high>
   <PARAM NAME=bgcolor VALUE=#000000>

<EMBED src="flashcow.swf" quality=high
   bgcolor=#000000 WIDTH=500 HEIGHT=110
   TYPE="application/x-shockwave-flash"
   PLUGINSPAGE="http://www.macromedia.com/shockwave/
   download/index.cgi?P1_Prod_Version =ShockwaveFlash">

</EMBED>
</OBJECT>

</BODY>
</HTML>
```

▶ Macromedia Generator

If you combine the Flash and Generator products, you can create dynamic Web sites in the second sense of the word. Here, dynamic does not refer to movement but to the fact that the data that appears in the animation is retrieved from a database. This technique is ideal for illustrations that constantly must be adjusted while the quality of the images has to remain intact. For example, think of maps used in weather-forecasting programs or road maps with traffic information. Such examples are ideal for Generator.

However, Macromedia has also equipped Flash 5 with the option of importing and processing variable information. Does that make Generator 2 superfluous? In many cases it does, for in Flash 5 you can pretty well work with the built-in script language. An additional advantage is that the database is accessed from the client rather than from the server.

Generator distinguishes itself because it is able to render images in real time into the GIF, Flash Player Movie, or QuickTime 4 file format. This option is specifically intended for most modern browser users groups. Generator can also independently create pie, bar, or other standard charts based on data retrieved from a text file, a database, or a URL.

▲ Macromedia Generator and Flash make it possible to create dynamically generated and animated sites. This is ideal for linking up-to-date information with high image resolution.

The database that is linked to Flash can be JDBC/ODBC compliant or can be ASP or Java compliant. Note that the Macintosh version does not support JDBC/ODBC; these are typical Windows standards.

There are also alternative solutions that enable dynamic modification of content in Macromedia Flash. The Swift Generator (www.swift-tools.com) is a free tool that enables you to connect databases to Flash content. The ASP Flash Turbine shareware program (www.blue-pac.com) is primarily geared toward producing dynamic Flash pages using Active Server Pages.

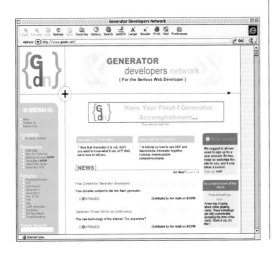

◄ On www.gendev.net you can find out everything about dynamic Flash sites.

▲ ScreenTime transforms Flash FLA files into screensavers.

▶ Flash Screensavers

Macromedia's triumphal march with its Flash product continues. The fact is, the product is an ideal tool for creating screensavers. A Flash FLA file can be saved as a screensaver, maintaining all its quality and dynamics, using special programs such as ScreenTime—this time, however, in full screen and with full motion!

Please note that you must have an original Flash work layout; an SWF file cannot be converted into a screensaver, because users can retrieve the Flash originals from their browser caches. This requires some searching on your hard drive. So look for .swf, and drag the cache file with the most recent date to the desktop.

The Flash .swf ▶ files can be found in the (temporary) browser cache.

The Shockwave ▶ Web site is a great online community builder for gamers.

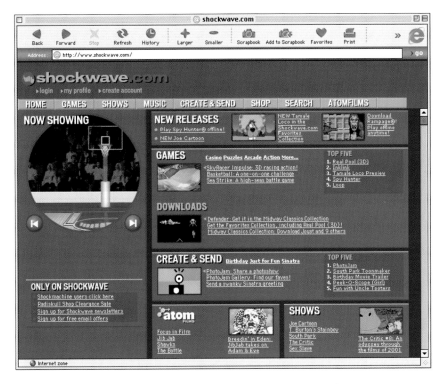

Home pages that consist only of text and static images are becoming less and less successful at attracting attention on the Web. Now, it seems, you have to include Shockwave animations in your pages. That's fine, but how is such a Director (DCR) file created? This chapter explains how, through both text and illustrations.

Shockwave Movies

Macromedia Director is the market leader in interactive productions for CD-based media. For years Macromedia has been amassing experience in interactive multimedia, so it's no surprise that the company has brought its knowledge and skills to bear on the Internet. Web pages with moving images, sound effects, and—extremely important—direct interaction with the user lend much added value to a site. Because these effects can be produced with Macromedia Director, creating dynamic Web pages is a seamless process for the large number of multimedia specialists who already use the program.

For the time being, you must install a special Macromedia Shockwave plug-in in order to view the movies in your Web page. But it is safe to expect that this engine will be included in the popular Web browsers as a standard in the future. Only then will we feel the real shocks on the Internet!

▶ **Director Equals Shockwave**

For the most part, producing a Shockwave animation is identical to creating a Director movie. In principle, the Shockwave process is nothing more than a common compression of the DIR file that Director uses as file format.

For this chapter a Macromedia Director file was created with the following components: text with the word Cyburger, two "brainburgers," and a slurping sound. All the images were prepared in Adobe Photoshop. The text lettering is based on Neville Brody's Fuse Font called Spherize. The letter R needs some adjusting to make it more legible.

The hamburger illustrations were saved in three versions: one straight on, a copy rotated 10 degrees to the right, and another copy rotated 10 degrees to the left. The three together were then saved as a PICT file.

▶ **Cast Members on the Stage**

In Director, all the images were first converted to the Apple Macintosh system color palette. This produces the best results on both Mac and Windows computers. Then the images in Director were imported into the "cast."

The background of the work area is set to 448 by 240 pixels and is assigned the same bright red color as the background for the lettering. The small cyburger images are 75 by 75 pixels. These images must be transparent, which means that the red background color must be changed to white. Do this with the Fill tool.

On the "stage," Director's work area, five positions are specified for the jumping cyburgers. Make them transparent by selecting all of them in the Score window and then choosing Matte ink. If you select the Space to Time option, Director will automatically calculate the intermediate images, producing a fluent animation.

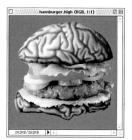 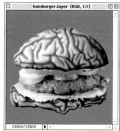

▲ Here are the two different Cyburgers.

▲ Using the Gaussian Blur filter, the Spherize lettering is given a blue aura. ▼

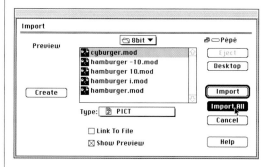

▲ The original cast members are imported from Photoshop. ▼

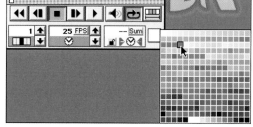

The background color is changed to bright red. ▶

▲ The Cyburger's red background is changed to white using the paint bucket tool.

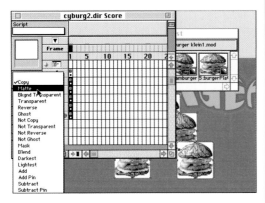

▲ The five images on the "stage" are selected and given a Matte in the score.

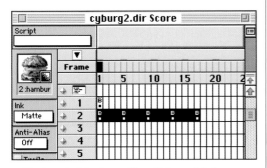

▲ Director calculates the position of intermediate frames based on four intermediate sprites.   ▼

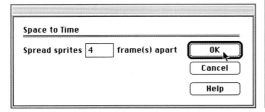

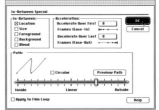

◄ The In-Between Special option ensures that the Cyburger's jumping movement appears realistic.

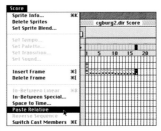

◄ The Paste Relative function is applied to the last frame of the series.

◄ The frame at the lowest point is used as a turning point in the movement.

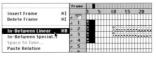

◄ The In-Between Linear option is applied to all four cells in frame 1.

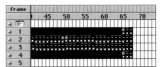

◄ The copied part from the score is pasted further down in time.

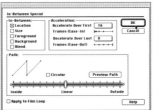

◄ The falling movement is achieved by using the In-Between Special option.

▼ The text is typed directly on the stage.

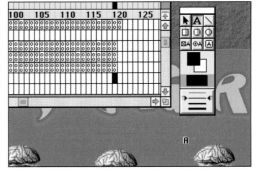

▶ Finishing

Once you have included all the animations and you know how long the movie is going to last, you have to apply a background drawing across the entire score.

I used the handy In-Between Special function for this. Subsequently, I added two text cast members and included the sound file in the cast. Then I inserted the sound in groups of four frames in the score at the spot where the cyburgers touch the "ground."

▶ Scripting

You cannot produce a Director movie without Lingo, the program's code language. One of the indispensable scripts, Script 7, specifies the end of the frame. Director's interactive options are illustrated with Script 11. In Lingo we indicate that "if one clicks on the cyburger with the mouse, the flat version will be displayed."

Script 8 goes one step further and describes the cyburger's behavior the moment the text is displayed, while the illustration wiggles. Anything you can imagine is possible. Now the definitive Director movie is finished and, in principle, it can be viewed in a compatible Web browser.

However, Macromedia Director has developed another compression mechanism that reduces the file size by about 40 percent. The Aftershock software that comes with Director completes the Shockwave DCR file and the HTML code.

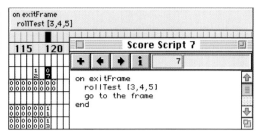

▲ The script starting with on exitFrame is intended for the last frame of the Director movie.

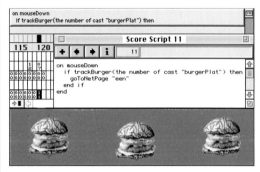

▲ This script ensures that the second flat version of the Cyburger is displayed when clicked on. ▼

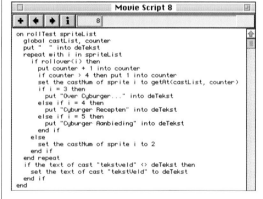

```
on rollTest spriteList
   global castList, counter
   put "   " into deTekst
   repeat with i in spriteList
      if rollover(i) then
         put counter + 1 into counter
         if counter > 4 then put 1 into counter
         set the castNum of sprite i to getAt(castList, counter)
         if i = 3 then
            put "Over Cyburger..." into deTekst
         else if i = 4 then
            put "Cyburger Recepten" into deTekst
         else if i = 5 then
            put "Cyburger Aanbieding" into deTekst
         end if
      else
         set the castNum of sprite i to 2
      end if
   end repeat
   if the text of cast "tekstveld" <> deTekst then
      set the text of cast "tekstVeld" to deTekst
   end if
end
```

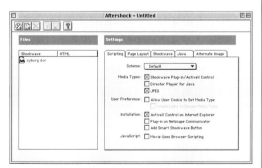

▲ Macromedia Aftershock generates all the required HTML code and Java scripting needed for the Shockwave movie.

▲ If the user does not have the Shockwave plug-in (or has the wrong version), a GIF image is displayed.

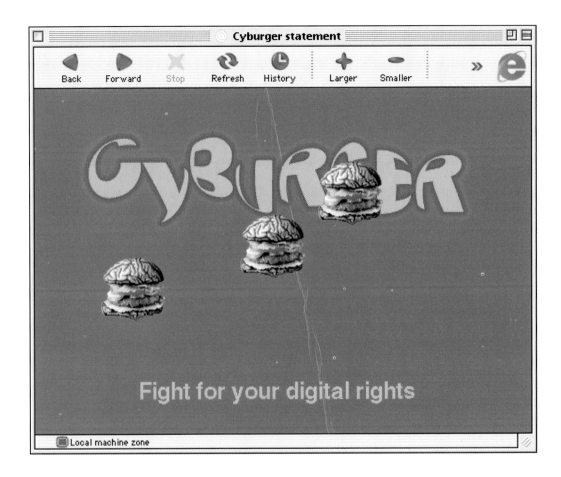

▶ Embedding

You can include a Shockwave movie in a Web page by using the <EMBED> tag. This tag also has attributes that can influence the entire course of the movement in the movie. The DCR extension indicates that it is a Shockwave file.

Allocate Shockwave DCR <EMBED> ▶

The animation is included in the page by using the <EMBED> tag and entering the name of the Shockwave file as the source. It is also wise to enter the width and height of the animation so that the browser can reserve the space in advance (this is a must for large Shockwave files). The size of the complete cyburg.dcr file is only 24K!

```
<HTML>
  <HEAD>
    <TITLE>Cyburger statement</TITLE>
  </HEAD>
<BODY bgcolor="#ff0000" text="#9CCEFF">
<BR>

<CENTER>

<EMBED SRC="cyburg.dcr" WIDTH=448
  HEIGHT=240 TEXTFOCUS=never>

<H1>Fight for your digital rights</H1>

</CENTER>

</BODY>
</HTML>
```

▶ Keep It Compact

The Shockwave movie file size should not exceed 200KB. You can use a number of techniques to restrict its size:

■ Limit the number of cast members and the number of colors in the palettes. Try to use the same image in various sizes, which is much more economical than preparing separate versions in Photoshop. The Transform Bitmaps option lets you set the dithering in Director very low. The program's drawing tools add a little extra "weight" to the movie, but can be used quite effectively to create cast members or a mask.

■ Try to keep sound files to a minimum of 11,025 kHz. Sound adds an important dimension to a movie but consumes an enormous amount of hard disk space. You can use loops to continually repeat a short sound fragment. A short sound that is heard when the user clicks on an object also works fine.

■ You can shorten the Shockwave movie itself and put it into a loop. However, this requires modifying the last frame using the following text:

```
on exitFrame
   go frame 1
end
```

The film will now repeat itself endlessly, so don't annoy the visitor with ear-piercing music fragments.

■ Give your Shockwave movie an attractive structure by using repeating background patterns, thus avoiding the large quantity of data that a huge PICT normally contains. The tiles used for the background pattern should be based on a height and/or width of 16, 32, 64, or 128 pixels. Director can save a maximum of eight separate patterns as a cast member.

■ You should exercise restraint with video clips. The QuickTime file size imposes this restriction. Try to use 1-bit PICT images as an alternative that can be put in a four-frame

loop. Adding color variations can disguise the limited number of images. You can also convert 3D animations into 1-bit frames to save space without compromising quality.

■ In the cyburger example, we used Director's greatest strength, the Lingo code language, only to a limited degree. Lingo's options are really endless and Macromedia continues to expand the language with each update. Lingo commands now allow URLs to be accessed directly from the movie.

■ Take a look in the cache of your Web browser after you have visited a number of Web sites containing Shockwave movies *(you can find them at www.shockwave.com)*. The DCR files in your cache are the Shockwave movies you have been viewing, there for your education and amusement.

▶ Shockwave Controller

Macromedia has added a special controller to Director that lets you save your favorite movies and access them again later. It lets you install a kind of remote control to play these movies on your computer desktop—a handy solution for storing your movies.

You can find ▶
advertising banners
of all sorts and
sizes on the Web.

This chapter shows how to create an attractive online ad bar quickly using Beatware's e-Picture Pro. We also examine the requirements for creating a successful banner and applicable related techniques.

Banner Advertising

Banner ads play the same role on the Internet as billboards do in a baseball stadium. They attract only a fraction of your attention, but they are impossible to overlook and are commercially valuable. However, one can have too much of a good thing, as we know. Just like Italian soccer stadiums, where you see billboards three or four rows deep almost entirely obscuring the players, not to mention the ball, commercial Web pages are becoming quite cluttered with ads. The reactions of visitors are just what you would expect, and the consequences are reflected in the statistics, as is everything on the Web.

The numbers of click-throughs continue to decline, and the regulations regarding banners are becoming more and more stringent. The DoubleClick Network and popular search engines such as AltaVista only accept banners that meet specific requirements. Other sites isolate the banners on their pages in order to keep the "noise" at an acceptable level.

▶ Rules and Tools

Of course, the cause of all this is the banner ad's disruptive form of communication. The image attempts to attract the reader's attention using striking *(read loud)* colors and irritating, continually repeating animations. This distracts the reader's attention from the rest of the content, for which the visitor had initially surfed to the page. A kind of disruptive communication, which explains the diminishing attention the banners receive. The objective for placing an online ad varies per advertiser.

Some banners merely communicate a specific message to entice the user to click. The user clicks the banner, and the rest of the process continues on another site. The number of times a banner is clicked can be measured precisely. The percentage of visitors who press the mouse button is expressed in the "click-through rate."

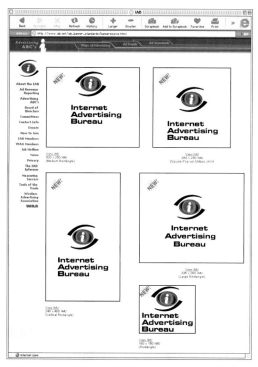

▲ An overview of all the official banner sizes and a visual example of all sizes is included.

▼ The site of the Internet Advertising Bureau (www.iab.net) offers rich information about online advertising.

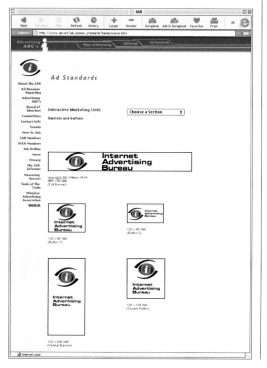

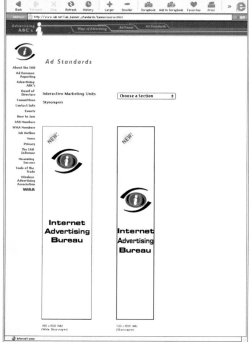

■ Beatware's e-Picture Pro Banner Production 1

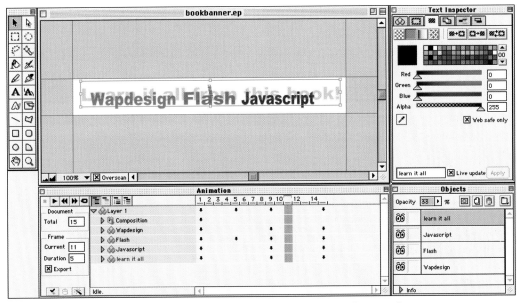

▲ ePicture is a professional Web media application specifically for online banners that lets you animate as you create.

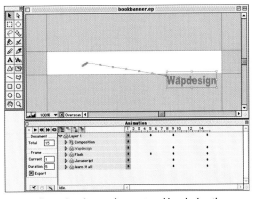

▲ An online animation can be creatured by placing the textual (or graphical) element at the first keyframe...

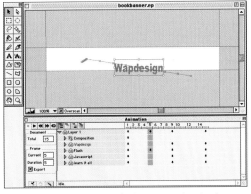

▲ ...and by simply dragging the image over the visual area (in this case the standard 468 x 60 pixels size).

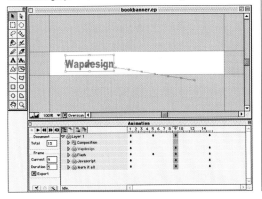

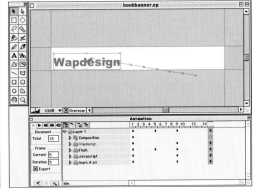

▶ Click-through Rate

A very successful banner, such as the famous Hewlett Packard's "pong," has reached a maximum click-through rate of seven percent! Nowadays a banner hardly reaches the half-percent mark... So you see what creativity can achieve. The HP banner gave the user the ability to play the Pong game inside the banner. A truly interactive experience, compared to the ordinary banner.

Some banners appear on the Web merely to promote name recognition; they don't request any specific action but create an awareness of the brand name displayed.

Other banners have simple interactive elements, such as pop-up menus or input fields. All banners have one feature in common, in spite of the considerable variety in their functions: conspicuousness. An online ad that does not catch the visitor's eye is a waste of money. A banner ad's appeal seems to depend to a large extent on its movement. A static bar results in about 25 percent fewer click-throughs than an animated banner.

In itself this is logical—a moving image attracts more attention. However, this has a number of practical consequences for the Web developer. A banner using GIF animation is subject to the limitations of the advertising medium. Aside from the

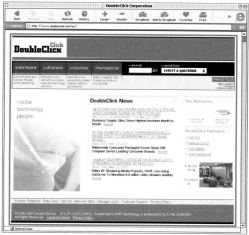

▲ On the DoubleClick Web site (www.doubleclick.com) you can find all sorts of information for an banner campaign.

most logical criterion—the ad bar's size expressed in pixels—the maximum size in kilobytes is increasingly becoming a restriction. From my own experience I know that AOL Time Warner's publications established a 15KB limit. This means that the design literally has to be processed pixel by pixel until the limit is reached. Yahoo even went one step further by setting a maximum of 4 seconds for the animation's duration. All this has been done expressly to avoid those irritating, endlessly repeating ad messages on the screen.

▼ Banners in Macromedia Flash format are becoming more and more fashionable. The combination of sound, moving images and interaction with the user is quite appealing.

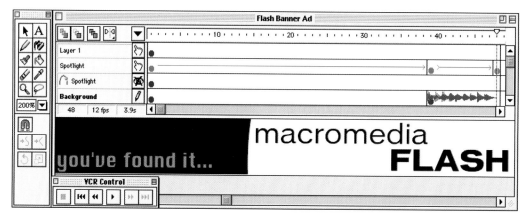

Beatware's e-Picture Pro Banner Production 2

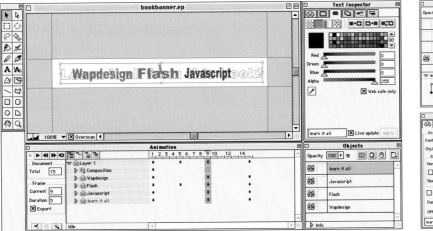

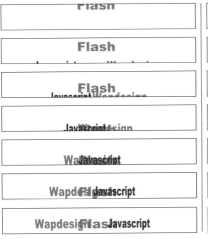

▲ e-Picture Pro is capable of creating all the textual elements in the banner design. The text stays fully editable even when graphical effects have been used.

◄ In this step-by-step sequence the effect of the banner is clearly visible. e-Picture Pro is able to emulate the final result from within in the program.

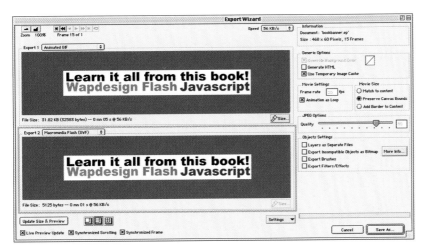

◄ When the creative part of the banner production process is finished, the finalization is done with the help of the Export Wizard. Again, a solid presentation of the end result is shown in e-Picture Pro before exporting the final GIF animation. If the usage of Macromedia Flash is allowed, the program can also facilitate this export format based on the same design and artwork!

▶ Typical Banner Requirements

The worldwide DoubleClick Network limited the number of animation loops to three repetitions. Therefore, the layout for a typical banner has to comply with the following requirements:

Width:	468 pixels
Height:	60 pixels
Maximum file size:	12 Kb
Extended file size:	15 Kb
Maximum animation loop:	3 x

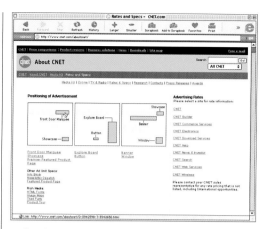

▲ C|Net has an online explanation of the commercial options regarding its banner positions and promotion facilities.

▲ This particular site, www.ilse.nl, uses fixed IAB sizes as basis for its design. The left- and right-hand columns are 120 pixels wide, just like the top button advertisement.

Of course, these measurements and conditions vary with the banner network of your choice. Individual sites have their own restrictions and enhancements, based on the specific site design. And due to the decreasing effectiveness of standard banners and buttons, new formats and positions are tried and tested. The beauty of the Web remains the sheer measurability of the medium. But in this instance, that particular virtue of the Web is held against it. If a client concludes that an online advertising campaign is unsuccesful because of a low click-through rate, the stats prove him right. But brand effectiveness is not solely measured by click-throughs!

▶ Successful Banner Techniques

In this chapter we are going to create a banner in the standard format by using the program e-Picture Pro from Beatware. This Windows- and Macintosh-compatible program is particlly suited for the creation of banners

The software automatically starts up in the standard 468-by-60-pixel setting. Of course, you can use the other IAB standard sizes: 392 by 72, 234 by 60, 120 by 240, 120 by 90, 120 by 60, 125 by 125, and 88 by 31 pixels, the Netscape and Microsoft browsers' well-known button format. These banner sizes are standard worldwide. Or you can specify your own size.

The e-Picture Pro program displays the interior dimensions of the banner inside a 1-pixel wide border with a wider margin around it—a sort of digital cropping. e-Picture Pro features an animation window, a text and color palette, a timeline with keyframes, and an objects/layers list. These are the ingredients with which the banners can be manufactured without the help of any other software. For the demo banner, we are going to use a white background with mostly RGB *(Red, Green and Blue)* colored text. Research has shown that strong colors result in a better click-through percentage.

One of the most successful ▶ banner ads of all time is the one on the HotWired site, shown here. The home page is completely black and white, and the visitor is invited to click "HotWired's true colors."

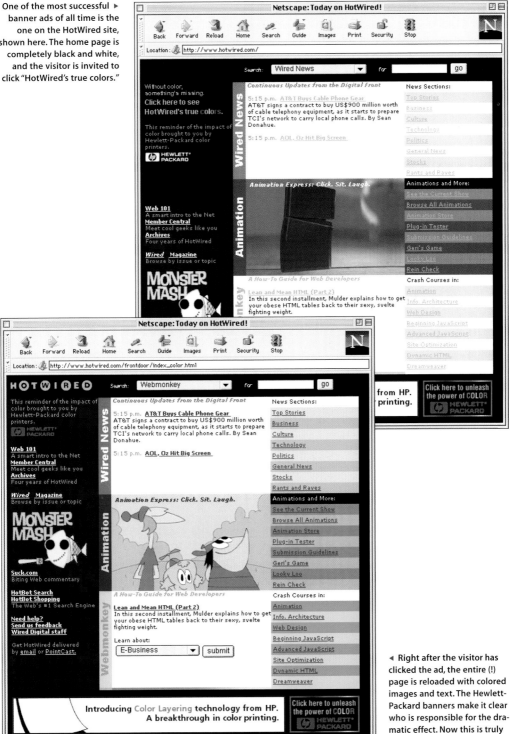

◀ Right after the visitor has clicked the ad, the entire (!) page is reloaded with colored images and text. The Hewlett-Packard banners make it clear who is responsible for the dramatic effect. Now this is truly integrated communication.

New Animation

Width: 234

Height: 60

Common Sizes

Full Banner (468 × 60)	Large Movie (320 × 240)
Full Banner (392 × 72)	Small Movie (160 × 120)
Half Banner (234 × 60)	Icon/Cursor (16 × 16)
Micro Banner/Button (88 × 31)	Icon/Button (32 × 32)

Cancel   New

▲ Extensis PhotoAnimator opens with a list of common banner sizes to facilitate and speed up the design process.

▶ Extensis PhotoAnimator

Of course there are other options to create effective and sophisticated online banners. Adobe Photoshop in combination with Adobe ImageReady is also a favorite of professional Web artists. alternative to e-Picture Pro is the offering from of Extensis. Their PhotoTools product features the Photo-Animator component, which is capable of creating complex GIF animations without losing track as a designer.

PhotoAnimator can automatically generate all the necessary frames and transitions for a particular special effect. In the process, the program alsoautomatically creates an optimal files size. The designer can focus on the creative process; Extensis PhotoAnimator worries about the details. An interesting option for the graphic artist who is not particularly interested in using keyframes.

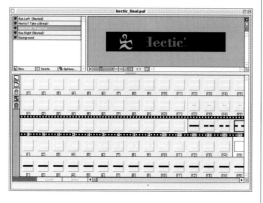

▲ Extensis PhotoAnimator is an alternative to e-Picture Pro.

The "virtual" ▶
documents can be
viewed online
using Acrobat.

Adobe developed the Portable Document Format, or PDF, as a system-independent solution for viewing and printing documents. This makes it a highly suitable product for both online and print-based publishing.

 ## Adobe Acrobat and PDF

HTML is not the only platform-independent file format. Adobe, which was part of the initial desktop publishing revolution, developed PDF years ago. Technically speaking, the Portable Document Format is a conversion of PostScript data.

The unique character of this file format is the fact that the "reader" of the PDF file does not have to have the typefaces installed that are used in the original PostScript document. A second advantage becomes clear when the information is printed on a PostScript printer: the print quality is perfect!

▲ The PDF file takes up less than 10 percent of the original image size of the QuarkXPress PostScript dump.

▶ Readers (Programs) and Readers (People)

In addition, the file's recipient can add comments to the text. It is even possible to copy parts of the text and paste them in a word processor. The fact that a PDF document is system-independent makes it suitable for producing files on CD-ROM as well. If the CD complies with the ISO 9660 norm, you can create a CD that any machine can read. Institutions or companies that wish to make information generally accessible can burn the information on a CD-ROM in the form of PDF documents.

Extra information such as comments, links, miniature displays, and bookmarks assist the person reading the text. Admittedly, it is no fun to read long texts from a computer screen. Only the text of the currently selected page is visible, while the rest of the document remains hidden. To address these objections, Adobe has built in a number of tools in the PDF file. The miniature display of all document pages and especially the ability to link to other pages create a better overview of all the digital information.

A page can be enlarged up to 800 percent. Adobe's ATM technology guarantees an extremely sharp screen display.

▶ Theory

The file format of a PDF document uses the PostScript page-description language to describe all external elements. Just like PostScript files, PDF files are resolution-independent and can be printed perfectly on any laser printer or photographic imagesetter. Only the screen information depends on the compression method chosen. The extent to which the images are compressed, of course, also determines the quality of the output.

▶ Image Compression

Acrobat Distiller is actually a virtual printer, a program with a built-in PostScript interpreter that allows the user to display a PostScript file directly onscreen. This technology is indispensable for creating PDF files. The Acrobat Distiller is a deceptively simple program—only a few menus and commands are available. The choice of the right image compression is important. You can set up separate compression techniques for color, grayscale, and black-and-white images in the Job Options window.

LZW compression guarantees the best quality, the so-called 'lossless' version. In addition, you have a choice of three JPEG compressions. Of course, the size of the PDF file decreases as the image compression increases.

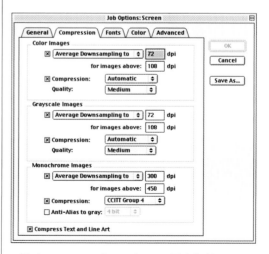

▲ The image compression can be set to 72 dpi without creating any problems.

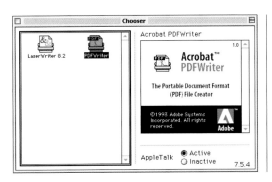

◄ You can make high-quality PostScript dumps from QuarkXPress using the Export for Prepress XTension.

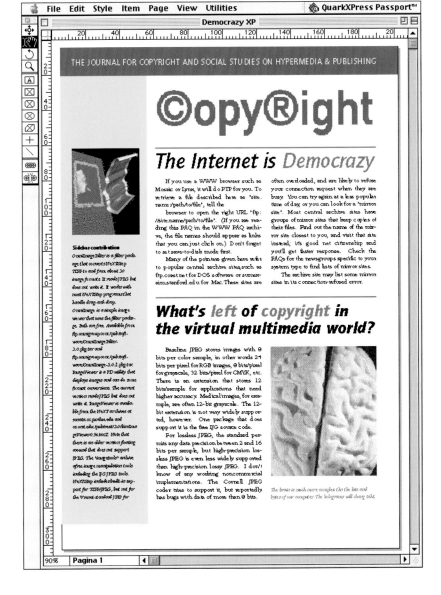

◄ The QuarkXPress file Democrazy XP is used as the basis for the PDF file. Two TIFF images and a PostScript document have been imported to the page. All this information must be displayed at an optimal resolution in the PDF file.

▶ Export for Prepress

A PostScript dump is always the starting point for Acrobat Distiller. This means that any program that can print to a hard disk can produce files that can be processed as PDFs.

These are not only the familiar page-layout programs such as QuarkXPress and Adobe InDesign, but also drawing programs such as Macromedia FreeHand and Adobe Illustrator and Photoshop. Even word processors, such as Microsoft Word, can generate PostScript.

The "Democrazy" newsletter was laid out in QuarkXPress and saved as a PostScript file, using Adobe's Export for Prepress XTension. Then Distiller was used to convert the PostScript dump to a PostScript file that takes up a little less than 1MB. However, after Distiller converted the document to a PDF file, the file size was reduced to 71KB! The miniature-page-display option in Acrobat Reader is extremely handy. To activate this, select Generate thumbnails in the Distiller Options window.

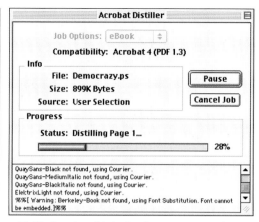

▲ Distiller in action with the QuarkXPress PostScript dump.

◀ Acrobat also works with "bookmarks." These can be referrals to other pages, files, or URLs.

Acrobat™ Weblink

▶ PDF and Multimedia

The PDF file format is an open format, just like the PostScript language. This means that other image techniques can be included as well. QuickTime, Apple's unsurpassed image and sound standard, is the first candidate, of course. By integrating this file format into a PDF document, you can add moving images and sound to universally readable documents.

It is also possible to create interactivity between the pages themselves and references to external URLs *(with or without PDF files)*. However, you must have installed the WebLink plug-in, which comes standard with the Acrobat Pro kit.

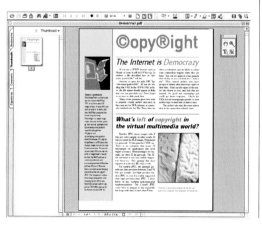

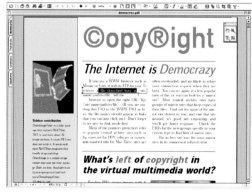

◀ You can copy text from the Democrazy PDF file.   ▲

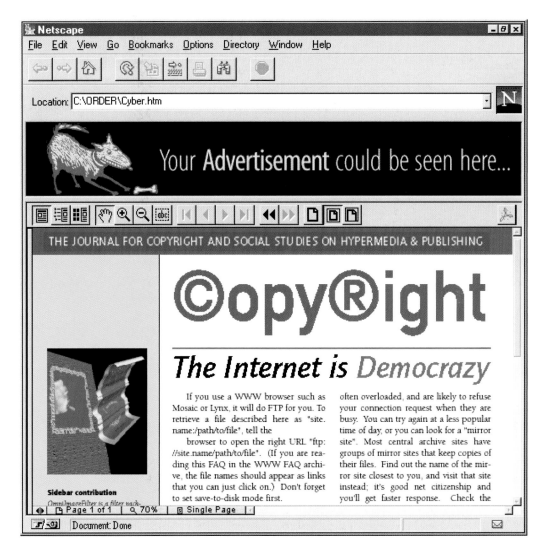

▶ PDF embedding

The Web page shown above was created using frames. This allows you to combine a changing advertising message with a PDF file. Using the <META> tag, you can have the advertising banner change every 'x' number of seconds.

Standard <HREF> Tag ▷

The <A HREF> tag is used to invoke the PDF file. The user can view the PDF in a browser window or move it to the hard disk with the Alt or Option key.

```
<!--Copyright Peter Kentie, frameset: Democrazy-->
<HTML>
  <HEAD>
    <TITLE>copyright.html</TITLE>
  </HEAD>
<BODY BGCOLOR="#FFFFFF">

<CENTER>
<A HREF="democraz.pdf">Download me now!</A>
</CENTER>

</BODY>
</HTML>
```

▲ Adobe Acrobat PDF files can be digitally watermarked.

▲ The question mark indicates a digitally "signed" document.

▶ Streaming Acrobat Files

When you create a PDF file from a large number of pages, at a certain point the file size will exceed a critical limit.

If you plan to put the document on a CD-ROM, this can be awkward; if the PDF file must be downloaded via a 14.4 kbps modem, you are in trouble. There are a number of ways to remedy the situation. If the PDF file is linked to the Web page, you can specify its size. Then the user can decide to retrieve the document or not, depending on the connection quality and the modem speed.

If the PDF file has been incorporated into the Web page, as shown on the previous page, this solution will not be sufficient. Realizing this, Adobe developed Supra to address this problem. In fact, what it does is "stream" the PDF file—the pages of the PDF file are sent over the Internet one by one. The loading time for the PDF files is shortened, and the user has the option of viewing the text as antialiased. Of course, the acceptance of this technology depends in part on the popularity of the Acrobat plug-in. Without that piece of software, the PDF page cannot be displayed.

This solution is also quite interesting for digital printing: Printing presses are directly linked to a computer that functions as a kind of super printer. This development is a giant step forward, because these machines also offer the option of "personalization."

▶ Linking to Offline Media

Each PDF file offers a unique way to combine online and offline techniques. Thanks to Acrobat's Weblink plug-in, you can create a hyperlink from the PDF file to a URL. This offers options that no other technique provides. Suppose you burn a CD-ROM with PDF files containing information about a product, and you establish hyperlinks from the CD files to a Web site where the latest prices are displayed. Wouldn't this be the perfect solution for many an information-publishing problem? The PDF files, optimized for printing, can be printed at a high resolution, like this book.

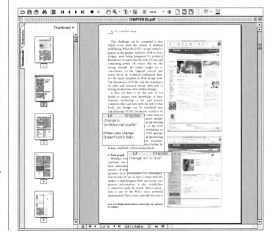

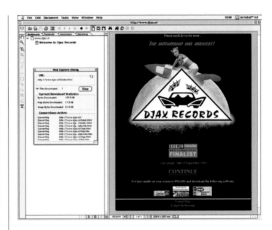

▲ In a single action, Acrobat converts a site to a PDF. ▶

▶ Web Site Conversion to PDF

Using Acrobat Exchange 5.0, an entire Web site can be retrieved and converted to PDF format. This is a useful application of the program, because Web sites are normally extremely volatile and change continually. By capturing a site, you create a picture of the content at a particular moment, which can be useful later. This Adobe invention is extremely beneficial for archival purposes. One reason is that all the site's links are included in the conversion, which makes the PDF document interactive as well.

This application offers many options for training developers because it resolves the question, Shall we give our course in HTML or not? The answer is yes, because this application makes it a living document!

The final PDF ▶
version for the
DJAX site with all
the underlying
Web pages.

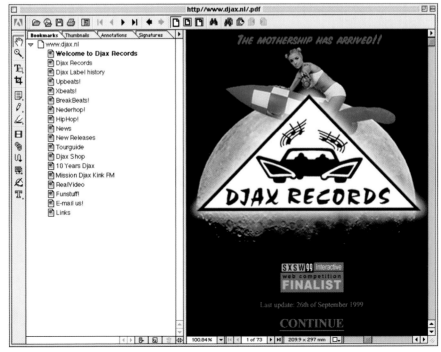

▲ E-paper and e-books will be hot words in the new economy.
Adobe is at the heart of this revolution.

▶ Web Buy and E-Books

Adobe can also use its PDF technique to
capitalize on the market for e-books. These
are the newest Internet devices with which
books, magazines, and other documents can
be read. The files are completely digital and
can easily be downloaded to the reader.

Of course, the reader has to pay a fee, and
that is why Adobe's Web Buy technology
comes in handy. It can lock a PDF document
and free it up again with an electronic key.
This creates a new business model for written
content.

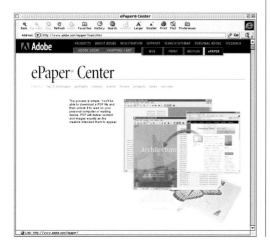

The home page ► of the Society for Radio Jingles and Tunes was created for a special-interest group.

Say you want to create a Web site that allows visitors to listen to music and other sounds. How do you achieve this? In this chapter, I explain how to convert professional radio jingles to an Internet-compatible file format.

Working with Sound

Moving images and sound—two elements of the broad category known as "multimedia"—may add liveliness to CD-ROM productions. But what works on a CD-ROM does not necessarily work on the Web: The generally large file sizes of video and sound clips can make them difficult to handle over the Internet. Fortunately, you can process an audio file in such a way that its size stays reasonable, and several technologies have emerged that permit "streaming" of sound files. One of them, RealAudio, enables you to listen to live broadcasts via the Internet.

▶ Audio File Formats

In contrast to image file formats, there is no universally accepted standard for audio data on the Internet, although a number of file formats—including AU, AIFF, WAVE, MIDI, MPEG audio, TrueSpeech, and the aforementioned RealAudio—compete for this honor. I will not attempt to explain the differences among these formats; rather, I will show you a practical way to add sound to your Web site using files saved in the WAVE *(.wav)* format. I chose WAVE because it is compatible with all mainstream computer platforms and because its ratio of file size to sound quality is acceptable. All jingles in the sample site have been saved as WAVE files.

▶ Analog to Digital

A jingle may be stored on a variety of media, from an analog record album to a digital CD-ROM, but must be digitized before you can use it on your Web site. In the example, an audio clip was transferred to hard disk using Astarte CD-Copy, unfortunately no longer available. Among the jingles is one transferred at 22KHz in 8-bit mono, using Adaptec *(Roxio)* Jam *(both of these are Macintosh applications).*

This ensures reasonable sound quality while keeping file size relatively small. Many alternatives to such software are available. On the PC, you can digitize your audio clips with a good sound card such as Creative Technology's Sound Blaster, then edit them using WaveStudio *(included with the Sound Blaster)* or a similar program.

▶ Sound Editing

Macromedia SoundEdit, popular with Macintosh users, offers several options for compressing the jingle files. Note, however, that a sound clip recorded at 22KHz and then converted to 11KHz will have a lower frequency range and, consequently, less volume. This effect is comparable to the way a scanner's range changes at various color

depths: The lower the scan range, the less detailed the image. To compensate for the lower frequency range, select the entire wave form and amplify it by 20 percent, then copy and paste it into a second track. Next, combine the two tracks using SoundEdit's Mix command. This editing process results in a much louder sound clip.

The example jingles have already been digitized in mono *(stereo is unnecessary for PCs)* and saved as 8-bit sound files.

▶ Reducing File Size but Not Audible Quality

Converting the sound file to 11KHz reduces its size from 187K to 89K. You can make it even smaller by reducing the duration of the data; accelerating the sound fragment has this effect.

The difference is not really audible, but the compression takes almost 1 second off the original eight beats and reduces the final file's size by 12 percent. *(Keep in mind that this trick does not always work as well as in our example, and not every sound is suitable for it.)*

Next, save the WAVE jingle file without compression and include it in the Web page using the standard HTML <A HREF> tag.

Frequency	Sound-Quality Range and Recommendations
5.564 kHz	Roughly the quality of a telephone call. Useful only for speech fragments, as the human voice is not very dynamic.
11.025 kHz	Television or broadcast-video quality. This is the level without Dolby noise reduction
22.050 kHz	FM radio broadcast quality (the signal still contains noise). Also known as broadcast audio.
44.100 kHz	CD quality, slightly below that of a digital audiotape recording (48KHz).

▲ An overview of sound quality at various frequencies.

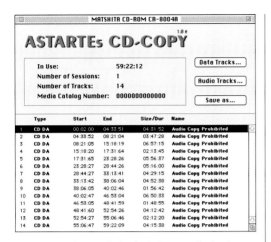

▲ Astarte CD-Copy reads the Jingle CD created using Jam.

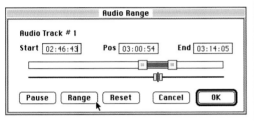

▲ Search for a specific fragment of sound with the Audio Range command.

▲ The audio sample shown below was created using these settings. ▼

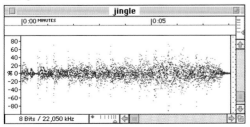

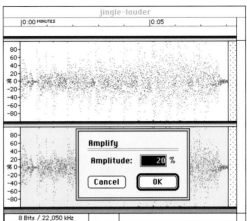

▲ A copy of a sound file is pasted into a second track.

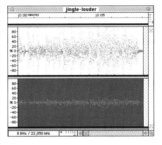

▲ After reduction to 20 percent followed by mixing, the file can be downsampled to 11KHz.

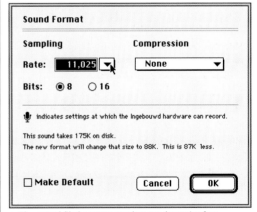

▲ The sound file becomes much more dynamic after modification and is converted to 11.025KHz.

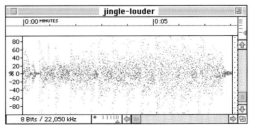

▶ Incorporating Sound Files

You can include sounds on a Web page in a number of ways. Use the standard <A HREF> tag to specify a sound; you should also indicate the clip's file size.

Creating a Structure Using <images/x.gif> ▷

You can keep your Web data organized by placing the images and sounds in separate folders. This will affect a page's URL, however.

By splitting the file into two ▶
types–six HTML documents
and two file folders–you create
a more logically structured
Web site.

The designation for the WAVE file now becomes <A HREF= "jingles/bfp.wav">, meaning that the bfp.wav file is located in the jingles folder. If you prefer working the other way around, you may find the Unix command ../ helpful: It tells a computer to search one level higher on the disk (../../ means two levels higher, and so on).

Playing Sound Using the <META> Tag ▽

You can also use the <META> tag to start playing a sound clip after a specific time interval (expressed in seconds) has elapsed. Make sure to place this code before the <BODY> tag.

```
<HTML>
<HEAD>
<META HTTP-EQUIV="refresh" CONTENT="1; URL=jingle.wav">
<TITLE>The Jingle Web: On Air</TITLE></HEAD> [and so on]
```

Playing Sound Using the <BGSOUND> Tag ▽

Microsoft has created an alternative tag that produces the same result as <META. The <BGSOUND> tag (short for "background sound") allows you to specify the number of times to repeat (loop) your sound clip, or even to specify an infinite loop.

```
<BGSOUND SRC="jingle.wav" LOOP=5>
<BGSOUND SRC="jingle.wav" LOOP=INFINITE>
```

```
<!--
All rights reserved, Creation date: 1995/11/01
Dino/The Society for Radio Jingles and Tunes
Text: Benno Roozen, Jelle Boonstra, Maarten Schutjes;
Design: Maarten Schutjes, Dino Design & Advertising
-->
<HTML>
<HEAD><TITLE>The Jingle Web: On Air</TITLE></HEAD>
<BODY bgcolor="#FFFFFF" link="#00CCFF">
<CENTER><IMG width=485 height=163 border=0
SRC="images/header.gif">

<TABLE width=490><TR><TD>
<FONT size=+1>On cue for you... the work of some of the
leading jinglecompanies in Europe. Read the descriptions
and push the 'play' button or click on the highlighted text to
download WAV files. And of course, all material is protected
under copyright! Enjoy... </FONT>
</TD></TR>
</TABLE>
<P>
<TABLE width=490 cellpadding=5>
<TR><TD>
<IMG width=490 height=33 border=0 align=center
SRC="images/chrome.gif" alt="green bar"><P>
<A HREF="jingles/bfp.wav"><IMG SRC="images/
button.gif" width=42 height=45 border=0></TD>
<TD>Ben Freedman Productions</A>(171 Kb WAV-file)<BR>
Some jingles from Maximum Fire Power made for WGEE. enz...
</TD></TR></TABLE>
<P>
<IMG width=490 height=33 border=0
SRC="images/chrome.gif" alt="greenbar"><P>
<A HREF="index.htm"><IMG hspace=10 border=0
SRC="images/main.gif" alt="Homepage"></A>
<A HREF="about.htm"><IMG hspace=10 border=0
SRC="images/ab.gif" alt="About JingleWeb"></A>
<A HREF="industry.htm"><IMG hspace=10 border=0
SRC="images/ind.gif" alt="Industry news"></A>
<A HREF="other.htm"><IMG hspace=10 border=0
SRC="images/other.gif" alt="Other sites"></A>
<A HREF="adres.htm"><IMG hspace=10 border=0
SRC="images/dir.gif" alt="Adres"></A>
</CENTER>
</BODY>
</HTML>
```

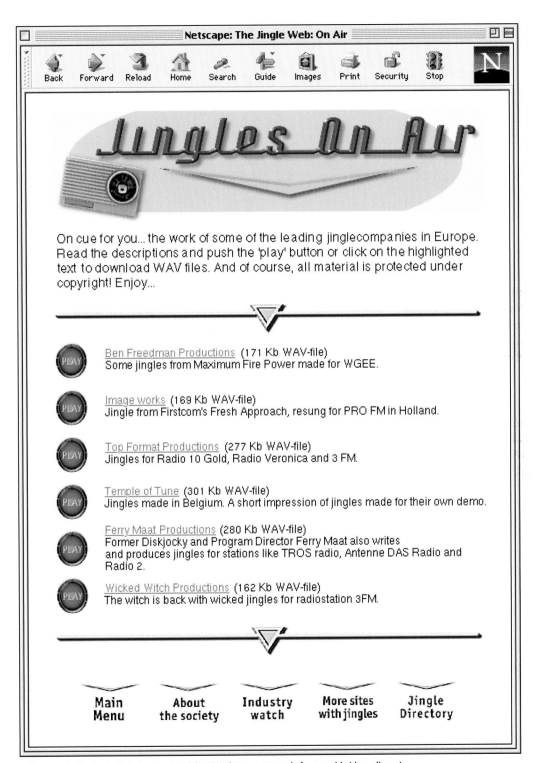

Back   Forward   Reload   Home   Search   Guide   Images   Print   Security   Stop

On cue for you... the work of some of the leading jinglecompanies in Europe. Read the descriptions and push the 'play' button or click on the highlighted text to download WAV files. And of course, all material is protected under copyright! Enjoy...

Ben Freedman Productions (171 Kb WAV-file)
Some jingles from Maximum Fire Power made for WGEE.

Image works (169 Kb WAV-file)
Jingle from Firstcom's Fresh Approach, resung for PRO FM in Holland.

Top Format Productions (277 Kb WAV-file)
Jingles for Radio 10 Gold, Radio Veronica and 3 FM.

Temple of Tune (301 Kb WAV-file)
Jingles made in Belgium. A short impression of jingles made for their own demo.

Ferry Maat Productions (280 Kb WAV-file)
Former Diskjocky and Program Director Ferry Maat also writes and produces jingles for stations like TROS radio, Antenne DAS Radio and Radio 2.

Wicked Witch Productions (162 Kb WAV-file)
The witch is back with wicked jingles for radiostation 3FM.

Main Menu   About the society   Industry watch   More sites with jingles   Jingle Directory

▲ The sample jingles, included on the "onair.htm" Web page, are ready for a worldwide audience!

RealAudio and Sound Compression

I noted earlier in this chapter that no standard for digital sound has been universally adopted. The frequencies have been specified, but the method for streaming audio data has not yet been settled on. The dream of all sound freaks—live audio on the Internet—requires a completely new technology because the WAVE, AU, and AIFF files cannot yet achieve a speed of 64Kbps. A rate of 10Kbps is a better starting point for live audio.

▲ RealAudio can convert data files to 8, 11, 22, and 44KHz mono.

▲ The conversion takes place without involving the user. The RealPlayer software is required to play the sound.

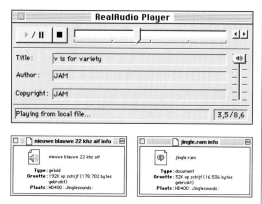

▲ The RealAudio file is only 10 percent of the size of the original file saved in AIFF (Apple's own sound format).

Several companies have attempted to tackle the problem by developing new Internet audio specifications. Currently, the most advanced is RealNetworks' RealAudio, whose associated .ra or .ram file format has become the de facto standard for streaming audio. In addition, many commercial Web sites *(notably those of broadcasting firms, radio stations, and the like)* use their own software.

Beyond its audio-streaming ability, RealAudio's biggest advantage is the compression technology it uses. The jingle test file prepared in this chapter is small—only 16.5K—due to RealAudio's 28.8Kbps mono quality; however, it does not sound as pristine as the 11KHz, 89K .wav file.

Real-time compression is undoubtedly the wave of the future. RealNetworks' free RealPlayer software, available for all computer platforms, allows an external server to start the data stream, eliminating the need for expensive server software. Real has not only swept the audio world; it has also simplified video-image transmission because the same player can be used for both sound and video. Microsoft Windows Media Player is of course its main rival in the online market, and is fighting for a stronger market share.

▲ RealPlayer works with both audio and video data and comes with a set of standard channels.

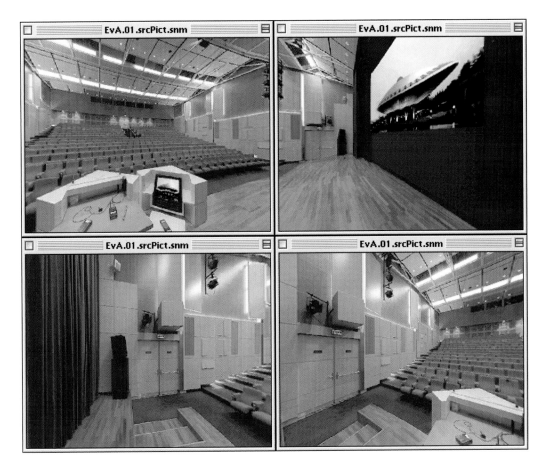

With the addition of video content to Web pages, the Internet becomes the ultimate form of television: millions of channels, and the ability to communicate directly with any of them. QuickTime VR allows a viewer to look over an unfamiliar space "virtually" from anywhere in the world via the Web.

QuickTime VR and Video

 When you build movie clips into a Web page, you simultaneously add moving images and audio data. The main disadvantage is the enormous size of the component video files, which can cause problems with data transfer. Yet bright minds are working hard on solutions that "stream" video images *(that is, make them viewable as soon as the first bytes of data are received by the computer)*. Apple has moved in another direction with its QuickTime VR, or QTVR for short. With this technology, users move through video clips by moving the mouse in the desired direction. The production process of a QTVR movie is explained in this chapter through a practical example.

▶ Virtual Sales

You can create a QTVR movie in a variety of ways, and several programs are available to help you do so. The standard procedure entails using specially prepared photographs, but you can also work with images created in a CAD or 3D graphics program, such as Corel Bryce. QTVR is suitable for multimedia applications because it allows creation of a "virtual world" and an almost magical impression of interior space. It is also very compact.

In this chapter, I explain how a QTVR panorama movie showing a conference center's auditorium was produced. The interior of Philips Hall is presented on the Web, giving potential rental customers around the world a detailed view from the inside.

This photo provides only a superficial glimpse of the ▶ Evoluon Congress Center's large Philips Hall.

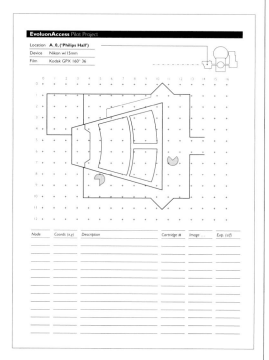

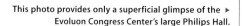

▲ Shots of the Philips Hall auditorium, along with photographic characteristics, are documented using this form.

▶ Production Planning

To present the room to best advantage, three QTVR movies are produced from three different angles. An architectural drawing helps determine the camera positions. Once the positions are determined, the actual photographs can be taken.

One shot, taken from the podium, gives an impression of the view from that position while also displaying the facility's equipment and other technical details. Twelve shots are taken using a mirror reflex camera equipped with a nondistorting ultrawide-angle (15mm) lens and placed on a special tripod from which the camera's angle can be set in degrees. The camera, which has an effective angle of 97 degrees, is moved backward so that the lens focuses above the center of the tripod, to avoid parallax distortion.

The disadvantage of such a "convex" lens is that light enters it from above and causes lens flare, which is clearly visible in the photos shown on the next page.

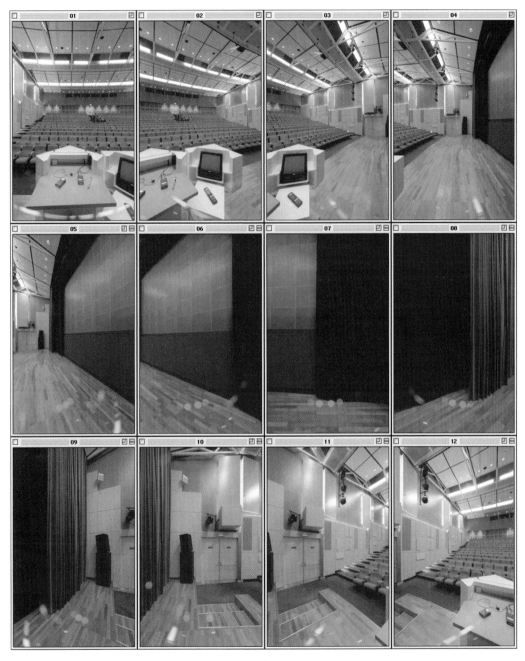

Setting up the individual shots meticulously now will save time later, when the photos will be combined into one image using the QTVR software. The lens, for example, is constructed to keep vertical lines in the images perfectly straight, and negative slide film is used because it can handle a wide range of lighting conditions. The 12 images are then digitized with a slide scanner and processed into a single image using "stitcher" software. At a later stage, the montage will be retouched to erase seams between the shots.

▶ The Stitcher

Apple's VR Authoring Tools Suite then "sews" the shots together. One way to do this is using the Stitcher. The Stitcher tool of the Macintosh Programmer's Workshop *(MPW)* software applies the cylindrical distortion of the source photos and then assembles them into a single image.

The overlapping parts are averaged out, and a 1248-by-384-pixel PICT file is generated. This size is adequate for a Web-quality QTVR movie *(for CD-ROM applications, 2496 by 768 pixels is more suitable)*. Note that the pixel measurements must be multiples of 96.

 The Stitcher is actually a script in which horizontal and vertical space for the photo montage is defined. It also specifies the path to the original image files, which are numbered from 01 to 12. If the file path is incorrect, problems will arise during the time-consuming and computer-intensive stitching process. To avoid introducing any typing errors, you can use DropPath; this handy drag-and-drop program allows you to easily place a file path on the Clipboard and then paste into the script in MPW.

Another way to achieve the same results is to follow the steps above, but use Apple's Quicktime VR Authoring Studio, which combines all of the operations of QuickTime VR authoring into a single program.

▶ Image Editing

As I mentioned earlier, the Stitcher should process the original unretouched scanned images. There are a number of reasons for this. Prior retouching of individual shots with Adobe Photoshop's Rubber Stamp tool, for example, will cause a change in the structure; retouching the auditorium's wooden floor, where the effect of lens flare is most obvious, will result in seam-stitching problems. Once the Stitcher has done its work you can modify the PICT image as you see fit. *(At the very least, be sure to increase its contrast.)*

▲ A standard Stitcher script is shown in an MPW Worksheet.

▶ Hot spots

QuickTime VR makes use of hot spots— areas in the movie that allow you to refer to a different "node" *(that is, another QTVR movie)*. And with all but the earliest versions of QuickTime, a hot spot can also link to a URL. This capability makes QTVR especially attractive for working with video on the Web. The Evoluon example includes two hot spots, which were created in Photoshop in a separate layer using a color from Apple's standard palette. The auditorium's Vidiwall bank of video monitors is designated with orange *(color number 16)*. When you include a QTVR movie in an HTML page through the <EMBED> tag, you can then link the hot spots to other Web pages.

```
<EMBED SRC="EvA_01.mov" WIDTH=320 HEIGHT=240
   HOTSPOT16="http://www.evoluon.com/comfort.htm"
   CONTROLLER=false>
```

The Stitch script must be expanded to combine the hot spots.

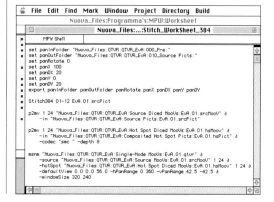

▲ The Stitcher tool "sewed" together the 12 photos shown on the previous page to create this unedited image.

▲ The lens-flare effects have been removed with Adobe Photoshop's Rubber Stamp tool, and a sample image is placed on the monitor screen.

▶ Scene Editor

Using the Scene Maker HyperCard stack, you can link nodes to one another to create a multinode scene. The process is not simple, however, and consumes a large amount *(about 20MB)* of RAM. Apple's free Make QTVR Panorama program, by contrast, makes it easy to create a single node based on a PICT image.

▲ This hot spot uses a color from Apple's basic palette. ▼

▶ Dicing and Assembling

Using MPW's p2mv *(PICT to movie)* dicer tool, the rotated panorama PICT image is divided into 24 tiles and compressed into a linear QuickTime movie. Then MPW's msnm *(make single node movie)* tool creates a playable QTVR movie. You can also perform these two steps using Make QTVR Panorama, although the settings will require some attention. The size of the image must be divisible by 4 pixels to ensure compatibility with Windows PCs as well as Macs. Thus, an image size of 320 by 240 pixels is a correct setting. The result is a QTVR movie that is only 158K yet contains a wealth of visual information.

▶ Cross-Platform Compatibility

The QuickTime file format works across computer platforms and, thanks to a variety of available plug-ins, is compatible with most Web browsers. But QuickTime is only one of many formats used for video images on the Internet. Among the alternatives are AVI, MPEG, and RealNetworks' RealVideo. One condition of using QuickTime is that the movie be saved in the Cinepak compression

The View Size must ▶ be a multiple of 4 pixels.

codec and, most important, be "flattened" to guarantee that it will play on non-Macintosh computers—including on Windows PCs, which have a different resource/data fork than the Mac's.

When the panorama movie is completed, it will have the extension .snm. The final step—

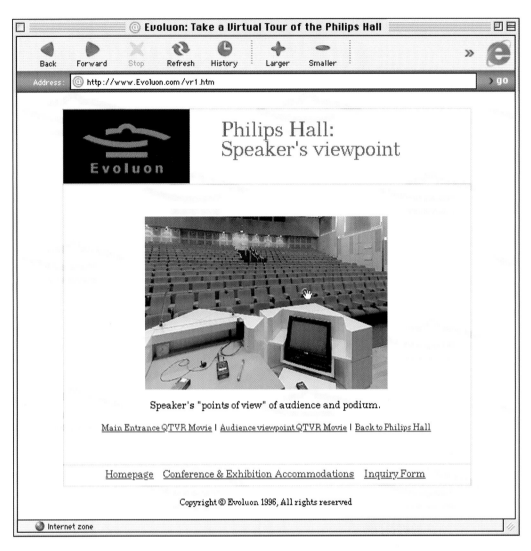

◄ A Web surfer first sees the QTVR page, then gets an overview of the hall (shown on preceding page). ▲

flattening the QTVR movie—is absolutely vital to ensure cross-compatibility. To flatten the movie, open it in Apple's QTVR Player and be sure to rename it with the general extension for films, .mov. To change the name, open the player's Save As window, check the box next to "Playable on non-Apple computers," rename the file in the text box, and click Save.

The movie is now ready to be positioned in your Web page using the <EMBED> HTML tag.

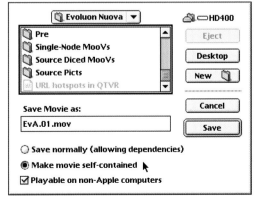

▲ The final movie is saved in the QTVR Player.

▶ Video Attributes

Adding a "normal" *(that is, non-QTVR)* movie to an HTML page is as simple as inserting an image; all you'll need is the <IMG> tag. Supported file extensions vary from platform to platform.

The .mov extension mentioned above is widely accepted, as is .avi, a Windows format that can be played directly in the Microsoft Internet Explorer browser without plug-ins.

Because the moving image has been assigned the same tag as the static images, the attributes are identical as well. You can use the well-known <ALIGN=left | right | middle | bottom>, for instance. Video images also have a number of their own attributes that affect how they look on a Web page.

Unfortunately, not all browsers recognize these attributes, although the situation improves with each browser update. Here are some examples of video attributes:

<CONTROLS>   Displays the buttons along the bottom of the movie screen.

<AUTOPLAY>   Automatically starts playing the film as soon as it is completely loaded on the Web page.

To add the movie exemplified in this chapter to your Web page, use the following code:

```
< IMG SRC="fantasy.mov" align=center width=160
   height=120 AUTOPLAY=true LOOP=true >
```

▲ To guarantee that the movie is compatible across platforms, you must turn on the Flatten option.

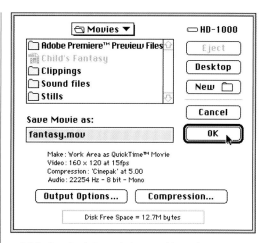

▲ Adobe Premiere's Save window provides various output options and compression settings.

▶ Streaming Video

New technologies are constantly being developed in the quest for a definitive Internet video standard. Two of them, "streaming video" and "QuickTime TV," currently hold the most promise.

▲ A movie can be played in a separate QuickTime window.

This interface ▶ is created in a 3D program and exported as an Flash file to maintain compatibility with the most popular browsers.

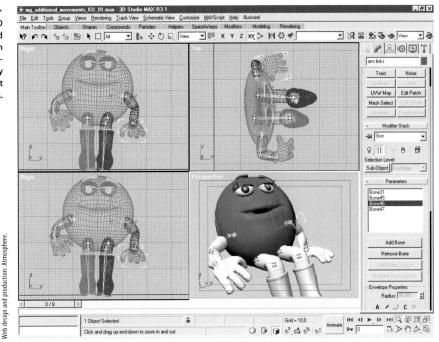

Web design and production: Atmosphere.

The Web is by nature a graphic-rich medium, though it can't live up to the nickname "Cyberspace" yet. There's far too little 3D online. The reasons are obvious; lack of bandwidth for the data-intensive 3D environments and no real Web standards for creating these environments.
This chapter explores an alternative for creating "fake" 3D with Macromedia Flash, and provides an introduction to VRML.

The Web in 3D

Initially the Internet was a text-based envionment. Today's Web is a visual medium; rich in form and color, but still flat. The next step, of course, is the third dimension: 3D-worlds in which the user navigates in real time. Flat products are becoming 3D objects to create an attractive shopping experience. That was the dream of VRML, short for Virtual Reality Modelling Language. Time has learned that this concept is not suitable for today's web environment.

Will the Web stay flat? No, emerging standards like Intel's Adaptive 3D technology and Shockwave 3D will provide solutions for the longer term. In the meantime, the Web developers have turned to practicality and have adopted Macromedia Flash as its real-world alternative for creating realistic and medium-quality 3D environments. In this chapter, I'll present an extensive Flash tutorial using Swift 3D, and will also cover the basics of VRML.

▲ The Miss Green character as seen in the M&M Web site. The model has a good balance between detail and filesize.

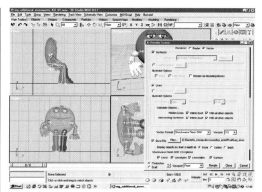

▲ The 'Miss Green' M&M model is drawn in 3DS MAX. Digimation Illustrate v5 is used for the export to Flash.

▶ Standard, what standard?

The promises VRML has made have yet to be fulfilled. In the real world the most viable option to bring a Web design to the third dimension is Flash. Macromedia Flash is not an genuine 3D-tool, it is a vector-based drawing environment whose success was based on the installation of the Flash plug-in. The acceptance of the plug-in is very broad. More than 90 percent of Web users have some version of Flash installed. And if the computer is using an older Windows operating system, the plug-in installs in a wink due to its small size *(approximately 90k)* so the user can see the Web site as intended.

▶ 3D models

The market reach of Flash and its concept of using vector-based lines and curves makes it an ideal platform for 3D. Flash has no modelling capabilities so the user has to start his 3D model in a dedicated drawing program. For this chapter we have used the software Cinema XL4D on a Macintosh computer and Discreet's 3DS MAX on a Windows PC. Both programs have the capabilities to create and export high-quality 3D-models that can be converted to Flash drawings. A popular Flash export filter for 3DS MAX is Illustrate, from www.digimation.com, as seen above in the M&M example. For Cinema 4D the conversion program Electric

Rain Swift3D is an interesting product because it is far more than a filter. It is also an editing environment for 3D Flash movies with interesting options.

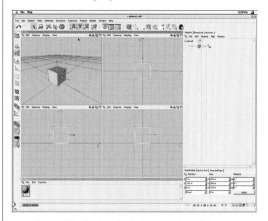

▲ In Cinema 4D a basic cube is drawn and carefully positioned on the grid using numerical input. ▼

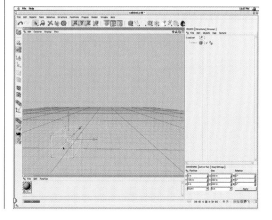

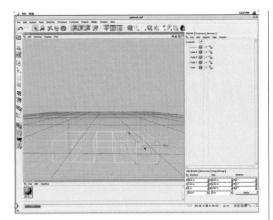

▲ Next the basic cube is copied four times to create the first row of the box. By using numerical input the cubes are tightly positioned next to each other.

▼ The complete box is drawn, five boxes wide and high.

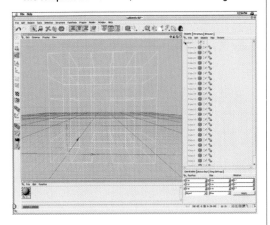

▼ A quick look in perspective is used to check the model for inconsistencies. The model is shown in skeleton form.

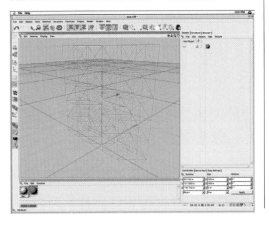

I'll present a rather elaborate example to illustrate the possibilities and restrictions of working with vector-based 3D programs. The construction of a Web site's main navigation environment is done in Flash with the aid of a modelling and export program.

▶ **Box design**

The design of the Web site is based on the concept of four large boxes that contain all navigational elements of the site. The boxes themselves slide from left to right in the browser's screen. The original boxes are drawn in Cinema 4D, an easy-to-use 3D modeller.

Each box is composed of five cubes side by side, and uses five layers stacked on top of each other. For the production of the box a single cube is drawn in Cinema 4D. Next the form is copied and positioned alongside the original cube. The dimensions are checked numerically to ensure the exact position of the individual cubes. When the final form is drawn the complete box is exported as an 3DS MAX file. The extension is ".3ds". This file format is becoming an industry standard and is accepted by the majority of the current 3D programs. The 3DS MAX file format is an ideal export choice to exchange models in 3D in between programs.

▼ The final model that has been drawn in Cinema 4DXL is exported in the 3DS MAX file format. The extension '.3ds' is automatically added to the file name.

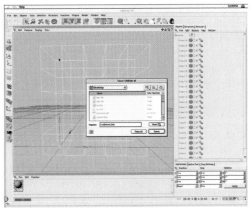

For our box the program of choice is Swift3D. The import of the ".3ds" file is simple and effective. Open a new document in Swift3D and select the Cinema file out of the file listing. In Swift3D the box model is imported and shown in its basic perspective settings. No color fills have been used, the wireframe is a basic black line. Coloring will be done in Flash so we can concentrate on the realistic movement of the model.

▶ Perspective

To create the movement from left to right we have to use key frames. This technique is similar to the one used in Macromedia Flash itself. Only the function keys are different. The model is placed to the far left of the drawing area with a small part of the box still visible. Now the key frame can be inserted. In the bar on top of the screen a key frame is placed at frame 40. This is the "end" position of the box movement.

Next we position the box to the far right hand side of the visible area. If we now move the slider you'll see the box panning from left to right. And it's not just a sliding movement. The perspective actually changes depending on the position of the box. When we're satisfied with the end result the file can be exported in the well-known ".swf" Flash file format. The edges of the box are preserved with the option called "Outlines" in the export settings of Swift3D.

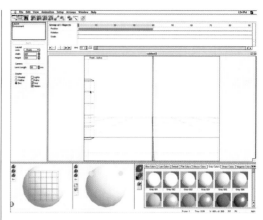

▲ The box is placed to the far left side at frame "1"...

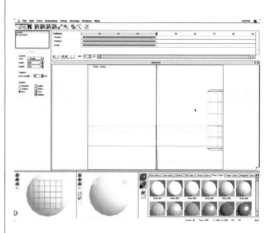

▲ ...and on frame "40" the box is positioned to the far right. The perspective of the model changes over time.

▼ The export settings of Swift3D are pretty basic.

◀ The imported model enters the desktop in the middle. No specific fillings or outline colors are added to the model.

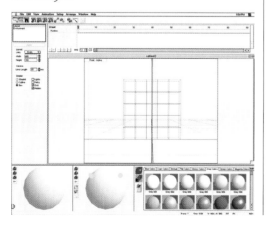

▲ The imported sequence in Flash at position "1".

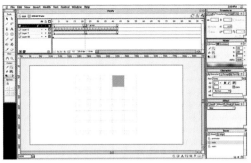

▲ Single areas are colored in Flash and made transparant.

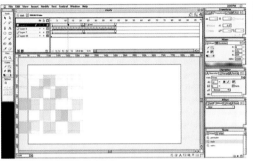

▲ As you can see the model gradually changes perspective...

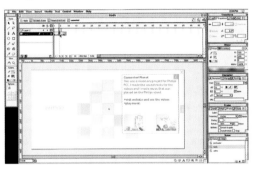

▲ When a user clicks on a colored area, hidden content appears.

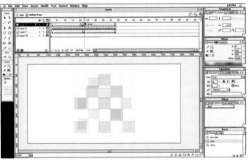

▲ ...during the movement to the middle section...

▶ Finishing Off in Flash

The ".swf" file is imported in Flash as a sequence of images in a dedicated layer. To create a smooth transition during the movement the number of "Frames Per Second", better known als FPS, is changed to 25. That will increase the file size somewhat, but the quality of the Flash movie increases significantly. Individual lines can be changed or even deleted in Flash. To bring some color to the environment, panels are given a tone.

To make this happen you'll need to convert the image to a graphic element in Flash as seen below.

▲ ...and the far right side of the working area. To enhance the effect of movement, the box starts to leave the visible area starting at frame "30."

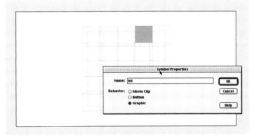

▶ A Virtual Standard

VRML 2.0 is based on collective efforts of a large group of enthusiasts. They determined the standard together and democratically decided which extensions would be used. Led by Mark Pesce and Tony Parisi, the group has come up with a spatial description language that enables visitors to a Web virtual world to look into it and navigate through it from every possible angle. The objects are coded in ASCII and are based on primitives. The actual description of a cube, called a base node, is quite simple. You save a text file as "cube.wrl" *(.wrl is the VRML extension)* and enter in the following text:

```
#VRML V1.0 ascii
Cube { height 2 width 2 depth 2 }
```

A VRML-compatible browser will then portray a 2 by 2 meter virtual cube on the screen. VRML is that simple. You can describe a sphere, bullet, or pyramid the same way. Despite its simplicity, you can do a lot with VRML. In the following example, the position, color, light source, and camera perspective are defined:

```
#VRML V1.0 ascii
Separator {
    DirectionalLight {
        direction 0.0 -1
    }
    PerspectiveCamera {
        position 0 8 15
        orientation 1 0 0 -0.4
    }
    Separator {
        Translation { translation 3 2 3 }
        Material { diffuseColor 1 0 0 }
    Cube { }
    }
}
```

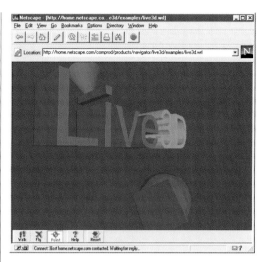

▲ Live3D is a Netscape plug-in which enables you to view VRML files in-line on a Web page.

The settings defined in VRML are fixed: Dimensions are always in meters, angles are expressed in "radians," and coordinates are always in the order x, y, z. Text preceded by a cross-hatch (#) is a comment code and not read by a VRML browser. On the following page, you can see a complete virtual office environment built using basic VRML. The floor surface is coded as follows:

```
Cube { height .01  width 8  depth 7 }
```

By keeping the height to a minimum, you effectively create a floor surface. You can also link a structure or texture to an object to create a realistic effect. You can use JPEG images to construct repeating background patterns, but that is most easily done with a WYSIWYG VRML program.

You can find VRML's unofficial logo on the Internet. ▶

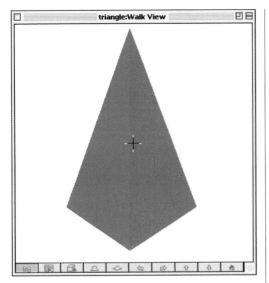

▲ In Virtus 3D Website Builder, you can click on one of the basic VRML forms in the library...

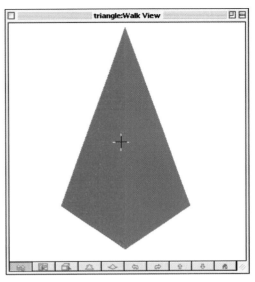

▲ ...and drag it onto the work space. If you click on the navigation buttons at the bottom, the object moves.

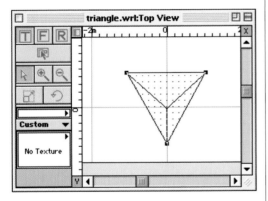

▲ You can view the pyramid object from three angles.

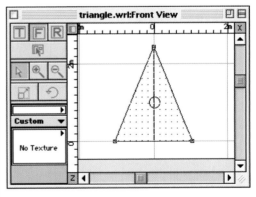

▲ You can change the size in this Artwork window.

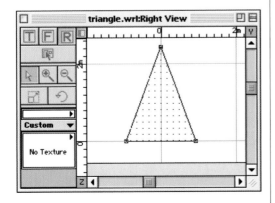

▲ The dimensions displayed on the rulers are in meters!

▶ Building Virtual Spaces

Using Virtus' 3D Website Builder, you can create simple objects as shown on this page. You can also build a complete interior in VRML by dragging and dropping without having to enter a single line of code. You can retrieve the objects from standard libraries, while Virtus creates the texture and floor fittings for you. The program supports the original VRML standard, so you can even include light and shadows in your virtual world. On the next page an example of a virtual space is shown.

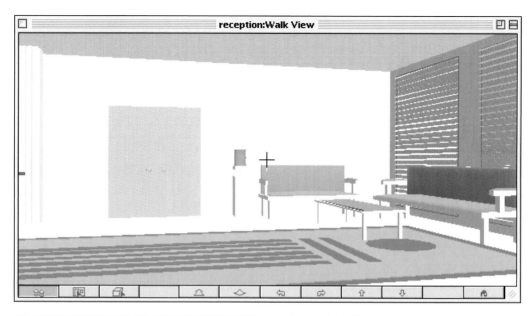

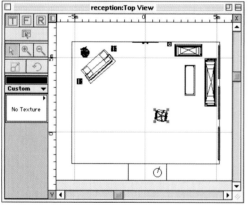

▲ The chair has been added to the scene by dragging the object from Virtus' clip art library to the virtual world. The various views are modified automatically. ▼

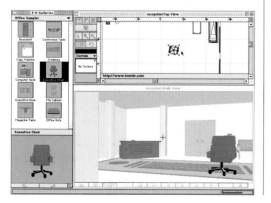

▲ The completed office as shown in a VRML preview program.

▶ Clip Art Libraries

The clip art libraries are extensive and have been designed for VRML worlds. In no time at all, you can construct an office, complete with floors, walls, and furniture. The method for creating a chair is illustrated on the page to your right. An additional chair can be added to the illustration above. To do this, select an executive chair from the Office Sampler, and drag it into the scene. The program automatically modifies the front, side, and top views accordingly. If the object is too big, you can alter its dimensions by clicking on the enlarge symbol and reducing the outline of the chair. The change is then displayed in the Walk View screen.

Every object can be displayed in a specific color or provided with a texture. For example, the carpet is actually an extremely flat "cube" to which a texture has been applied. You can see the layout of the room by selecting Top View. VRML also allows you to link a URL to an object. If you click on the chair in the virtual world, you will jump to the site contained in the hyperlink.

The XML-versus- ▶
HTML battle for
hegemony on the
Web has begun.

Extensible Markup Language (XML), the universal layout format for structured documents and data on the Web, is having a major impact on Web-design process. XML's possibilities impact the heart of the process by structuring the actual data. This chapter introduces Web designers to the rules and tools of XML and related languages.

Web Design and XML

Imagine if television programs had to be viewed on TV screens of different sizes and color depths without any way to adjust to various screen formats and without a clear and valid agreement on a technical standard. Such a scenario is unimaginable for the television medium, but it is everyday reality for the World Wide Web. Fortunately, Extensible Markup Language *(XML)* was developed to provide a possible solution. This universal layout format for structured documents and data on the Web was standardized by the World Wide Web Consortium *(W3C)* and is replacing HTML as the Web-design language of choice. Using practical examples and applications, this chapter explains the basic principles and some of the possibilities offered by XML.

▶ A Separate Version for Each Surfer?

One of the biggest challenges in designing for the Web is the huge diversity of software and hardware that must be supported. On the hardware side, for example, an ever-growing range of monitor sizes and color densities is available; on the software side is a wide variety of operating systems and browsers, each with specific differences in the way it interprets seemingly "standardized" HTML content. Due to the increasing use of mobile Internet devices, as well as the continuing popularity of TV set-top boxes and similar devices, the standardization gap will only widen in the future.

Does this mean, then, that Web designers must provide separate versions of their pages for every computer platform? Clearly, HTML cannot universally address this explosion of users' needs. "Portable" Web users need a quick and light version that they can view on a screen that is just 200 pixels wide and with only a 2-bit color depth.

On the other hand, users who grab their Web content from a TV screen will want the complete experience, with all the flashy graphics and animations. The core of the problem is that although both types of users can view the exact same Web content, the page presentation must somehow be tailored for optimal viewing on their specific device or platform.

To do this, a separation must be made between the actual content and the form in which the Web content is presented. XML offers a solution by combining structural information with a flexible, descriptive presentation. In contrast to HTML, for example, XML gives you the freedom to create your own tags and labels. This makes it a suitable language for creating all kinds of documents, not just Web pages: metadata, database files, and even message traffic can be stored in XML.

Will the freedom to create custom tags lead to Web-design chaos? In theory it could, because designers are not obligated to use a tag in a particular way: you could use the <WEBBOOK> tag exactly like this, or you could create, say, a <WEB_BOOK> or <WEBOOK> tag, as you prefer. For small-scale applications, the advantages of such free-form creation may outweigh the drawbacks.

However, bigger problems can occur when Web data is exchanged between large entities, like corporations. If applications are to work together, tags must be defined uniformly. The document type definition, or DTD, was invented for this purpose. In fact, HTML is itself a DTD; you can read it the source code of well-constructed Web pages. Let's go back to basics to clarify the entire theoretical spectrum.

▶ XML in Context: SGML and HTML

HTML is by far the most popular language for publishing documents on the Web, but it mostly just specifies how text is to be displayed. HTML is considered an application of Standard Generalized Markup Language *(SGML)* application—a standardized, generalized language for describing the markings of text. HTML is, in fact, a language that makes it possible to describe the syntax of other languages.

Many of HTML's characteristics are copied from SGML; among the most striking are its way of describing tags, and the start and end tags. Tag nesting is also derived from SGML. Here is a very basic example of HTML page construction:

```
<html>
<head>
<title>...</title>
</head>

<body>
<p>...</p>
</body>

</html>
```

Another characteristic copied from SGML is the use of so-called entities for special symbols, including < *(smaller than)*, > *(greater than)*, and & *(ampersand)*, which are coded <, >, and &, respectively. Although the first version of HTML had more logical descriptive tags *(H1 through H6, address, quote)*, the lack of decent style sheets caused its transformation into a markup language. HTML elements such as table, frameset, and div*(ision)* ensure that a Web browser will know how to render a document page but, unfortunately, not the document's actual content.

▶ A Simple XML Example

When displayed in the browser, the following HTML description only gives a value to the name of director Ridley Scott. To state it more emphatically, the name is coded for bold type.

The life of <b>Ridley Scott</b> is ...

The following description tells us more about Ridley Scott's function and makes it possible to search the file for the term movie director.

The life of <moviedirector>Ridley Scott</moviedirector> is best known...

If we tell the browser to display everything between the start and end tag in bold, the layout and description will be linked. This example clearly illustrates that XML assigns a meaning to information, while HTML only describes the information display.

XML is actually a digital "label." Now, if the terminology and semantics of the labels are standardized, you get a universally understood description of information that offers an enormous number of perspectives.

Thanks to product descriptions in XML, products can be compared to each other and catalogs can be brought in line with one other.

If the corresponding product prices are also labeled using XML, then international price comparison becomes an option. In a world that is moving toward two standard currencies—the U.S. dollar and the euro—such an ability offers enormous opportunities.

▶ Find the Differences...

In essence, XML is a stripped-down version of SGML. Whereas SGML is designed for working with extremely large and complex documents, XML is specifically geared for simple database-like storage of information on the Internet.
Here are some of the notable differences between SGML and XML:

▪ SGML lets you indicate that an element's start and end tag can be left out. (*See the* <!ELEMENT P - 0 ...> *example, below.*) The minus sign specifies that the start tag is mandatory, and a zero indicates that the end tag can be left out. In XML, however, both tags are mandatory; for "empty" elements such as the description of an image, the end tag is written as <IMG.

▪ XML is always case sensitive; SGML and HTML are not. Therefore <B>...</b> is acceptable in HTML, while only <b>...</b> or <B>...</B> will work in XML.

▪ With SGML, you need to choose a specific character set. XML uses only Unicode *(UTC-8 or UTC-16)*, a character set that attempts to include all the text characters in the world, and is the basis for a new font standard.

▪ SGML features the "AND connector," with which you can specify that certain elements occur within another element in random sequence. When many elements are "linked" in this manner, the number of combinations is extremely large, making the document very complex. XML does not recognize the AND connector.

► XML Building Blocks

An XML document can be as small as a listing of name, address, and city—or as large as a Web page, a book, or a description of all the products a company sells. Here is one example of an XML document:

```
<? XML version="1.0"?>
<! DOCTYPE product_sheet SYSTEM
"http://www.domain/dtds/product_sheet.dtd">
<product_sheet >
   <prod_name>Dynamax</prod_name>
   <prod_typenumber>RX-567-78</prod_typenumber>
   <prod_group>portable audio</prod_group>
   <prod_family>audio</prod_family>
   <prod_price currency="EURO">300</prod_price>
   <prod_photo src="http://www.domain/images/
      dynamax.gif"/>
</product_sheet >
```

The heading <? XML version="1.0"?> is a mandatory construction for opening a document. XML uses process instructions, or PIs, which are orders sent directly to an application *(for instance, to lay out text that XML and a corresponding style sheet cannot handle)*. PIs are always bracketed between <? and ?>. The heading of an XML document can be called a "special PI."

Regardless of size and content, all XML documents have the characteristic appearance shown above.

► My First XML File

To create an XML file, you start by naming its elements, the terms that describe the logical parts of the document. One such term—the root element—marks the start and end of the document and is mandatory in XML. So, for instance, if you're creating a product information sheet, you might name the root element PRODUCT_SHEET. According to the rules of XML, an element is defined in the form <!ELEMENT PRODUCT_SHEET>.

You'll also want to record other data, such as the category or product family the item belongs in, its subgroup within the product family; the actual product name, and where a corresponding photo can be found. These elements are shown in the following XML code:

```
<! ELEMENT prod_name #PCDATA >
<! ELEMENT prod_typenumber #PCDATA >
<! ELEMENT prod_group #PCDATA >
<! ELEMENT prod_family #PCDATA >
<! ELEMENT prod_price #PCDATA >
<! ELEMENT prod_photo EMPTY >
```

The entry #PCDATA represents normal *(body)* text, and EMPTY simply indicates that an element has no content, comparable to the <IMG> tag in HTML. In the example, an important piece of information is thus still missing: the location of the product photo. To supply this information, you add attributes to the element in a so-called attribute list. Take a look at this example:

```
<! ELEMENT prod_photo EMPTY >
<!ATTLIST   prod_photo
            src     CDATA #required >
<! ELEMENT prod_price #PCDATA >
<!ATTLIST   prod_price
            currency CDATA #required >
```

The attribute CDATA represents each character that can be placed between tags; for instance, you can include http://, $, or Dollar in the element as well. The attribute #REQUIRED means that it is mandatory.

► The DTD (Document Type Definition)

Each XML document belongs to its own specific category, whether you're creating a book, a Web page, or an e-mail file.

This category specification is usually reflected in the root element: <BOOK>...</BOOK>, <HTML>...</HTML>, <EMAIL>...</EMAIL> are all possible examples. In our product-sheet example, of course, we use

```
<PRODUCT_SHEET> ...</PRODUCT_SHEET>.
```

A document type definition is thus a collection of descriptions of elements, attributes, and entities. The compulsory logical structure for the document is specified in the DTD as well. The program that processes the document will later use these rules to determine whether the document is constructed correctly.

```
<! ELEMENT    product_sheet
              (prod_name, prod_typenumber,
              prod_group, prod_family, prod_photo?)>
<! ELEMENT    prod_name #PCDATA >
<! ELEMENT    prod_typenumber #PCDATA >
<! ELEMENT    prod_group #PCDATA >
<! ELEMENT    prod_family #PCDATA >
<! ELEMENT    prod_photo EMPTY >
<!ATTLIST     prod_photo
              src
              CDATA  #required >
<! ELEMENT    prod_price #PCDATA >
<!ATTLIST     prod_price
              currency
              CDATA  #required >
```

The definition of the XML element PRODUCT_SHEET is adjusted by adding a line that includes every other element *(between parentheses)* from the DTD to indicate that each must appear in the product sheet. This is the only way a valid document can be created. The sole exception being the element PROD_PHOTO, which follows with a question mark to indicate that the element is optional. The DTD file is saved in an ASCII text file named PROD_SHEET.DTD. You can write a set of rules for the document's formal structure by specifying the elements and their mutual relationships according to fixed XML instructions. This determines the compulsory structure of the document.

▶ Well-Formed and Valid

In XML you aren't really required to use a specific DTD. Any document that complies with basic tree-structure and nesting rules and that includes a root element can be a good XML document—one that we call "well-formed." If the construction is incorrect, for example, <ROOT><TAG></ROOT></TAG>, the document is invalid and therefore unusable as an XML file.

A document with a DTD at its core is one we call "valid." XML-compatible browsers such as later versions of Microsoft Internet Explorer render documents that are both well-formed and valid. Such a browser will not display an invalid XML document.

▶ Mark-up

"Marking up" means tagging elements *(that is, enclosing them between a start and end tag)*. A tag and an element are not synonymous in XML, even though people often use the two terms interchangeably. Elements are the logical parts of the document; the element ADDRESSEE in a letter is the name of the person to whom the letter is sent. A tag is the "label," or invisible code, such as <ADDRESSEE>...<ADDRESSEE>.

The DTD PRODUCT_SHEET will be used to write an XML document with the type PRODUCT SHEET. This XML file must always start with the current XML version; currently the W3C approves only version 1.0.

▲ ElfData's XML Editor is a great (Macintosh) program for creating and editing XML data.   ▼

▲ The WAP Forum can keep you up to date.

Here is a "filled-in" XML document based on the product sheet introduced earlier:

```
<?XML version = "1.0"?>
<! doctype product_sheet system

  "http://www.domain/dtds/product_sheet.dtd">
<product_sheet >
  <prod_name>Dynamax</prod_name>
  <prod_typenumber>RX-567-78</prod_typenumber>
  <prod_group>portable audio</prod_group>
  <prod_family>audio</prod_family>
  <prod_photo src=
      "http://www.domain/images/dynamax.gif"/>
  <prod_price currency="EURO">300</prod_price>
</product_sheet >
```

Glancing through this code, you can see that the product Dynamax is a portable audio player selling for 300 euros. What makes XML unique is that computers can read this text as well. With such a powerful capability, XML is becoming the lingua franca of the computer world.

▶ To the Browser: Style Sheets

What can you do with the XML file now? Well, you can parse it, or retrieve the original data from the document. Or we can render it, causing it to display legibly onscreen along with the corresponding photo.

A Web browser is used for rendering. Because an XML tag does not, in principle, convey anything about how a browser must show a page, in contrast to many HTML tags such as <B>, <I>, and <P>, information must be linked to the tag to tell the browser how an element should be displayed. You can use style sheets for this purpose. You know about CSS *(Cascading Style Sheets)*, but did you

know that its current successor is XSL? Short for eXtensible Stylesheet Language, XSL is the W3C specification for denoting XML style sheets. Its notation style is similar to XML's, and it looks much like the style sheets now used in HTML. Because XSL is still under development, it so far constitutes one of the weaker chapters in the XML success story.

Here is one example of XSL code:

```
(p {font-weight : bold;})
```

If we wish to display the product name in bold in our product-sheet example, we then indicate so with an XSL Style Sheet:

```
<xsl>
  <rule>
  <target-element type="prod_name"/>
    <P font-weight="bold">
      <children/>
    </P>
  <rule/>
<xsl/>
```

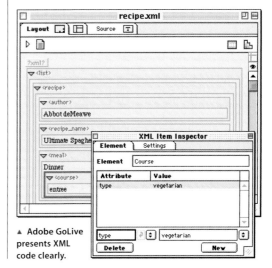

▲ Adobe GoLive presents XML code clearly.

The notation <CHILDREN/> communicates to the application that if multiple PROD_NAME elements occur, they should also be displayed in bold. The reference to the style sheet can be placed in the document in a just like the DTD reference.

```
<? xml:stylesheet href=
"http://www.domain.com/stylesheets/prod_sheet_style.xsl"
type="text/xsl" ?>

<table>
  <tr>

<td><prod_name>Dynamax<prod_name/></td>
  </tr>
</table>
```

To ensure that XML documents are viewable with older browsers, you can replace XML tags with HTML tags, or enclose them in HTML tags using a script before you finalize the documents. Fortunately, all browsers ignore tags they don't recognize; thus the product sheet will be displayed as an ordinary HTML page.

The latest versions of Internet Explorer and Netscape Navigator are capable of reading and displaying both XML documents and the XSL style sheets linked to them

▶ WAP and UMTS Surfers

In the beginning of this chapter, I pointed out that we're starting to see the first signs of a schism in Web use. People view Web pages on a variety of equipment. Besides computer monitors and TV screens, there are micro-browsers, Internet-enabled devices such as mobile phones and handheld computers, that are perfectly suited for receiving information through the Internet.

The Wireless Application Protocol *(WAP)* and Universal Mobile Telecommunications System *(UMTS)*, the successor to GSM, both offer wireless data transmission at up to 2 megabits per second.

▲ Microsoft's free Windows-based XML Notepad in action.

This high speed means that an Internet-enabled mobile telephone could send moving images in color. Soon the long-held dream of portable "picture phones" may finally become a reality.

Of course, this reality hasn't quite happened yet—UMTS will not be fully operational until 2002—but we should take it into account before the fact. By storing data in XML right now, for instance, we will later need only to write a separate XSL style sheet to accommodate handheld devices.

▶ Tailored Content for the Mobile User

Then, when a user invokes a Web page enabled for mobile Internet display, the handheld device transmits that it is equipped with, say, a small black-and-white screen. Based on XML labels attuned to this information, an XSL style sheet composes the page and sends it to the user. The mobile user, therefore, receives only content tailored to his or her device, without large images and unnecessary colors. Because the actual content is structured in XML, the separation between form and content is achieved—an absolute necessity in a case like this.

▶ XML's Strengths

Here are the main advantages of XML:

▪ XML is simple to use, and programs that can process the language can be written quickly.

▪ It is completely "media and medium" independent; in theory, writing something once in XML means publishing it infinitely

▪ XML documents can be read by both human and machine.

▪ XML's logical "content-descriptive" tags make it easy to check a document's quality.

▪ XML permits structured data storage without the complexity of a database, yet it allows you to search and select content. Example: GIVE all products from GROUP "portable audio" starting with "B".

▪ Once the XML file has been read into a late-model browser, data can be manipulated without requiring contact with the server. Example: GIVE all "portable audio"devices cheaper than 300 euros.

▶ One-to-One Marketing and XML

Almost all data types can be translated into XML, so future browsers will need to understand only one language. You can address all browsers, even older versions, by simply using an XSL style sheet and by embedding XML data in an HTML file. With a simple click on a hyperlink, a user can request a Web page from the server.

Suppose a user fills in a form, enters a name and password, and requests specific information. Behind the scenes, data sources are summoned to collect data for the Web page to be transmitted. If the requested page is a template in a content-management system, then all the other layout elements—such as navigation, page header, copyright data, and corresponding images—must be gathered as well.

From the collected material, a Web page is then composed and sent to the browser. With many Web sites functioning like this, the process can take a long time—and it takes

even longer when "personalized" pages are used for one-to-one marketing communications. In these situations, a cookie containing the user's preferences and previous Web-surfing behavior is interpreted as well. The time it takes to generate a perfectly tailored page may well exceed the limits of the surfer's patience—in which case he or she simply disconnects. Although such scenarios are a nightmare for the information supplier, customized content based on personal preferences is nevertheless the model of the future, and XML will play a key role.

Here, XML's power lies in its "extensibility." Any element can be added to a DTD, so all the data from any source can be translated to

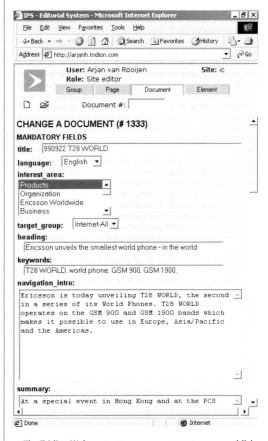

▲ The Tridion Web content-management system can publish XML-based content to a standard browser, such as Internet Explorer, as shown here, as well as to a WAP-enabled mobile phone, as shown on the right hand page. ▶

a new XML format without any trouble. XML's specific tree-structure and nesting rules have so much in common with those of a relational database that a table from such a database can easily be translated to XML without modification. An additional advantage is that the browser needs to understand only one language.

▶ The Three-Tier Model

The newest concept for the Web is called the Three-Tier Model. In contrast with the Two-Tier Model—which involves just the client *(the user's computer)* and the Web server sending the data—the Three-Tier Model uses a third layer sandwiched between the data and the client. This layer translates the data to XML and then sends it to the client. Many content-management systems use the Three-Tier Model to avoid the problems described above. Publishing and content management are considerably simplified when using separate page layouts or templates filled with content stored in databases—much less time-consuming than when manually hard-coded HTML pages are used.

Until fifth-generation browsers become standard, XML will primarily be used as an intermediary language.

These examples from Ericsson's ▶ news site clearly show how XML-coded data adjusts to the medium. Now this is state-of-▼ the-art Web publishing!

▶ XML and EDI

XML will play a large role in Electronic Data Interchange *(EDI)*. These days, companies exchange data such as inventory lists, prices, and orders through formats and forms they developed together. Account and package numbers have thus become standardized in EDI format and can be sent in digital form. Such a system has been in operation for years and is the force driving the rise of electronic commerce, including Web-based shopping and online money transfer.

EDI makes it possible to connect disparate corporate systems that were previously used only within each company. By including EDI information in XML, companies can now settle their accounts through the Web.

The use of XML even enables corporate alliances within an industry sector or vertical market—for instance, supermarkets and their suppliers—to develop their own versions of a DTD to exchange data.

▶ Working DTDs

All kinds of Document Type Definitions are currently being developed. A wonderful example is a specific DTD for classified advertisements in newspapers.

If all newspaper publishers used the same DTD, people all over the world could search through the online versions of these ads. A new challenge for Ebay, perhaps?

A number of working DTDs already exist:

■ Channel Definition Format *(CDF)* was written by Microsoft and implemented in Explorer 4 and later versions. CDF describes so-called metadata or "push channels" such as the URL, page summary, corresponding logos, and broadcasting schedule.

■ Mathematics Markup Language, or MathML, is a W3C effort to develop a language that can describe mathematical formulas in XML.

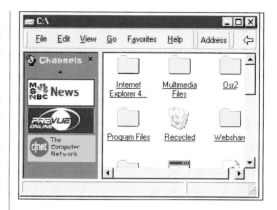

■ Wireless Markup Language *(WML)* is an initiative of the WAP Forum to support browsers for Global System for Mobile Communications equipment and handheld computing appliances. These devices all have very specific demands and technological limitations *(for instance, extremely small display screens)*. In addition, GSM employs proprietary navigation tools that are accessible through the devices' Accept, Up/Down, Left/Right, and Back buttons. In this way, GSM functions can be used for Web applications, and the telephone becomes a mobile Internet station.

■ Synchronized Multimedia Integration Language *(SMIL, pronounced "smile,")* is an XML subset that allows users to synchronously invoke various media and play the

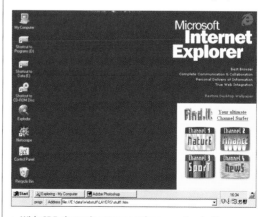

▲ With CDF, channels appear on the computer desktop.

▲ **RealPlayer can process SMIL content beautifully.**

content simultaneously. Image, speech, music, and dynamic text can thus be used together in harmony. A SMIL file can even be viewed "streaming" in RealNetworks' RealPlayer.

■ **Directory Service Markup Language** *(DSML)* is a data model being jointly developed by Microsoft, IBM, Netscape, and Novell to describe directory data such as name and address listings.

▶ BizTalk

Some people see the Microsoft-developed BizTalk as yet another effort by the Redmond giant to dominate a platform—in this case, XML. But this is not the case: BizTalk is actually more an XML platform for collaboration in application integration and e-commerce. Moreover, Microsoft has transferred BizTalk to an independent organization.

Currently, the biggest obstacle for collaboration between applications is that the programs communicate with one another in different languages. Where one says "abc," another understands "xyz"—yet it is possible that they mean the same thing. The physical solution would be to build a bridge to close

the gap. In the virtual equivalent, an application must link external data to internal *("abc" for System A = "xyz" for System B)*.

The way applications express themselves is based on a data model called a blueprint. Once we know the blueprint for an external data bank, we also know how to ensure its connection with our own data model.

In this context, the BizTalk initiative includes several important elements. The underlying principle is as follows: Make a number of agreements on how applications present themselves, and then all applications that adhere to the agreements can understand one another. To realize this goal, companies need to choose a location for publishing their blueprints. They can do this on the official BizTalk site *(www.biztalk.org)*. In addition, Microsoft has established a framework that contains a general structure for describing this blueprint data.

Microsoft is approaching all major consumer-electronics manufacturers to promote BizTalk. Several large companies— including Microsoft, SAP, Baan, and PeopleSoft have become BizTalk members,

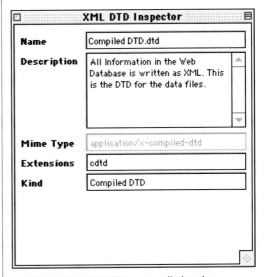

▲ Adobe GoLive's XML DTD Inspector displays the classifications.

and a steering committee of sorts will monitor the initiative's execution. Thanks to BizTalk, electronic business and data exchange has become much simpler.

▶ XML Data Server

The newest XML development, XML Data Server, is characterized by replacing the previously discussed Three-Tier Model with a complete XML-based two-layer model. In this model, data is not first retrieved from a database or other source. Rather, it comes right from the data server in XML format and is sent directly to the client. This model applies Extensible Query Language, XQL—similar to Standard Query Language, or SQL—to retrieve specific data from an XML Data Server while enabling simultaneous client-side data manipulation. XQL is currently in the same spot as XSL: There is no XQL standard yet, so the language is completely subject to change. The European site for Dell Computer is one of the first Web sites to use XQL.

▶ XLink

Finally, I want to call your attention to developments that affect the basic principles of Web surfing. Hyperlinks made the Web. The simple action of clicking on a specially formatted graphic or piece of text to bring up another document has revolutionized the world in many ways. You can thank Alan Kay, a former employee of the prolific Xerox PARC technology-development lab, for making hyperlinks what they are today.

However, not every click on a hyperlink produces the desired result. Wrong pages surface quite often, especially with search engines. And having to first click on a link before an image is displayed can be time-consuming, especially if that click doesn't bring forth the information you were seeking in the first place.

XML's contribution to the hyperlink realm is a useful one. A new standard called XLink, in which hyperlinks are based on the XML data model, is now under development. When implemented, XLink will allow a single hyperlink to return multiple results, and it will let you view images when clicking on a link without having to navigate to another Web page. XLink will also make possible the linking of hyperlink content to database information. It will record the disappearance of a Web page and inform all references to the page that it no longer exists.

One of XLink's most obvious advantages is that people will be better able to find the proverbial needle in that haystack known as the Web.

▶ Conclusion

XML is not only well conceived; it also has no real technological drawbacks. In fact, the only negative thing I can say about XML is that there is no full-fledged standard, certainly not an ISO standard such as SGML. So far there is no fixed standard for style sheets, either, although XSL remains the most common. However, the W3C organization has completed development of XML in collaboration with large companies including Microsoft, Sun Microsystems, and Netscape. This inspires hope, but offers no guarantee that the language will not undergo big

XHTML

The W3C body has recommended adopting a hybrid of XML and HTML 4.0. Extensible Hypertext Markup Language (XHTML) was proposed as a standard that would simplify Web-page viewing on nontraditional devices such as handheld computers and GSM appliances, as well as on set-top boxes equipped with WebTV and similar services.

A more rigid structure distinguishes XHTML from HTML. For instance, a start tag without an end tag is not accepted, all tags and attributes must be in lowercase, and all values have to be placed inside quotation marks. The following examples hint at the basic differences between XHTML and HTML:

HTML:

```
(P><FONT SIZE=1
COLOR="$ffffff>Alinea<p></FONT>
```

XHTML

```
(p><font size="1" color="$ffffff>Alinea</font></p>
```

XHTML addresses the demand for compact, select content by dividing a Web page into "modules." When an Internet-enabled portable device invokes a Web page, XHTML instructs the server to display only the relevant modules that will fit on the device's small screen. You can find more information about XHTML at the W3C Web site (www.w3c.org).

changes, as occurred when HTML broke off into various "dialects" such as the W3C, Internet Explorer, and Netscape versions of the language. Time will tell...

▶ Avenue.quark XML XTension

Million copies of the popular QuarkXPress page-layout program have been sold to date. Because the application dominates the graphics and publishing industries, almost all of these companies store their content in QuarkXPress documents. This storage is not structured, of course. In most cases style sheets are used, but the textual content is mostly in the Quark document itself.

To structure the content and store it in XML, Quark has developed a product called avenue.quark. The product name can be taken literally, because in effect avenue.quark moves the publishing industry onto a new avenue leading to the Web. Avenue.quark's biggest advantage is its simple method for generating XML output.

As long as two conditions are met–you must have a DTD, and your QuarkXPress files must have been created using style sheets–the conversion entails nothing more than simple dragging and dropping.

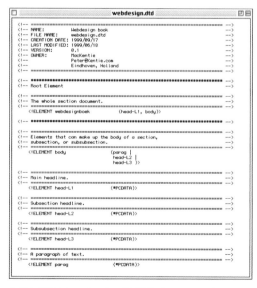

▲ This DTD is based on Quark's White Paper example.

The Tagging Rule Set is based on the style sheets from ▶ the QuarkXPress file.

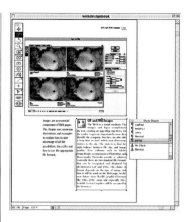

◀ This QuarkXPress file uses style sheets.

◀ The QuarkXPress DTD example is used to create a custom Tagging Rule Set called "Webdesign rules."

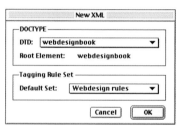

◀ Before creating a new XML, you must select a DTD and a default Tagging Rule Set.

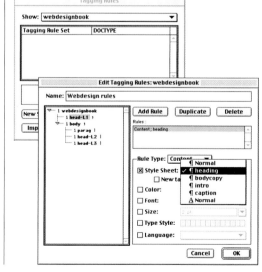

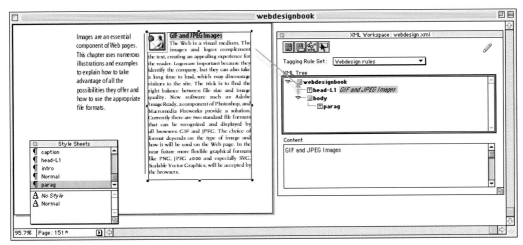

▲ To save text in the XML file format in accordance with the Webdesign.dtd document structure, simply drag the text to the HEAD-L1 icon.

▶ Document Structure Is Decisive

One important characteristic of XML is that it describes not only the data layout but also its meaning. In the following example, the style sheets for the chapter heading (HEAD-L1), body text (PARAG), and s ubheads (HEAD-L2) are used as self-made tags. By dragging the heading to HEAD-L1, the following XML code is created:

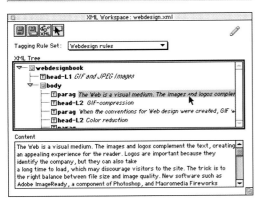

`<head-L1>GIF- en JPEG Images</head-L1>`

The `<HEAD-L1>` tag would be particularly suited to the translation of this book into XML. In the XML Workspace, you can see a clear hierarchy between the parts of the page. The chapter heading is followed by the subhead and then by the body text.

This structure can maintain a fixed order for all text when it is translated to another medium, such as the Web. By using Cascading Style Sheets, you can translate the hierarchy to HTML without any manual input. You can easily convert the content into databases as well.

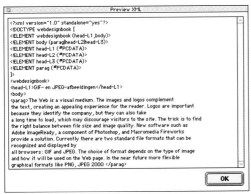

◀ Avenue.quark can present a preview of the XML code.

```
┌────────────────────────────────────┐
│ □ ▭▭▭▭ webdesign.css ▭▭▭▭ 目       │
│ ┌──────────────────────────────────┤
│ │ head-L1  {                        │
│ │     font-size : 18pt;             │
│ │     font-family : Arial;          │
│ │     font-weight : bold;           │
│ │     color : Blue;                 │
│ │     background-color : Aqua;      │
│ │     display : block;              │
│ │     line-height : 40pt;           │
│ │ }                                 │
│ │                                   │
│ │ head-L2  {                        │
│ │     font-size : 14pt;             │
│ │     font-family : Arial;          │
│ │     font-weight : Bold;           │
│ │     color : Blue;                 │
│ │     display : block;              │
│ │     line-height : 36pt;           │
│ │ }                                 │
│ │                                   │
│ │ parag  {                          │
│ │     display : block;              │
│ │ }                                 │
└─┴───────────────────────────────────┘
```

webdesign.xml

webdesign.dtd

▶ XML and CSS: The Ideal Combination

In the example above, all QuarkXPress content has been converted to XML, and I stored a file called Webdesign.xml to the hard disk. Now we will create a CSS file in which the heading, subhead, and body text have their own separate descriptions in an HTML style sheet. In this example the heading, HEAD-L1, is displayed in 18-point Arial Bold; a background color (BACK-GROUND-COLOR) called Aqua is applied to further accentuate the heading. The subhead, HEAD-L2, is a bit smaller (14 point) and has no background color. The body or paragraph text, defined by the style sheet PARAG, is set to Justified.

You can now display the text with this layout on a Web page by invoking the style sheet Webdesign.css. By creating or using different style sheets, you can publish the same content with a new look for different online publications. The XML data remains untouched—only the CSS file has to be changed.

As you have seen in the previous pages, the process of converting text is both simple and efficient. Naturally, the ability to reuse the information provides added value to the content. Thanks to avenue.quark, it takes only a little extra effort to export the data to XML.

Handheld ▶ computers and mobile phones are the infor- mation carriers of the future.

A prediction: Mobile telephones will become the most important point of access to the Internet, and telephone service will be a free component of Internet service. "Unwired" Web access will be available everywhere, giving rise to product-service combinations that promote and expand mobile e-commerce.

WAP Design and WML

Wireless Markup Language (WML) is a page-markup language comparable to HTML but developed specifically for mobile telephones and handheld computing devices. With WML, you can compose Web pages for mobile use. WML is based on Extensible Markup Language and is part of the open Wireless Application Protocol *(WAP)* standard. WAP can be thought of as the HyperText Transfer Protocol of the wireless world. Both HTTP and WAP handle the transfer of Web-based data, but in the case of WAP the destination is Internet-enabled mobile devices—with all the limitations they entail. Because WAP is optimized for mobile data communications, it is more efficient than HTTP at compressing Web pages. WAP also works with familiar data-link protocols such as the Global System for Mobile Communications *(GSM)* and its upcoming successor, Universal Mobile Telecommunications System *(UMTS)*.

The broad penetration of mobile phones and of handheld computers such as the Palm and Psion devices has fueled an increasing interest in using wireless devices to browse the Web. HTML-based applications are not suitable on mobile phones because their miniature screens can display only four 20-character lines at a time. A typical mobile phone's screen size is 96 by 65 pixels, and it can display only 1-bit monochrome images. A Palm organizer's screen is a bit larger: 160 by 160 pixels. WML addresses the display-size limitation by ensuring that data gets buffered before it appears on the tiny screen.

The enormous growth in the mobile-appliance market guarantees that developers will devote more and more attention to the specific challenges of viewing Web content on these devices.

▶ WAP and Operating Systems

WAP is simultaneously a data communications protocol and an application environment. This dual-purpose design means that developers don't have to create separate versions of a WAP application for each specific OS—the same program can be used with all competing mobile operating systems, including PalmOS, Windows CE, JavaOS, OS/9, and Psion's EPOC.

▲ Buy concert tickets online while waiting for a bus? Thanks to WAP, WML, and a mobile phone, it's no longer fiction.

▶ WML Decks

In WML parlance, a complete Web page is a deck, divided into cards. When a mobile user requests a Web page, the first card in the deck is displayed. To navigate through a page, the user presses keys on the mobile device or phone to bring up subsequent cards.

▶ WML Script

WAP has its own scripting language, WMLScript, which is very similar to Java-Script for HTML in terms of both design and possibilities. WMLScript is used as a separate file in the WML document. The script-file extension is .WMLS, to distinguish it from the regular .WML extension. The scripts are invoked using a URL, just as is the WML content itself. The WMLScript syntax is as follows:

```
<go href="currency.wmls">
```

The scripting options are truly infinite. WMLScript allows even complex calculations, such as mortgage costs, to be performed on mobile devices.

▶ WAP Server

Publishing the WML data requires a so-called WAP server, which large telecommunications companies will offer to secure their share of the mobile-services market.

▶ WAP Design in Practice

The WML code shown in the right-hand column exemplifies the design of this compact markup language and includes several standard tags, such as <B>...</B>, <I>...</I>, <P>...</P> and <EM>...</EM>. Note the structure's handy similarity to HTML.

WML-version 1.1 ▷

The XML version is listed in the Document Type Definition, or DTD. (In this case it's version 1.1, which is part of WAP 1.1.) The Web address for the WAP Forum is also listed.

Card IDs ▷

When the Web page is invoked, the first card of the deck appears.

Placing an Image ▷

Positioning an image in WML is similar to the procedure in HTML except that the image can be only 1-bit. (Newer WAP versions will support color.) If the image is not loaded, the Alt text appears. The <TITLE> contents are kept "outside" the scroll field. The ASCII entity © displays the copyright symbol.

Telephone Operation ▷

To scroll through the page, users can press the keys on a mobile phone. (The <TITLE> contents remain on the screen.) The two function keys on either side of the up and down block can also be used, so rather than using only the standard Open and Close options, the display could be made to read, say, "Buy" and "Skip" using a WML script. The wide range of functions offered by WML—and by WAP in general—can translate virtually any form of e-commerce to work within the tight confines of a mobile-phone screen.

```
<?xml version="1.0"?>
<!DOCTYPE wml PUBLIC "-//WAPFORUM//DTD WML 1.1//EN"
"http://www.wapforum.org/DTD/wml_1.1.xml">

<wml>

    <card id="card1" title="Wapdesign&#169; tips">
        <p>
            <img src="wapdesign.gif" alt="Wapdesign"/>
            <em>
                Hello mobile wapdesigners<br/>
                <i>
                    Wireless Application Protocol<br/>
                </i>
                Toolkit for you!
            </em>
        </p>
    </card>

</wml>
```

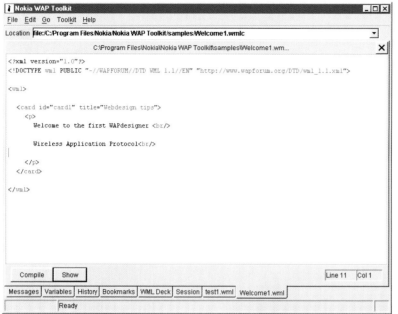

▶ Nokia WAP Toolkit

The mobile-phone manufacturer Nokia offers a simulator, written entirely in Java, that allows developers to create and test WML applications and scripts. The Nokia WAP Toolkit also includes support for graphics display on mobile phones. In the example shown, the "Wapdesign" image originated as a GIF file and is displayed in two dithered colors.

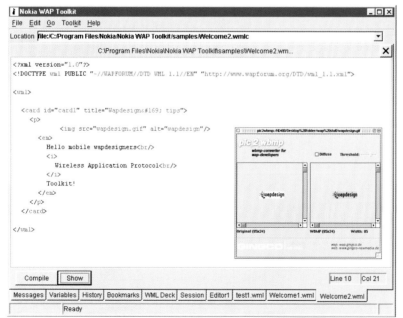

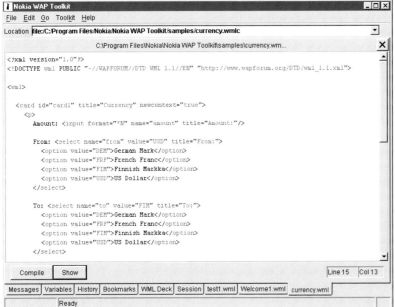

▶ Using the Mobile Phone's Keypad

The conversion example shown above makes fresh new use of function keys that are normally used to initiate and terminate calls: They are displayed on the WML page as "OK" and "Clear."

The Nokia WAP Toolkit offers ▶ built-in WML validation.

The scroll function remains intact, leaving four buttons available for use.

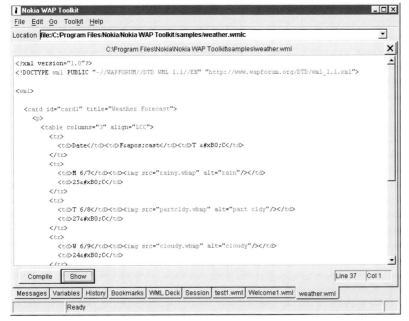

▶ The Product-Service Combination

Mobile Internet services represent only one of the many offerings made possible through the business model of the future: inseparable combinations of a hardware product and an interactive service. Under this business model, neither the product or the service exist without the other. In a world in which the Internet is expanding enormously, but is simultaneously becoming less visible since it is included in almost every device that  can communicate, its ubiquity guarantees a constant stream of income for providers of the service.

A perfect example of product-service interdependence is the sale of subscriptions to proprietary news services that are accessible only from specific devices. If subscribers must use, say, a mobile phone to view or listen to a particular news service's content, the provider of the phone service is also the content provider. Customers will pay *(continually, through subscriptions)* for the services; the requisite products—access tools such as Internet access and the phone itself—may even be offered for "free" to make the service possible.

▶ Opportunities of the Mobile Internet

The Internet has redefined how commerce is conducted worldwide. Entrepreneurs can now capitalize on the growing demand for mobile Internet services by developing and maintaining creative product-service combinations. This "networked economy" offers businesses ample opportunities for both success and failure. Surviving and thriving will require creativity and an enterprising spirit.

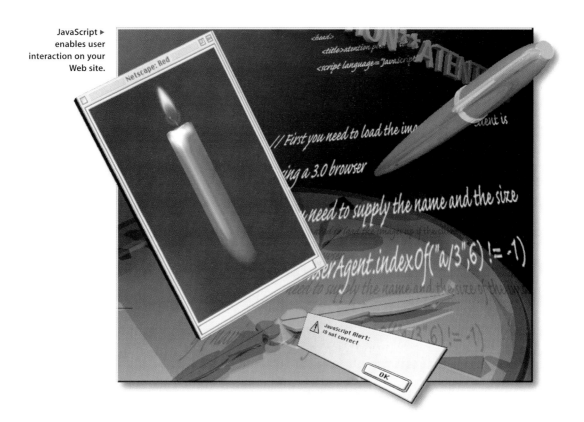

JavaScript ▶ enables user interaction on your Web site.

About the only thing that JavaScript has in common with the Java programming language is the name. But that does not restrict the applicability of JavaScripts. You can add functionality to your Web site by including bits of code in your pages.

Programming with JavaScript

Although its name suggests that JavaScript is derived from the full-fledged Java programming language, that is a misconception. Like the Sun Microsystems-developed Java language, JavaScript comes from the C++ language and exhibits some similarities to Java in its notation method, but that is where the resemblance ends. For Web and graphic designers, JavaScript is an ideal way to add interactivity to a site without having to learn a complicated programming language.

The beauty of this scripting language is that the code can be included in the Web page itself—in contrast to Java, which calls for using separate applets that must be compiled. The JavaScript code placed in your own Web page can be "played" without the need for an external server connection, which means that it runs faster.

▶ JavaScript

JavaScript is thus a very simplified version of Java. Although it offers fewer options, JavaScript can be very handy for such tasks as filling out Web-based forms. It allows you to warn users that they entered an incorrect value, for instance, and amounts can be calculated immediately and input fields can be filled in automatically. With JavaScript you can also create "dynamic" pages, such as those that change several times a day. Another advantage is that JavaScript can be typed directly into the HTML code, and you can view your results quickly. Take a look at the following examples.

■ Clock-script

JavaScript can be this simple: One line of code, and the time appears in the page.

```
<HTML>
<HEAD><TITLE>It's time for Java!</TITLE></HEAD>
<BODY bgcolor="#FFFFFF">
<SCRIPT>document.write("The current time
  is "+Date()+"<P>")
</SCRIPT>
</BODY>
</HTML>
```

You can use JavaScript in two ways. The first is dynamic construction of a page, in which part of the HTML code comes from the script. The disadvantage of this method is that the HTML code cannot be modified once the page has been created.

■ Update-script

The following is a sample script that is executed during page construction. It calculates how old the page is and then displays the result *(in days)*. The comment symbols <!--' and '--> are for use by browsers that do not support scripts—they interpret the JavaScript as comments and simply skip over it without generating any error messages.

```
<script language="JavaScript">
<!--
    today = new Date()
    lastmod = new Date(document.lastModified)
    diffdays = Math.ceil( (today.getTime()-
    lastmod.getTime())/(24*60*60*1000) )
    document.writeln( diffdays+" since last modified.")
// end -->
</script>
```

This line appears where the script is inserted:

'17 days since last modified.'

■ Text and explanation script

A script for displaying text and explanations at the bottom of the page is shown below.

```
<HTML><HEAD>
<TITLE>Comment in window</TITLE></HEAD>
<BODY bgcolor="#FFFFFF">
<a href="/tips" onMouseOver="window.status='text ¶
  and explanation';return true">text</a>
</BODY>
</HTML>
```

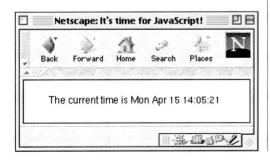

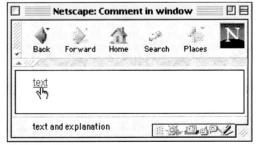

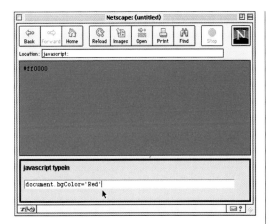

▲ By typing the word javascript: in Netscape Navigator's Location window...

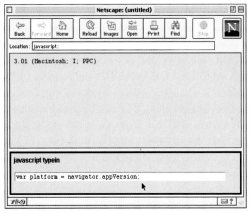

▲ ... you can look at the coding syntax immediately in the browser. To check a complete script, you'll need an editor.

The second application suited to JavaScript is for user interaction with a form. Some interactions can take place only in particular areas of a form—for example, "onFocus" can occur in a text area but not in a checkbox.

The possible events are:

Event	Situation
onBlur	the cursor leaves a text input field
onChange	the value of a form element changes
onClick	the user clicks on an element
onFocus	the cursor appears in a text-input field
onLoad	a page (or frame) loads
onMouseOver	the mouse moves over an element
onSelect	an element is selected
onSubmit	the form is sent
onUnload	the user exits a page

You can use a JavaScript to check, for instance, that user data in all form fields is entered correctly.

▲ Visitors to your site won't appreciate an error message, so test your JavaScripts in more than one browser.

▶ **Testing One, Two, Three...**

You need quite a bit of programming knowledge to write a JavaScript, but copying a script isn't nearly as difficult. By replacing the references in an existing JavaScript with your own, you can add simple scripting to your Web page. Check out the JavaScripts listed in this chapter as a good starting point.

Keep in mind that the JavaScript language is still being developed, and be aware of the differences in the way that scripts are interpreted by the Microsoft Internet Explorer and Netscape Navigator browsers.

▼ **Adobe GoLive has a built-in JavaScript editor.**

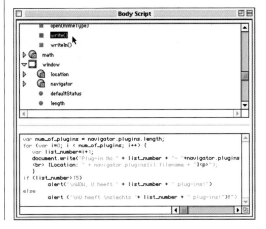

■ JavaScript Welcome Message

```
<HTML>
<HEAD>
<TITLE>Welcome  message</TITLE>

<script language="JavaScript">
<!--
var temp="enter your name here";
var user_name=prompt(temp,"your name");
if (user_name)
document.write("<H2>Hello " + user_name + "! Thanks ¶
for visiting!</H2>");
else
document.write("<H2>Thanks for your visit!</H2>");
// end -->
</script>
</HEAD>

<BODY bgcolor="#FFFFFF">

<A HREF="/tips">Back to the Javascript index.</A>
</BODY>
</HTML>
```

▶ User-Interactive Design

When users visit a Web page containing the script shown above, they will first be asked to enter a name. Only after they do this will they see the actual page with their name in context.

▲ A Web page personalized for every visitor is simple to create in JavaScript.

■ JavaScript for Automatically Opening a Window

```
<HTML>
<HEAD>
<TITLE>Automatic window open</TITLE>

<script language="JavaScript">
<!--
function WinOpen() {
  window.open('find.htm', 'newWin');
}
// end-->
</script>
</HEAD>

<BODY BGCOLOR="#FFFFCC"
onLoad="window.open('find.htm', 'newWin', '
resizable=no,menubar=no,directories=no, toolbar=no,
scrollbars=no,status=yes,width=140,height=220')")>

<IMG SRC="finditkl.gif" WIDTH=90 HEIGHT=40 >
Remaining text and image...
</BODY>
</HTML>
```

▶ Open Browser Window

You can use the JavaScript listed above to open a new window of a specific width and height. This way, you can have your Web presentation fill the entire screen.

▲ A mouse-click on online presentation introduces a separate full-screen image that appears above the opened window.

■ JavaScript for a browser check in frames display

```
<HTML>
<HEAD><TITLE>Browser sensitive frames</TITLE>

<script language="JavaScript">
<!--
browser = navigator.appName;
version = parseInt(navigator.appVersion);

if    (browser=="Netscape" && version >=3) ver="Netscape3plus";
else if (browser=="Netscape" && version ==2) ver="Netscape2";
else if (browser=="Microsoft Internet Explorer" && version >=2) ver="Explorer3";

if (ver=="Netscape3plus") {
document.write('<FRAMESET ROWS="100%,*" FRAMEBORDER=NO BORDER=0>' +
      '<FRAME NAME="main" SRC="netscape3.htm" SCROLLING=AUTO MARGINHEIGHT=10 MARGINWIDTH=10>' +
      '</FRAMESET>');
}
if (ver=="Netscape2") {
document.write('<FRAMESET ROWS="100%,*" FRAMEBORDER=NO BORDER=0>' +
      '<FRAME NAME="main" SRC = "netscape2.htm" SCROLLING=AUTO MARGINHEIGHT=10 MARGINWIDTH=10>' +
      '</FRAMESET>');
}
if (ver=="Explorer3") {
document.write('<FRAMESET ROWS="100%,*" FRAMEBORDER=NO BORDER=0>' +
      '<FRAME NAME="main" SRC="explorer3.htm" SCROLLING=AUTO MARGINHEIGHT=10 MARGINWIDTH =10>' +
      '</FRAMESET>');
}
// end -->
</script>
</HEAD>
<BODY bgcolor="#FFFFFF">
<FONT SIZE="4">This text is being displayed in a browser that does not support JavaScript.</FONT>
</BODY>
</HTML>
```

▶ Adjusting to the browser

Through a clever combination of a "framed" Web site and a good JavaScript (developed by Nick Heinle and Athenia Associates), Web surfers using Internet Explorer will see an entirely different page than those using Navigator. Adding the code FRAMESET ROWS=100%,* to the HTML page ensures that only one frame is visible.

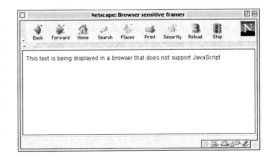

```
┌──────────────────────────────────────────┐
│ □ ░░░░░░░░░░░ Action Inspector ░░░░░░░░░ ▤ │
├──────────────────────────────────────────┤
│  Exec. [ OnLoad    ◆ ]  Name [ B40BA06D0 ]│
│                                            │
│  ┌──────────────┐  ┌─┐                     │
│  │ ? Action ▾   │  │□│ Open Window (NS 3, IE 3)│
│  └──────────────┘  └─┘                     │
│  Link   [ index.html                     ] │
│         [◎]          □ Absolute [ Browse...]│
│  Target [                                ] │
│  Size   [ 300    ] [ 200     ]  Resize □   │
│  Scroll □      Menu  □     Dir. □          │
│  Status □      Tools □     Loc. □          │
│                                            │
└──────────────────────────────────────────┘
```

▲ With a WYSIWYG editor such as Adobe GoLive, you don't have to code the JavaScript manually.

▶ JavaScript Editors

Writing a JavaScript takes skill. Extensive scripts in particular require a great deal of both programming knowledge and practical experience. Not surprisingly, commercial software packages are available to streamline the process. Netscape, for example, created a JavaScript application-development tool called Visual JavaScript that includes a WYSIWYG HTML editor. Similar editors are available with built-in functions for JavaScript editing, including Adobe's GoLive, which can also generate complex JavaScript code based on predefined windows.

The Web and TV ▶ are moving closer together—both literally and figuratively—giving Web designers a newly converged medium to exploit.

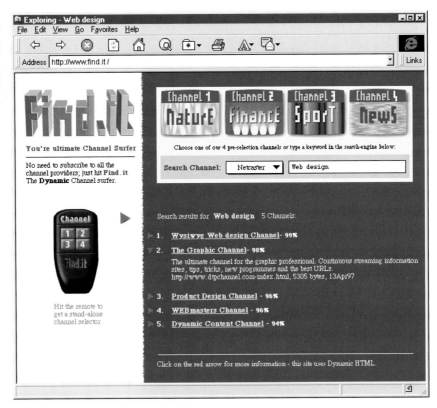

On the World Wide Web, "interaction" has usually meant clicking and waiting. Dynamic HTML has changed all of this. It allows a Web page to assume different forms after it is loaded. Moreover, this technique adds "dynamics"—like those from CD-ROM applications —to the modern Web page.

Dynamic HTML and TV Browsers

The World Wide Web is not standing still. New browsers and other Web applications are being developed so rapidly that keeping up with them is a challenge even for professional Web designers. With their fourth generation of browsers, Netscape and Microsoft implemented Dynamic HTML *(DHTML)* and Cascading Style Sheets. Technologically, these developments offer attractive creative and interactive possibilities, but the compatibility problems they cause make the earlier "browser wars" pale by comparison.

The World Wide Web Consortium *(W3C)* acts as a referee between the two companies in creating a uniform standard for DHTML. Nevertheless, creating dynamic pages that are fully downward-compatible is still quite a job for Web designers.

▶ Positioning with CSS1

Microsoft has made a proposal to the W3C to expand Style Sheets to include positioning characteristics—meaning that the style determines not only the physical display of the text elements but also their location on the Web page.

```
<STYLE type=text/css>
#start { position: absolute; left: 100; top: 50;
</STYLE>
```

```
<DIV ID="start">
<FONT SIZE="+2" COLOR="Red">The first text</FONT>
</DIV>
```

▲ The code as it appears in Internet Explorer 4.0.

▶ The Function of the <DIV> Tag

The <DIV> tag in the example above isolates a page element from the general settings. For example, an image that must be right justified in a centered page.

▶ CSS1 versus Layers

At first glance, specifying page elements with the help of styles seems a simple process. Using clear attributes such as left and top, with values expressed in pixels, you can specify the exact location of text and graphic elements on a Web page. The color, size, cropping, and sequence can be specified using a Style Sheet.

When you start combining these elements, the Style Sheets become increasingly extensive and complex, making the process more difficult. If on top of that you also add JavaScript or Visual Basic Script commands, you can certainly create very attractive Web pages, but the effort required to program them is considerable. To complicate matters, Netscape's method for method for creating Web pages using layers is incompatible with Microsoft's.

▶ The <LAYER> Tag

The Layer concept was invented by Netscape programmers to simplify the positioning of elements on a Web page. Unfortunately, Microsoft's Internet Explorer browser does not support the <LAYERS> tag, and Microsoft has proposed to the W3C an alternative based entirely on Style Sheets.

Now, Web designers must choose between the two alternatives. An example of the syntax is shown below:

```
<LAYER VISIBILITY=SHOW TOP=100 LEFT=100>
The first level
</LAYER>
```

The possible attributes are:

name	The layer name
left	The layer location (in pixels) in relation to the left side of the browser window
top	The layer location (in pixels) in relation to the top of the browser window
Z-index	The hierarchical sequence of the layers
visibility	The layer visibility, expressed by the values HIDE and SHOW
clip	The visible part of the layer, expressed in pixel coordinates
bgcolor	The layer's background color
background	The layer background

By default each layer is transparent and behaves like a table cell. If a 200-by-200-pixel image is placed in a layer with smaller dimensions, the layer will adjust itself. Transparent GIF images remain transparent; however, if a background color is applied, the layer will no longer be transparent.

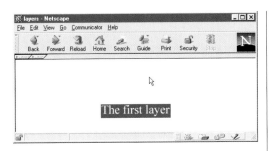

```
<HTML>
<HEAD><TITLE>layers</TITLE></HEAD>
<BODY BGCOLOR="#ffffff">

<LAYER VISIBILITY="SHOW" BGCOLOR="NAVY"
  LEFT=150 TOP=150>
<FONT COLOR="WHITE" SIZE="+2">The first layer</FONT>
</LAYER>

</BODY>
</HTML>
```

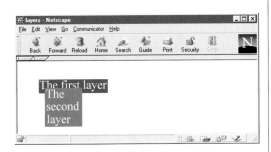

```
<HTML>
<HEAD><TITLE>layers</TITLE></HEAD>

<BODY BGCOLOR="WHITE">

<LAYER VISIBILITY="SHOW" BGCOLOR="NAVY"
  LEFT=50 TOP=50>
<FONT COLOR="WHITE" SIZE="+2">The first layer</FONT>
</LAYER>

<LAYER VISIBILITY="SHOW" BGCOLOR="FF0000"
  LEFT=60 TOP=60 HEIGHT=100 WIDTH=60>
<FONT COLOR="WHITE" SIZE="+2">The second layer</FONT>
</LAYER>

</BODY>
</HTML>
```

```
<HTML>
<HEAD>
<TITLE>layers</TITLE>

<script language="JavaScript">
<!--
   function showHide() {
   if (document.layers["layer1"].visibility == "show")
     document.layers["layer1"].visibility = "hide"
   else document.layers["layer1"].visibility = "show";
   }
// end-->
</script>

</HEAD>
<BODY BGCOLOR="#ffffff">

<LAYER NAME=laag1 VISIBILITY=show LEFT=150 TOP=50>
<FONT COLOR="RED"  SIZE="+2">The second layer</FONT>
</LAYER>

<FORM>
<INPUT type="button"  VALUE="Show/Hide layer"
  onClick="showHide()">
</FORM>

</BODY>
</HTML>
```

▶ Layers and Scripting

The layers lend themselves perfectly to manipulation when you use a scripting language such as JavaScript. With a script like the one in the example above, the visibility of the layer can turn on and off at the click of a button. Note that the page is retrieved without contact being made with the server.

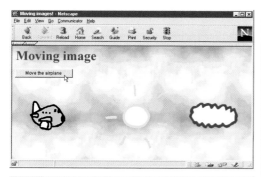

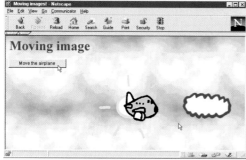

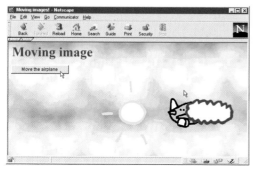

▲ A user can play this animation at will without any server intervention.

▶ Moving Layers

In the following example, the script ensures that the airplane moves and that it flies in front of the sun but behind the cloud. The function moveplane works as follows:

```
var plane = document.layers["plane"];
```

This line means that the official syntax for the layer —document.layers["plane"]— is abbreviated to the word (in fact, the variable) plane. So the word plane can be used in the rest of the function, even if the layer is modified.

■ Animation using layers and JavaScript

```
<HTML>
<HEAD><TITLE>Moving images!</TITLE>
</HEAD>
<BODY BGCOLOR="#CCFFFF" BACKGROUND="back.jpg">

<LAYER NAME="cloud" LEFT=250 TOP=100>
    <IMG SRC="cloud.gif" WIDTH="149" HEIGHT="79">
</LAYER>
<LAYER NAME="sun" LEFT=450 TOP=150>
    <IMG SRC="sun.gif" WIDTH="183" HEIGHT="186">
</LAYER>
<LAYER NAME="plane" LEFT=50 TOP=100  ABOVE="sun">
    <IMG SRC="plane.gif" WIDTH="152" HEIGHT="107">
</LAYER>

<SCRIPT LANGUAGE="JavaScript">
    function moveplane() {
        var plane = document.layers["plane"];
        if (plane.left < 500) {plane.offset(5, 0);}
        else {plane.left = 10;}
        setTimeout("moveplane()", 10);
        return;
    }
</SCRIPT>
<H1>Moving image</H1>
<FORM>
    <INPUT type=button value="Move the airplane"
    OnClick="moveplane(); return false;">
</FORM>
</BODY>
</HTML>
```

```
if (plane.left < 500) {plane.offset(5, 0);} else {plane.left = 10;}
```

Here a feature of the abbreviated layer is entered: plane.left. The .left part is a property —it defines the horizontal position for the left side of the layer relative to the browser window. The offset method handles the placement. Thus plane.offset (5,0) translates as "move the plane layer five pixels to the right and down zero pixels."

```
setTimeout("moveplane()", 10);
```

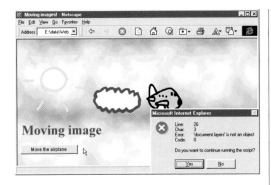

In this example, setTimeout repeats the entire cycle every 10 milliseconds, which keeps shifting the layer.

▶ Moving Style Sheets

The script on the left-hand page works only with Netscape Navigator 4.7 or later, in Internet Explorer 4.0 it generates an error message. With Style Sheets and modified scripting, however, you can still create an animation in DHTML that will function in both browsers.

The animation is more difficult to program this way than with Netscape's layers method, but the payback is that you will need to create only one version of the page.

▶ ECMA Script

The DHTML solution shown in the adjacent column works in version 4.0 and later of both Navigator and Internet Explorer. Because both browsers support Style Sheets and because the JavaScript uses no browser-specific functions, the animation plays without any problems.

Had you used Visual Basic Script commands, the animation would work only in the Microsoft browser. Developing uniform scripts is more difficult because three versions of JavaScript are currently in use, and not all browsers support the same script versions.

The ECMA Script project is an attempt to make order out of the impending chaos by standardizing JavaScript.

■ Animation with Style Sheets and JavaScript

```
<HTML><HEAD><TITLE>Moving images!</TITLE>
<STYLE>
.cloud {position: absolute; left: 250; top: 100;}
.sun {position: absolute; left: 450; top: 150; z-index: 2;}
.plane {position: absolute; left: 50; top: 100; z-index: 1;}
</STYLE>
</HEAD>

<BODY BGCOLOR="#CCFFFF" BACKGROUND="back.jpg">
<DIV CLASS="cloud">
<IMG SRC="cloud.gif" WIDTH="149" HEIGHT="79"></DIV>
<DIV CLASS="sun">
<IMG SRC="sun.gif" WIDTH="183" HEIGHT="186"></DIV>
<DIV CLASS="plane" ID="bewegend">
<IMG SRC="plane.gif" WIDTH="152" HEIGHT="107"></DIV>
<SCRIPT LANGUAGE="JavaScript">
   var nN = (navigator.appName == 'Netscape');
   var moving = (nN) ? document.moving:
document.all.moving.style ;
   function movePlane(){
      if (parseInt(moving.left) < 500){moving.left =
      parseInt(moving.left) + 5} else {moving.left = 10};
      setTimeout('movePlane()', 10)
   }
</SCRIPT>

<H1>Moving image</H1>
<FORM>
<INPUT TYPE=BUTTON VALUE="Move the airplane"
  OnClick="movePlane()">
</FORM>
</BODY>
</HTML>
```

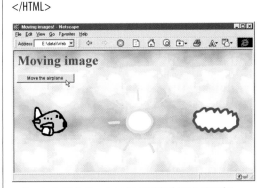

▲ Thanks to Style Sheets and a modified JavaScript, the animation is displayed correctly in Internet Explorer 4.0.

▶ WYSIWYG versus Manual JavaScripting

If all of this JavaScript code is too much for you, remember that there are alternatives for generating good JavaScripts. The familiar WYSIWYG HTML editors all include a JavaScript code generator. The advantage of these editors is that you can indicate which browser you want the script to function in, and you can also exclude older browser versions. Thus, you do not need to write the complex and hypersensitive browser check yourself; rather, you simply specify it in the program. (*Adobe GoLive works well this way.*) Of course, nothing beats manually inputting script code in editors such BBEdit and HomeSite. Manual coding is always more compact and thus runs quickly, but not everyone is comfortable working with straight computer code.

▶ JavaScripting and Layers

The example on the right-hand page illustrates the power of a WYSIWYG program such as GoLive. These applications allow you to construct an entire dynamic Web page without writing a single line of code. The animation, coded entirely in JavaScript, is created using simple drag-and-drop actions. After the code and the accompanying images are loaded, the separate halves of the images are combined into one whole. This process employs only Adobe GoLive's standard solutions.

Adobe GoLive can estimate a Web page's download time. ▶
The modem type and Internet connection are reported.

▶ WYSIWYG Uploading

The GoLive Timeline is a powerful tool that can register movements manually and then convert them to JavaScript code. It requires that you use layers, however, and that immediately poses a problem if you need your pages to work with older browser versions such as Navigator 3.0, as they do not recognize the <LAYER> tag. Fortunately, later-generation browsers do not have this limitation.

Uploading is also simple and efficient with GoLive. The site is managed from the program itself, and GoLive remembers what must and must not be modified.

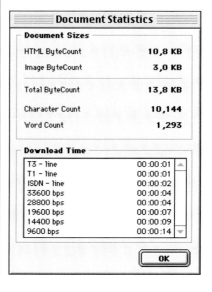

■ Dynamic HTML in Adobe GoLive

❶ Place a layer in the work area and import the image.

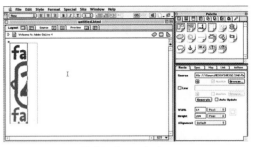

❷ Place the left half of the face in the layer.

❸ The layer is positioned in the Floating Box Inspector.

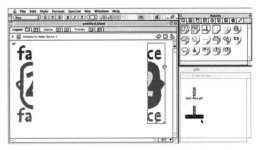

❹ The right half of the illustration is placed in the second layer.

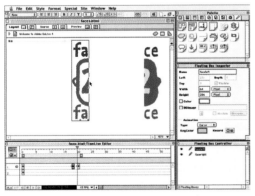

❺ The first movement is recorded using Record...

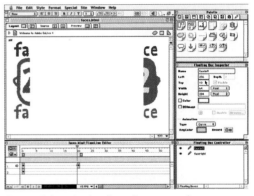

❻ ... and the redundant "jumps" are removed.

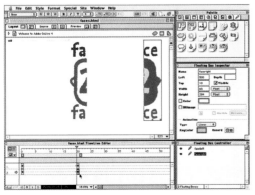

❼ The right half is animated the same way...

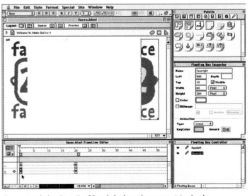

❽ ... and the "top" of both halves is set to 10 pixels.

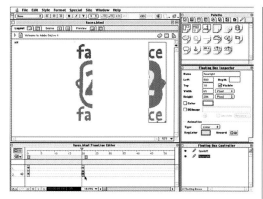

⑨ The starting position for the right half is specified…

⑩ … and then the final position. GoLive calculates the steps.

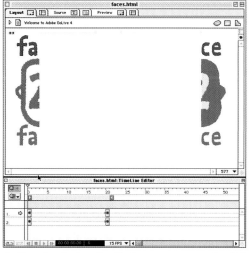

⑪ The animation in action. The images are apart at time "0."

⑫ At time "9" the two images move closer together…

⑬ …at time "18" they almost touch each other…

⑭ …and at time "20" they come completely together.

▶ Site Composition

By using three frames, you can place the JavaScript code generated by Adobe GoLive into a separate HTML file. The top and bottom frames are used for the heading and the site navigation, respectively. All in all, this strongly visual approach creates a striking effect.

The production time is relatively short thanks to the WYSIWYG editor and a sophisticated typography. Choosing a font that has attractively drawn symbols results in a consistent appearance.

A good Web site must be attractive and timely, and the cyberchat café in this example is right on target with both qualities.

▲ FF Kosmik, from the Dutch font designers Just van Rossum and Erik van Blokland, is the basis for the navigation symbols and the face.　　　　▶

▲ GoLive indicates where older browsers falter.

▲ If you select "Check Syntax," the error messages are displayed line by line—including the associated line number.

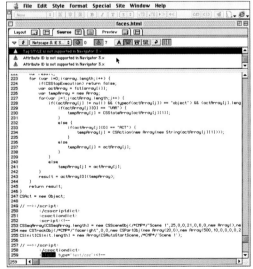

▶ Dynamic HTML and VBScript

A script that dynamically manipulates the HTML code is not JavaScript-specific; it can be written just as well in VBScript *(Visual Basic Script)*. Because the following example only works in Internet Explorer, we will use VBScript for a change.

The script cannot do much without making several modifications in the HTML code. Therefore, it adds a special class attribute to the <IMG> tag that places a large arrow button on the screen. This class is read later in the script to determine which button a user has clicked on.

```
<IMG SRC="btn.rightarrow.on.gif" VSPACE=10 WIDTH=19
  HEIGHT=19 BORDER=0 CLASS="ExpandAll" ALT="Expand">
```

A similar class attribute, arrow, is also added to each little arrow. Moreover, each arrow is assigned a unique ID attribute *(ID="Item1")*; this tells you which arrow gets clicked, so you can display the text that goes with it.

```
<IMG SRC="sm.right.gif" VSPACE=5 WIDTH=9 HEIGHT=9
  BORDER=0 ID="Item1" CLASS="Arrow">
```

The next arrow gets the attribute ID="Item2", but the class remains the same (arrow). Finally, a unique ID is added to the <TR> (table row) tag containing the long description. This ID is linked to the arrow ID.

```
Arrow <IMG> ID="item1" Text <TR> ID="item1txt"
```

You don't have to use this method, but it makes scripting easier and gives you a better overview of your script. To hide the text when the Web page is being loaded, a style is added to the <TR> tag with display:none. This works only with browsers that understand the function. The script influences the style as soon as a user clicks one of the arrows. The browser displays the new text, and the rest of the content is shifted down the page.

▲ The standard page shows a compact version of the information. When you click on an arrow, the full information appears.   ▼

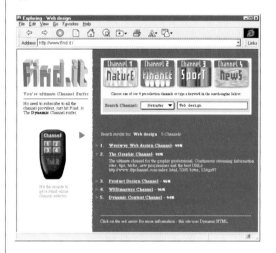

```
<TR ID="item1txt" style="display:None">
```

▶ The VBScript in Action

Each time a user clicks on the page, the browser automatically invokes the Document_OnClick() routine (shown to the right). Using the window.event.srcElement.className we ask what type of button was pushed, Arrow or ExpandAll. Depending on the type, or class name, the program performs a different action.

The text associated with the clicked-on arrow must be visible; if text is already visible, it must be made invisible. If a user clicks on the first arrow, the ID is requested *(Item1)*. Then the text is displayed to combine the ID with the <TR> tag that must be made visible.

Check the <TR> tag to determine whether it should be hidden or displayed. The appearance of the image will then change *(opened=down, closed=right)*.

▶ ExpandAll

If a user clicks on this button, all the items must be either opened or closed. Moreover, you must change the <ALT> attribute for the large arrow so that you can later request the status *(opened or not)*.

Changing the <ALT> attribute is proof that Microsoft's Dynamic HTML implementation is very advanced and has few restrictions. You can request the status of *(and modify)* each attribute for every tag even while the page is displayed on the screen.

▲ Browsers that do not support VBScript get a text-only page.

```
<HTML>...
<SCRIPT LANGUAGE="VBSCRIPT">
sub ExpandAll(State)
    on error resume next
    For i = 1 to 10
        Err.clear
        set ClickItem = document.all("Item" & cstr(i))
            if (err.number = 0) and (ClickItem.className = "Arrow")
            then
                TextID = ClickItem.id & "txt"
                set TextElement = document.all(TextID)
                if (State = True) then
                    TextElement.style.display = ""
                    ClickItem.src = "down.gif"
                else
                    TextElement.style.display = "none"
                    ClickItem.src = "right.gif"
                end if
            end if
    next
end sub
sub Document_OnClick()
    set ClickItem = window.event.srcElement

    select case ClickItem.className
        Case "Arrow"
            TextID = ClickItem.id & "txt"
            set TextElement = document.all(TextID)
            if (TextElement.style.display = "none") then
                TextElement.style.display = ""
                ClickItem.src = "down.gif"
            else
                TextElement.style.display = "none"
                ClickItem.src = "right.gif"
            end if
        Case "ExpandAll"
            select case ClickItem.alt
                case "Expand"
                    ExpandAll(true)
                    ClickItem.alt = "Collapse"
                    ClickItem.src = "downarrow.on.gif"
                case "Collapse"
                    ExpandAll(false)
                    ClickItem.alt = "Expand"
                    ClickItem.src = "rightarrow.on.gif"
            end select
    end select
end sub
</script>
```

▶ Internet + Television = WebTV

The Internet is gradually opening up to the public at large. A medium that provides easy access to online information is an important instrument. The personal computer remains an extremely technical device, but television bombards virtually every living room and teenager's bedroom and thus offers much greater potential in terms of penetration. With new distribution options—particularly Web access via television cable—the advance of the Internet gains an entirely new dimension. Not surprisingly, several companies, including Philips Electronics, are now bridging the gap between online information and the TV set, and one result is called WebTV. Clearly, viewing a Web page on a 26-inch TV screen from across the living room is a completely different experience than sitting with one's nose pressed against a PC monitor. Displaying Web content properly and ergonomically on a television screen thus presents enormous challenges on various levels.

Nevertheless, WebTV effectively gives its subscribers millions of stations (*sites*) to choose from. If Web designers take into account this medium's idiosyncrasies, the convergence or fusion of the various media will be that much closer to fruition. Given that Web sites increasingly feature multimedia content, a mature medium is coming into being. WebTV is the perfect instrument for broadening the scope of the Internet.

▶ I Want my WebTV

The WebTV appliance consists of a so-called set-top box with a 64-bit RISC processor. It supports several interfaces and comes with an integrated browser that supports HTML tables, frames, and many mul-

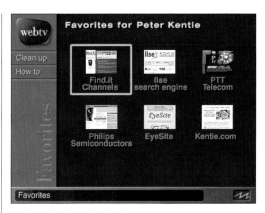

▲ The WebTV interface for the Favorites screen.

timedia extensions such as RealAudio, MIDI, and Macromedia Flash. With WebTV and the almost limitless offerings of Internet-based radio stations, a television set becomes the ultimate radio receiver.

▶ Taking WebTV into Account

The WebTV browser does have some limitations, however. It cannot play Java applets, for instance, so television-screen width is a serious consideration. The browser is 564 pixels wide and up to 384 pixels high. The software reduces Web sites that are too wide, which means that text is sometimes displayed much too small to be read from across the room. WebTV's standard font size is 18 point. This rather large size is necessary

▼ The startup screen of the WebTV Viewer simulator.

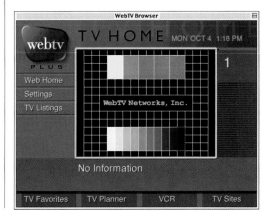

▲ The WebTV dimensions are specified in pixels. Larger sites get reduced automatically.

to keep the Web content legible at typical television-viewing distance. Consequently, WebTV can display only a few text lines at a time. Set your computer-based browser to this font size, and you will get an idea of what happens.

Interpretation of tables and frames must also be taken into account. The WebTV browser has the nasty habit of compressing a page made up of multiple table cells by shifting the outermost cell to the left. This compression affects the overlap and thus the legibility of Web pages. Web designers who use pseudoframes on their sites are no doubt familiar with pages that place navigation elements in a table in a narrow left-hand column.

A final consideration is the way that WebTV uses color. When you design a site geared specifically toward WebTV users, using darker background colors and light-colored text will result in a much more appealing image on a TV set. Also, avoid thin borders, as the background color may overpower them.

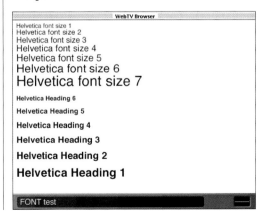

▲ With WebTV, interactive television takes a giant step closer to reality. The information icon is transmitted along with the TV program...

▲ ...and when the WebTV user clicks on the icon, the box displays a Web-page selection bar. The user then has the option of requesting that page.

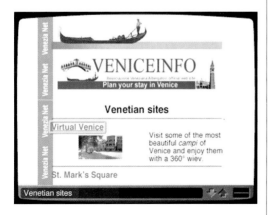

▲ If the Internet content is selected, the user is switched to a specific URL that the television station has transmitted along with the TV signal.

▶ Optimizing for WebTV

You can use WebTV's own tags without disrupting the page display on a standard browser. Some of these tags are quite specialized and are needed only for certain situations. <BLACKFACE>...</BLACKFACE>, for example, ensures that the text placed between the tags is displayed "extrathick." <SHADOW>...</SHADOW> is more commonly used; text inserted between these tags shows as a black shadow in the WebTV browser.

▶ WebTV Simulator

The WebTV.com site provides detailed description of all relevant tags and the results they produce on the television screen. Serious WebTV designers may also want to download a free WebTV Viewer "simulator" for PCs or Macs from the developer site (*developer.WebTV.net*). The simulator is extremely handy, but it does have its limitations.

For example, it offers only three font sizes and thus will not reduce the text to fit as in the "live" situation with a real television set. Also, the range of available colors for content display is, naturally, that of the PC or Mac rather than the TV. In most other ways, however, the simulator is similar to a real WebTV connection.

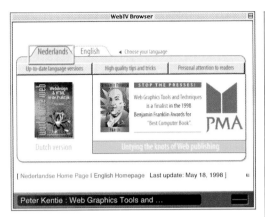

▲ The Web site for this book, displayed on a WebTV.

▶ Design Guidelines

Developing a site attuned to WebTV users can certainly challenge a Web designer's adaptability, but the challenge comes not only from the medium itself but also from the perceptions and expectations of the public. After all, WebTV puts online content in a "living,"rather than computing, environment; and accommodating a much broader target group puts certain limitations and requirements on the designer. The age distribution of TV viewers differs from that of PC users. For example, a study conducted in the United States reveals that WebTV subscribers tend to be significantly older than Web surfers who use a PC. As a group, older people would generally rather use WebTV for Internet access than invest in—and learn to use—a computer.

Compared with PC surfers, TV viewers are not accustomed to the still images and array of links and buttons found on many Web sites. Television focuses the viewer's attention much more on a single point, whereas a typical Web page offers plenty of choice and thus distraction. This is just one more reason to make sure that your home page (and preferably subpages as well) will fit on the TV screen without scrolling. Also, use text sparingly—no more than a few short paragraphs with a clear message. And light-colored text

on a dark background is much easier on the eyes than the other way around; avoid bright colors such as clear red, as they tend to "dominate" on the TV screen and may look peculiar.

▶ Integrating WebTV with Television

WebTV users navigate a site using a remote control or a wireless keyboard (or both). URLs can be typed in from the keyboard or—much less handy—by selecting individual letters on the remote control. But how will WebTV users' surfing behavior develop? If the entire family is sitting in front of a TV set in the living room, democracy will play a role, even if only in the battle over whether they should watch television or check out sites on WebTV. Such possibilities are not lost on WebTV Networks, which provides the service: In collaboration with the television industry, it now offers a seamless connection between television and the Internet.

The company calls its approach "Web page with TV overlay" and is already testing it in practical situations. Making use of so-called crossover links, the system displays an icon in the image that alerts WebTV users that they can find more information about the TV program on the Internet. When users click on the icon, a bar appears on the screen asking if they wish to view the Web content; if the answer is yes, the WebTV browser starts and the page is loaded.

▼ The state of the art WebTV viewer with code checker.

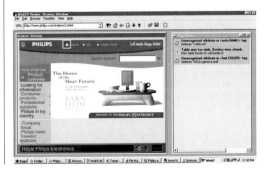

▶ TeleVision Markup Language

At this point the regular television image disappears. To avoid disrupting the continuity of the TV program, WebTV can use TVML *(TeleVision Markup Language)* code to display the TV image in the Web page. A WebTV page can even include a real Picture-In-Picture window in which the active TV channel is displayed. The TVML coding for this feature consists of HTML tags and attributes that were custom-developed by WebTV Networks.

For example, to include a link that causes the WebTV browser to switch immediately to CNN *(provided the channel is available from the viewers' cable service)*, you would use the following HTML code. The attribute tv: is part of TVML.

```
<A HREF="tv:cnn"> CNN
```

To incorporate a small Picture-In-Picture screen that displays CNN, use the following code:

```
<img src= "tv:13" height=90 width=120>
<object data= "tv:CNN" height=90 width=120>
<body background="tv:">
```

A TV station can send a link with its signal. A TVML example would be:

```
<a href="http://cnn.com/newslink.html" view=WEB>
```

The attribute view=WEB ensures that WebTV is activated if you click on the standard "I" icon that appears at the top right of the television screen during transmission.

▶ WebTV and E-Commerce

Although the techniques described are still in their infancy, WebTV is clearly a complete and functional concept in which the television industry can join in. With support from Microsoft, Philips, and Sony, the dream of media convergence can become a reality. The electronic-commerce possibilities are almost infinite. WebTV is SSL-compliant and thus is tailor-made for e-commerce. A travel program on television can provide links to the an opportunity for the viewer to book and pay all at once. A soap-opera episode ends with the option of clicking through to the actors' fan-club sites. An episode of a series about cars takes viewers to a special Web site where they can read detailed test reports on various automobiles. These ideas are based on existing content; creative media entrepreneurs can only hope that WebTV and similar technologies will soon reach critical mass in the consumer marketplace. The combination of broadband Internet, bringing personalized content to the individual consumer is nirvana for all marketeers!

A cup of coffee ▶ for the Web designer? Java is the programming language of the future.

Ever since Java took the programming world by storm several years ago, the saying "Think globally, act locally" has become increasingly relevant in reference to the World Wide Web. With Java, you can create applets—small programs that add real interactivity to your Web pages and even update software applications for you. Java offers true "internetworking."

Java Programming

The Java programming language allows you to enhance your Web pages with software programs that visitors can execute from their own computers. This ability offers possibilities that creative spirits once only dreamed of—such as drawing a picture or playing a game on a Web page, or filling out an online form with the help of a digital "assistant." All of this can happen with Java.

Now, a graphic designer might think, "A programming language? I don't know how to program, and I have no desire to learn." If that sounds familiar, you should read this chapter, because Web design is increasingly becoming "interactive design"—and to do that, you'll need to know the basic principles of Java.

▶ Confusion of Terms?

When the subject turns to Java, several different concepts are frequently confused with one another: Java and JavaScript. Java is an extensive programming language developed by the network-computer maker Sun Microsystems. JavaScript is a scripting language originally developed by Netscape. Check out the chapter "Programming with JavaScript" for further information.

Originally, Java was not developed for the Internet. In early 1991—before the World Wide Web even existed—Sun wanted to develop software for set-top boxes, those electronic devices placed on top of a TV set that give viewers "interactive" options. The boxes had to be programmed in a robust language that could one day be used to program other household appliances, such as CD players, refrigerators, and even toasters. As it turns out, set-top boxes never quite set the world on fire.

▶ A Truly Versatile Language

In the process, however, Sun had developed a versatile language that far exceeded the capabilities of other programming languages in a number of ways. Eventually it became clear that Java was perfectly suited for distribution on the Internet.

So why did Sun develop a whole new programming language when so many others—such as C, C++, and Perl—were already in wide use? The most important reason was that the language had to be both robust and secure. After all, you can't have your TV freeze up or your toaster crash! Also, it had to be system-independent: Because various computer platforms support common standards and formats such as HTML and Adobe's Portable Document Format (PDF), a common language among them would be helpful for cross-compatibility.

The following concepts were taken into account in developing Java.

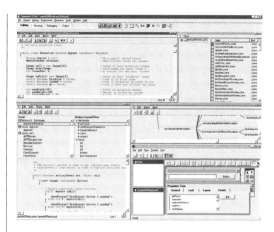

▲ Symantec Café is a complete WYSIWYG Java development environment.

■ Relative simplicity

Programmers familiar with the concept of "object-oriented" programming will find Java fairly easy to master. The same cannot be said of the most commonly known object-oriented language, C++. And many applications have been developed to simplify Java programming.

■ Object orientation

A Java program consists of objects. An object can be anything—for example, an animated button that users can click on with a mouse. The advantage of building a program with objects is that they are simple to modify. For instance, to make your program continually repeat a button's animation, you need only modify the object rather than all the locations in the program where the button is used. You can also the reuse objects over and over again.

■ Platform independence

The fact that Java is platform independent is extremely important for Web-based applications. It means that the same programs can be run under Unix just as easily as under Windows PC or a Macintosh.

Safety and robustness

Of course, a Java program in a Web page isn't meant to read data from a site visitor's hard disk and send it to the program's creator, nor can any errors occur that cause the computer to crash. Yet because "executables" are sent to the user, Java still entails a small security risk.

Speed

Java is comparable to an "interpreter" programming language such as Basic. Only the code is emulated. Java programs are relatively slow at the moment, but that problem is being addressed. In addition, processor chips keep getting faster, and chips developed especially for Java are on the market. With a just-in-time compiler, a Java program can be quickly converted to an "ordinary" program before it is executed.

Multithread capability

The term multithreaded means that more than one program *(or program component)* can be executed simultaneously. For example, an animation can be run and the data processed while the program waits for a mouse-click.

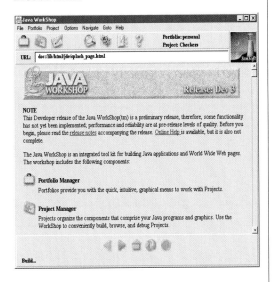

▲ One of the first Java development kits: Java Workshop!

▶ The Network Is the Computer

The concept of network-as-computer is fascinating, but unfortunately it remains more a concept than a reality. Computers based on different platforms that only mildly tolerate one another are often connected to a network, yet files residing on, say, a Windows PC may be unusable by a Unix workstation on the same network.

With Java, however, the same applications and files can be used on all the common computing platforms without modification. Such platform independence is possible because a Java program is made up of so-called byte code.

There are two main ways to distribute a program: as a script and as machine code. A script is generally a small program consisting of text in the form in which the programmer typed it. If you load this script into a text editor, you can view it. In some cases a script can be executed on different computing platforms. Often, though, scripts run slowly and are not secure.

▶ Java Virtual Machine

Most programs, however, are made up of machine code. If you attempt to load this type of program into a text editor, either the attempt will fail entirely or you will just see strings of strange-looking characters. Machine code is meant to run on computers that use a specific microprocessor—therefore, machine code for a Motorola processor will not run on an Intel-based PC. The Java byte code can be regarded as a sort of machine code for a Java Virtual Machine.

You may wonder whether a Java program in a Web page can read data from a visitor's hard disk and send it over the Internet without the visitor's knowledge.

It can't. But if Java can't read a user's hard drive, then how can you create a serious program with it? The answer lies in the two different types of Java programs: the applet and the application.

▶ Stand-alone Applications

An applet is a small bit of program code that can be included in a larger program *(such as a Web browser)*. Because they can be distributed by anyone via the Web, applets must comply with strict security rules that severely limit an applet's possibilities. For instance, applets are not allowed to read from a hard disk—nor are they permitted to contact just any computer. However, Java programs can be used as full-fledged applications as long as they are stand-alone programs *(that is, not part of the larger program)*. In that case, the security rules no longer apply. An example of a stand-alone Java application is the HotJava browser.

▶ Source File

To include a Java applet in a Web page, you use the tags <APPLET>...</APPLET>. As with the <IMAGE> tag, you must specify the source file and the dimensions *(if relevant)*. The applet file is specified with the <CODE> tag, and its extension is always .class.

You can add HTML code between the Java tags in cases where the browser used does not support Java.

```
<APPLET CODE="EngineDemo.class" width=490 height=400>
<I> This demo requires a Java-compatible browser.</I>
</APPLET>
```

■ Demo Applet

Parameters can be passed on with many Java applets. The mouse-sensitive HighLightImage applet, whose code is listed below, is such an example. When a mouse is moved across the image, its appearance changes; and if a user clicks on the image, a different page opens. The HTML code for this page looks like this:

```
<HTML>
  <HEAD>
    <TITLE>Image Highlight Example</TITLE>
  </HEAD>
<BODY bgcolor="#FFFFFF">
<H2>Image Highlight Example </H2>
<APPLET CODE="HighLightImage.class" WIDTH=260
  HEIGHT=75>
<PARAM NAME="image" VALUE="product.gif">
<PARAM NAME="highlighted" VALUE="h-product.gif">
<PARAM NAME="url" VALUE="products.html">
<A HREF="products.html"><IMG SRC="product.gif"
  border=0 width=260 height=75 alt="products"></A>
</APPLET>
</BODY>
</HTML>
```

▶ Compiler

The parameters are passed on using the <PARAM> tag. You'll have to know which parameters the applet will read in advance; in the HighLightImage example they are image, highlighted, and url. The image parameter must specify which image will appear when the mouse moves outside of the image *(in this case, product.gif)*.

You must specify a separate "highlighted" version of this image in the highlighted parameter, and specify in url the URL to jump to when a user clicks on the image. Even if Web surfers can't see the Java applet, they'll still see a linked image in the browser window. Both current versions of Netscape Communicator and Microsoft Internet Explorer have built-in Java support into the core of their respective browsers.

▶ The Pure Java Initiative

One of Java's biggest strengths is that it can run the same code on multiple computing platforms. When Microsoft introduced Java extensions that could run only under Windows, Sun mounted a counterattack. Under Sun's 100% Pure Java Initiative, a program is considered "pure Java" only if it is truly platform independent. Many large computer makers have lined up behind the initiative, but Microsoft still has not.

Microsoft cofounder Bill Gates says that "Java is a lovely language, but programs that do not use the specific capabilities of the operating system will lose ground to those that do." Time will tell which camp is right.

▶ Java 1.1

The demand for more options arose soon after Java's introduction and continues to this day. Less than two years after Java arrived on the scene, Sun released Java 1.1, which included the following important new features.

▦ Java Archive

The different files that make up a Java applet can now be combined into a single compressed Java Archive *(JAR)* file. With this capability, loading an applet over the Internet is much quicker.

Even more important, JAR files can also contain "digital signatures" that show clearly who owns an applet. Armed with this information, a user may feel more secure about an applet's origin and can then permit a given applet to read and write files to and from the hard disk, for example, or establish a connection with another computer.

▦ Java Database Connectivity

Java Database Connectivity (JDBC) allows users to read and modify database contents in a uniform way using common SQL commands.

▦ Internationalization

With Java you can develop programs for every language, whatever the alphabet or writing system.

▦ User-interface improvements

Among the many improvements to Java's user interface is the ability to print from Java programs.

▶ JavaBeans

JavaBeans are simply independent bits of a Java program *(also called "components")*. One example is the animated button mentioned earlier. A JavaBean can also be a calendar, a calculator, or a search method. All user-interface elements in Java, such as buttons and input fields, are JavaBeans themselves. One advantage of these components is that they help developers to program visually: You can add new options to a program simply by dragging a JavaBean between two lines of code using the mouse.

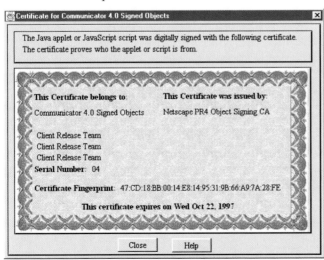

◀ An original digital certificate from Netscape.

▶ The Spacemen Applet

The Spacemen applet illustrates the harmony between programming and design. A complete listing of the source code will not fit in a single column, but the most important code is shown in the adjacent column. (See the facing page for the complete Web page.) The Java code allows Web surfers to play a game online; the highest scores are shown in a separate frame. The complete applet is quite tiny—only 15K—and yet it offers all the facets of a full-fledged computer game.

Class Sprite extends Object

This is the core of the Spacemen applet. With the help of this Java "class," Sprite objects (small bits of graphics) are created and drawn on the screen. During creation, the Sprite objects are "cut" out of the GIF file and placed in the computer's memory. A Sprite object can consist of multiple frames, so you can create animations. Once the class is created, you can make as many Sprite objects as you wish in different sizes and with varying numbers of frames. This capability clearly shows the advantage of Java's object-oriented approach to programming.

This applet ▶ consists of two "class" files and invokes the GIF files.

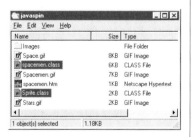

Mainship = new Sprite

This example shows that the Sprite object named Mainship is created and then used in the program. The instruction Mainship,paint (Doublebuffer) draws the Sprite object on the screen at the x and y positions specified.

```
class Sprite extends Object
{
  spacemen parent;

  public int xpos;
  public int ypos;
  public Image IMGsprite[];
  public int frames;
  public int currentframe;
  public int framespeed;

  Sprite(spacemen parent,int xpos,int ypos,Image
  IMGsprite, int frames, int sx,int sy,int w,int h)
  {
    this.parent=parent;

    this.IMGsprite=new Image[frames];
    this.xpos=xpos;
    this.ypos=ypos;
    this.frames=frames;
    this.currentframe=0;
    this.framespeed=2;

    for(int x=0;x<frames;x++)
    {
      this.IMGsprite[x]=parent.createImage(new
      FilteredImageSource(IMGsprite.getSource(), new
      CropImageFilter((sx+x)*w,sy*h,w,h)));
    }
  }

  public void paint(Graphics g)
  {
    g.drawImage(this.IMGsprite[this.currentframe],
    this.xpos, this.ypos, null);
  }
}
```

```
mainship = new Sprite(this,size().width/2-8,size().
height-30,imgs,1,0,0,24,24);
```

The Java applet is seamlessly integrated into the Web page. The online game increases the page's appeal. ▶

▶ **Wysiwyg Java Products**

Several programs have been introduced that help developers create Java applets. One of these is PageCharmer Pro, an extensive sample library. With PageCharmer Pro, you need only replace the supplied samples with your own images; the program then generates the applet and the requisite Java and HTML code.

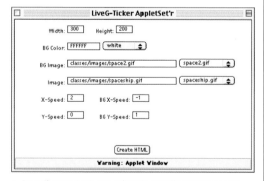

▲ PageCharmerPro's Java editor is actually written in Java.

```
<applet codebase="classes" code=GABillboard width=300 height=150 name="gabillboa
<param name=LoadMsg value="Loading Example... ">
<param name=Rate value=70>
<param name=BGColor value=#FFFF9F>
<param name=Image0 value="classes/images/paddle.gif">
<param name=Vector0 value="P 10;S;H 0 -1 1 47;H 0 1 1 47;L">
<param name=Image1 value="classes/images/paddle.gif">
<param name=Vector1 value="P 286;S;H 0 1 1 47;H 0 -1 1 47;L">
<param name=Image2 value="classes/images/orb.gif">
<param name=Tiles2 value=3>
<param name=Vector2 value="P 15;S;H 5 1 1 47;E 'splayer:a0';H -5 -1 1 47;E 'spla
</applet>
```

With ActiveX ▶
controls, Web
pages can be
much more
dynamic.

ActiveX, a technology that Microsoft introduced with Internet Explorer, is a powerful way to extend a Web browser's standard functions. This chapter explains how ActiveX controls work and offers a real-world example in which it excels.

All About ActiveX Controls

Microsoft has done more than any other software maker to popularize the Basic, C, and C++ programming languages. The company's Visual Basic and Visual C/C++ development environments enable programmers to write not only complete programs but also OLE *(Object Linking and Embedding)* applications.

When the success and ubiquity of Sun Microsystems's Java proved that a full-featured programming language could be used to enhance Web pages, Microsoft expanded OLE into a "universal", that is, system-independent, technology called ActiveX. It has radically altered the way people use the World Wide Web.

▶ Automatic Downloads and Updates

Falling somewhere between a plug-in and a Java applet, an ActiveX program is known as a control, just as a Java program is called an applet. These reusable software components can be used in special programming environments, including Microsoft Access, Borland's Delphi, and Sybase's PowerBuilder. Using this software, developers can, for example, create players for movie clips and add user-interface enhancements such as text highlights and buttons with images.

When an ActiveX-enabled Web browser loads a page containing a reference to an ActiveX control, the program first checks whether that particular component is already installed on the user's computer. If it isn't, the browser downloads the control and installs it automatically. If the component already exists on the machine, it is not retrieved again but simply activated. This all happens at such lightning speed that it doesn't cause a performance lag; in fact, the user is not even aware of the activity.

In terms of complexity, ActiveX controls can do anything that Java applets can. They can add a variety of functions to a Web page—from a simple highlight for a button, to an automatic scrolling menu, to a full-blown player for Shockwave animations. With the wide range of available tools for creating Windows programs, the number of ActiveX controls continues to grow. Microsoft Internet Explorer was the first Web browser to support all ActiveX control functions, and makers of other browsers have been compelled to follow suit. Newer versions of Visual Basic make the programmer's job considerably more pleasant. The automatic loading of an ActiveX control is comparable to a Java applet's "installing"; in both cases, enhancements to the Web page are evident only after the component code is completely loaded. But unlike a Java applet—which displays a gray area onscreen for a few seconds after loading—ActiveX controls go into action immediately.

▶ Cache Flow

Another difference between ActiveX and Java is that an ActiveX control is permanently stored on a user's hard disk. Internet Explorer keeps a separate cache directory, named Occache, just for storing the controls. This cache is never "flushed," so what happens if a new version of a control has the same filename as one that is already stored in the Occache directory?

Microsoft has come up with a solution that is as simple as it is functional: The author can add an internal version number to the ActiveX control *(placed at the end of the <CODEBASE> attribute)*. Here is an example:

```
< OBJECT ID="StatistiX1"
  WIDTH=600 Height=181
  CODEBASE="StatistiX.ocx#version=1,0,0,1">
```

If, while loading an HTML page, the browser determines that an ActiveX control already exists on the user's computer, it will not load the control from the Web. But if an older version of the same control does reside on the hard disk, the browser will load the newer version and install it over the old one. On a Windows-based PC, the older control gets backed up to Occache\Conflict.1. If this directory already contains a control with the same name, it is then automatically copied to the Occache\conflict.2 directory, and so on. Comparable backup strategies have been devised for the Macintosh and Unix operating systems.

■ Security

By now you're probably wondering whether all the ActiveX controls installed on your hard disk without your knowledge are safe. In fact, just like Java applets, ActiveX controls are potentially unsafe. In the case of Java, Sun Microsystems has done everything in its power to limit the negative consequences of these miniprograms by allowing a Java "virtual machine" to determine which computer functions can and cannot be used. This technique is called Sandboxing. Moreover, Java can't write any files to the local hard disk, so no configuration settings can be modified.

ActiveX controls are potentially more unsafe than Java applets because they have access to all system functions, including the hard disk and the network. One rogue ActiveX control circulating on the Web at least demonstrates this danger in a civilized fashion: It simply restarts your computer. The only protective mechanism that Microsoft has in place is to "certify" ActiveX controls, whereby so-called trusted servers can issue certificates to a control's recipients guaranteeing the component's origin.

However, certifying a control as safe says nothing about its contents or function. Also, the certification process itself is full of hurdles *(including fees)* that make it unappealing for individual ActiveX producers to register their work.

▓ Functionality

The main drawback to ActiveX controls is their extensive functionality at the system level. Users of Windows PCs can get access to the entire operating system from an ActiveX control. Files can not only be read but also written and erased, and data can even be transmitted. The power of ActiveX controls can thus be seen as both a great advantage *(flexibility)* and a huge disadvantage *(lack of security)*. This also applies to the limitations of the system software: An ActiveX control can access a Windows machine at file level.

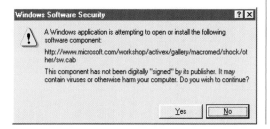

Other operating systems, such as Unix and the Mac OS, do not use this process. If Microsoft wishes to export its controls to other platforms, it must create a separate version for each. Java applets are not encumbered by this restriction, but they have only limited access to system-specific features.

For example, Java can invoke just four fonts, cannot harness the right mouse button, and cannot invoke printer routines. These limitations are due to the fact that Java is a platform-independent language, and these routines differ from platform to platform. Have you ever seen a Macintosh with three mouse buttons?

▓ Speed

Because the applicationis compiled to native machine code, ActiveX controls offer maximum speed on computers with Intel *(or Intel-compatible)* processors. Java applications, on the other hand, are compiled to a completely platform-independent byte code that must then be converted *("interpreted")* by the virtual machine into instructions the computer can understand.

The extra processing time means that Java applets are often not as fast as ActiveX controls. So-called JIT *("just in time")* compilers, available for both Internet Explorer and Netscape Navigator, translate byte code back into native machine code, giving Java applets a considerable speed boost and thereby undercutting one of the key advantages of ActiveX controls.

▓ File size

File size is also important. A typical ActiveX control, though relatively small, is not as compact as a Java applet. However, ActiveX applications can be downloaded in a compressed form called a .cab file *(similar to a .zip archive)* that bundles all necessary components such as DLL and configuration files. A Java applet cannot do this, but then again, users already have a large portion of

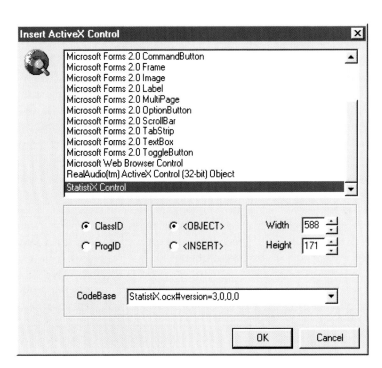

◄ HomeSite 2.0 is a great tool to incorporate an ActiveX control in a Web page.

the libraries on their computers—Netscape Navigator and Microsoft Internet Explorer place this information on the hard disk when the program is installed. Thus, a Java applet can be written in extremely compact form because its functions are called from this stored software library upon execution.

▶ What About Plug-ins?

After all of this talk about Java applets and ActiveX controls, you may think that plug-ins are now obsolete. However, they will surely not disappear. Plug-ins continue to be well suited to complex functions that are too large to download from the Internet every time they are called on. Instead, plug-ins are downloaded once and then install themselves from the Web browser into the proper folder. Macromedia Shockwave is a good example of a plug-in that is simply too large to download every time a user wants to play a Shockwave movie with the ActiveX Viewer.

The procedure for assigning a "ClassID" *(more on this below)* to an ActiveX control is not simple, but you can automate the process with a good HTML editor such as HomeSite.

▶ HTML Syntax

To add an ActiveX control to a Web page, you use the <OBJECT> tag, perhaps combined with one or more <PARAM> tags. Following is a description of the <OBJECT> syntax, based on the World Wide Web Consortium specifications:

```
<OBJECT                          NAME=url
                                 SHAPES
    ALIGN=left | center | right  STANDBY=message
    BORDER=n                     TYPE=type
    CLASSID=id                   USEMAP=url
    CODEBASE=url                 VSPACE=n
    CODETYPE=codetype            WIDTH=n>
    DATA=url
    DECLARE                      <PARAM NAME="name"
    HEIGHT=n                       VALUE="value">
    HSPACE=n
    ID=id                        </OBJECT>
```

▶ A Practical Example

An ActiveX control's function can also be influenced from an HTML page using properties and methods from JavaScript or VBScript. A control called StatistiX offers a practical example—a visual overview of a visit to a Web site. Normally, this is done by running a program on the server that interprets the "log file" and creates a GIF image showing the statistical results; the log file records when an external browser requests a page or any other object.

Many Internet service providers, however, do not permit users to place their own programs on the servers because of the load they may place on the server processors. The solution is to let a program that runs on the client *(user)* side process the information. This can be done using an ActiveX control.

The StatistiX control's operation involves several steps:

1. The page is requested by a Web browser.
2. The browser sees that an ActiveX control is on the page and retrieves it.
3. Once the control is retrieved, it loads automatically.
4. On the Web page, a property (more on this later) is specified in which the statistics can be found in the form of text. For comparison purposes, the statistics for multiple pages may be specified in these properties.
5. The control retrieves and then examines the statistics to locate the information regarding number of visitors to the site.

The statistics file looks something like this:

```
Number of hits per day:<p>
<SS>
<pre>
1 Sep 1996    1017  (9176Kb)
2 Sep 1996    1177  (10377Kb)
3 Sep 1996    1249  (10692Kb)
4 Sep 1996    1044  (8956Kb)
5 Sep 1996    1016  (9193Kb)
</pre>
<ES>
```

The <SS> *(Start Statistics)* tag is made up and indicates that the statistics we are seeking start at this point. When the ActiveX control encounters the <SS> tag, it will know exactly where those statistics can be found. The subsequent lines specify the total number of "hits"—site visits—per day. The control keeps reading the statistics until it comes to the <ES> *(End Statistics)* tag. After all of the information has been read and interpreted, it must be converted into graphic form.

▶ Image Tags

The resulting StatistiX screen is shown below. What if someone else also wants to use the control, but wants a yellow background rather than a black one? The source code is not available, and the user may well lack the programming skills to make such a change independently. Fortunately, the programmer thought of this situation in advance and built a property into the StatistiX control.

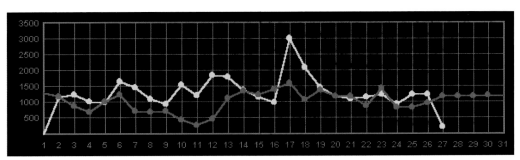

▲ Using primary colors from Windows' basic palette results in a clear display of the StatistiX "score."

▶ Properties

Properties are "program variables" accessible from outside the program even after it has been compiled. Examples of properties include background color, font name, location of a file, update interval, and the like. The StatistiX control's properties include a color per line, a URL per line *(the location of the file containing the statistics)*, and the background color for the image. The properties are set by including a bit of VBScript in the HTML file:

```
<HTML>
<HEAD>
  <SCRIPT LANGUAGE="VBScript">
    <!—
    Sub window_onLoad()
      StatistiX.URL(0) = location.href
      StatistiX.URL(1) =
      "http://www.xs4all.nl/~jarit/stats/index0896.html"
    end sub
    —>
  </SCRIPT>
<Title>Statistics for www.xs4all.nl/~jarit</Title>
</HEAD>
<BODY BGCOLOR="#ffcccc">
```

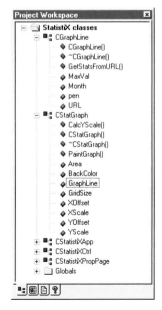

The Visual C++ ▶
ClassView window
displays the methods
and properties of
C++ objects.

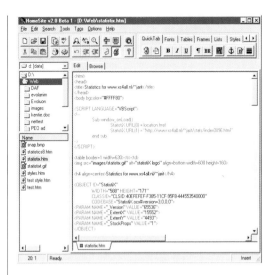

▶ HTML Code

Building an ActiveX control into a Web page is not a simple matter. As you've already learned, this is done using the <OBJECT> tag. However, Microsoft's "registration" process requires that a ClassID property be added.

It must be entered separately and thus can pose a challenge to HTML editors, but HomeSite *(shown above)* automates this complex process. Using the <PARAM> tag, you can set the object's foreground color, font, line color, and other specific parameters.

```
<OBJECT
  ID="StatistiX"
  WIDTH=588 HEIGHT=171
  CLASSID="CLSID:40EFEFEF-F385-11CF-95F8-444553540000"
  CODEBASE="StatistiX.ocx#version=3,0,0,0">
    <PARAM NAME="_Version" VALUE="65536">
    <PARAM NAME="_ExtentX" VALUE="15552">
    <PARAM NAME="_ExtentY" VALUE="4493">
    <PARAM NAME="_StockProps" VALUE="1">
  <IMG SRC="images/statistix.gif"
    WIDTH=600 HEIGHT=181 BORDER=0><BR>
  You need an ActiveX enabled browser like
    <A HREF="http://www.microsoft.com/ie/">Microsoft
    Internet Explorer 3</A> to properly display this page.
</OBJECT>
```

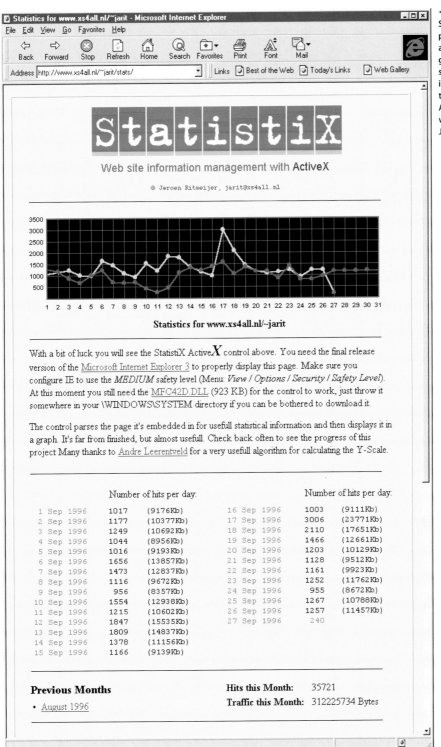

◄ The complete StatistiX Web page includes the automatically generated statistical information, thanks to an ActiveX control written by Jeroen Ritmeijer.

▶ Internet Explorer Security Settings

Internet Explorer comes with several features that help protect users against aggressive ActiveX controls.

The browser provides the following three security settings:

■ **High** Controls that lack a certificate are not loaded.

■ **Medium** If Internet Explorer encounters a control without a certificate, it warns the user and asks whether it should load the control or not.

■ **Low** Internet Explorer loads every control, with or without a certificate, and never alerts the user.

▶ Authenticode

If the programmer built Microsoft's Authenticode security into an ActiveX control, users will see a "digital certificate" message onscreen when the control starts to load from a Web page. Authenticode identifies a control's publisher and is meant to assure users that the code has not been altered prior to download.

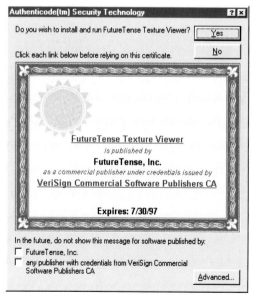

▲ An Authenticode digital certificate looks impressive and offers a measure of safety for ActiveX controls and other software components.

This complex, ▸ database-driven page was published live on the Web without using any HTML or scripting commands.

Many people see the World Wide Web as the future of database publishing. Instead of manually coded and static pages, databases could be automatically generated and continually updated online. This chapter demonstrates how to take on such an apparently complex task with ease.

FileMaker Database Publishing

Not long ago, putting a database on the Internet was a job reserved for experienced programmers, who had to write complex scripts in languages such as C and Perl to ensure that the database contents were translated accurately to the Web. But Web developers' demands changed this situation; now, programs such as NetObjects Fusion and ColdFusion offer easy, standard ways of linking a Web page template to a database.

FileMaker Pro 5 goes a step further. With this comprehensive database software from FileMaker Inc., Web developers can publish a database online with only a few modifications of settings. It can't get any simpler, yet the result is powerful and efficient. Read on for step-by-step tutorial!

▶ Database Design

FileMaker Pro 5 is very easy to use. With little effort or expertise, users can set up a database—even a relational database—and include links to Microsoft Excel, Access, and other common files. And because FileMaker Pro supports Open Database Connectivity *(ODBC)*, virtually any commonly used database format is accessible, including Microsoft SQL.

▶ Fixed IP Number

Although publishing a FileMaker Pro database on the Web is simple to do, the process can seem rather illogical. Therefore, we will approach it step-by-step.

An initial requirement *(apart from having a database, of course)* is an Internet connection. Most connections today use "dynamic" IP addresses that change each time you connect to the Internet. When this happens, the access code changes as well. It's better to have a "fixed" IP address to ensure that the database is continually accessible. If you can't get a fixed connection, you should consider a cable connection. Although the providers usually assign dynamic IP addresses, these numbers do not change as frequently as with dial-up Internet access because the subscribers have an "always-on" connection. If you need a persistent connection because you use it to earn a living, you will have to check in with your Internet service provider.

▼ The IP address can be obtained from the TCP/IP window.

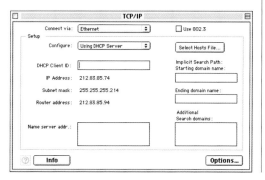

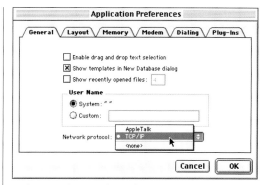

▲ The network protocol must be set to TCP/IP.

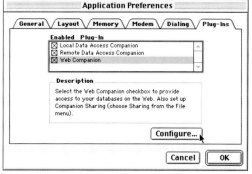

▲ The Web Companion plug-in is then configured.

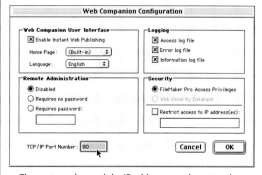

▲ The port number and the IP address must be entered. ▼

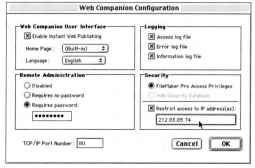

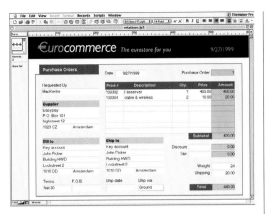

▲ The database contains several layouts, but the Web site's startup screen is Form.

▶ Setting Up the Web Companion

The key to success with FileMaker Pro is using the Web Companion, a plug-in that

▲ You can activate the database by turning Sharing on.

converts the application into a Web database server, complete with security and access privileges. Configuring the Web Companion is quite simple. Once you have found your IP address *(on Macs, go to the TCP/IP control panel)*, go to FileMaker's Application Preferences. On the General tab, set the network protocol to TCP/IP; and from the Plug-Ins tab check the Web Companion box and click on Configure. In the window that appears, enter the IP address and— option, but a good idea—a password for remote administration.

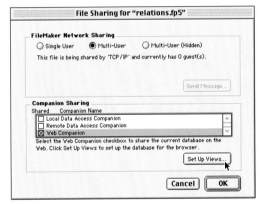

▲ Select Multi-User, then click on Set Up Views for the correct layout.

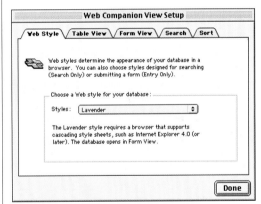

▲ The Lavender style best suits the database layout. ▼

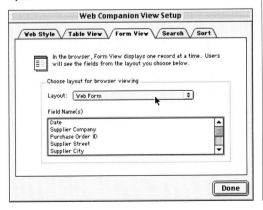

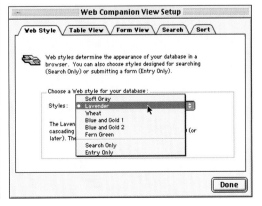

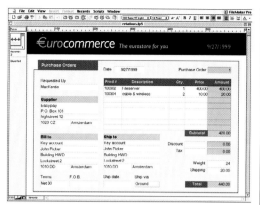

▲ Both the FileMaker Pro layout and the online version visible in the browser window have identical functions.

▶ Common Use of the Database

If you are behind a firewall, you must set the TCP/IP port number separately. If you don't have a firewall, use port 80. For logging, FileMaker Pro offers three options: Access, Error, and Information log files. You should select all three because they record valuable information about visits to your site and any problems encountered.

By default, FileMaker Pro uses the Enable Instant Web Publishing option to specify the layout for both the contents of the database itself and the Web grid. The option's Home Page default is *(Built-in)*; deselect this option. The following step is to specify the layout to be displayed for both the contents of the database itself and the layout of the Web grid.

FileMaker Pro uses the option "Enable Instant Web Publishing" by default. The popup menu contains "Home page: built-in". If you are going to create your own design for presenting your database, click this option off. Using a WYSIWIG Web editor, you can design your own home page for the database designs. And, of course, edit it further in a different editor. For this chapter we have used a standard layout since this not only looks good, but is also equipped with a sophisticated user interface. For commercial Web sites it is advisable to use a more distinctive layout. Once you've entered all

the required values, FileMaker Pro can then publish the database on the Web. You now need to set up the File Sharing attributes. From the File menu, select the Sharing option. From the File Sharing window that appears, check the Web Companion box and make sure that Multi-User is selected for network sharing. Once the site is accessible, the number of connected users will be displayed at the bottom of the screen; at this point the number is still zero.

▶ Modifying the Database Layout

By default, you specify the database design in FileMaker Pro itself. The program offers an almost infinite variety of options for customizing the way your database will look online. You can also import images, such as the logo for Eurocommerce, which lends its name to our sample site. The design of the database should be completely attuned to its end users. After all, they will have to fill in quite a few fields, so clarity and ease of use are extremely important.

One condition for a Web link is that at least one layout be selected, but all of the Web pages don't have to use the same layout. In the Eurocommerce example, you see that the display of the central overview screen has

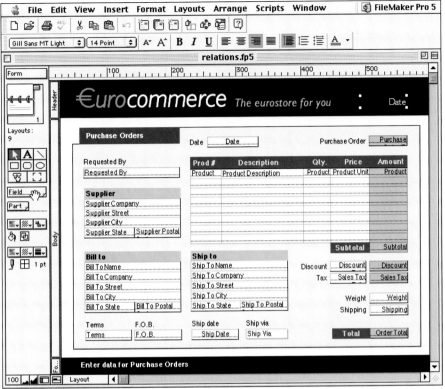

◀ The Form layout consists of a header, a body, and a footer, all of which FileMaker Pro translates to the Web. The logos are converted to GIF files.

many more options than the customer input screen. Both use the same data, but they have different layouts. Clicking on FileMaker's Set Up Views option brings up the layout options. Select Lavender as the Web style.

▶ Database Publishing

Now it's time to view the results in the browser. One of the less logical aspects of FileMaker Pro is that it doesn't provide a Publish button, so you'll need to do the

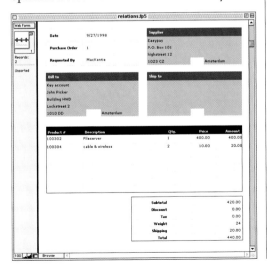

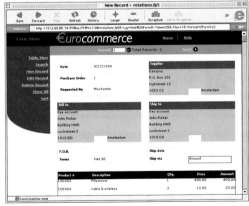

▲ A completely different layout called Web Form is employed for user input.

◀ Here, too, the translation to the Web is successful.

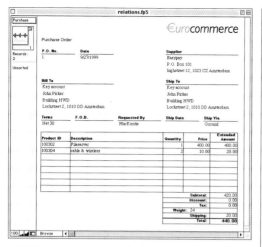

▲ This layout is used to print the form.

following: Open the browser, make sure you have an Internet connection, and paste your IP address in the browser's address box. Once you establish contact, you'll see a standard screen with the name of our database —relations.fp5—as the only hyperlink. If you click on this link, the database will be published in the layout you selected previously. As you can see in the examples, FileMaker Pro has meticulously translated the Eurocommerce database to the Web. The examples shown are from a Macintosh, but the process is exactly the same in the Windows version of FileMaker Pro. Of course, the speed of the system on which the database runs is a

factor in its accessibility: The more popular your site, the bigger the load it puts on your computer.

Luckily, FileMaker offers various growth paths—in Internet lingo, this is known as a "scalable solution". Instead of using the Web Companion plug-in that comes with the application, you can select a dedicated FileMaker Server. The link can also be improved by using products such as Tango and Lasso. Even some larger e-commerce firms use these products to publish their databases on the Web. Tango also offers cross-platform support and can with work with all current Web servers.

▶ **XML Support**

FileMaker Pro comes with built-in support for Extensible Markup Language *(XML)*. The layout in our lavender.fth example is described using XML, and the database itself can also generate output to XML. Selecting this option offers you perspectives for the long term. With this program in its product line, Apple, FileMaker's owner, has made a fine entry into online database publishing.

Although you can opt for Apple's WebObjects development platform, many database publishers will find a mature solution in FileMaker Pro 5 Unlimited. This upgrade to FileMaker 5 supports Secure Sockets Layer *(SSL)* connections, enabling you to protect your content with reliable security. You can also use FileMaker as groupware by expanding it to FileMaker Server 5, which allows 250 users to be linked to the database simultaneously. FileMaker Server is ideal as an inexpensive groupware product for small companies that need a way for multiple employees to work on the same database.

▲ The log file meticulously registers the site's usage statistics.

The Direct E-Mail ▶
site is based on
Microsoft's Active
Server Pages (ASP)
technology.

E-commerce is actually constructing a shell around relational and product databases. International electronic trade is made possible by putting this data on the Internet. This chapter explains the development process for a Microsoft Active Server Pages (ASP) database link.

Database Linking with ASP

Not all Web pages are manually coded in HTML. More and more URLs now have rather mysterious extensions, such as .asp and .stm. Some pages consist merely of numbers, like 8002336.htm. These are typical peculiarities of the database-driven Internet, in which Web pages are only generated the moment when the user selects a specific link. This form of online publishing offers several advantages and heralds such developments as online commerce and merchant servers. The interaction between the designer of such a site and the technical responsibilities must be carefully arranged. The designer has to create HTML files such as templates or grid pages in which reciprocal, structurally identical data can be placed. This work thus requires some understanding of the underlying process.

The site exemplified in this chapter is for a fictional online supplier of office equipment. Because the target group for the company is located in both the Netherlands and Belgium, end users must be able to indicate in which currency they want prices displayed.

A separate option lets bargain hunters type in the maximum price they are willing to pay for a product, so any prices that are higher will not be shown to them.

▶ Task Allocation

The programmer isn't generally skilled in using layout programs and applying house styles. By contrast, the Web designer typically is experienced in these aspects but may lack programming knowledge. Once the designer and the programmer establish clear agreements, they can start working together. Parts of the work they can do simultaneously, whereas with other parts they will be dependent on each other's progress.

▶ The Programmer's Tasks

As mentioned above, the designer creates HTML files such as templates or grid pages in which reciprocal, structurally identical data are placed. The programmer handles the following tasks *(generally in the order presented)*.

■ Analyzing the database

By talking with customers, programmers must determine which information is already available and what data must be stored and be available for requests. We also need to take a good look at the quantity of data. Based on these observations, we can deduce the required hardware *(server)* and software *(database environment)*. This analysis should be very thorough because modifications made later will often involve a lot of extra work.

■ Communicating with the designer

The programmer tells the designer which available information must be included on the Web site. It is then up to the designer to

▲ Figure 1: The search form screen.

▲ Figure 2: The result screen. Figure 3: The detail screen. ▼

display that information in an efficient and user-friendly way. An optimal database design is created based on the information acquired in the analysis phase.

The Direct E-Mail sample site specifies the following:

- Table names *(products, categories, customer information, etc.)*
- Relationships among the tables
- Fields per table *(name, price, description, etc.)*
- Field properties *(data type, validations, etc.)*

The database is implemented in whatever database the programmer chooses, using the basic design.

Converting the existing data

To cut down on errors and unnecessary work, the programmer should reuse as much existing information as possible by converting any data already present in the customer's existing *("legacy")* system to the new system.

Creating the input program

If the customer itself does not have the capability to do so, the programmer must create a user-friendly input program that hides the database's complexity from the people who will enter new data. With an effective input program in place, most of the data-entry work can be performed inexpensively by typists.

Programming the link between database, templates, and search form

Once the database includes all the necessary information and is properly structured, the programmer needs to create a link between the database and the Web site.

Which Web server and linking software you select will depend on the specifications of the Web site, the complexity of the database, and the anticipated number of visitors to the site. Frequently, these two options are integrated.

▶ Setting Up the Design

At the core of our design assignment is the need to display various search options as clearly as possible. The idea is not to overwhelm the user with too many options but to present an efficient and user-friendly search form screen *(see Figure 1)*.

Designing the result screen

The designer must also create a template for the result screen *(see Figure 2)*, which shows a summary of products found that satisfy the criteria entered by the user on the search form. The result screen is most often line-oriented—meaning that one line of data is displayed for each relevant article found. A line-oriented approach puts restrictions on the designer, who will need to take possible exceptions into account. How should the screen look, for instance, if the information found does not fit on one line? To localize the exceptions, the designer must take a close look at all possible results the database may present.

Designing the detail screen

The detail screen *(see Figure 3)* comes up when the user clicks on a product summary from the result screen or when only one article is found, in which case a result screen is not displayed. Depending on the amount of information in the database, the detail screen can be rather complex. As with the result screen, the designer should take potential exceptions into account. How should the detail screen look, for example, if no image of a product exists? Should the text move to the side to fill the empty space, or should a "placeholder" graphic be displayed instead? The detail screen is the last in our sample application; real-world situations, however, may require specialized buttons, such as Order or Add To Shopping Cart, to be displayed on this screen. Now that the design is ready and the inventory of all data complete, we will invoke the help of support software.

▶ Database Engine

For our Direct E-Mail example, we use Microsoft Access as the database engine. Access is a component of the Microsoft Office suite of business software and thus already enjoys a huge base of installed users. Although Access isn't well suited to high-volume Web applications, it is perfectly sufficient for the average database-driven site.

The first step involves creating a table in which the data is stored. We won't get into the details of database development here, but this example should be easy to follow. In addition, we will create tables to accommodate all the required categories and groups, and we will define the relationships among these tables and the MAIN_ITEMS table on the Relationships screen.

▶ Input Screen

No database is complete without an input screen. Using this screen, people with no technical knowledge of HTML or computers in general can keep the Web site up to date. When a price gets adjusted in the database, the change is immediately displayed on the Internet. An input screen, properly designed, is one of the biggest advantages of a database-driven Web site.

▶ Web Server

Our Web pages have now been designed, the database set up, and all the data entered. All we need at this point is the proverbial "glue" that connects these elements to one another.

HTML itself does not address these issues, but Web server software such as Microsoft Internet Information Server *(IIS)* and Netscape Enterprise Server can handle the task. For our example, we will use IIS.

The Active Server Pages element of IIS makes it possible to place meaningful processing codes for the server among the HTML. These codes can be written in VBScript or JavaScript.

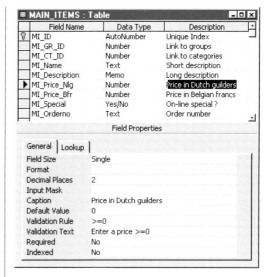

▲ The setup is created in the MAIN_ITEMS table.

Here is a simple example:

```
<HTML>
<HEAD><TITLE>ASP Demo</TITLE></HEAD>
<BODY>
<H1>ASP Demo</H1>
<% for i = 1 to 3
  response.write("<FONT SIZE=" & i & ">Hello ¶
    World</FONT><BR>")
  next
%>
</BODY>
</HTML>
```

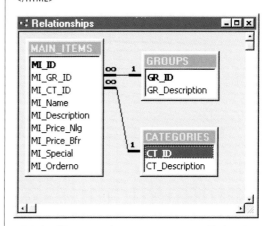

▲ Relationships among the components are specified on the Relationships screen.

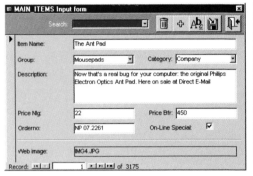

▲ The input form has been created especially for the link.

This demo will be immediately clear to someone with knowledge of Visual Basic. The <%...%> tag tells the Web server to execute the commands that follow before loading the page to the browser. This technique is browser-independent. The new commands are intended for the Web server. All pages that include possible ASP commands must have the extension .asp. When the server executes the program, the result is pure HTML, as shown below.

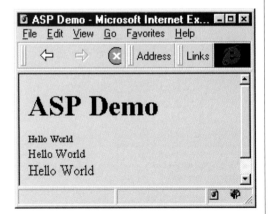

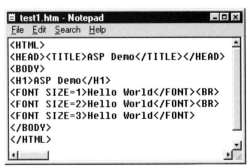

▶ The Search Form Screen (Figure 1)

The most important feature of the search form screen is the input form in which search criteria can be entered. For the sake of clarity, all formatting codes have been stripped from this example.

```
<FORM ACTION="result.asp" METHOD="get">

Group:
<INPUT TYPE="radio" NAME="group" VALUE="1"
  CHECKED> Computers
<INPUT TYPE="radio" NAME="group" VALUE="2"> Printers
<INPUT TYPE="radio" NAME="group" VALUE="3"> Modems
<INPUT TYPE="radio" NAME="group" VALUE="4"> Pads
<INPUT TYPE="radio" NAME="group" VALUE="5"> Faxes
<INPUT TYPE="radio" NAME="group" VALUE="6"> Tablets
Category:
<INPUT TYPE="radio" NAME="category" VALUE="1"
  CHECKED> Private
<INPUT TYPE="radio" NAME="category" VALUE="2">
  Non-profit
<INPUT TYPE="radio" NAME="category" VALUE="3">
  Commercial
<INPUT TYPE="radio" NAME="category" VALUE="4"> Profit
Max:
<INPUT TYPE="TEXT" NAME="max" SIZE="5">
Currency:
<INPUT TYPE="RADIO" NAME="currency" VALUE="nlg"
  CHECKED> Nlg
<INPUT TYPE="RADIO" NAME="currency" VALUE="bfr"> bfr
Buttons
<INPUT TYPE="SUBMIT">
<INPUT TYPE="RESET">

</FORM>
```

In this example we use only radio buttons, and just one button can be selected per group *(the three groups are Group, Category, and Currency)*. Thus, when the Printers option is selected, Computers is deselected. The number entered in the Value attribute corresponds to the value of each database category *(Computers=1, Printers=2, etc.)*.

The contents of the search form are automatically sent to the result.asp page, where we will compose a search using the filled-in criteria, which will get passed on to the database.

▶ The Result Screen (Figure 2)

This result screen processes the information generated on the search form screen, composes a search order for the database, and formats the information found in the HTML code. The search criteria are passed on from the search form by the so-called query string on the URL. The string looks like this:

http://www.directemail.com/result.asp?group=1&
    category=1&max=50&currency=nlg

Using SQL (Structured Query Language), we will now construct a search order based on the query string. SQL is supported by almost every database software maker; therefore our Web pages will be database-independent. Should our site become so successful that we need a faster database, we can easily exchange Microsoft Access, say, for an Oracle server without having to reprogram. The ASP code required to do this is shown on the right. *(Again, the formatting code is left out for better clarity.)*

```
<HTML>
<HEAD><TITLE>Result Page</TITLE></HEAD>
<BODY>

<% set Conn = server.createobject("ADODB.Connection")
   Conn.Open "DirectEMail"

   SQLQuery = "SELECT * FROM main_items"
   SQLWhere = " WHERE mi_gr_id = " & request("group")
   SQLWhere = SQLWhere & " AND mi_ct_id = " &
       request("category")
   if request("max") <> "" then
      SQLWhere = SQLWhere & " AND mi_price_nlg <= " &
      request("max")
   end if

   set RSItems = Conn.Execute(SQLQuery & SQLWhere)

   if RSItems.eof then
%>
   There are no articles that satisfy your criteria.<P>
<% else %>
   The following items satisfy your criteria:<P>
   <%   while not RSItems.eof
         response.write(RSItems("mi_name") & " - fl." &
            RSItems("mi_price_nlg") & "<BR>")
         RSItems.movenext
      wend
   %>
<% end if
   RSItems.close
   Conn.close
%>
</BODY>
</HTML>
```

Here is a brief explanation of this ASP code:

```
set Conn = server.createobject("ADODB.Connection")
Conn.Open "DirectEMail"
```

Generate a Connection object that refers to the Open Database Connectivity (ODBC) database

```
SQLQuery = "SELECT * FROM main_items" SQLWhere = "
WHERE mi_gr_id = " & request("group") SQLWhere =
SQLWhere & " AND mi_ct_id = " & request("category")
 if request("max") <> "" then
SQLWhere = SQLWhere & " AND mi_price_nlg <= " &
request("max") end if
```

Compose the search query for the database using the query string...

```
set RSItems = Conn.Execute(SQLQuery & SQLWhere)
```

...and execute it.

```
if RSItems.eof then
```

Do any records satisfy the criteria?

```
while not RSItems.eof
response.write(RSItems("mi_name") & " - fl." &
RSItems("mi_price_nlg") & "<BR>")
RSItems.movenext wend
```

Go through the records found and "print" them until no records remain.

```
RSItems.close Conn.close
```

Close everything properly.

For every line found, we also have to make a hyperlink that users can click on to invoke a product-information detail screen. To do this, we add another query string to this hyperlink. which will tell the detail screen which product it must display. We compose the link as follows:

```
<A HREF="detail.asp?id=<% =RSItems("mi_id") %>">
Productname </A>
```

In the browser, the link looks like this:

http://www.directemail.com/detail.asp?id=4

▶ The Detail Screen (Figure 3)

The detail screen is comparable to the result screen, except that it displays information about only one product at a time. It gets a product's "ID" from the query string in the result screen. The detail screen should include all data about the relevant product in an attractive way—after all, just because information comes from a database does not mean that it should look boring.

We have complete freedom to design the database data as we choose. To emphasize of this point, the formatting codes are included this time.

```
<% set Conn = server.createobject("ADODB.Connection")
  Conn.Open "DirectEMail"

  SQLQuery = "SELECT * FROM main_items"
  SQLWhere = " WHERE mi_id = " & request("id")

  set RSItem = Conn.Execute(SQLQuery & SQLWhere)
%>
<P>
<FONT SIZE="4" COLOR="#FF0000"><B>Detailed
information about your selection:</B></FONT>
<P>
<TABLE BORDER="0" CELLPADDING="3" WIDTH="343">
  <TR>
    <TD WIDTH="52%" VALIGN="TOP">
      <IMG SRC="/images/img<% =RSItem("mi_id")
      %>.jpg" WIDTH="164" HEIGHT="164"
      ALIGN="BOTTOM" BORDER="1"></A>
    </TD>
    <TD WIDTH="3%"> </TD>
    <TD VALIGN="TOP" COLSPAN="3">
      <FONT SIZE="4" COLOR="#0000AA">
      <% =RSItem("mi_name")
      %></B><BR><BR></FONT>
      <FONT SIZE="4"><%= RSItem("mi_description")
      %><BR><BR>fl <%= RSItem("mi_price_nlg")
      %></FONT>
    </TD>
```

As we can see from the <IMG> tag, the image is composed of data in the database.

Of course, the entire image isn't stored in the database, but we can retrieve it through its unique "record ID." We paste /images/img in front and .jpg behind it for a complete path to the image.

▶ Using the Search System Starting From Other Pages

Now we have put together the search form, result, and detail screens. However, we are not dependent on the search form screen to give commands to the database: We can also invoke the result screen or the detail screen from ongoing text on a random HTML page, complete with parameters for display of a product. Thus, the home page can contain the following text:

This site contains our product line of <A HREF="result.asp?group=1&category=3">computers</A> and other <A HREF="result.asp?group=2&category=3">peripheral equipment</A>. This week's special offer<A HREF="detail.asp?id=4">Ant Pad</A>.

The first two hyperlinks jump to the result screen and display an overview of all the computers and printers available for sale. The third link goes directly to the Ant Pad detail screen. On every page, we also apply this technique to the icons that refer to the relevant product groups.

▶ Other Examples

This technique is not restricted to database links, of course. And its browser-independence means that we can create interactions that are impossible to do in JavaScript or VBScript.

■ Shifting background patterns

Creating Web sites that work with more than one browser has its challenges. Netscape Navigator, for example, background-shifts one pixel more to the left than Microsoft Internet Explorer does. This one-pixel shift can be a problem if we want to connect foreground images seamlessly with the background. But thanks to server intelligence, an annoying complication of Web design can be solved simply: First we create two separate backgrounds—one for Navigator and one for Internet Explorer—and then we place some ASP functions in the HTML code. The server can then ask which browser is being used, and depending on the answer, one of the two backgrounds is loaded. Here is an example of the coding:

```
<% Agent =Request.ServerVariables("HTTP_USER_AGENT")
   if instr(Agent, "MSIE") then %>
<BODY background="images/back_ie.gif" bgcolor="red">
<% else %>
<BODY background="images/back_ns.gif" bgcolor="red">
<% end if %>
```

■ "Reset" Problem in Internet Explorer

We can apply the same technique to another browser-related problem. Internet Explorer cannot use a graphic button to erase contents from a form, so this button is not loaded to Internet Explorer but it is sent to Netscape Navigator. This way, users of the Microsoft browser won't be confused by a button on their screens that doesn't work.

Index

< > (angle brackets), 23, 27, 54
" " (quotation marks), 54
& (ampersand), 54
* (asterisk), 87
<!—> (comment tags), 27, 54, 104, 360
(number sign), 65, 84
/ (slash character), 27
3D animations, 298
3D buttons, 190, 191
3D graphics, 255–258, 280–281
3D lettering, 226
3D models, 330–333
3D programs
    Corel Bryce program, 255–258
    Poser program, 195, 196–200
3D Web environments, 329–336
3D Website Builder, 335
.3ds extension, 331, 332
3DS MAX, 330, 331
8-bit sound files, 316
100% Pure Java Initiative, 385

A

<A HREF> tag, 318
<A STYLE> attribute, 104
<A> tag, 64, 104
access privileges, 22
Acrobat. *See* Adobe Acrobat
<ACTION> attribute, 59
Active Server Pages. *See* ASP
ActiveX controls, 389–396
    adding to Web pages, 392–395
    advantages, 389–390
    Authenticode, 396
    cache flow, 390
    cross-platform issues, 391
    described, 389, 390
    disadvantages, 391
    example, 393
    file size and, 391–392
    functionality, 391
    HTML code, 392, 394
    image tags, 393
    plug-ins and, 392
    properties, 394
    security and, 390–391, 396
    speed of, 391
    vs. Java applets, 390, 391
ActiveX programs, 390
Adaptec Jam, 316

Adaptive 3D technology, 329
Adobe Acrobat, 307–314
Adobe Acrobat Distiller, 308, 310, 312
Adobe Acrobat Exchange, 313
Adobe Acrobat Reader, 308
Adobe After Effects, 286–287
Adobe ATM technology, 308
Adobe Dimensions, 280–281
Adobe GoLive, 134–140
    DHTML and, 370, 371–372
    GoLive Timeline, 370
    image maps, 183
    JavaScript and, 361, 362, 364, 370
    uploading sites, 370
    XML and, 342
Adobe Illustrator
    converting Flash files to, 285, 287–289
    Flash animations and, 282
    image creation, 250
    importing Flash files from, 284
Adobe ImageReady, 306
Adobe InDesign, 116–117
Adobe PageMaker, 115
Adobe PageMill, 90
Adobe Photoshop
    banner creation, 306
    color adjustment, 157, 203, 209
    deleting background edges, 214
    designing home page, 134–136
    filters, 188, 189
    GIF files, 203
    importing files, 142
    inputting flattened versions of, 142
    JPEG files, 158, 161
    prototyping in, 141
    Quick Mask mode, 208–209, 231, 232
    removing edges in, 214
    Rubber Stamp tool, 324, 325
    table creation, 202
    testing patterns, 170
Adobe Premier, 328
Adobe Streamline, 287, 288–289
advertising. *See also* banner ads; marketing
    Internet Advertising Bureau, 300
    online, 17
    on Web sites, 9
After Effects, 286–287
Aftershock software, 296
Agency.com Web site, 128
.ai format, 280
AIFF format, 272, 316, 320

Alexa initiative, 126
Alien Skin filters, 191, 245
<ALIGN> attributes, 70–73, 100
<ALIGN> tag, 78
alignment
    dot.gif alignment, 198
    images, 71, 195–200
    invisible, 198
    table text, 78
    text, 70–72, 78, 195–200
<ALINK> tag, 110
alpha channels, 256
<ALT> attribute, 67, 96, 375
ampersand (&), 54
anchor tag, 64
anchors, 27, 64–65, 66
AND connector, 339
angle brackets (< >), 23, 27, 54
animated rollovers, 273–275
animations. *See also* Flash animations; GIF
    animations; movies; video
    3D animations, 298
    animated buttons, 273–275, 276
    cross-platform compatibility, 369
    Extensis PhotoAnimator, 306
    with layers and JavaScript, 368–369, 370
    size of, 272–273
    sprite objects and, 386
    with style sheets and JavaScript, 369
    text, 275, 276, 278–279
    Ulead GIF Animator, 270
    vs. layers method, 369
Asarte CD-Copy, 316
ASCII text, 27
ASP (Active Server Pages), 291, 403–409
ASP Flash Turbine program, 291
asterisk (*), 87
ATM technology, 308
attributes
    <A STYLE> attribute, 104
    <ACTION> attribute, 59
    <ALIGN> attributes, 70–73, 100
    <ALT> attribute, 67, 96, 375
    <AUTOPLAY> attribute, 328
    <BIG> attribute, 100
    <cellpadding> attribute, 80, 81, 206
    <cellspacing> attribute, 81
    <CHECKED> attribute, 59
    <COL> attribute, 88
    <CONTROLS> attribute, 328
    COORDS attribute, 184

<EXPIRES> attribute, 97, 98
Flash attributes, 276
font attributes, 100
frame attributes, 91
<HREF> attributes, 65
line attributes, 62–63
<MARGINHEIGHT> attribute, 89
<MARGINWIDTH> attribute, 89
<MAXLENGTH> attribute, 59
<METHOD> attribute, 59
MULTIPLE attribute, 60
<NAME> attribute, 59, 64, 89, 96
<NORESIZE> attribute, 89, 94
<NOSHADE> attribute, 63
<ROW> attribute, 88
<ROWS> attribute, 87
<SCROLLING> attribute, 89, 94
<SIZE> attribute, 59
<SMALL> attribute, 100
spacer attributes, 200
<STYLE> attribute, 104
<SUB> attribute, 100
<SUP> attribute, 100
table tag attributes, 82–83
<TYPE> attribute, 59
<VALUE> attribute, 59
video attributes, 328
AU format, 316, 320
audio. *See* sound
Authenticode security, 396
<AUTOPLAY> attribute, 328
avenue.quark XML XTension, 350, 351, 352
.avi extension, 328
AVI format, 326, 328

B
<B> tag, 27, 52
B2B (business-to-business) world, 16
<BACKGROUND> tag, 165
backgrounds
    cluttered, 6
    color of, 6, 46, 136–138, 203
    complex, 163
    contrast of, 210
    deleting, 163
    deleting edges, 214
    designs for, 171–176
    GIF animations, 180
    images for, 177–180, 224

integrating with foreground, 192, 207–214, 254, 410
lines, 171–174
masks, 209–210, 211
music, 6
patterns. *See* patterns
shadows, 227–228
sharpness of, 210
Shockwave movies, 296
sounds, 6
tables, 82
text and, 46
bandwidth, 43–44
banner ads, 299–306. *See also* advertising; marketing
click-through rates, 300, 302–303, 304
creating, 304–306
ePicture Pro program, 301, 303–304
Extensis PhotoAnimator, 306
Flash format, 302
GIF animations, 302
interactive elements, 302
requirements, 304
rules, 300–301
search engines and, 299
successful techniques for, 304–305
tools for, 300–301
banners, 4
<BASEFONT> tag, 51, 100, 252
BBEdit, 121, 122
BeyondPress XTension, 118–119
<BGCOLOR> tag, 82, 212
<BGSOUND> tag, 318
<BIG> attribute, 100
binary mode, 33
BizTalk initiative, 347–348
<BLACKFACE> tag, 378
<BLINK> tag, 248
<BLOCKQUOTE> tag, 58
<BODY> tag, 29, 101, 102, 246
bold text, 27, 52
bookmarks, 15, 17, 37, 86
Bookmarks list, 10
<BORDER> tag, 66, 77, 91
<BORDERCOLOR> tag, 82
borders
frames, 91
images, 66–67, 214
tables, 77, 80–82, 198, 204, 205, 212
WebTV and, 377
bots, 115

box design, 331–333
<BR clear=all> tag, 72, 73, 74, 198, 222

 tag, 50, 51, 73, 94
browsers. *See also* Internet Explorer; Netscape
adjusting, 363
browser check, 363
browser wars, 29
BrowserWatch Web site, 28
cache, 38, 97, 98, 298
check in frames display, 363
colors and, 147–152
compatibility issues, 28, 410
DHTML and, 369, 370
differences in, 24–26
extensions, 28
Flash and, 290
fonts and, 24–26, 108
frames and, 86, 88, 91, 94
GIF animations and, 180
HTML versions and, 28, 48
identifying, 180
image maps and, 184
interlacing, 44
Java support for, 384
JavaScript and, 362–363, 370
JPEG format and, 158
logical *vs.* physical styles, 52
Lynx browser, 25
margins, 175–176
Mosaic browser, 158
opening new window, 362
Opera browser, 28
playing movies in, 328
plug-ins. *See* plug-ins
progressive rendering, 109
registering visitor browsers, 12
Reset button and, 410
sending e-mail from, 32
spacing and, 200
style sheets and, 103, 342–343
tables and, 84
tracking developments, 28
VBScript and, 375
versions of, 3
viewing database results in, 401–402
VRML-compatible, 334
WebTV browser, 376
width of, 42
XML and, 341–345
BrowserWatch Web site, 28
bullets, 55, 56, 58

Bush, Vannevar, 27
business-to-business (B2B) world, 16
button bars, 188–193, 194
buttons, 188–194
   3D buttons, 190, 191
   animated, 273–275
   creating, 188–191
   download speed and, 192
   home page button, 31–32
   navigation buttons, 31–32, 188–193, 194
   Reset button, 410
   Submit button, 60
   text-based, 191
   three-dimensional, 190, 191

C

C language, 59
C++ language, 59, 382
.cab files, 391
cache
   ActiveX controls, 390
   image display and, 38
   pragma no-cache, 97
   Web browsers, 38, 97, 98, 298
<CAPTION> tag, 78
captions, tables, 78
cascading style sheets. *See* CSS
CDF (Channel Definition Format), 346
CD-ROMs
   PDF files and, 308, 312
   QTVR movies and, 324
   sound on, 315
cell padding, 80, 81, 206
cell spacing, 81
CellAnimator, 272
<cellpadding> attribute, 80, 81, 206
cells
   blank, 79
   padding, 80, 81, 206
   spacing, 81
<cellspacing> attribute, 81
<CENTER> tag, 218
CERN maps, 182, 183
CGI (Common Gateway Interface), 59
CGI scripts, 59
Channel Definition Format (CDF), 346
character shape player (CSP), 109
characters
   sets, 98
   special, 54, 112, 339

charts, 291
<CHECKED> attribute, 59
Cinema XL$_4$D, 330, 331
Cinepak compression codec, 326
.class extension, 384
<CLEAR=all> tag, 94
clip art libraries, 336
CLUT (color look-up table), 148–151
C|Net, 304
<CODE> tag, 384
<COL> attribute, 88
color
   adjustment, 147–152, 157, 203
   automating color process, 234
   backgrounds, 6, 46, 136–138, 203, 252
   basic palette, 150
   browsers and, 147–152
   cross-platform issues, 147, 148, 150–151, 224, 294
   custom palette, 150
   defining, 250
   deviations, 224
   DitherBox feature, 151
   file size and, 176
   foregrounds, 252
   GIF animations, 262, 264–265
   hexidecimal values, 150, 224
   hyperlinks, 110
   Image Hose feature and, 238
   images, 250
   indexed, 148, 157, 203, 264–265
   names, 150–151
   patterns and, 229
   photos and, 156
   Photoshop and, 157
   quality of, 147
   random color replacement, 234
   RGB colors, 150, 251
   table cells, 82
   text, 110
   Unix systems and, 151
   Web-safe colors, 147–148, 151, 152
   WebTV and, 377
color cards, 148, 150, 154
color look-up table (CLUT), 148–151
color palette, 251
<COLSPAN> tag, 79, 204
comment tags (<!—>), 27, 54, 104, 360
comments
   adding to hyperlinks, 67
   <META> tags for, 96
Common Gateway Interface. *See* CGI

compression
    Cinepak compression codec, 326
    GIF, 154–155, 160, 161, 172, 176
    images, 308
    JPEG, 44–45, 158–161
    LZW, 155, 156, 308
    PDF files, 308
    sound files, 316, 320
content
    converting existing content to Web, 129
    importance of, 8, 128
    quality of, 37
    reloading, 97
    on Web pages, 2, 6, 21, 36–37
controls, ActiveX, 389–396
    adding to Web pages, 392–395
    advantages, 389–390
    Authenticode, 396
    cache flow, 390
    cross-platform issues, 391
    described, 389, 390
    disadvantages, 391
    example, 393
    file size and, 391–392
    functionality, 391
    HTML code, 392, 394
    image tags, 393
    plug-ins and, 392
    properties, 394
    security and, 390–391, 396
    speed of, 391
    vs. Java applets, 390, 391
<CONTROLS> attribute, 328
cookies, 344
COORDS attribute, 184
Corel Bryce, 255–258
Corel Bryce program, 255–258
Corel KPT filterset, 188–189, 190, 210
Corel Painter, 166, 191, 226–228, 233–242
Corel stock photos, 244
counters, Web page, 186
cross-platform issues. See also Mac OS–based sys-
        tems; Unix-based systems; Windows-based
        systems
    ActiveX and, 391
    animation, 369
    color issues, 147, 148, 150–151, 224, 294
    filename conventions, 34
    font issues, 106
    Java and, 382, 383, 385
    margins, 175

QuickTime file format, 326–327
    rendering, 257
    special characters, 54
    tables, 84
    Tango program and, 402
    Web browsers, 28, 410
    Web page display, 101, 106, 338
CSP (character shape player), 109
CSS (cascading style sheets), 102–105, 106, 351,
    352
CSS files, 352
CSS1, 366
Cuisine Web site, 215–224
Curious Lab Poser, 195, 196–200
customer database, 16
customer feedback, 132

D
database engine, 406
databases
    analyzing, 404
    ASP (Active Server Pages), 291, 403–409
    common uses for, 400
    converting existing data, 405
    customer, 16
    detail screen, 405, 409–410
    engine, 406
    FileMaker Pro, 397–402
    input screen, 406
    Java Database Connectivity (JDBC), 385
    linking internal databases, 22
    linking to Flash, 291
    linking with ASP, 403–409
    links to, 22, 397–402
    Microsoft Access, 406
    modifying layout of, 400–401
    Open Database Connectivity (ODBC), 398
    publishing, 401–402
    result screen, 404, 405
    search form screen, 404, 407–408, 410
    speed of, 408
    tables in, 406
    viewing results in browser, 401–402
dates, adding to Web pages, 74
DCR (Director) files, 293–298
DCR extension, 297
<DD> tag, 57
definition lists, 57
desktop publishing (DTP), 8

DHTML (dynamic HTML), 365–375
  Adobe GoLive, 371–372
  CSS1, 366
  <DIV> tag, 366
  <LAYER> tag, 366–367
  site composition, 373
  VBScript and, 374–375
digital certificates, 385, 396
digital printing, 312
digital signatures, 312, 385
Dimensions, 280–281
<DIR> tag, 58
Director, 293, 294–296
Directory Service Markup Language (DSML), 347
DitherBox feature, 151
dithered items
  images, 250
  photos, 156
  text, 110
dithering, 148, 250
<DIV> tag, 72, 100, 366
<DL> tag, 57, 58
document type definitions (DTDs), 338, 340–341,
    346–347, 350
dot.gif alignment, 198
DoubleClick Network, 304
downloading
  ad banners and, 4
  images and, 3, 4, 43, 44
Dreamweaver, 141, 143, 183
DropPath program, 324
DSML (Directory Service Markup Language), 347
<DT> tag, 57
DTDs (document type definitions), 338, 340–341,
    346–347, 350
DTP (desktop publishing), 8
dynamic fonts, 108–109
dynamic HTML. See DHTML
dynamic Web pages, 92, 93, 95, 291, 370

E
e-books, 314
ECMA Script project, 369
e-commerce
  ASP and, 403
  BizTalk, 347–348
  e-books, 314
  Web Buy technology, 314
  WebTV and, 380

e-commerce Web sites, 15–17
  customer confidence, 130
  customer feedback, 132
  design techniques, 131
  preparation for, 15–16
  shopping carts, 130–131, 405
  tracking navigation, 130–131
EDI (Electronic Data Interchange), 346
editors, HTML
  Adobe GoLive. See Adobe GoLive
  Adobe InDesign, 116–117
  Adobe PageMaker, 115
  Adobe PageMill, 90
  Allaire Homesite, 122
  BBEdit, 121, 122
  described, 24
  HotMetal Pro program, 120, 121
  Macromedia Dreamweaver, 141, 143
  Macromedia UltraDev, 123
  Microsoft FrontPage, 31, 86, 114–115, 248
  Microsoft Word 2000, 114
  NetObjects Fusion, 124–125
  professional HTML editors, 119–126
  QuarkXPress, 118–119
Electronic Data Interchange (EDI), 346
electronic mail. See e-mail
ElfData XML Editor, 341
<EM> tag, 52
e-mail (electronic mail)
  intranets and, 20
  links to, 31, 38
  Mail To protocol, 32, 218
  responding to, 14–15
  sending from browser, 32
  sent to Web site manager, 14
  Web servers and, 20
<EMBED> tag, 276, 278, 297, 327
environment variables, 59
e-paper, 314
e-Picture Pro, 299
ePicture Pro program, 301, 303–304
EPOC operating system, 354
error messages, 6, 17
<ES> tag, 393
events, JavaScript, 361
<EXPIRES> attribute, 97, 98
exporting
  Flash animations, 275–277
  Flash files from Illustrator, 284
  PICT images, 286–287
  for prepress, 310

extended HTML (XHTML), 28, 349
Extensible Markup Language (XML), 337–352
  advantages of, 344
  BizTalk, 347–348
  cascading style sheets and, 352
  described, 337
  document structure, 351
  EDI and, 346
  elements *vs.* tags, 341
  examples, 339, 340
  FileMaker Pro and, 402
  HTML and, 338–339
  hyperlinks and, 349
  markups, 341–342
  mobile users and, 343
  one-to-one marketing and, 344–345
  process instructions (PIs), 340
  QuarkXPress documents and, 350
  SGML and, 338–339
  special characters, 339
  vs. HTML, 338, 339
  vs. SGML, 339
  Web browsers and, 341–345
  XLink standard, 348–349
  XML Data Server, 348
  XML Editor, 341
  XML files, 340
Extensible Query Language (XQL), 348
Extensible Stylesheet Language (XSL), 342–343,
    344
extensions
  .3ds extension, 331, 332
  .avi extension, 328
  browser extensions, 28
  .class extension, 384
  DCR extension, 297
  file extensions, 34
  font extensions, 100
  HTML extensions, 54, 58
  Microsoft extensions, 28, 29, 48
  .mov extension, 286, 328
  Netscape extensions, 28, 29, 48, 55–58
  paragraph, 100
  paragraph extensions, 100
  .snm extension, 326
  .swf extension, 332, 333
  .WML extension, 354
  .wrl extension, 334
Extensis DrawTools, 234
Extensis Mask Pro, 163
Extensis PhotoAnimator, 306

extranets, 20, 22
extrude action, 281
Eye Candy, 191, 245
EyeSite Web site, 207–214

F

Favorites list, 7, 10
feathering, 227
feedback, 132
file transfer protocol. *See* FTP
FileMaker Pro, 397–402
FileMaker Server, 402
files
  .cab files, 391
  CSS files, 352
  DCR files, 293–298
  FLA files, 292
  Flash files, 284
  GIF files. *See* GIF files
  HTML files, 27
  importing into Flash, 285
  JAR files, 385
  JPEG files. *See* JPEG files
  MP3 files, 272
  multimedia files, 33
  naming conventions, 34
  PDF files. *See* PDF files
  PICT files, 324
  PostScript files, 308, 309, 310
  quality of, 156
  QuickTime files, 286–287, 298
  Shockwave files, 297–298
  size of, 156, 163
  sound files, 298, 315, 316, 318, 320
  streaming. *See* streaming files
  SWF files, 275, 277, 284, 285, 292
  transferring, 33–34
  video files, 321
  XML files, 340
firewalls, 22, 400
Fireworks, 141–143, 163, 164, 191
FLA files, 292
Flash
  3D Web design and, 333
  advantages of, 278–279
  attributes, 276
  banners, 302
  cinematic effects in, 286–287
  considerations, 290
  converting files to Illustrator, 287–289

Flash, *continued*
   creating 3D environments, 330–333
   described, 272
   drawing options, 272–273
   embedding movies, 290
   Generator and, 291
   importing files into, 285
   importing QuickTime movies into, 286–287
   linking databases to, 291
   objects in, 282
   screensavers, 292
   sound and, 272
   text quality, 276
   vs. Shockwave, 271
   vs. SVG, 164
   Web browsers and, 290
Flash animations
   Adobe Illustrator and, 282
   Dreamweaver and, 143
   exporting, 275–277
   generating sequences, 281
   gradients, 275–276
   importing as movie clips, 282
   placing movie in work area, 283
   rollovers, 273–275
   text animation, 278–279
Flash files, 284
Flash movies
   embedding, 290
   vs. Shockwave movies, 272
Flash Player Movie format, 291
Flash plug-in, 290
Flashwriter, 143
floaters, 182, 237, 238
focus groups, 128
<FONT COLOR> tag, 82
font extensions, 100
<FONT FACE> tag, 102
<FONT SIZE> tag, 82, 218
<FONT> tag, 49, 50, 218
Fontfonts collection, 226
fonts. *See also* text
   attributes, 100
   browsers and, 24–26, 108
   dynamic, 108–109
   fixed, 53
   Fontfonts collection, 226
   guidelines, 6
   HTML, 49–51
   improving legibility with, 111
   monospaced, 53

nonproportional, 53
number of, 6
pixels and, 106–107
portable, 109
PostScript, 101, 278
size of, 6, 42, 49–51, 100, 106–107
tips for, 42
TrueDoc font format, 108–109
TrueType, 101, 278
WebTV and, 376–377, 378
width of, 42
foregrounds
   color, 252
   integrating with background, 192–193,
      207–214, 254
<FORM> tag, 59, 60
forms, 59–61
   CGI and, 59
   eliciting responses with, 16
   input types, 59
   sample form, 60–61
   WYSIWYG forms, 140
Fractal Design Painter, 166–167, 188
Fractal Design Poser, 196
frame sets, 88, 98
<FRAME SRC> tag, 94
<FRAMEBORDER> tag, 91
frames
   bookmarks and, 86
   borders, 91
   browsers and, 86, 88, 91, 94
   defining, 87–88
   dividing Web pages into, 86
   height of, 87
   <META> tag and, 85, 92–98
   Microsoft attributes for, 91
   nested, 89
   problems with, 86
   scroll bars and, 86
   search engines and, 86, 98
   size of, 91
   specifying for URLs, 90
   targets, 90
   WebTV browsers and, 377
   width of, 88
frames, picture, 241–248
<FRAMESET> tag, 88–89
<FRAMESPACING> tag, 91
FreeHand, 234
FrontPage, 31, 86, 114–115, 248
FTP clients, 33

FTP (file transfer protocol), 33
FTP programs, 140
FutureSplash Animator, 272

G

Generator, 291
<GET> method, 59
GIF animations, 261–270
　as background image, 180
　banners, 302
　colors, 262, 264–265
　creating, 266–270
　described, 261
　GIF Construction Set, 268
　GIF89a format, 262
　GIFBuilder, 262–264
　guidelines, 6
　high source after low source, 269
　interlacing, 264–265
　number of, 6
　race car animation, 266–267
　size of, 275
　stand-alone, 262
　Ulead GIF Animator, 270
　Web browsers and, 180
GIF Animator, 270
GIF compression, 154–155, 160, 161, 172, 176
GIF Construction Set, 264, 268, 269
GIF Converter, 157
GIF export plug-in, 216
GIF files
　color table in, 178
　converting images to, 136
　digit GIFs, 186
　displaying text as, 211
　efficient design of, 172
　interlacing, 44, 45
　size of, 156, 251
GIF format, 154–155
　combined images and, 161
　described, 154
　graphics files and, 136, 160
　interlacing and, 44
　photos, 158
　transparency and, 155, 162
　uses for, 155, 160
GIF images, 153–164
　as background element, 177–180
　changing Photoshop files to, 203
　combining with JPEG images, 161, 215–224

consistent use of, 21
creating, 45
guidelines, 6
quality of, 156, 157
referencing, 66
size of, 44, 156, 251
uses for, 160
using with tables, 82
GIF89a format, 44, 262
GIFBuilder, 262–264
Global System for Mobile Communications
　(GSM), 346, 353
GoLive. See Adobe GoLive
gradients, 275–276
graphics. See images
GSM (Global System for Mobile
　Communications), 346, 353

H

handheld computers, 353–358
HCI (human-computer interaction), 127
<HEAD> tag, 29
headings, 48, 49–51
hit counters, 186
hits, Web page, 12, 186, 393
home pages, 3, 130
HomeSite program, 394
hot spots, 324, 325
HotMetal Pro program, 120, 121
HotWired Web site, 305
<HR> tag, 62
<HREF> attributes, 65
<HREF> tag, 311
<HSPACE> tag, 68, 197, 252
HTML, 23–34
　ActiveX controls, 392–393, 394
　anchors, 64–65, 66
　ASP functions and, 410
　automating layout, 74
　backward compatibility of, 28
　basic concepts, 47–74
　color. See color
　complexity of, 27
　converting text to, 113–126
　described, 23
　example, 338
　extensions to, 54, 58
　fonts, 49–51
　forms, 59–61
　headings, 48, 49–51

HTML, *continued*
    hyperlinks. *See* links
    image tags, 66–73
    input types, 59
    learning, 24, 47
    limitations of, 8
    lines, 55–58, 62–63
    lists, 55–58
    Netscape extensions, 55–58
    paragraph extensions, 100
    preformatted text, 53
    special characters, 54
    text styles, 52
    versions of, 28, 29
    vs. desktop publishing, 8
    vs. XHTML, 28, 349
    vs. XML, 338, 339
HTML 3.0, 100
HTML attributes
    <A STYLE> attribute, 104
    <ACTION> attribute, 59
    <ALIGN> attributes, 70–73, 100
    <ALT> attribute, 67, 96, 375
    <AUTOPLAY> attribute, 328
    <BIG> attribute, 100
    <cellpadding> attribute, 80, 81, 206
    <cellspacing> attribute, 81
    <CHECKED> attribute, 59
    <COL> attribute, 88
    <CONTROLS> attribute, 328
    COORDS attribute, 184
    <EXPIRES> attribute, 97, 98
    font attributes, 100
    frame attributes, 91
    <HREF> attributes, 65
    line attributes, 62–63
    <MARGINHEIGHT> attribute, 89
    <MARGINWIDTH> attribute, 89
    <MAXLENGTH> attribute, 59
    <METHOD> attribute, 59
    MULTIPLE attribute, 60
    <NAME> attribute, 59, 64, 89, 96
    <NORESIZE> attribute, 89, 94
    <NOSHADE> attribute, 63
    <ROW> attribute, 88
    <ROWS> attribute, 87
    <SCROLLING> attribute, 89, 94
    <SIZE> attribute, 59
    <SMALL> attribute, 100
    spacer attributes, 200
    <STYLE> attribute, 104
    <SUB> attribute, 100
    <SUP> attribute, 100
    table tag attributes, 82–83
    <TYPE> attribute, 59
    <VALUE> attribute, 59
    video attributes, 328
HTML containers, 29
HTML editors
    Adobe GoLive. *See* Adobe GoLive
    Adobe InDesign, 116–117
    Adobe PageMaker, 115
    Adobe PageMill, 90
    Allaire Homesite, 122
    BBEdit, 121, 122
    described, 24
    HotMetal Pro program, 120, 121
    Macromedia Dreamweaver, 141, 143
    Macromedia UltraDev, 123
    Microsoft FrontPage, 31, 86, 114–115, 248
    Microsoft Word 2000, 114
    NetObjects Fusion, 124–125
    professional HTML editors, 119–126
    QuarkXPress, 118–119
HTML files, 27
HTML standard, 28, 48, 248
<HTML> tag, 29
HTML tags
    <!—> (comment tags), 27, 54, 104, 360
    <A HREF> tag, 318
    <A> tag, 64, 104
    <ALIGN> tag, 78
    <ALINK> tag, 110
    anchor tag, 64
    <B> tag, 27, 52
    <BACKGROUND> tag, 165
    <BASEFONT> tag, 51, 100, 252
    <BGCOLOR> tag, 82, 212
    <BGSOUND> tag, 318
    <BLACKFACE> tag, 378
    <BLINK> tag, 248
    <BLOCKQUOTE> tag, 58
    <BODY> tag, 29, 101, 102, 246
    <BORDER> tag, 66, 77, 91
    <BORDERCOLOR> tag, 82
    <BR clear=all> tag, 72, 73, 74, 198, 222

 tag, 50, 51, 73, 94
    <CAPTION> tag, 78
    <CENTER> tag, 218
    <CLEAR=all> tag, 94
    <CODE> tag, 384
    <COLSPAN> tag, 79, 204
    comment tags (<!—>), 27, 54, 104, 360

<DD> tag, 57
<DIR> tag, 58
<DIV> tag, 72, 100, 366
<DL> tag, 57, 58
<DT> tag, 57
elements *vs.* tags, 341
<EM> tag, 52
<EMBED> tag, 276, 278, 297, 327
<ES> tag, 393
<FONT COLOR> tag, 82
<FONT FACE> tag, 102
<FONT SIZE> tag, 82, 218
<FONT> tag, 49, 50, 218
<FORM> tag, 59, 60
<FRAME SRC> tag, 94
<FRAMEBORDER> tag, 91
<FRAMESET> tag, 88–89
<FRAMESPACING> tag, 91
<HEAD> tag, 29
<HR> tag, 62
<HREF> tag, 311
<HSPACE> tag, 68, 197, 252
<Hx> tags, 49, 103
<I> tag, 52
image tags, 66–73
<images/x.gif> tag, 318
<IMG SRC> tag, 66
<IMG> tag, 212, 328, 374
<INCLUDE> tag, 74
<INPUT> tag, 59, 60
Internet Explorer tags, 82–83
<ISMAP> tag, 68–69, 182, 184
<LAYER> tag, 366–367, 370
LEFTMARGIN tag, 175
<LI> tag, 55
<LINK> tag, 103, 104, 110
list tags, 58
<MARQUEE> tag, 248
<MENU> tag, 58, 222
<META> tags, 311. *See* <META> tags
<NOFRAMES> tag, 86, 94, 98
<OBJECT> tag, 392, 394
<OL> tag, 55
<P> tag, 51, 100
<PARAM> tag, 384, 392, 394
<PRE> tag, 53, 76
RIGHTMARGIN tag, 175
<ROWSPAN> tag, 79, 204
<SELECT> tag, 59, 60
<SHADOW> tag, 378
<SPACE> tag, 68

spacer tag, 200
<SPAN> tag, 103, 104
<SS> tag, 393
<STRONG> tag, 52
<STYLE> tag, 104
<TABLE> tag, 75, 76–82, 198, 205
table tag attributes, 82–83
table tags, 76
<TARGET> tag, 90
<TD> tag, 76, 78, 204, 205, 218
<TEXT> tag, 110
<TEXTAREA> tag, 59, 60
<TH> tag, 76
<TITLE> tag, 49
TOPMARGIN tag, 175
<TR> tag, 76, 78, 374, 375
<TT> tag, 53, 76
<UL> tag, 55, 246
<USEMAP> tag, 69, 184
<VALIGN> tag, 78
<VLINK> tag, 110
<VSPACE> tag, 68, 197
<WIDTH> tag, 200
HTTP, 32
human-computer interaction (HCI), 127
<Hx> tags, 49, 103
hyperlinks
    adding comments to, 67
    anchors and, 64–65
    color, 110
    to databases, 22, 397–402
    databases to Flash, 291
    databases to Web pages, 403–409
    "dead ends," 43
    display of, 3
    within documents, 64
    to e-mail address, 38
    to external servers, 65
    hotspots to URLs, 324, 325
    to images, 65
    images as, 68–69, 140, 181–186
    location of, 5
    navigational, 6, 36, 37, 64
    number of, 43
    to offline media, 312
    to other sites, 37
    PDF files to URLs, 312
    power of, 30–32
    to style sheets, 103
    text as, 181, 184, 197
    URLs to objects, 336
    to Web pages, 37, 38

hyperlinks, *continued*
  WebTV links, 380
  XLink standard, 349–350
  XML and, 349
hypertext, 30
hypertext markup language. *See* HTML

I

<I> tag, 52
IIS (Internet Information Server), 406
Illustrate filter, 330
Illustrator. *See* Adobe Illustrator
Image Hose feature, 237–242
Image Map Editor, 183
image maps, 181–186
  browser support for, 184
  clickable, 140
  client-side, 183–184, 185
  creating, 182–185, 258
  described, 181
  specifying URLs for, 68–69, 140, 181–186
  standard, 182–183, 184
image tags, 66–73
ImageReady, 151, 306
images. *See also* vector graphics
  3D graphics, 280–281
  alignment, 71, 195–200
  as background patterns, 177–180
  for backgrounds, 177–180, 224
  bandwidth and, 43–44
  borders around, 66–67, 214
  clip art libraries, 336
  color, 250
  compression, 308
  creating in Illustrator, 250
  digit GIFs, 186
  dithered, 250
  download time of, 3, 4, 43, 44
  editing, 230–232, 324
  GIF. *See* GIF images
  graphic images, 249–254
  grouping elements, 238
  height of, 44, 68
  hyperlinks to, 65, 68–69
  integrating text with, 161, 215–224
  interlacing, 44, 45
  JPEG. *See* JPEG images
  linking to URLs, 68–69, 384
  as links, 65, 68–69, 140, 181–186
  navigation bars, 38

  picture frames for, 241–248
  placing in WML, 355
  plug-ins for, 162–163
  positioning, 197
  PostScript images, 211, 235
  quality of, 158
  rasterizing, 235
  resolution of, 229–230
  rollovers, 138–139, 143
  size of, 229–230
  specifying in pixels, 211
  tools for, 162–163
  transparent, 155, 179, 212
  vector graphics, 164
  width of, 44, 68
<images/x.gif> tag, 318
<IMG SRC> tag, 66
<IMG> tag, 212, 328, 374
importing
  files into Flash, 285
  Flash animations as movie clips, 282
  Photoshop files, 142
  PICT images, 288
  QuickTime movies into Flash, 286–287
<INCLUDE> tag, 74
InDesign, 116–117
indexed colors, 148, 157, 203, 264–265
<INPUT> tag, 59, 60
inranets, 18
Interactive Bureau, 111
interactive navigation, 187–194
interactivity, 16, 129, 302, 362
interlacing, 44, 45, 155, 264–265
International Standards Organization (ISO), 24
Internet. *See* Web
Internet Advertising Bureau, 300
Internet Engineering Task Force, 100
Internet Explorer. *See also* Web browsers
  ActiveX controls and, 390
  bookmarks and, 15, 86
  browser cache and, 97
  compatibility issues, 28, 29
  DHTML and, 369
  frames and, 91
  playing movies in, 328
  Reset problem, 410
  security settings, 396
  table tag attributes, 82–83
  XML and, 343
Internet Information Server (IIS), 406
intranets, 19–22

intranet-specific conditions, 21
IP addresses, 398, 399
<ISMAP> tag, 68–69, 182, 184
ISO (International Standards Organization), 24
italic text, 52

J

JAR (Java Archive) files, 385
Java 1.1, 385
Java applets, 381, 384, 386–392
Java applications, 384
Java Archive (JAR) files, 385
Java Database Connectivity (JDBC), 385
Java language, 381–388
    100% Pure Java Initiative, 385
    browser support for, 384
    CGI and, 59
    cross-platform support, 382, 383, 385
    described, 382
    error messages, 6
    features, 382–383
    multithread capability, 383
    sandboxing, 391
    scripts vs. machine code, 383
    security and, 383
    Spacemen applet, 386–387
    speed of, 383
    vs. JavaScript, 382
    WYSIWYG Java products, 388
Java Virtual Machine, 383
JavaBeans, 385
JavaOS operating system, 354
JavaScript, 359–364
    alternatives to, 370
    animating with, 368–369, 370
    browser operations, 362–363
    browser versions, 370
    control panels, 194
    copying scripts, 361
    described, 359, 360, 382
    error messages, 6
    events, 361
    examples, 360–361
    layers and, 367, 370
    user-interactive design, 361, 362
    vs. Java, 382
    vs. WYSIWYG editors, 370
    welcome message, 362
JavaScript editors, 364
JDBC (Java Database Connectivity), 385
JIT (just in time) compilers, 391

JPEG 2000 initiative, 164
JPEG compression, 44–45, 158–161
JPEG files
    editing and, 159
    image degradation, 158, 159
    Photoshop and, 136, 158, 161
    size of, 158
JPEG format, 44–45
    photos, 136, 158
    transparency and, 160
    Web browser support, 158
JPEG images, 153–164
    combining with GIF images, 161, 215–224
    file size, 158
    graphics files and, 160
    quality of, 158
    referencing, 66
    repeating backgrounds, 334
    using with tables, 82
just in time (JIT) compilers, 391

K

Kai's Power Tools, 188
Kay, Alan, 27, 349
key frames, 332
key words, 96
KPT Seamless Welder, 166, 168–169

L

Lasso program, 402
layer masks, 196
<LAYER> tag, 366–367, 370
layers
    adding content to, 135–136
    animating with, 368–369, 370
    converting Photoshop layers, 136
    converting table cells to, 143
    DHTML, 366–367
    exporting, 116–117
    JavaScript and, 367, 370
    moving, 368
    scripting and, 367
    transparent, 366
    turned off, 141
    vs. animation, 369
    vs. CSS1, 366
layout
    automating, 74
    databases, 400–401
    improving legibility through, 110–111

LEFTMARGIN tag, 175
<LI> tag, 55
libraries
    clip art, 336
    Top Drawers Art Library, 216
lines
    attributes, 62–63
    background, 171–174
    horizontal, 62
    new, 51
Lingo, 296, 298
<LINK> tag, 103, 104, 110
links
    adding comments to, 67
    anchors and, 64–65
    color, 110
    to databases, 22, 397–402
    databases to Flash, 291
    databases to Web pages, 403–409
    "dead ends," 43
    display of, 3
    within documents, 64
    to e-mail address, 38
    to external servers, 65
    hotspots to URLs, 324, 325
    to images, 65
    images as, 68–69, 140, 181–186
    location of, 5
    navigational, 6, 36, 37, 64
    number of, 43
    to offline media, 312
    to other sites, 37
    PDF files to URLs, 312
    power of, 30–32
    to style sheets, 103
    text as, 181, 184, 197
    URLs to objects, 336
    to Web pages, 37, 38
    WebTV links, 380
    XLink standard, 349–350
    XML and, 349
lists
    alternative list structures, 58
    definition lists, 57
    HTML, 55–58
    nesting, 56, 57
    Netscape extensions, 58
logos, 153
loops
    Shockwave movies, 298
    sound clips, 318

Lynx browser, 25
LZW compression, 155, 156, 308

M
Mac OS 9 operating system, 354
Mac OS–based systems. See also cross-platform
        issues
    ActiveX controls and, 391
    color palette, 294
    converting between platforms, 34
    dithering and, 148
    file size and, 163
    filenames and, 34
    QuickTime. See QuickTime
    rendering and, 257
    WebObjects, 402
    Windows emulation software, 144
Macintosh Programmer's Workshop (MPW), 324,
        326
Macromedia Aftershock software, 296
Macromedia Director, 293, 294–296
Macromedia Dreamweaver, 141, 143, 183
Macromedia Fireworks, 141–143, 163, 164, 191, 258
Macromedia Flash. See Flash
Macromedia FreeHand, 234
Macromedia Generator, 291
Macromedia Homesite, 122
Macromedia SoundEdit, 316
Macromedia UltraDev, 123
mail, electronic
    intranets and, 20
    links to, 31, 38
    Mail To protocol, 32, 218
    responding to, 14–15
    sending from browser, 32
    sent to Web site manager, 14
    Web servers and, 20
Mail To protocol, 32, 218
Make QTVR Panorama program, 325
Map This program, 182
<MARGINHEIGHT> attribute, 89
margins
    frames, 89
    tables, 81
    Web browsers, 175–176
<MARGINWIDTH> attribute, 89
marketing. See also advertising; banner ads
    communication problems, 17
    e-commerce, 15–16
    e-mail and, 14–15
    measuring Web site effectiveness, 10–11

niche markets, 13–14
one-to-one, 10, 16–17, 344–345
online advertisements, 17
online project site, 18–19
online style guide, 19
paperless offices, 20–21
promotional elements, 16
scope, 10
search engines and, 17
target groups, 10
vertical markets, 13–14
Web Buy technology, 314
Web design and, 7–22
Web marketers, 15, 16
Web page hits and, 12
zapping, 13
<MARQUEE> tag, 248
masking text, 226–227
masks, 208–211, 244–245, 258
Mathematics Markup Language (MathML), 346
MathML (Mathematics Markup Language), 346
<MAXLENGTH> attribute, 59
Media Player, 320
<MENU> tag, 58, 222
menus, scrolling, 60
Merck | Vel Web page, 114
<META> tags
    banners and, 311
    for comments, 96
    dynamic Web pages, 95
    frame sets and, 98
    frames and, 85, 92–98
    PDF files and, 311
    playing sound, 318
    search engine performance and, 97, 98
    specifying character sets, 98
    specifying language, 98
MetaTools Sphere program, 189
<METHOD> attribute, 59
Microsoft Access, 406
Microsoft Authenticode security, 396
Microsoft FrontPage, 31, 86, 114–115, 248
Microsoft Internet Explorer. See also Web
    browsers
    ActiveX controls and, 390
    bookmarks and, 15, 86
    browser cache and, 97
    compatibility issues, 28, 29
    DHTML and, 369
    frames and, 91
    playing movies in, 328

Reset problem, 410
    security settings, 396
    table tag attributes, 82–83
    XML and, 343
Microsoft Internet Information Server (IIS), 406
Microsoft Windows Media Player, 320
Microsoft Word 2000, 114
MIDI format, 316
MIME types, 63, 109
mobile Internet services, 338, 343, 353–358
mobile telephones, 353–358
modems, 43
Mok, Clement, 124
monitors, 39–42. See also screen
    browser width and, 42
    limited color options, 152
    resolution of, 41, 229–230, 257
    settings, 40, 41
    size of, 6, 39, 40–42
    SVGA monitors, 161
    XVGA monitors, 161
Mosaic Web browser, 158
Motion Blur filter, 262
.mov extension, 286, 328
movie clips, 282
movies. See also animations; Flash movies; video
    embedding in Web pages, 297, 327–328
    panorama movies, 322–327
    QTVR movies. See QuickTime VR
    Shockwave movies, 293–298
MP3 files, 272
MPEG format, 316, 326
MPW (Macintosh Programmer's Workshop), 324, 326
multimedia
    animations and, 262
    PDF format and, 310
MULTIPLE attribute, 60
multithread capability, 383
music, 6, 298

N

<NAME> attribute, 59, 64, 89, 96
naming conventions, 34
navigation, 37–38
    buttons, 188–193, 194
    consistency of, 15, 132
    continuous display of, 132
    ease of, 9
    GIF images and, 21
    guidelines, 5

navigation, *continued*
  home page button, 31–32
  hyperlinks and, 6, 36, 37
  importance of, 3, 128
  interactive, 187–194
  link-based navigation, 64
  page design as, 37
  programming languages and, 194
  tools for, 37–38, 132
  tracking, 130–131
navigation bars, 38, 132, 188, 191
  entity, 79, 104, 200, 222
NCSA maps, 182, 183
nesting
  frames, 89
  lists, 56, 57
Netiquette, 14–15
NetObjects Fusion, 84, 124–125
Netscape Communicator, 25
Netscape Enterprise Server, 406
Netscape Navigator. *See also* Web browsers
  color look-up tables, 148–150
  compatibility issues, 28, 29
  DHTML and, 369
  extensions, 28
  font extensions, 100
  list tags, 58
  Reset button and, 410
  scrolling and, 86
  spacing and, 200
  XML and, 343
network computer, 383
newsletters, 14
niche markets, 13–14
Nielsen, Jakob, 128
Nielsen Media Research, 20
<NOFRAMES> tag, 86, 94, 98
Nokia WAP Toolkit, 356, 357
<NORESIZE> attribute, 89, 94
<NOSHADE> attribute, 63
number sign (#), 65, 84

O

Object Linking and Embedding (OLE), 389
<OBJECT> tag, 392, 394
objects
  in Flash, 282
  Java and, 382
  linking to URLs, 336
  sprite objects, 386

  WebObjects, 402
ODBC (Open Database Connectivity), 398
<OL> tag, 55
OLE (Object Linking and Embedding), 389
onBlur event, 361
onChange event, 361
onClick event, 361
onFocus event, 361
online shopping. *See* e-commerce
onLoad event, 361
onMouseOver event, 246, 361
onSelect event, 361
onSubmit event, 361
onUnload event, 361
Open Database Connectivity (ODBC), 398
Opera browser, 28
operating systems. *See also* cross-platform issues;
    Mac OS–based systems; Windows-based systems
  EPOC operating system, 354
  JavaOS operating system, 354
  PalmOS operating system, 354
  Web technology and, 3
  Windows CE operating system, 354
  Wireless Application Protocol and, 354

P

<P> tag, 51, 100
PageCharmer Pro program, 388
PageMaker, 115
PageMill, 90
Painter, 166, 191, 226–228, 233–242
PalmOS operating system, 354
panorama movies, 322–327
paperless offices, 20–21
paragraph extensions, 100
<PARAM> tag, 384, 392, 394
patterns
  background, 136–138, 177–180, 258
  color and, 229, 234
  combining with shadows, 225–232
  creating, 230–232, 236
  feathering, 227
  random color replacement, 234
  repetitive, 171–176
  single GIF images as, 177–180
  tiled, 165–170
  transparent images and, 179
  unusual, 228–229
PDF files, 307–314
  Adobe InDesign and, 116

built-in tools in, 308
CD-ROMs and, 308, 312
compression and, 308
digital signatures, 312
embedding in Web pages, 311
FTP and, 33
linking to URLs, 312
PostScript and, 308
printing, 312
QuickTime format and, 310
resolution of, 308, 309, 312
size of, 308, 310, 312
streaming, 312
watermarks, 312
PDF format
  Adobe Web Buy technology, 314
  advantages of, 307
  converting Web sites to, 313
  described, 307
  e-books and, 314
  multimedia and, 310
PDFViewer, 312
Perl language, 59
perspective, 332
PFR (Portable Font Resource), 109
Phillips Semiconductors Web page, 8, 9
photo frames, 241–248
PhotoAlto, 216, 221
Photo-CDs, 244
PhotoDisc, 208
PhotoGIF plug-in, 162, 212
photos
  color and, 156
  dithered, 156
  GIF format, 158
  JPEG format, 136, 158
  masks for, 244–245
  Polaroid photos, 242–243
  resolution, 244
  stock photos, 208, 216, 244
  in Web pages, 216, 220–221
PhotoTools product, 306
PICT format, 159, 324
PICT images
  dividing, 326
  exporting, 286–287
  importing, 288
  modifying, 324
  QuickTime and, 286–287
  Shockwave animations and, 272
  size of, 298

PICT previews, 282
pixels
  font size in, 106–107
  printing, 36
  spacing with, 197–200
  specifying images in, 211
plug-ins
  ActiveX and, 392
  alternatives to, 3
  browsers and, 63
  button creation, 188–189
  Flash plug-in, 290
  GIF export plug-in, 216
  images, 162–163
  KPT Seamless Welder, 166, 168–169
  missing, 3, 7
  need for, 392
  PhotoGIF plug-in, 162, 212
  Shockwave plug-in, 272, 293, 296, 392
  Terrazzo plug-in, 166
  Web Companion plug-in, 398, 399
  WebLink plug-in, 310, 312
PNG (Portable Network Graphics) format, 164, 258
Polaroid frames, 242–243
Portable Document Format. See PDF
Portable Font Resource (PFR), 109
Portable Network Graphics (PNG) format, 164, 258
Poser program, 195, 196–200
<POST> method, 59
PostScript files, 308, 309, 310
PostScript fonts, 101, 278
PostScript images, 211, 235
PostScript language, 116, 250, 308
PostScript printers, 307
pragma no-cache, 97
<PRE> tag, 53, 76
preformatted text, 53
Premier, 328
printing
  digital printing, 312
  optimizing for, 312
  PDF files, 312
  pixels, 36
  PostScript printers, 307
  Web pages, 43
problems
  dead URLs, 112
  frame problems, 86
  Reset problem in, 410
products, ordering. See e-commerce

programmers, 404
programming languages, 194. *See also specific languages;* specific languages
promotional elements, 16

Q

QTVR Player, 327
QuarkXPress, 118–119, 309, 310, 350, 352
Quick Mask mode, 208–209, 231, 232
QuickTime 4 format, 291
QuickTime files
    cross-platform issues, 326–327
    exporting PICT files from, 286–287
    size of, 298
QuickTime format, 310
QuickTime movies, 286–287
QuickTime TV, 328
QuickTime VR, 321–328
    adding movies to Web page, 325, 327
    assembling images, 326
    creating movies, 322–324
    cross-platform issues, 326–327
    described, 321
    editing movies, 324–325
    flattening movies, 326–327
    stitching movies, 324, 325
    streaming video, 328
    video attributes, 328
QuickTime VR Authoring Studio, 324
QuidProQuo program, 109
quotation marks (" "), 54

R

Random Color Replace filter, 234
rasterizing images, 235
RealAudio, 315, 316, 320
RealPlayer software, 320, 347
RealVideo format, 326
Reset button, 60, 410
resolution
    images, 229–230
    monitors, 41, 229–230, 257
    PDF files, 308, 309, 312
    photos, 244
RGB colors, 150, 251
RIGHTMARGIN tag, 175
rollovers, 138–139, 143, 273–275
<ROW> attribute, 88
<ROWS> attribute, 87

<ROWSPAN> tag, 79, 204
Rubber Stamp tool, 324, 325
rulers, 42, 43

S

sandboxing, 391
Scalable Vector Graphics (SVG), 153, 164
Scene Maker HyperCard stack, 325
screen. *See also* monitors
    displaying PostScript files on, 308, 309, 310
    rulers, 42, 43
    size of, 6
screensavers, 292
ScreenTime program, 292
scripting. *See also* JavaScript
    layers and, 367
    with Lingo, 296
    Wireless Application Protocol (WAP), 354
    WMLScript, 354
scroll bars, 86, 89
scrolling, 6, 42–43, 86
<SCROLLING> attribute, 89, 94
scrolling menus, 60
search engines
    banners and, 299
    bots, 115
    frames and, 86, 98
    generating visits via, 9
    improving performance, 97, 98
    on intranets, 20–21
    <META> tags and, 97, 98
    for navigation, 5
    power of, 17
search form screen, 404, 407–408, 410
search function, Web sites, 5, 17, 404, 407–410
Secure Sockets Layer (SSL), 402
security
    ActiveX and, 390–391, 396
    Authenticode security, 396
    digital certificates, 385, 396
    Internet Explorer settings, 396
    Java and, 383
    Secure Sockets Layer (SSL), 402
<SELECT> tag, 59, 60
servers. *See also* Web servers
    FileMaker Server, 402
    Internet Information Server (IIS), 406
    links to external servers, 65
    Netscape Enterprise Server, 406
    testing Web sites on, 109
    WAP server, 354

Web database servers, 399
XML Data Server, 348
set-top boxes, 382
SGML (Standard Generalized Markup Language),
    23, 24, 338–339
<SHADOW> tag, 378
shadows, 225–232
Shockwave animations, 294–296
Shockwave controller, 298
Shockwave files, 297–298
Shockwave Flash animations, 271–292
Shockwave movies, 293–298
    background for, 296
    controller for, 298
    embedding, 297
    looping, 298
    size of, 298
    vs. Flash movies, 272
Shockwave plug-in, 272, 293, 296, 392
Shockwave technology, 271, 329
shopping, online. See e-commerce
shopping carts, 130–131, 405
Simac home page, 30, 31
site maps, 38, 129
<SIZE> attribute, 59
slash character (/), 27
slicing, 142
<SMALL> attribute, 100
SmartSketch, 272
SMIL (Synchronized Multimedia Integration
    Language), 346–347
.snm extension, 326
sound
    adding to Web pages, 318–319
    analog to digital, 316
    audio file formats, 316
    background, 6
    on CD-ROMs, 315
    editing, 316
    Flash support for, 272
    mono, 316
    music, 6, 298
    playing, 318, 320
    quality of, 316–317
    RealAudio, 315, 316, 320
    reducing file size, 316–317
    stereo, 316
    on video, 315
    working with, 315–320
Sound Blaster, 316
sound cards, 316

sound clips, 315, 316, 318
sound files, 298, 315, 316, 318, 320
SoundEdit, 316
<SPACE> tag, 68
Spacemen applet, 386–387
spacer attributes, 200
spacer tag, 200
spacing, 197–200
    Netscape Navigator and, 200
    tables, 78, 80–81
    white space, 110
<SPAN> tag, 103, 104
special characters, 54, 112, 339
splash pages, 129
sprite objects, 386
SQL commands, 385
SQL (Structured Query Language), 408
<SS> tag, 393
SSL (Secure Sockets Layer), 402
Standard Generalized Markup Language. See
    SGML
statistics, Web site, 4
StatistiX control, 393–395
StatMarket Web site, 152
Stitcher tool, 324, 325
storyboards, 2
streaming files
    Acrobat files, 312
    PDF files, 312
    sound files, 315
    video, 328
    video files, 321
Streamline, 287
strikeout text, 54
<STRONG> tag, 52
Structured Query Language. See SQL
<STYLE> attribute, 104
style guides, 18, 19
style sheets, 102–105
    animating with, 369
    browser compatibility, 103, 342–343
    combining elements, 366
    Extensible Stylesheet Language (XSL), 342–343
    moving style sheets, 369
    W3C style sheets, 104
<STYLE> tag, 104
styles, 27, 52
<SUB> attribute, 100
Submit button, 60
subpages, 43
<SUP> attribute, 100
Supra technology, 312

SVG (Scalable Vector Graphics), 153, 164
SVGA monitors, 161
.swf extension, 332, 333
SWF files, 275, 277, 284, 285, 292
Swift Generator, 291
Swift₃D program, 330, 332
Symantec Cafe, 382
Synchronized Multimedia Integration Language
    (SMIL), 346–347

T

table cells
    blank, 79
    padding, 80, 81, 206
    spacing, 81
<TABLE> tag, 75, 76–82, 198, 205
table tags, 76
tables, 75–84
    aligning text in, 78
    backgrounds, 82
    benefits of, 75–76
    blank cells, 79
    borders, 77, 80–82, 198, 204, 205, 212
    browsers and, 84
    captions, 78
    cell padding, 80, 81
    cell spacing, 81
    color, 82
    columns, 79
    composition of, 204
    converting cells to layers, 143
    creating, 76–79, 202–203
    cross-platform issues, 84
    database, 406
    diagram of, 205
    fixed width, 206
    FrontPage and, 115
    HTML editors and, 84
    Internet Explorer tags, 82–83
    Microsoft Word and, 114
    modifiable code, 77
    monospace fonts and, 53
    QuarkXPress and, 119
    rows, 79
    seamless, 201–206
    spacing, 78, 80–81
    tabs in, 202
    tips and tricks, 84
    using GIF images with, 82
    using JPEG images with, 82

    WebTV browsers and, 377
    width of, 84
tags, HTML
    <!—> (comment tags), 27, 54, 104, 360
    <A HREF> tag, 318
    <A> tag, 64, 104
    <ALIGN> tag, 78
    <ALINK> tag, 110
    anchor tag, 64
    <B> tag, 27, 52
    <BACKGROUND> tag, 165
    <BASEFONT> tag, 51, 100, 252
    <BGCOLOR> tag, 82, 212
    <BGSOUND> tag, 318
    <BLACKFACE> tag, 378
    <BLINK> tag, 248
    <BLOCKQUOTE> tag, 58
    <BODY> tag, 29, 101, 102, 246
    <BORDER> tag, 66, 77, 91
    <BORDERCOLOR> tag, 82
    <BR clear=all> tag, 72, 73, 74, 198, 222

 tag, 50, 51, 73, 94
    <CAPTION> tag, 78
    <CENTER> tag, 218
    <CLEAR=all> tag, 94
    <CODE> tag, 384
    <COLSPAN> tag, 79, 204
    comment tags (<!—>), 27, 54, 104, 360
    <DD> tag, 57
    <DIR> tag, 58
    <DIV> tag, 72, 100, 366
    <DL> tag, 57, 58
    <DT> tag, 57
    elements vs. tags, 341
    <EM> tag, 52
    <EMBED> tag, 276, 278, 297, 327
    <ES> tag, 393
    <FONT COLOR> tag, 82
    <FONT FACE> tag, 102
    <FONT SIZE> tag, 82, 218
    <FONT> tag, 49, 50, 218
    <FORM> tag, 59, 60
    <FRAME SRC> tag, 94
    <FRAMEBORDER> tag, 91
    <FRAMESET> tag, 88–89
    <FRAMESPACING> tag, 91
    <HEAD> tag, 29
    <HR> tag, 62
    <HREF> tag, 311
    <HSPACE> tag, 68, 197, 252
    <Hx> tags, 49, 103
    <I> tag, 52

image tags, 66–73
<images/x.gif> tag, 318
<IMG SRC> tag, 66
<IMG> tag, 212, 328, 374
<INCLUDE> tag, 74
<INPUT> tag, 59, 60
Internet Explorer tags, 82–83
<ISMAP> tag, 68–69, 182, 184
<LAYER> tag, 366–367, 370
LEFTMARGIN tag, 175
<LI> tag, 55
<LINK> tag, 103, 104, 110
list tags, 58
<MARQUEE> tag, 248
<MENU> tag, 58, 222
<META> tags, 311. See <META> tags
<NOFRAMES> tag, 86, 94, 98
<OBJECT> tag, 392, 394
<OL> tag, 55
<P> tag, 51, 100
<PARAM> tag, 384, 392, 394
<PRE> tag, 53, 76
RIGHTMARGIN tag, 175
<ROWSPAN> tag, 79, 204
<SELECT> tag, 59, 60
<SHADOW> tag, 378
<SPACE> tag, 68
spacer tag, 200
<SPAN> tag, 103, 104
<SS> tag, 393
<STRONG> tag, 52
<STYLE> tag, 104
<TABLE> tag, 75, 76–82, 198, 205
table tag attributes, 82–83
table tags, 76
<TARGET> tag, 90
<TD> tag, 76, 78, 204, 205, 218
<TEXT> tag, 110
<TEXTAREA> tag, 59, 60
<TH> tag, 76
<TITLE> tag, 49
TOPMARGIN tag, 175
<TR> tag, 76, 78, 374, 375
<TT> tag, 53, 76
<UL> tag, 55, 246
<USEMAP> tag, 69, 184
<VALIGN> tag, 78
<VLINK> tag, 110
<VSPACE> tag, 68, 197
<WIDTH> tag, 200
Tango program, 402

target groups, 10
<TARGET> tag, 90
targets, 90
TCP/IP protocol, 20, 24, 399, 400
<TD> tag, 76, 78, 204, 205, 218
telephones, mobile, 353–358
television, integrating WebTV with, 379
TeleVision Markup Language (TVML), 380
templates, 21
Terrazzo plug-in, 166
text. *See also* fonts
    3D lettering, 226
    alignment, 70, 71–72, 78, 195–200
    animating, 275, 276, 278–279
    background color and, 46
    bolded, 27, 52
    case of, 6
    centering, 51
    color, 110
    converting to HTML, 113–126
    displaying as GIF files, 211
    dithered, 110
    indenting, 58
    integrating with images, 161, 215–224
    italic, 52
    as links, 181, 184, 197
    logical styles, 52
    masking, 226–227
    monospaced, 53
    new lines, 51
    physical styles, 52
    on picture frames, 243
    positioning, 71–73, 197
    preformatted, 53
    size of, 6, 42, 49–51, 100, 106–107
    special characters, 54, 112, 339
    strikeout, 54
    subscript, 100
    superscript, 100
    transparent, 211
    typewriter, 53
    underline, 54
    WebTV and, 378, 379
text boxes, 60
text mode, 33
<TEXT> tag, 110
<TEXTAREA> tag, 59, 60
<TH> tag, 76
ThirdVoice initiative, 126
TIFF format, 155, 159, 164
<TITLE> tag, 49
Top Drawers Art Library, 216

TOPMARGIN tag, 175
<TR> tag, 76, 78, 374, 375
transparent items
   button bars, 192–193
   GIF format and, 155, 162
   images, 155, 179, 212
   JPEG format and, 160
   layers, 366
   text, 211
Tridion Web content-management system, 344
troubleshooting
   dead URLs, 112
   frame problems, 86
   Reset problem in, 410
TrueDoc font format, 108–109
TrueSpeech format, 316
TrueType fonts, 278
<TT> tag, 53, 76
TVML (TeleVision Markup Language), 380
tweening, 274
<TYPE> attribute, 59
typography, 99–112

U

<UL> tag, 55, 246
Ulead GIF Animator, 270
UltraDev, 123
UMTS (Universal Mobile Telecommunications
   System), 343, 353
underline text, 54
Unicode, 339
uniform resource locators. *See* URLs
Universal Mobile Telecommunications System
   (UMTS), 343, 353
Unix-based systems. *See also* cross-platform
   issues
   ActiveX controls and, 391
   color and, 150–151
   filenames and, 34
   FTP clients, 33
   Netscape Navigator and, 150
URLs (uniform resource locators), 32
   Bookmarks list, 10
   clickable image maps, 68–69, 140, 181–186
   "dead URLs," 112
   Favorites list, 7, 10
   "floaters," 182
   linking hotspots to, 324, 325
   linking to images, 68–69, 384
   linking to objects, 336
   linking to PDF files, 312
   references to, 88, 140
   search engines and, 9
   specifying as targets, 90
   specifying frames for, 90
   typing errors and, 112
   WebTV and, 379
   working with, 64
usability design, 127–132
<USEMAP> tag, 69, 184
user interactivity, 362
user testing, 128

V

<VALIGN> tag, 78
<VALUE> attribute, 59
VBScript (Visual Basic Script), 369, 374–375, 394
vector graphics, 164, 280–281. *See also* images
vectors, converting PICT images to, 272
vertical markets, 13–14
video. *See also* animations; movies
   formats for, 326
   playing, 320
   QuickTime VR, 321–328
   sound on, 315
   streaming, 328
video clips, 298, 315
video files, 321
Virtual Reality Modelling Language. *See* VRML
virtual spaces, 335
Virtus 3D Website Builder, 335
VisiBone classification, 150
Visual Basic, 59, 390
Visual Basic Script (VBScript), 369, 374–375, 394
<VLINK> tag, 110
VR Authoring Tools Suite, 324
VRML 2.0 standard, 334
VRML (Virtual Reality Modelling Language),
   329–336
<VSPACE> tag, 68, 197

W

W3C style sheets, 104
W3C (World Wide Web Consortium), 28, 29, 54,
   100, 349
WAP server, 354
WAP (Wireless Application Protocol), 343,
   353–356
watermarks, 312
WAVE format, 272, 316, 318, 320

WaveStudio, 316
Web
  competition on, 2
  firewalls, 400
  IP addresses, 398, 399
  mobile devices and, 353–358
  mobile Internet services, 338, 343, 353–358
  one-to-one communication and, 129
  Three-Tier Model, 345
  Two-Tier Model, 345
  typography and, 99–112
Web browsers. *See also* Internet Explorer;
    Netscape
  adjusting, 363
  browser check, 363
  browser wars, 29
  BrowserWatch Web site, 28
  cache, 38, 97, 98, 298
  check in frames display, 363
  colors and, 147–152
  compatibility issues, 28, 410
  DHTML and, 369, 370
  differences in, 24–26
  extensions, 28
  Flash and, 290
  fonts and, 24–26, 108
  frames and, 86, 88, 91, 94
  GIF animations and, 180
  HTML versions and, 28, 48
  identifying, 180
  image maps and, 184
  interlacing, 44
  Java support for, 384
  JavaScript and, 362–363, 370
  JPEG format and, 158
  logical *vs.* physical styles, 52
  Lynx browser, 25
  margins, 175–176
  Mosaic browser, 158
  opening new window, 362
  Opera browser, 28
  playing movies in, 328
  plug-ins. *See* plug-ins
  progressive rendering, 109
  registering visitor browsers, 12
  Reset button and, 410
  sending e-mail from, 32
  spacing and, 200
  style sheets and, 103, 342–343
  tables and, 84
  tracking developments, 28

  VBScript and, 375
  versions of, 3
  viewing database results in, 401–402
  VRML-compatible, 334
  WebTV browser, 376
  width of, 42
  XML and, 341–345
Web Buy technology, 314
Web Companion plug-in, 398, 399
Web database servers, 399
Web design
  3D aspects of, 329–336
  custom design, 134
  drawing programs and, 134–136
  dynamic design, 6
  extranets, 20
  intranets, 20
  marketing and, 7–22
  modifying, 6
  rules for, 1–6
  setting up, 405
  slicing, 142
  WYSIWYG design, 133–144
Web designers, 404–405
Web Embedding Fonts Tool (WEFT), 108–109
Web marketers, 15, 16
Web pages
  adding ActiveX controls to, 392–395
  adding dates to, 74
  adding Java applets to, 384
  adding sound to, 318–319
  attracting visitors, 9
  automatic update of, 93
  cache and, 97, 98
  content on, 2, 21, 36–37
  dynamic, 92, 93, 95, 291, 370
  embedding movies in, 297, 327–328
  embedding PDF files into, 311
  error message pages, 17
  frames. *See* frames
  graphic Web pages, 249–254
  hits, 12, 393
  home pages, 3, 130
  information accessibility and, 130
  on intranets, 21
  jumping from page to page, 12
  layout of, 110–111
  length of, 42–43, 110
  links. *See* links
  mobile display of, 343
  niche markets, 13–14
  Phillips Semiconductors page, 8, 9

Web pages, *continued*
  printing, 43
  prototyping, 144
  recording visits to, 11–12
  relevance of, 15
  scrolling and, 6, 42–43
  site maps, 129
  splash pages, 129
  style guides for, 19
  subpages, 43
  tabs in, 202–203
  templates for, 21
  title of, 37
  vertical markets, 13–14
  zapping, 13
Web programmers, 404
Web servers. *See also* servers
  ASP and, 406–407
  company items placed on, 20–21
  e-mail and, 20
  on intranets, 20–21
  QuidProQuo program and, 109
  setting up, 21, 406–407
Web sites
  advertising, 9
  alternative views of, 3
  anonymous visitors and, 12
  attracting visitors to, 2, 15, 127, 128
  box design, 331–333
  building, 35–46
  composition, 373
  content, 2, 6, 36–37
  converting existing data, 405
  converting to PDF format, 313
  customer feedback, 132
  e-commerce. *See* e-commerce Web sites
  eliciting responses, 16
  e-mail, 14–15
  growth of, 37
  hits *vs.* visits, 12
  image flow, 4
  links. *See* links
  management of, 140
  measuring effectiveness of, 10–11
  monitors and, 39–42
  navigation. *See* navigation
  online project site, 18–19
  previewing, 138
  promotional elements, 16
  publishing, 140
  search function on, 5, 17, 404, 407–408, 410

  site guidelines, 18–19
  site maps, 38
  site overview, 139
  size of, 4
  statistics, 4
  storyboards, 2
  structure of, 2, 38, 138, 139
  style guides, 18, 19
  target visitors, 35
  testing, 2, 109, 131
  tracking number of visitors to, 186
  updates to, 6
  uploading, 370
  usability design, 127–132
  visits *vs.* hits, 12
WebLink plug-in, 310, 312
Webmasters, 15, 17
WebObjects, 402
Web-safe colors, 147–148, 151, 152
WebTV, 376–380
WEFT (Web Embedding Fonts Tool), 108–109
white space, 110
<WIDTH> tag, 200
Windows 95 systems, 34
Windows CE operating system, 354
Windows-based systems. *See also* cross-platform
    issues
  converting between platforms, 34
  filenames and, 34
  monitor resolution and, 229–230, 257
  rendering and, 257
Wireless Application Protocol. *See* WAP
Wireless Markup Language. *See* WML
WML decks, 354
.WML extension, 354
WML (Wireless Markup Language), 346, 353–358
WMLScript, 354
World Wide Web. *See* Web
World Wide Web Consortium (W3C), 28, 29, 54,
    100
.wrl extension, 334
WS-FTP, 33
WYSIWYG
  editors, 24, 84
  forms, 140
  Java products, 388
  JavaScript code generator, 370
  uploading, 370
  vs. manual JavaScripting, 370
  Web design, 133–144

X

XHTML (extended HTML), 28, 349
XLink standard, 348–349
XML Data Server, 348
XML Editor, 341
XML (Extensible Markup Language), 337–352
  advantages of, 344
  BizTalk, 347–348
  cascading style sheets and, 352
  described, 337
  document structure, 351
  EDI and, 346
  elements *vs.* tags, 341
  examples, 339, 340
  FileMaker Pro and, 402
  HTML and, 338–339
  hyperlinks and, 349
  markups, 341–342
  mobile users and, 343
  one-to-one marketing and, 344–345
  process instructions (PIs), 340
  QuarkXPress documents and, 350
  SGML and, 338–339
  special characters, 339
  vs. HTML, 338, 339
  vs. SGML, 339
  Web browsers and, 341–345
  XLink standard, 348–349
XML files, 340
XQL (Extensible Query Language), 348
XSL (Extensible Stylesheet Language), 342–343, 344, 349
XVGA monitors, 161
x/y coordinates, 69

Z

zapping, 13

ACKNOWLEDGEMENTS:

Rob Kouwenberg, Eric Bruinewoud, Mike Camerling, Richard Heesbeen, Jeroen Ritmeijer, Edwin Martin, Mark Ossen, Maarten Schutjes, Sander Kessels, Ton Daamen, Paul Keltjens, Ilse van Kuijck, Marijke den Ouden, Marlou Wijsman, Frits Bonjernoor, Wouter Betting, René van den Bichelaer, Willem Jan Withagen, Hans van Rossum, Marieke Verspaandonk, Marc de Kruijf, Thomas Marzano, Eric van der Linden, Cor Steenstra, Hans Frederiks, Martin Mes, Just van Rossum, Erik van Blokland, Albert Kiefer, Marc Hagers, Rob Mooij, Dennis de Poorter, Kees Metzger, Stephen Atkinson, Pieter van Twisk, Ruud Kluivers, Martin van den Berg, Michael Baumgardt, Jouk Pleiter, Douglas Jacobson, Peter Buiks, Herbert van Staveren, Ronald Baart, Ton Frederiks, Adelheid van der Werf, Loek Schönbeck, Joop Krijvenaar, Nathalie Melotte, Jacqueline K. Aaron, Whitney Walker, Lester Nunnellee, Marjorie Baer, David Boelen, Nancy Ruenzel, Becky Morgan, Robert Klep and Marjan Kentie.

A special word of thanks to Kate Reber and Wouter Vermeulen.